Sir Thomas Wyatt and His Background

Sir Thomas Wyatt
and
His Background

by

PATRICIA THOMSON

STANFORD UNIVERSITY PRESS

STANFORD, CALIFORNIA

Stanford University Press
Stanford, California
© *Patricia Thomson 1964*
Library of Congress Catalog Number: 64–7650

LIBRARY

AUG 1 3 1965

UNIVERSITY OF THE PACIFIC

140173

Printed in Great Britain

Dedicated to the memory of
JOHN GORDON THOMSON

Contents

Preface   *page* ix
Abbreviations   xiii

PART ONE:
WYATT'S ENVIRONMENT AND LIFE

I.   Introductory   3
II. Courtly Love   10
III. Courtly Wisdom   46

PART TWO:
WYATT'S POETRY AND PROSE

IV.   Classical Philosophy and English Humanism, with
      a Note on Prose Style   79
V.   English Lyrics   111
VI.   The First English Petrarchans   149
VII. Wyatt and the School of Serafino   209
VIII. Neo-Classical Satire   238

APPENDICES

A. The Wyatt MSS   273
B. Wyatt's 'Daughter Besse'   274
C. Sir Francis Brian   274
D. Wyatt's May Day Sonnet   275
E. Opinions on Wyatt's Affair with Anne Boleyn   276
F. Boethius, Chaucer, and Wyatt   277
G. Clichés in the Medieval Lyric   278
H. Italian Sonnet Theory   279
I. Wyatt and Ariosto   280

Index   285

Preface

THE purpose of this study is to look at Sir Thomas Wyatt's life and work against his social and literary background. His life has an interest to some extent independent of his work, for he was a diplomat and courtier, and by no means a professional author. Hence my first section touches on his poetry and prose only where they relate to his biography. In the succeeding chapters they become the centre of attention, and here my chief interest is in their relation to literary tradition and to specific literary sources. Wyatt's borrowings in the foreign market claim special attention because they account for his well deserved reputation as a pioneer. Before him, only Chaucer showed the same kind of enterprise. While Wyatt is in some ways the heir to the English Middle Ages, he is in others the Tudor 'new man'—the adventurer who brings the Italian Renaissance into England. From the start his is an essentially innovative genius, and even with his early attempt to translate Plutarch he does something new.

It must not, of course, be assumed that Wyatt's work is excellent simply because it is innovative. A judgement of value based on a 'historic estimate' is, as Arnold long since warned us, fallacious. Nevertheless, unless my partiality deceives me, Wyatt has, in fact, intrinsic as well as historical importance—not, certainly, always in just proportion, and, where that appears the case, I try to acknowledge it.

The major groups of Wyatt's poems are treated in chapters V to VIII, with one important exception. His translations of the Psalms have been so recently and so thoroughly discussed in H. A. Mason's *Humanism and Poetry in the Early Tudor Period* (1959) that I can find nothing left to say about them. Certain other omissions should also be noted. Obviously I stress some aspects of Wyatt at the expense of others. For a full account of his rhythmical and metrical purpose, I must gratefully refer the reader to the numerous studies of it, and particularly to Sergio Baldi's *La Poesia di Sir Thomas Wyatt* (1953) and John Thompson's *The Founding of English Metre* (1961). His independent sonnets deserve more attention than I give them, but chapter VI, where they would find a place, is long enough as it stands. Finally, there is my virtual omission of his debt to French poetry, and this requires a fuller explanation. I think the French debt small, but it might, in the opinion of some scholars, demand more than the few notices I give it. Common conventions and, in the case of 'Like to these vnmesurable montayns', a common Italian original, account for many of the similarities between Wyatt's poems and what were once supposed to be their sources in Marot and Saint-Gelais. Nevertheless, there exists a fair case for the dependence of 'Madame, withouten many wordes' upon Saint-Gelais's 'S'amour vous a donné mon cœur en gage', while the view that Wyatt's rondeaux are influenced by the French form has yet to be discredited. He spent two years in Calais. He was fluent in French, which he used, for example, in his far from simple conversations with the Emperor Charles V. For all that, Wyatt's French debt seems to me to be overshadowed by his major Italian one, and I am content to leave some other student to investigate the matter more fully than I have done, and to supply, if need be, a scholarly correction.

I should also explain that the arrangement of my material in chapters V to VII is not intended to infer a Wyatt chronology. I cannot accept W. E. Simonds's dating of the poems by their style and emotional content, or A. K. Foxwell's dating by the order in which they stand in the Egerton MS. Only a few dates are known and a few others conjecturable. The Plutarch translation was completed by 31 December 1527. A handful of poems seems to be connected with Anne Boleyn and may therefore belong within the period in which Wyatt knew her (c. 1525–36). The first satire was written some time after 1532, and seems to refer to Wyatt's withdrawal from court in 1536. Mr Mason would allocate the Psalms to the same year. Three poems clearly belong to Wyatt's residence in Spain between 1537 and 1539, while the succeeding years produced a sonnet lamenting Cromwell's fall (1540), as well as providing an alternative 'period' for the Psalms. Finally, in the winter of 1540–1, just before or during his imprisonment, Wyatt wrote his 'Defence' and 'Declaration to the Council'. For the rest, it cannot even be assumed that his translations from Italian poetry precede the apparently more mature imitations. For 'So feble is the thred', a plodding translation of Petrarch, was done 'In Spayne', that is, late in Wyatt's career.

My numerous debts to Wyatt scholars are, I hope, sufficiently indicated in the text, and, in spite of the drastic pruning they have undergone, in the footnotes. The books already mentioned have all proved useful, and, with Mr Mason's, I would couple the equally stimulating *Music and Poetry in the Early Tudor Court* (1961) by John Stevens. I have presumed, in one chapter, to dissent from these authors' opinion of Wyatt's courtly lyrics, but I am far from wishing this dissent to obscure the fact of my gratitude to them. In addition, I should like to speak of some editions of Wyatt. G. F. Nott's text, published in 1816, was a monumental and pioneer work. Still, the poems continued, throughout the nineteenth century, to be studied in the 'edited' text of Tottel's 'Miscellany' of *Songs and Sonettes* (1557). In 1913 A. K. Foxwell effected a great change. She not only produced the best text to date, but, in establishing the importance of the Egerton MS and tracing the history of the Devonshire, put all later students in her debt. If I find occasion to disagree with a few of her comments, it will not, I trust, suggest disrespect. Her edition was, in 1949, superseded by Kenneth Muir's *Collected Poems of Sir Thomas Wyatt*, and herewith I acknowledge my greatest debt. This debt is not only to Professor Muir's text, which I use throughout this study, but to his most generous assistance. Though my book was completed before the publication of his *Life and Letters of Sir Thomas Wyatt* (1963), I have been able to incorporate quotations from and references to his text of the letters and speeches. He kindly sent me the proofs of that section of his book. The alternative would have been to quote the letters from Nott's edition, the 'Declaration' from Miss Foxwell's, and the 'Defence' from Thomas Gray's transcript, published by Horace Walpole as long ago as 1772. These three sources are, in fact, alike in being out of print and generally inaccessible. The advantage of using the new text must be obvious.

Parts of this study have appeared in the form of articles, and for permission to use them I thank the editors of *The Huntington Library Quarterly*, *Comparative Literature*, *English Miscellany*, and *The Review of English Studies*. I also acknowledge gratefully the assistance of Dr J. H. P. Pafford and his staff in the University of London library, of the Earl of Romney, who has allowed me to use the Wyatt MSS, and of the Principal and Governors of Queen Mary College, who have given me generous support, including a term's study leave. Last but by no means least, I thank Mr Francis Berry for his most friendly encouragement. I have not, however, inflicted a reading of my typescript on any friend or colleague, and so, by no stretch of imagination, can anyone but myself be held to blame for errors in it.

Abbreviations

BESIDES the usual abbreviations for periodicals and reference books, the following are used:

Blage Sir Thomas Wyatt and his Circle, *Unpublished Poems*, ed. from the Blage MS by Kenneth Muir. English Reprints Series: no. 18 (Liverpool, 1961).

Foxwell *The Poems of Sir Thomas Wiat*, ed. A. K. Foxwell, 2 vols. (London, 1913).

Letter(s) Kenneth Muir, *Life and Letters of Sir Thomas Wyatt* (Liverpool, 1963).

LP *Letters and Papers of Henry VIII*, ed. J. S. Brewer, R. H. Brodie, and J. Gairdner, 21 vols. (London, 1862 &c.).

Merriman *Life and Letters of Thomas Cromwell*, ed. R. B. Merriman, 2 vols. (Oxford, 1902).

Muir *Collected Poems of Sir Thomas Wyatt*, ed. Kenneth Muir (London, 1949; repr. 1960).

Padelford *The Poems of Henry Howard Earl of Surrey*, ed. Frederick Morgan Padelford. University of Washington Publications, Language and Literature: no. 5 (Seattle; rev. ed. 1928).

Petrarch Francesco Petrarca *Le Rime*, ed. Giosuè Carducci and Severino Ferrari (Florence, 1899; repr. 1957).

Quyete of Mynde Plutarch *Quyete of Mynde*, trans. Thomas Wyat. Reproduced in facsimile from the copy in the Henry E. Huntington Library, with an introduction by Charles Read Baskervill (Cambridge, Mass., 1931)

SL *Secular Lyrics of the XIVth and XVth Centuries*, ed. Rossell Hope Robbins (Oxford; 2nd ed. 1955).

Tottel *Tottel's Miscellany*, ed. Hyder E. Rollins, 2 vols. (Cambridge, Mass., 1928-9).

Wyatt MSS   The manuscript volume, with this title, in the British Museum (See Appendix A).

REFERENCES, where possible, are to the numbers of the items in the above publications; otherwise, to the page numbers.

EDITIONS. The above list includes the editions most frequently used. Quotations from the Latin authors, Boethius, Seneca, Horace, Persius, and Juvenal are taken from the texts published by the Loeb Classical Library; and from Chaucer, from *The Complete Works*, ed. F. N. Robinson (Boston and London, 2nd ed. 1957).

QUOTATIONS. In quotations from early printed books, the usual contractions are expanded, and archaic symbols, such as the long s, have been modernized.

PART ONE
Wyatt's Environment and Life

CHAPTER I
Introductory

And consider wel your good grandfathir what things ther wer in him,
and his end; and they that knew him notid him thus: first and chiefly to
haue a great reuerens of god and good opinion of godly things, next
that ther was no man more piteful, *no man more trew of his word, no man
faster to his frend, no man diligenter nor more circumspect, which thing
both the kings his masters notid in him greatly.* And if thes things, and
specially the grace of god that the feare of god alway kept with him, had
not ben, the chansis of thes troublesome worlde that he was in had long
ago ouirwhelmid him. This preseruid him in prison from the handes of
the tirant that could find in his hart to see him rakkid, from two yeres
and more prisonment in Scotland, in Irons and Stoks, from the danger
of sodeyn changes and commotions diuers, till that welbelouid of many,
hatid of none, in his fair age and good reputation godly and Christenly
he went to him that louid him for that he always had him in reuerens.
(Sir Thomas Wyatt's description of his father, from a letter to his son,
15 April 1537: Letter no. 1, with my italics.)

SIR THOMAS WYATT's solemn filial piety is, perhaps, unusual in
that it accurately matches the facts of his father, Sir Henry Wyatt's life.
He interprets these facts—and this is less surprising—in accordance
with Tudor ideals of service. Service to God and service to the King
are found in perfect harmony. Wyatt, like his father, is remote from
Sir Thomas More's experience of their disharmony. He describes the
perfect royal servant, a man pious and mindful of God, but also endowed with virtues useful in the world, like friendliness, diligence,
and circumspection. His father, first of influences upon him, also set a

standard by which Wyatt himself would, in his own time, have been judged. If posterity remembers only the courtly love poet, Wyatt's contemporaries regarded also, and more keenly, the servant of the state, his father's heir.

Henry Wyatt, born about 1460, early linked his destiny to the house of Tudor, and this obscure Yorkshire gentleman thereby founded his own and his family's fortunes. In 1483 he took part in the Duke of Buckingham's unsuccessful revolt against Richard III and in favour of Henry Tudor, Earl of Richmond, then biding his time in Brittany. 'Wyat why are thou such a foole? thou servest for moonshine in the water, A beggarly fugitive, forsake him, and become mine, who can reward thee and I Swear unto thee, Will.' With these words, Richard, according to the Wyatts' domestic chronicler, attempted to seduce him. But Henry Wyatt preferred to endure cold, starvation, and torture in the Tower. 'If I had first chosen you for my Master,' he replied, 'thus faithfull would I have been to you, if you should have needed it, but the Earle, poor and unhappy, tho he be, is my Master, and no discouragement or allurement shall ever drive, or draw me from him, by Gods grace.'[1]

This sublime argument for feudal loyalty was too simple for all participants in the struggle which culminated on 22 August 1485 at Bosworth Field; and especially for those already established in the governing class, like Thomas Howard, grandfather of the other great early Tudor poet, Henry, Earl of Surrey. Thomas Howard's father, the Duke of Norfolk, died fighting for the 'tyrant' Richard, and he himself was also present at Bosworth. Called to account by Henry Tudor, now *de facto* King Henry VII, he offered an explanation which breathes the respect, not of the retainer, but of the maintainer: 'He was my crowned King, and if the Parlamentary authority of England sette the Crowne vppon a stocke, I will fight for that stocke. And as I fought then for him, I wil fight for you, when you are established by the said authoritie.' And William Camden, who tells the tale, adds 'And so hee did'.[2]

Howard rode the storm, the enormous disadvantages of his royal blood, and Yorkist allegiance. If he won a measure of Tudor confidence, regaining the Dukedom of Norfolk and Earldom of Surrey, he and his heirs remained always suspect as possible hotheads, and always inclined to oppose upstarts, like Wolsey and Cromwell. Henry Wyatt,

[1] Wyatt MSS, no. 29. f. 33ʳ. For a note on the MSS and their contributors, see Appendix A.

[2] *Remaines of a Greater Worke, concerning Britaine* (London, 1605), p. 217.

on the other hand, was the creature of the hour. He was a mere 'private gentleman', and one, moreover, who had stood the test of service. By birth and worth alike, such men were eminently suited to the role of new Tudor official. They could be relied upon to work under the up-starts.

After Bosworth there was no more moonshine. Henry Wyatt won the profitable position of Keeper of Norwich Castle and Gaol, to be promoted, in 1486, to Constable. He secured court office as assistant to the Master of the King's Jewels, whom he shortly succeeded: there to remain until, in 1524, having installed his son in a warm nook as clerk, he became Treasurer of the King's Chamber. He served also as Clerk of the King's Mint, from which he was promoted to Keeper of the Change and Comptroller of the Mint. Clearly he was a 'diligent' ad-ministrator and financier, as skilful as the notorious Empson and Dud-ley in building up the King's resources, and either more skilful, or, simply, luckier, in looking after himself.

With money saved and some borrowed from the King, Henry Wyatt, in 1492, bought and set about restoring Allington Castle in Kent, henceforward the chief of the family properties. He established himself as a Kentish gentleman, on good terms with his neighbours, the Cheneys of Shurland, the Brookes of Cobham, the Boleyns of Hever, and the Poynings of Westenhanger. He served on the commission of the peace for Kent and several other home counties. In about 1500 he married Anne, daughter of John Skinner of Reigate, who bore him a son, Thomas, and a daughter, Margaret, and who, during his frequent absences on royal business, kept up the hospitality for which Allington had soon become famous. Of Lady Wyatt's lively personality, one anecdote deserves to be told. Among her visitors was the Abbot of the neighbouring Boxley Abbey, renowned for its miraculous 'Rood of Grace', an imposture destined to be exposed not long before, in 1540, the dissolved abbey itself fell into Wyatt hands.[1] This fraudulent abbot took to playing 'pranks' with my lady's maids. She 'set a watch upon him', caught him out, and, ignoring the privilege of his cloth, set him in the stocks before the castle. He complained to the Privy Council and Wyatt was applied to. He laughed the matter off, asking what man was responsible for his wife's actions in his absence.[2] Judgement is not recorded, but Wyatt, himself a Privy Councillor from 1504, was cheer-fully secure in the royal favour. In the family chronicle he is the simple, unselfish servant who would even admonish the King if he thought his

[1] *V. C. H. Kent*, ii. 154.   [2] Wyatt MSS, no. 29, ff. 35ʳ–36ʳ.

conduct 'not for his worship'. But clearly he was, after all, no 'fool'. The 'circumspection' noted by his son mingles with the simplicity and courage of Richard's victim.

Yet the soldierly virtues remained. Wyatt fought all three of the traditional English enemies: rebels against the crown, the Scots, and the French. In 1487 he assisted in the defeat of Lambert Simnel at Stoke on Trent, to be rewarded with the office of Bailiff and Constable of Conisborough Castle in Yorkshire. Appointed, in 1494, Governor of the city and castle of Carlisle, Wyatt engaged in the recurrent border warfare and was taken. The 'two yeres and more prisonment . . . in Irons and Stoks', which his son records, followed, and his release probably dates from the Scottish truce of 1497. Much later, in 1513, Wyatt was made a knight banneret for service in France with Henry VIII at the victorious Battle of the Spurs. Only a week later, on 22 August, Thomas Howard, true to his Bosworth promise, demolished the Scots at Flodden. Doubtless the anniversary of Bosworth in 1513 was a peak moment for both the aristocratic hothead and the private gentleman.

But this is to anticipate. Henry VII died in April 1509, to be succeeded by his second son, Henry VIII, a boy not yet eighteen. The last and not least of the old King's acts was to secure, by his will, the continuity of the government. And the last and not least of Wyatt's services to his master was as one of his executors. The members of the old Privy Council, Wyatt among them, were admitted to the new one: there was little change, except that Wolsey now joined them. The government was carried on in the old way, except that the council was forced to sacrifice the unpopular royal extortioners, Empson and Dudley. Most offices were confirmed, and some new honours were showered on the trusty old servants through whom the gay and as yet unpolitical young King was at first content to rule. At the coronation on 24 June Wyatt was made a knight of the Bath. He retained all his other offices. The years to follow brought new honours. In 1511, jointly with Sir Thomas Boleyn, Wyatt was made Constable of Norwich Castle. In 1510 and 1511 he obtained substantial grants of land in Middlesex, Northamptonshire, and Berkshire. He won the new King's respect at the Battle of the Spurs, was present in his courtly office as Master of the King's Jewels at the Field of the Cloth of Gold, and in 1527 entertained Henry at Allington. And meanwhile he was also grooming his son for the royal service.

Thomas Wyatt was born in 1503 at Allington 'in kente . . .

where . . . is spoken as brode and rude englissh as in ony place of englond'.[1] And his only reminiscence of early days, if not 'rude', is pleasantly homely:

> My mothers maydes when they did sowe and spynne,
> They sang sometyme a song of the feld mowse.   (no. 197)

Little, in fact, is known of his childhood in the renovated thirteenth-century castle on the Medway, except a family tale of his courage. A lion's whelp, which he had reared as a pet, one day 'ran roaring' upon Wyatt, who 'drew forth his Rapier, and ran it into the Rebels heart'. The story impressed Henry VIII, who remarked of its hero 'Oh, he will tame Lyons'.[2]

In childhood Wyatt laid the foundations of one of his three great friendships. Thomas Poynings was the illegitimate son of Sir Edward Poynings, who as leader in the 1483 rebellion and later Comptroller of the Household had much in common with his neighbour Sir Henry. The two boys were introduced by their fathers at court in 1516, when they served as ewers extraordinary at the christening of Princess Mary. For both it was the beginning of a successful courtly career, throughout which their friendship would last. When abroad Wyatt would write to Poynings, and even as late as 1541, a Lady Poynings, probably his wife, is found living at Allington castle. 'Excoluit largi Poyningi pectus.'[3] Valued for his generosity, this rather inconspicuous man became a friend as dear as the learned John Mason and the witty George Blage.

For Wyatt, Princess Mary's christening was only a brief foretaste of the court, and he was sent, in the same year, to the newly founded college of St John at Cambridge. The contribution of the university to his education is a matter of surmise only, for, beyond the fact that he met there his friend and elegist, the scholarly John Leland, there is no record of his activities. The study of Latin may be taken for granted. Wyatt read it easily, and, years later, recommended Seneca and Epictetus to his son. Greek was almost certainly not at his command, for he displays no first-hand knowledge of it. On the other hand he was at least well placed to appreciate the value of all the new learning, classical and scriptural. When he went to Cambridge, the humanistic

---

[1] William Caxton's preface to Raoul Lefevre's, *The Recuyell of the Historyes of Troye* (c. 1474), ed. H. O. Sommer (London, 1894), i. 4.

[2] Wyatt MSS, no. 29. ff. 30ʳ–32ʳ.

[3] See John Leland's elegies on Wyatt: *Naeniae in Mortem Thomae Viat* (London, 1542), sig. A 3ʳ.

reforms of the Chancellor, John Fisher, had been under way for some years. Between 1511 and 1514 Erasmus had taught Greek and Divinity in the university. And, after his departure, he wrote approvingly of the spread of 'Good Letters' there, of the study of Greek and 'a renovated Aristotle'. 'Cambridge,' he added, 'is a changed place.'[1] The change, furthermore, received no more ideal expression than at St John's. For its foundation had been almost entirely the work of Fisher, in his role as executor to its benefactress Lady Margaret Beaufort, and it was in the spirit of Christian Humanism that he drew up its statutes. He conceived St John's as an austere, religious community, where the poor scholar was specially welcome, and where, while Theology was the crown of all studies, 'Good Letters' were also prominent. The college rapidly expanded, and Fisher's own chaplain Nicholas Metcalfe became master in 1518.

Anthony à Wood claims that Wyatt was in due course 'transplanted' to Oxford 'purposely to advance himself in knowledge', and that 'Afterwards being sent to travel, he return'd an accomplish'd gentleman.'[2] Though no evidence exists to support this story, Wood is correct in his emphasis on gentlemanly accomplishment. For all the monastic influence of St John's, Sir Henry Wyatt's son was not brought up to pursue learning as a career, but, like many other young gentlemen of his era, to use it for the benefit of court and government. Like George Herbert's his 'birth and spirit rather took, The way that takes the town'.

Accordingly, the next step was marriage, which (almost certainly) took place in 1520, when Wyatt was still only seventeen. The bride was Elizabeth Brooke, daughter of the Wyatts' neighbour Lord Cobham. A son, Thomas, was born the following year, and one of his godfathers was the Duke of Norfolk, the friendly connection with whom arose, probably, through the Boleyns.

Meanwhile, by 1523 Wyatt was already helping his father with the royal finances. His first official appointment followed in 1524, when he was made clerk of the King's Jewels. By 1525 he was also an 'esquire of the body'. Yet if he owed this start in life to Sir Henry Wyatt, he lived henceforth by his own wits and went his own way. He became less the soldier and administrator, and more the diplomat and accomplished courtier. He inherited little of his father's skill with money. The family

---

[1] *The Epistles of Erasmus*, trans. F. M. Nichols (London, 1901–18), ii. 331 and iii. 177.

[2] *Athenae Oxonienses*, ed. Philip Bliss (London, 1813–20), i. 124.

chronicler contrasts them, describing Thomas as a great housekeeper and 'rather wastfull than thrifty'.[1] In 1528 Sir Henry resigned the Treasurership of the Chamber to Sir Brian Tuke, who henceforward had a good deal to do with Thomas Wyatt's debts to the King. (It would be interesting to know if their communications extended beyond such dull matters. For Tuke, like Wyatt, admired Chaucer, writing a preface to the edition produced in 1532 by William Thynne, the chief clerk of the King's kitchen.)

In the last eight years of his life, before his death in 1536, Sir Henry retired to Allington, regretting that he was too infirm to serve any longer, and insisting that his son must supply his place. So he told the King, while admonishing Thomas to give attendance on his grace day and night, and begging Cromwell to be as a father, that the son might 'fly vice' and yet—one reads easily between the lines of his letters—and yet still succeed as a royal servant.[2] He wrote as though unaware, not only of the dangerous quicksands of Tudor favouritism, but also of any incompatibility between service to God and service to the King. 'By the Mass,' said the Duke of Norfolk to More, 'it is perilous striving with Princes, and therefore I would wish you somewhat to incline to the King's pleasure. For by God's body (Mr More) *Indignatio principis mors est.*'[3] The problem did not even enter the Wyatts' consciousness, so perfectly did the ideal and prudential motives in their service to Henry VIII coincide.

The splendid example of his father was that part of Thomas Wyatt's legacy which, he told his own son, was of more value than all the family properties. Fate, indeed, had dealt him a strong hand and, with some lapses, he played it well. The following study of his life and its background falls into two sections: the first dealing with Tudor love and marriage, leading to Wyatt's career as a courtly lover, the second dealing with Tudor learning and government, leading to Wyatt's diplomatic career.

[1] Wyatt MSS, no. 29. f. 35ʳ.

[2] For the letters, all of 1536, to the King, Wyatt, and Cromwell, see, respectively, LP, xi. 1492, x. 819, and x. 840.

[3] William Roper, *Life of More* (Paris, 1626), Everyman edition, p. 49.

CHAPTER II

Courtly Love

Loue wel and agre with your wife, for where is noyse and debate in the hous, ther is unquiet dwelling. And mitch more wher it is in one bed. Frame wel your self to loue, and rule wel and honestly your wife as your felow, and she shal loue and reuerens you as her hed ... And the blissing of god for good agrement between the wife and husband is fruyt of many children, which I for the like thinge doe lack, and the faulte is both in your mother and me, but chieflie in her. (Wyatt's advice to his newly-married son, 15 April 1537: Letter no. 1.)

Come on now, my lorde of Londone, what is my abhominable and viciouse livinge? Do ye know yt or have ye harde yt? I graunte I do not professe chastite, but yet I vse not abhomination. Yf ye knowe yt, tell yt here, with whome and when. Yf ye harde yt, who is your autor? Have you sene me have anye harlet in my howse whylst ye were in my companie? (Wyatt's 'Defence' against the Bishop of London's charge of loose living, January 1541: see Letters no. 37, p. 206.)

T HE Italian author of a *Relation of England*, written about 1500, thought the English licentious, cold, and mercenary in love and marriage.[1] Among gentry, as well as royalty and nobility, marriages were, of course, bargains. 'Hath Leonato any son, my lord?' Claudio's shrewd inquiry into Hero's prospects is nothing to the ruthless probing revealed in the late fifteenth-century *Paston Letters*. Edmund Paston inspects a widow for his brother William: a 'fayer jantylwoman', with a hundred marks in cash, besides household stuff, plate, and land, and

[1] *A Relation, or Rather a True Account, of the Island of England*, trans. Charlotte Augusta Sneyd. Camden Society (London, 1847), p. 24.

only two children.[1] There are years of delay before Anne Paston marries William Yelverton who 'seyde but late that he wold have hyr, iff she had hyr mony, and ellis nott'.[2] And meanwhile her brothers, like humdrum versions of the Duchess of Malfi's, are hard at work to see 'that the olde love of Pampyng renewe natt'. Pampyng is a family servant, and neither his, Anne's, nor Yelverton's feelings are much to the point.

Yet the shocked Italian's is not quite the whole story, and Shakespeare, be it noted, presents Claudio as a lover. The desideratum is, really, a marriage where prudential and affectionate impulses coincide, and where there is good hope of children. Margaret Paston desires her son to marry a kinswoman of the Queen, that, through her, he may regain his lands; but only, the anxious mother adds, 'yf ye can fynde in yowyr harte to love hyr, so that sche be suche one as ye can thynke to have issu by, or ellys, by my trowthe, I had rather that ye never maryd in yowyr lyffe'.[3] There is some giving in to lovers' feelings. Sir John Kendal opposes his cousin John Clippesby's suit to Constance Paston only at first: 'At that tyme I knewe not what love was bitwix them, but now I undrestand that bothe there myndes is to mary to geders.'[4] It was not, one gathers, actually an unsuitable match.

Many moralists feared undue independence as immoral, unfilial, and anti-social. Roger Ascham deplored the fact that 'not onelie yong ientlemen, but euen verie girles dare without all feare, . . . where they list, and how they list, marie them selues in spite of father, mother, God, good order, and all'.[5] But Sir John Kendal's more humane view was shared by others, like Miles Coverdale:

> For an vngodly and vnhappy thyng is it in the cause of mariage to compel a yong man agaynst his wyl, to take such one as he hath no harte vnto. For in mariage ought to be the full consent of both parties with the consent of theyr parentes.[6]

Writing on *The Christen State of Matrimony* (1543), Coverdale goes on to echo Margaret Paston in advising a young man to choose a girl fit 'to beare children, and to kepe an house, euen such a persone as thou canste fynde in thyn herte to loue, and to be contente withe all'.[7] Compare Wyatt's advice to his son. The picture in both cases is one of

---

[1] *The Paston Letters*, ed. James Gairdner (Edinburgh, 1910), iii. 278.
[2] *Ibid.*, iii. 102–3.　　　[3] *Ibid.*, iii. 231.　　　[4] *Ibid.*, iii. 397.
[5] *The Scholemaster* (1570), ed. Edward Arber, English Reprints (London, 1920), p. 50.
[6] *Op. cit.*, f. 14ʳ.　　　[7] *Ibid.*, f. 40ᵛ.

domestic, rather than romantic, bliss. Is it tacitly agreed that the young husband may seek romance elsewhere? The distinction implied in Wyatt's 'I graunte I do not professe chastite, but yet I vse not abhomination' has, indeed, 'almost the air of the distinction between an Honours School and a Pass School'.[1] It also involves a distinction between the morality proper to men and that proper to women. Whatever his tremblings before God, a gentleman is not ashamed to confess, among his worldly equals, to romantic lack of chastity, but his wife's adultery is a blot on the family escutcheon; and this is, in fact, the matrimonial 'fault' to which Wyatt refers. For Coverdale, all 'inordinate affeccion' is dangerous. Adultery is 'horrible, both in men & women, yet in women it is moost hurtfull & destable'.[2] Notice, too, Ascham's shocked observation that the young gentleman's habit of doing what he list has spread to 'verie girles'. This traditional double morality Erasmus was almost alone in attacking as unfair to women and indulgent to men.

Similarly, the Church's view, backed by Aristotle's, of women's inferiority, generally prevails. 'Woman in her greatest perfection, was made to serue and obey man'.[3] John Knox, in one of his less virulent 'blasts' against women, merely echoes St Paul. On the other hand, St Thomas More's enlightened treatment of wife and daughters shows, at least, that they need not be mere chattels. Even the Church was sometimes willing to generalize from Mary as well as from Eve. And many a medieval poem, in the form of a *disputatio*, argues the issue. Sir Thomas Elyot takes it up in a serious prose *Defence of Good Women* (1545), which is in the form of a debate. Caninius supports the opinion that 'a woman is a worke of nature vnperfecte'; but Candidus, who gains the 'preheminence', shows that this is 'cankred malice', and that women are perfect in their kind.[4] Elyot is still at a good distance, however, from the poetic and Platonic idealization of women's superiority, which, in some aristocratic circles of his day, was becoming popular. Wyatt, too, ignores modern theorizing and sticks to the orthodox view: his son is 'head' over his wife, but must love her as his 'fellow'.

These are the views of moralists and guardians. How do the lovers themselves feel? Margery Brews nags her parents to improve her poor

---

[1] C. S. Lewis, *The Allegory of Love* (Oxford, rev. ed. 1938), p. 42 n.

[2] *Op. cit.*, ff. 17ᵛ and 34ʳ.

[3] *The First Blast of the Trvmpet Against the Monstrvovs Regiment of Women* (Geneva, 1558), f. 13ʳ.

[4] *Op. cit.*, sigs. B 3ᵛ, A 1ᵛ, and B 5ᵛ.

dowry, while pleading with her prospective husband to be content with it: 'But yf that ye loffe me, as I tryste verely that ye do, ye will not leffe me therefor; for if that ye hade not halfe the lyvelode that ye hafe . . . I wold not forsake yowe.' For he is her 'ryght welebeloved Voluntyne', to whom she sends love poems, in whose absence she is as sick in heart as body: 'there wottys no creature what peyn that I endure'.[1] The very picture of the courtly lover, only appearing in the guise of a middle-class girl, and in life, not in literature. Margery is still far from the social rebel, but, in a world of unromantic prices, she pleads for romantic values. Hers is also a protest against the stock notion of girls as chattels.

Sir John Paston understands the paradox that girls are and are not chattels. True, he can drive a shrewd bargain. Yet he either believes or makes belief that Anne Haute is the object of much chivalrous devotion:

> I beseche yow, let me not be forgotyn when ye rekyn up all yowr ser-vaunts, to be sett in the nombyr with other. . . . And I prey yow, Mastresse Annes, for that servyse that I owe yow, that in as short tyme as ye goodly may that I myght be assarteynyd of yowr entent. . . . And now farewell, myn owne fayir lady.[2]

Love as 'service', with rivalry among servants for the favour of fair ladies, is, of course, among the most deeply entrenched conventions of courtly love literature. What we have to notice is that the courtly idiom has currency in life as well as in literature. It is a mode of expressing real feelings. The point, essential to this study, needs to be laboured because it is so often assumed that the conventional literary terms make a poor job of masking insincere or unreal feelings, that, in fact, they have nothing to do with life. But conventional people like the Pastons —that is, most people—invariably use conventional terms. A non-literary example of love-convention is the giving of a ring as a pledge. No one thinks the feeling behind this unreal, much less insincere, simply because it has, for centuries, been the thing to do.

Margery Brews's breaking out into poetry is relatively uncommon. Yet *The Paston Letters* also include verses which are (editorially) de-scribed as 'written by a Lady in the reign of Henry VI. or Edward IV. to an absent Lord with whom she was in love'.[3] Needless to say, these verses are decidedly conventional, and, were it not for their context, would doubtless be explained away as 'literary exercises'. This lady is shaken as with a 'fevyr . . . now hot, now cold'. She envies 'thys rude

---

[1] *Paston Letters, ed. cit.*, iii. 170.   [2] *Ibid.*, ii. 321–2.   [3] *Ibid.*, iii. 302–3.

byll', for it will see her 'most knyghtly gentyll knyght' before she does. She writes, meanwhile, her 'peynys to apease', an interesting suggestion that poetry can relieve, by expressing, unhappiness. But, of course, the Paston lady could have got a poet, say Lydgate, to write for her, or, simply, dipped into a commonplace book. Either way, however, the poem's *use* is non-literary. In endless array late medieval love lyrics employ the 'Go little bill' formula, apologize (unnecessarily) for 'rudeness', discourse of the fever of love and pains of absence. The inference is that some, at least, were in reality love letters.

Thomas Whythorne (1528–96), whose autobiography has recently been brought to light, records how he made his 'first entrance' into his suit to a maiden by singing his love songs to her, with virginals or lute.[1] Another young lady made advances to him by leaving verses within the strings of his gittern, and he replied to her in verse. At other times he used his poetry, not in the game of wooing, but as a means of personal expression and relief. 'I should have been very sawcy with my mistress, if I had delivered it or sung it unto her, it being so plain as it is.'[2] In fact Whythorne's poetry is autobiographical. Equally it is very stilted:

> Remember him that hath not you forgot,
> Ne your promise out of remembrance blot.[3]

Again, if these verses were encountered outside the context of autobiography, they might be thought mere essays of an apprentice to poetry.

For a certain group of early Tudor courtiers, the Devonshire Manuscript has long been recognized as a vehicle for love messages, chiefly on the grounds that it contains Lord Thomas Howard's addresses to his wife, written, probably, while both were in the Tower. This manuscript is associated not only with these two lovers, but with the Earl of Surrey, his sister, and her husband, and it contains poems not only by Thomas Howard, but by Wyatt, Surrey, Sir Antony Lee (Wyatt's brother-in-law), and other courtiers. One could certainly wish for more evidence that this courtly poetry is autobiographical, but there is sufficient to cast doubt on the impersonal theory. Outside love poetry evidence is abundant. Tudor satire and elegy provide numerous examples. A glance through Surrey's poems shows that he frequently builds on actuality:

[1] *The Autobiography of Thomas Whythorne*, ed. James M. Osborn (Oxford, 1962), p. 64.

[2] *Ibid.*, p. 46.   [3] *Ibid.*, p. 88.

his experiences as a boy at Windsor with Henry Richmond the King's son, as a prisoner in the Fleet, as the absent husband of a loving wife and son, and so on.[1]

It is unfortunate that, with one exception, the love letters of early Tudor courtiers are not easily discoverable. The few surviving from the later Tudor period confirm my belief in the social currency of the literary love idiom. Sir Christopher Hatton, the cousin of the Chancellor, writing in about 1601, floods his future wife with torrents of romantic clichés, part-Petrarchan, part-Platonic, and part from the common source of courtly love literature. He declares that he differs from the ordinary 'amorous gallants of our tyme', for 'fine beautie can pearce, and compleate perfections ravish, my admiringe soule'. His 'fancies', Cupid-like, 'are flowne abroade and have burnte theire winges in affections flame'. The 'true property' of Hatton's 'fierie soule' is to 'honour chast beauty where ever it harbers'. He pursues Alice, 'soe woorthy a game', like a huntsman. His 'stammeringe' letter is his 'atturnie' in the 'court of beautie'. He must live 'discontented' till his 'longinge desires' are satisfied. And, naturally, he concludes with verses.[2]

The exception, mentioned above, is the collection of love letters written by Henry VIII to Anne Boleyn. The King, with all his *droit du seigneur*, is a courtly lover and directs his feeling in what, did they occur in the context of fiction, would be thought purely literary channels. He is, in fact, a stiff, stilted, letter-writer. Always he is Anne's 'loyall et plus assure serviteure'. Absence is wearisome, more so, of course, to servant than to mistress. 'Je suffre' is Henry's constant refrain, while the uncertainty whether to construe Anne's letters to his advantage or otherwise, brings on a 'grand agonye'. He pleads for a favourable response, for he is struck with the dart of love—'attaynte du dart damours'—and, of course, he apologizes for the ineptness of his 'rude lettre'.[3]

To generalize about love and marriage at Henry's court is no easy matter, for the evidence is varied, and it seems best to proceed by means of examples. These will confirm what *The Paston Letters* tell us, with this difference: the romantic atmosphere at court was distinctly more

[1] See, for example, Padelford nos. 31, 32, and 33.
[2] *Correspondence of the Family of Hatton*, ed. Edward Maunde Thompson. Camden Society (Westminster, 1878), i. 1–2.
[3] *The Love Letters of Henry VIII*, ed. H. Savage (London, 1949), nos. 2, 4, and 5.

heady than among the country gentry, and the marriage contracts were under an even stricter surveillance. Among kings, Henry VIII was almost eccentric in considering his personal inclinations as he entered the marriage market. And he certainly did not extend the privilege to his relatives and friends. The bewildering way in which the dauphins, princes, and infants of sixteenth-century Europe were contracted and re-contracted in marriage is merely an illustration of political manoeuvres and shifting alliances. At the age of two, Henry's daughter Mary was engaged to the Dauphin of France, only the first of many matches mooted for her. In 1529, for instance, the poet Surrey, then only twelve, was put forward. But he, or rather his father, the ambitious Duke of Norfolk, was disappointed, and in 1532 Surrey was married off to Frances Vere, the Earl of Oxford's daughter. He appears to have been perfectly happy in this arranged marriage. For personal feelings did not always conflict with 'good order'. And headstrong feelings also sometimes triumphed. To seal the peace treaty of 1514 Henry's sister Mary went off, in high dudgeon, to marry Louis XII of France. The gay princess is said to have exhausted her elderly husband, who died only two months later. Early in 1515 Mary married Charles Brandon, Duke of Suffolk, as she had always said she would. Henry was ostensibly furious when he heard of their private wedding in Paris, but soon accepted the situation. The instructive point, here, is that he had really favoured the match and the bridegroom for some time. Had he not done so, catastrophe would have resulted, as it did in the case of his niece, Lady Margaret Douglas and Lord Thomas Howard. Howard, 'without the kynges assent', married Margaret, 'for whiche presumpteous acte he was attainted of treason'.[1] Henry's reactions had little enough to do with morals. Howard was honourable in his private actions. Suffolk was not. Indeed, Suffolk's married life and love life were not unlike those of the King who was his bosom friend and, in appearance, strikingly resembled him. For when he married Princess Mary he committed bigamy. Lady Mortimer claimed connubial rights in 1524, and was not silenced till 1528, when Suffolk obtained a divorce from the Pope. He soon began to neglect Mary, and had various mistresses and bastards. None of this in the least affected his high standing at court.

The premier noble family of England, the Howards, regarded marriage merely as a means of empire-building. The Duke and Duchess of

[1] Edward Halle, *Chronicle; containing the History of England* (1548 and 1550) (London, edn. 1809), p. 819.

Norfolk (Surrey's parents) hated each other, and by 1533 he was openly living with Elizabeth Holland, 'a churl's daughter'. They inculcated no idea of the sacredness of marriage into the younger generation, but leaped at every chance of a royal alliance. Their daughter Mary was wedded in childhood to the King's bastard, Henry Duke of Richmond. Of their nieces, Mary Boleyn became the King's mistress, Anne Boleyn and Catherine Howard his wives. A recent biographer of Catherine Howard suggests that her attitude to love and marriage was that of her clan, her time, and her situation.[1] In youth she was unchaste, as were her fellow maids of honour in the household of the Dowager Duchess of Norfolk. First her music master, Henry Manox, flirted with her. After, a young gentleman-retainer of the family, Francis Dereham, made yet more headway, calling Catherine his wife, and visiting her in the girls' dormitory at night. Finally, after her marriage to the infatu-ated King, Catherine was foolish enough to take Thomas Culpeper as lover, and this, in combination with her earlier affairs, finally ruined her. All the ashes were raked over at her fall, and Dereham was reported to have said that if the King 'were dead I am sure I might marry her'.[2] The kind of evidence on which Catherine was convicted is strikingly like that produced at the trial of her predecessor, Anne Boleyn. It is mentioned here partly for the light it throws on that event, an event which impinges on the life of Wyatt. In both cases gossip serves as evidence, but it may safely be said that the case against Catherine was much more concrete than that against Anne. At the same time, both these Howard ladies have the same careless vanity and thirst for admiration.

There is little, so far, to suggest that the graceful art of loving was given, as it were, official recognition at court. Yet it was so. Not only courtly love letters but courtly love poems flowed from Henry's pen. 'Loue enforcyth all nobyle kynd,' he declares in a stock attack on dis-dain.[3] And the same *motif* is found in the elaborate entertainments in which he delighted, and which kept alive the outward forms of chivalric love. On Shrove Tuesday 1522 Wolsey entertained the King to supper and a show, in which his Majesty took part.[4] A castle had

[1] See Lacey Baldwin Smith, *A Tudor Tragedy: the Life and Times of Catherine Howard* (London, 1961).

[2] LP, xvi. 1414.

[3] Henry VIII, *Songs, Ballads, and Instrumental Pieces*, ed. Lady Mary Trefusis. Roxburghe Club (Oxford, 1912), no. 9.

[4] Halle, *Chronicle, ed. cit.*, p. 631.

been rigged up. It was held by ladies with 'straunge names', as, Beauty, Honour, Perseverance, Kindness, Constancy, Bounty, Mercy, Pity, while underneath the 'basse fortresse' were others called Danger, Disdain, Jealousy, Unkindness, Scorn, 'Malebouche', and Strangeness. Lords approached, by name, Amorous, Nobleness, Youth, Attendance, Loyalty, Pleasure, Gentleness, Liberty, and their leader, dressed in crimson satin, was Ardent Desire. They moved the ladies to yield. Desire encouraged them, Scorn rebuffed, and so on. Edward Halle's account transports the reader back to the *Romance of the Rose*, but at court the allegory of love is working itself out, not in words, but in action and on a social occasion. The purpose is for the men and women to show themselves knightly servants and gracious mistresses. The pantomimic garishness of these Tudor shows is, no doubt, an instance of 'The Waning of the Middle Ages', to use the title of J. H. Huizinga's classic study. With all their childishness and decadence they were undoubtedly very highly stimulating to the feelings and senses. And this applies to all the pompous occasions, even the solemn funerals, christenings, and coronations. What young courtier could fail to be impressed by the abundance of allegorical devices, the white palfreys, the cloth of gold and ostrich feathers, and the constant 'noise of minstrelles' that still haunt us in the pages of Halle's *Chronicle*? I turn now to the one young courtier, Thomas Wyatt.

Much of what follows will have to do with the affair of Wyatt and Anne Boleyn. It is as well, therefore, to deal at the outset with the once-popular notion that they were childhood sweethearts. Anne, daughter of Sir Thomas Boleyn and niece of Thomas Howard, third Duke of Norfolk, was born about 1507, the year in which her family moved to Hever Castle in Kent. Her father and Wyatt's were now neighbours, and from 1511 they also shared office in Norfolk. However, any progress of affection between their children would suffer an interruption on Anne's departure abroad. She may have gone as early as 1514, accompanying her sister Mary, the 'Madamoyselle Boleyne' appointed to attend Princess Mary on her marriage-journey. But, according to some authorities, it was not until 1518 or 1519 that her father took her over to the French court to complete her education, in which case the childhood romance would stand a better chance. Yet, whatever the truth of that matter, there can never have been any question of a marriage between Wyatt and Anne, who, as one of the ambitious Howard clan, was well beyond his reach.

About two years after his marriage, Anne did appear on Wyatt's

horizon. It was on the threat of war, late in 1521, that she returned
to England. She was now a dark-eyed beauty, fluent in French, and
witty, while even her enemies were to acknowledge her skill in dancing
and music. Wyatt was tall, fair, and handsome, with a luxuriant beard,
and superior to most men in wit and accomplishments. Anne was at
court by March 1522, but the discovery, in 1523, that she was in love
with Lord Henry Percy hurried her home, in disgrace, to Hever.
Thus a meeting between Wyatt and Anne, in 1522–3, either at court
or in Kent, is probable enough. Yet he was newly married and she
in love, so that, unless they undertook to console each other, a love
affair is not particularly likely. The idea that Anne caused an early
break-down of Wyatt's marriage receives little support. Had she done
so, the later Spanish abuse of the 'concubine' (as Catherine of Aragon's
countrymen termed Anne) would surely not have missed this tit-bit.

Nevertheless Wyatt's marriage did prove a failure. He and his wife
separated in due course, probably early, since no child was born after
the first.[1] Somewhat before 1526 is the time suggested by a Spanish
observer.[2] He adds that Wyatt repudiated his wife for adultery, while
Wyatt himself declares that the 'fault' was 'chiefly' on her side. The
impression uniformly given is that he was, indeed, badly wronged, but
that he thereupon behaved with extreme rabidity. He is said to have
'defamed' his guilty wife, thus incensing her family.[3] He certainly grew
to hate her. The frantic appeals to maintain her which, in 1537, her
brother made through Thomas Cromwell, Sir John Russell, and Sir
William Hawte—men of influence with Wyatt—were 'all to no purpose'. He reluctantly made a half-promise, then withdrew it, to George
Cobham's intense irritation.[4] Finally, in 1541, when Wyatt was in
trouble with the council, a condition for his pardon was that he should
take back Lady Wyatt, an awkward situation, for, by this time, he was
living with Elizabeth Darrell, a former maid of honour to Queen
Catherine Howard.[5]

These are the facts, and, before embarking on the mystery—for such
it is—of Wyatt's entanglement at court, it is as well to consider what
they yield. These facts admirably match the Wyatt who declared, 'I
graunte I do not professe chastite, but yet I vse not abhomination.'

---

[1] See Appendix B.   [2] C.S.P., Spanish, vi (i), 155.
[3] LP, xvi. 467.   [4] LP, xii (i), 766.
[5] E. K. Chambers gives a useful account of Elizabeth Darrell, correcting the
D.N.B., in Sir Thomas Wyatt and Some Collected Studies (London, 1933),
pp. 141–5.

Life at court was not conducive to austerity, especially in a man passionately resentful of his wife's unfaithfulness. But for 'abhominable and viciouse livinge' there is no shred of evidence. I do not refer to Bishop Bonner's ridiculous faultiness in charging Wyatt with seducing nuns, but to his constancy, in later years, to Elizabeth Darrell, for whom he provided in his will. In Wyatt's love poetry, whether as a result of literary convention or actual experience or (as I think) both, rabid bitterness, disillusion with women, and a strong sense of betrayal are present. Yet to judge by his advice to his sixteen-year-old son, he did not lose faith in the possibility of happy, fruitful, and, as the custom was in his day, early marriages: 'Frame wel your self to loue' &c. I should judge, therefore, that Wyatt's broken marriage, though embittering, was far from demoralizing him, and that, while he did not conduct himself as 'nobly' towards women as Miss Foxwell supposes, he was not depraved. As for his other affairs, we cannot go far wrong in assigning them to the period between the break-down of his marriage and the formation of the permanent attachment to Elizabeth Darrell in about 1536—in fact, to his early years at court.

Wyatt's début at court in 1523, followed by his first official appointment in 1524, has already been recorded. The Christmas of 1524–5 finds him well launched and participating in 'a chalenge of feactes of armes', a popular Tudor display, in the traditional allegorical form.[1] 'The castle of Loyaltie' was set up in the tiltyard at Greenwich. A herald announced to Queen Catherine of Aragon that the King had presented it to four maidens. They, in turn, gave the custody to a captain and fifteen gentlemen, who vowed to defend it 'against all commers, beeyng gentlemen of name and armes'. Accordingly, one day, 'twoo ancient knightes'—the King and his brother-in-law the Duke of Suffolk in disguise—arrived to do battle. They were followed by others, including the two royal favourites, Sir Francis Brian and Henry Norris. Another day George Cobham and John Poynz joined in the attack, which continued off and on until 8 February, so enjoyable was it. Wyatt, at the Castle of Loyalty, was among friends and enemies: the King, his master; the Queen, patroness of his only published work; Suffolk, his 'heavie adversarie'; Cobham, his brother-in-law; 'Myne owne John Poynz,' to whom he addressed two satires; the notorious sycophant Brian,[2] to whom he addressed another; and Norris, with whom he was to be implicated in the affairs of Anne Boleyn.

The year 1525 offers the likeliest date not only for Anne's reap-

---

[1] Halle, *Chronicle*, ed. cit., pp. 688–9.   [2] See Appendix C.

pearance at court as handmaid to Queen Catherine, but for the beginning of Wyatt's intimacy with her. It was of short duration—two
years at most—and ended on Henry's appropriation of Anne and
warning to Wyatt to leave her alone. When did this occur? Henry,
who had long since favoured the Boleyns, conferred a signal honour
in 1525 when he created Sir Thomas Viscount Rochford. But he does
not seem to have distinguished Anne openly until 1527. He could, of
course, have privately hinted to Wyatt, say, as early as 1526, that Anne
was his. But on the whole it is unlikely that Wyatt's information would
be much in advance of others'. Wolsey was in the dark until May 1527,
and the first divorce proceedings took place before him on the 17th.[1]
The news then spread, and by July the whole court knew that the
King's affair with Anne differed from the infidelities of his earlier
married life. Henry's love letters are usually assigned to the period
starting July 1527. One promises to make Anne his 'sole mistress', 'to
remove all others from my affection'.[2] Now Wyatt was in Italy from
January to May 1527, with Sir John Russell's embassy. The travellers
were 'detained' at Civitavecchia until 4 May, and in Savona on 11th.[3]
After this there is no news of their homeward journey, but probably
they arrived in England before the end of May. Then would be the
moment for Wyatt to receive his shock and warning, an idea to which
some colour is lent by his poetic description of May as his unlucky
month, especially in affairs of the heart:

> Let me remember the happs most vnhappy
> That me betide in May most comonly,
> As oon whome love list litil to avaunce.
> Sephame saide true that my natiuitie
> Mischaunced was with the ruler of the May.   (no. 92)[4]

The evidence for Wyatt's love for Anne and the King's veto on it,
amounts to an accumulation of references in his poems and of sometimes more, sometimes less, reliable reportage, taken in combination
with his imprisonment in 1536, at the time of the fall of Anne and her
'lovers'.

First there is the Devonshire MS in circulation among the group at
court to which Anne and Wyatt belonged. 'An' is inscribed on one

---

[1] LP, iv (ii), 3140.
[2] LP, iv (ii), 3218.   Cp. *Love Letters*, ed. cit., no. 4.
[3] LP, iv (ii), 3110 and 3111.   [4] See Appendix D.

page (f. 69^r) and 'I ama yowres An' on another (f. 67^v).[1] The last phrase is echoed in a poem (f. 17^r), possibly by Wyatt, in which a lover records how

> in my boke wrote my maystresse:
> *I am yowres, yow may well be sure,*
> *And shall be whyle my lyff dothe dure.*   (no. 114)

That was in a time of 'myrthe', now exchanged for 'hevines' and 'dystresse', and hence appropriate to a fool's paradise of 1525–6 before Wyatt irrevocably lost Anne. The poem continues in the stock vein of melancholy complaint. The poet asserts that his own love is 'fermly sett', but cannot sustain his momentary faith in the renewal of his mistress's.

Other poems suggest that the lover's suit was hopeless. Courtly love suits nearly always sound so, so that the fact, of itself, proves nothing about Wyatt's love for Anne. Only those complaints with more precise reference to her can be taken in evidence. For example:

> What wourde is that that chaungeth not,
>   Though it be tourned and made in twain?
> It is myn aunswer, god it wot,
>   And eke the causer of my payn.
>   A love rewardeth with disdain,
> Yet is it loved. What would ye more?
> It is my helth eke and my sore.   (no. 50)

This is a poem from Wyatt's own manuscript, the Egerton, and therefore to be taken more seriously than the Devonshire poems. The answer to his riddle is, or could be, the palindrome 'Anna'. This has, in fact, been inserted as the title in the manuscript 'by a later hand'. It reappears in Tottel's *Miscellany*, in which the poem is entitled 'Of his loue called Anna'. Tottel has also read 'it is myn aunswer' as 'it is mine Anna', or used a manuscript in which that variant appeared. So much would show, at least, that near-contemporaries believed that Wyatt loved a lady called Anna.

In the remaining 'Anne' poems a more worldly and knowing tone is apparent. There is no more talk of a love 'fermly sett', so that the mood

[1] R. C. Harrier challenges this reading of the inscription, in his 'Notes on Wyatt and Anne Boleyn', *J.E.G.P.*, liii (1954), 581–4. Hence I would not wish to make too much of this piece of 'evidence', especially as poem no. 114 is not indisputably Wyatt's.

described above was (if it existed at all) evanescent. The contradiction is perfectly acceptable, for whatever a man's first reactions to disappointment, hopeless love always withers eventually. ('Men have died,' sighs Rosalind, 'but not for love.') Accordingly Wyatt describes a transference of his affection:

> then do I love agayne,
> If thow aske whome, sure sins I did refrayne
> Her that ded set our country in a rore,
> Th'unfayned chere of Phillis hath the place
> That Brunet had. (no. 95)

Brunet is surely the dark-eyed Anne, who set England in a roar twice: in 1527–33 when she superseded Catherine of Aragon, and in 1536 when she was 'proved' to have cuckolded the King. Furthermore, as though to cover up Anne's tracks, Wyatt has altered the revealing line to 'Brunet, that set my welth in such a rore'. This, as Kenneth Muir points out, provides the most 'striking' evidence that Wyatt wrote poems about Anne Boleyn.[1]

It must be recalled that Wyatt had, at no time, any chance of marrying Anne. He was married to Elizabeth Brooke, and she was a Howard lady. Their situation resembles that of the courtly 'servant', one among many, *vis à vis* the great lady. It could be idealized, and it could be seen for the folly it was. Wyatt probably had not even much chance of monopolizing Anne's attention for long. The great court lady entertains a crowd of servants, whom she may encourage to the extent of accepting their love, but, in return, need only give occasional favours, or, if she prefers, disdain. The promiscuity of Henry's court was not conducive to a love 'fermly sett', and this is bound to be recognized in the end. Wyatt and the King were probably not Anne's only suitors. This dizzy and futile situation is, it is suggested, used in the sonnet

> Who so list to hount, I knowe where is an hynde,
> But as for me, helas, I may no more:
> The vayne travaill hath weried me so sore.
> I ame of theim that farthest commeth behinde;
> Yet may I by no meanes my weried mynde
> Drawe from the Diere: but as she fleeth afore,
> Faynting I folowe. I leve of therefore,
> Sins in a nett I seke to hold the wynde.

[1] Muir, p. xi.

> Who list her hount, I put him owte of dowbte,
> As well as I may spend his tyme in vain:
> And, graven with Diamonds, in letters plain
> There is written her faier neck rounde abowte:
> *Noli me tangere*, for Cesars I ame;
> And wylde for to hold, though I seme tame.   (no. 7)

The fact that this sonnet derives from Petrarch's 'Una candida cerva' is far from confounding the theory that it is personal. For several of Wyatt's versions of Italian poems strike a distinctly autobiographical note. Furthermore, this is not a translation, but a free and daring adaptation. Petrarch describes his solitary vision of a hind (Laura), who disappears (dies), because appropriated by Caesar (God). Wyatt's crowded chase, figuring Anne as the wild hind, Henry as Caesar, and the lovers as huntsmen, could hardly be more different.

This completes the survey of poems which appear specifically connected with Anne. There are others which may or may not bear upon Wyatt's experience of loving her. For example,

> Some tyme I fled the fyre that me brent,
> By see, by land, by water and by wynd;
> And now I folow the coles that be quent
> From Dovor to Calais against my mynde.   (no. 59)

Wyatt 'fled' Anne and the court on journeys abroad in 1526, 1527, and 1528.

No poem so far cited (except perhaps no. 114) contains the least inference that Wyatt and Anne were lovers. They do not give substance to the tradition that she was his mistress. On the other hand, they do not rule out the possibility. One Devonshire poem remarks

> My songes ware to defuse, . . . (*i.e.* vague)
> Theye shall be song more plaine,

and goes on, with the new plainness, to plead for the lover's rights:

> Let not the frute be lost
> That is desired moste; . . .

> Vndrestonde me who lyste;
> For I reke not a bene,
> I wott what I doo meane.   (no. 138)

This poem is to be noted, not because it proves anything about Wyatt and Anne, but because it comments on the comparative rarity of open sexual pleading in Tudor courtly poems. Love pleas are dark and oblique. Whythorne's refraining from presenting a 'plain' statement of his love to his mistress exemplifies the same reticence. Plainer speaking will be found in the prose comment on Wyatt's affair with Anne.

The gossiping chroniclers and tract-writers all concur in one point: that Wyatt courted Anne before the King stepped in. Otherwise their ideas vary, and the particular bias of each must be carefully kept in mind. None of these was an eye-witness or courtier. Only one was a contemporary. This is the unidentified Spaniard resident in Henry VIII's London, who wrote the *Chorónica del Rey Enrico Otavo de Ingalaterra*. He has a rough, unliterary style, and was perhaps a merchant. He hints that he was the one man to evade the ban on foreigners at Anne's execution. Here and wherever possible he records first-hand information. He has therefore rightly been taken as a comparatively reliable witness, and it is particularly unfortunate that, not being a courtier or even known to such courtiers as the ambassador Eustace Chapuys, he was sometimes forced back on hearsay. On the one hand he reports wrongly that Anne's father died a few days after her execution. On the other, he gives an accurate impression of Wyatt's friendly relationship with Cromwell. He has no axe to grind. He merely sets down a private record, not meant for publication. He is naturally partial to the 'sainted Queen Katharine' and hence against Anne. But, unlike Nicholas Harpsfield and Nicholas Sander, he is not a Catholic propagandist. Like many Spaniards, he respects 'the good Wyatt', who, he records, was in love with Anne before her marriage. He depicts a hero, rather like the 'hero' of Wyatt's own poems—one who told Anne of his 'torment' and pleaded for 'consolation'. He visited her in her bedchamber, 'kissed her', and 'even to still greater familiarities she made no objection'. On learning of Henry's intention to marry Anne, Wyatt warned him that she was a 'bad woman'. But the King refused to listen, and banished him for two years. (If the banishment was a reality, this must refer to Wyatt's posting to Calais from 1528 to 1530.) In 1536, declares the chronicler, Wyatt was able to remind the King of his earlier warning.[1]

Nicholas Harpsfield (1519–75) wrote *A Treatise on the Pretended Divorce between Henry VIII and Catherine of Aragon* well after the event, in the reign of Mary. As Catholic Archdeacon of Canterbury he

[1] *Chronicle of King Henry VIII of England*, trans. Martin A. Sharp Hume (London, 1889), pp. 68–9.

was concerned to reinstate his Queen's mother as Henry's 'true, most loving, chaste, tender wife'.[1] But, though a Marian propagandist, he does not take leave of evidence. His story, he claims, came from 'Anthony Bonvise', who was 'very likely to know the truth thereof'. This is Antonio Bonvisi, an Italian merchant resident off and on in London, part-time intelligence agent of Cromwell's and capable, to judge by his dutiful references to the 'Bishop of Rome', of entertaining Protestant sympathies. His story of Wyatt's warning to the King is on the same lines as the Spanish chronicler's:

> she is not meet to be copled with your grace, her conversation hath been so loose and base; which thing I know not so much by hear-say as by my own experience as one that have had my carnal pleasure with her.[2]

Nicholas Sander (1527–85) was an Elizabethan Catholic propagandist, whose *De Origine ac Progressu Schismatis Anglicani* was published in Cologne in 1585. He is the least reliable witness so far, for he does not cite authorities, and is credulously prone to melodramatic nonsense. Thus he believes the tale that, on her father's admission, Anne was not his child, but Henry VIII's, and that the latter, with this knowledge, still went ahead with his marriage to her. Sander, too, describes Wyatt's warning to the King. He went, it seems, to the council 'and confessed that he had sinned with Anne Boleyn'. Then, on meeting with incredulity, he offered to 'put it in the king's power to see with his own eyes the truth of his story, if he would but consent to test it, for Anne Boleyn was passionately in love with Wyatt'. The Duke of Suffolk bore the message to the King who merely exclaimed 'Wyatt was a bold villain, not to be trusted'. The King told Anne, who therefore shunned Wyatt, and this was afterwards to his advantage.[3] The story of Wyatt's offer of ocular proof strains credulity. One would be tempted, indeed, to dismiss Sander from the witness box altogether, were it not that he seems to hit on the truth twice. Anne's shunning of Wyatt is convincing, and receives support from the poems. More important, the Duke of Suffolk is included in Sander's story. This depraved nobleman, the King's brother-in-law and Wyatt's 'heavy adversary', has already received mention. It is necessary to my reading of

[1] *Op. cit.*, ed. Nicholas Pocock. Camden Society (London, 1878), p. 255.
[2] *Ibid.*, p. 253.
[3] *Rise and Growth of the Anglican Schism*, trans. David Lewis (London, 1877), pp. 28–30.

Wyatt's story that Suffolk be regarded, not only as the bane of Wyatt's life, but as the King's *alter ego*. In support of this last is a French report: 'he is a second king, . . . it is he who does and undoes'.[1] That was said in 1513, before Suffolk married Henry's sister, an alliance which brought him yet closer to the monarch who was never, in fact, to turn against him permanently. If he did so temporarily, it may, according to the Spanish ambassador, have been on Anne's account. Chapuys's letter[2] of 10 May 1530 retails the rumour that Suffolk's recent absence from court was the result of his having denounced her intimacy with 'a gentleman of the Court', that the gentleman (? Wyatt) had also been sent away at her request, and that the King had eventually interceded for the gentleman's return. Curiously enough, the next witness, though one diametrically opposed to Sander, is also to introduce Suffolk, and to puzzle over the enmity between Suffolk and Wyatt which, if the Spanish rumour be true, may find its explanation there.

George Wyatt (1554–1624), the poet's grandson, wrote his 'life' of Anne Boleyn at the end of the sixteenth century, and for two reasons. First, he had information deriving from Anne Gainsford (Anne Boleyn's maid) and from an unnamed lady ancestor of his own. Second, he was encouraged by the Archbishop of Canterbury, who shared the zeal of all Elizabeth's servants in reinstating her mother, 'the excellent lady' and 'spotles Queene'. His access to first-hand material must inspire confidence in George Wyatt. But his partisanship is evident too. The Wyatt Manuscripts reveal him as an ardent vindicator of the Reformation as well as of his family's loyalty, which had been called in question by 'Wyatt's Rebellion' (1554) and re-recognized on the accession of Elizabeth.[3] Obviously he has as much reason to suppress scandal as Harpsfield and Sander have to spread it. Indeed, he writes partly to refute the 'Romish fable-framer' Sander. He throws his weight on the side of courtly romance. Anne is the heroine. Many 'brave spirits' honoured her, the two chief being the King and Wyatt, whose 'hart seemed to say, *I could gladly yeald to be tiede for ever with the knot of her love*', as expressed 'somewhere in his verses'. (The common 'knot' metaphor is frequently used by Wyatt, and his grandson's sanction for a personal reading of the poems is welcome.) George Wyatt is suspect of white-washing when he goes on to say that Anne hesitated to accept the King's suit out of love for Queen Catherine, and that she rejected Wyatt's because he was a married man. True to the principle of courtly

---

[1] LP, i (ii), 2171.   [2] *C.S.P. Spanish* IV, (i), 302.   [3] See Appendix A.

gentleness, Anne, we are told, did not scorn Wyatt. She was not, in fact, 'my Lady Disdain', though, inevitably, she left him a disappointed lover. One day Wyatt, 'in sportinge wise', snatched a jewel from her, thrust it in his bosom, and kept it as a favour. George Wyatt now differs from the other reporters in describing, not Wyatt's warning to the King, but the King's to Wyatt. The royal veto came at a famous game of bowls between various courtiers, including Henry, Wyatt, Suffolk, and Brian. The King affirmed a cast to be his that plainly was not, pointing with a finger on which was Anne's ring. Wyatt took his meaning, but boldly produced Anne's jewel and said, 'I hope it will be mine.' The King angrily broke up the game—'then am I deceived'— but Anne soon settled his doubts. (This would lead naturally to her shunning Wyatt, as in Sander's account, though George Wyatt does not mention the fact.) Sander's 'fable' of Wyatt's confession to the council is then dismissed, and his account of Suffolk's meddling softened. George Wyatt has 'heard' that Brian confessed such things of another lady, whom the King gave up to him. But he does think that Suffolk, 'upon the sight of that which happened at bowles', may have tried to dissuade the King from marriage to Anne. Then, having earned their 'misliking', he turned his own 'heave displeasure . . . ever after' on Wyatt. This is put forward as a hypothesis, George Wyatt confessing to his failure to discover the cause of Suffolk's 'perpetual grudge'.[1] It is a convincing hypothesis, not damaged by the fact that Suffolk eventually became a supporter of the Boleyns. In due course he also assisted in their downfall. He was a trimmer. Furthermore, there is no doubt that he did hate Wyatt, who makes much of his 'vndeservyd evyll will' in the 'Defence'.

George Wyatt, the last witness properly in touch with Wyatt's life, is already baffled or vague at certain points. It is therefore not surprising that later historians have failed to solve the mystery of the affair with Anne. The matter is still fiercely fought over, and will undoubtedly never be settled to everyone's satisfaction.[2]

In the face of all the controversy, the present writer can only hope to set out the evidence fairly and to make a few suggestions, leaving the reader to agree or disagree. To recapitulate, and add to, what has been said: That Wyatt was in love with Anne and that the King learned of it is generally agreed. I think that the officious Suffolk was a party to the

---

[1] *Extracts from the Life of the Virtuous, Christian, and Renowned Queen Anne Boleigne* (London, 1817), pp. 4–10.

[2] For some opinions, see Appendix E.

communication, even if the Spanish chronicler's and Harpsfield's description of a private interview between Wyatt and the King be correct. Secrets at court were not well kept, and Suffolk was the King's confidant. How far and for how long Anne responded to Wyatt's suit cannot be finally settled, but it is to be noticed that even George Wyatt does not paint her as utterly cold. Given her Howard background and the court background itself, given her love of romantic admiration, Anne is more likely than not, first to have flirted with, after to have shunned, Wyatt. Her feeling for him might well resemble Catherine Howard's for Francis Dereham: she was glad to satisfy his desire for the time being, but ready to deny him for prudential reasons.

One apparent contradiction in the foregoing account remains to be explained. On the one hand, Anne has appeared as the disdainful *princesse lointaine*, from whom her henchmen can expect only 'pity'. On the other, she is the possible (not certain) mistress of Wyatt, her social inferior. This contradiction expresses a paradox, which the Renaissance would recognize more readily than the twentieth century. Venetia Stanley was not a chaste woman, but Kenelm Digby made her his wife and courtly heroine, the image of his romantic idealism. All Tudor courtly comment and love poetry is informed with similar contradictions. On the one hand the humble suitor expects only his small share of grace. On the other he aims at seduction. The woman of whom he has begged 'consolation' turns out not to be 'meet to be copled with your grace'. The courtly lover can sue humbly and sneer in turn. The effect of the sixteenth century's double morality is also noticeable in all the accounts of Wyatt's affair with Anne. The Catholic writers see the unchaste Anne as a 'bad woman', while her equally unchaste lover remains the 'good Wyatt'. George Wyatt, though observing the fact that Wyatt was married, is far from condemning him for the attempt to engage Anne's affection. He sees his grandfather's life as a romance. So indeed it is. But a sordid construction could easily be put upon it. Does he not see that, for all her supposed love of Queen Catherine, Anne did not deny Henry for ever? Even in his version the story is, to quote the Victorian lady on *Antony and Cleopatra*, 'unlike the home-life of our own dear Queen'.

To go further, the Tudor image of the court, like the sixteenth-century portrait of Anne, is Janus-faced. The opponents, Nicholas Sander and George Wyatt, both perceive a Tudor truth. Courtly comment is ambivalent in feeling. On the one hand the court represents, for the whole Renaissance, an image of a perfect society. On the other it is the chief object of satire. Spenser's *Faerie Queene* and *Mother Hubberds Tale* show the two sides of the coin, the lovely and the sordid. Elizabeth's favourites adored (and it is not all flattery) the Virgin Queen and Queen of Love. They also endured the tyrannies of an ill-tempered, black-toothed hag. Sir Walter Raleigh would have had less difficulty than we have in stomaching both Sander's and George Wyatt's stories.

Possibly Wyatt was banished the court as a result of the Anne Boleyn affair. But, if so, he was by no means utterly disgraced. In the nine years from 1527 to 1536 history is rather silent on the subject of Thomas Wyatt. This could mean that he was out of favour during the period of the royal divorce (1527–33) and reign of Anne (1533–6). But he was not unemployed or unsuccessful. In 1528 he was appointed Marshal of Calais, which office he held till 1532. His superior was John Bourchier, Lord Berners, who whiled away the hours in Calais by translating French and Latin books. Wyatt's post carried responsibility for troops, and earned fees and perquisites. The Calais posting can be taken, alternatively, as merely a prelude to a career as ambassador. For that was the case with Wyatt's colleague there, Sir John Wallop. Furthermore, Wyatt was not bound to Calais for more than the two years suggested by the Spanish chronicler. In 1530 Sir Edward Ringley was appointed his vice.[1]

Wyatt was back in English public life by early 1532. In February he was appointed commissioner of the peace for Essex.[2] By this time, too, he was probably known to the rising power, Thomas Cromwell. Two letters of 1532 mention a 'Mr Wyatt' as intermediary between Cromwell and his client Henry Lockwood, one mentioning a parsonage in Kent.[3] In the same year, Wyatt's debts to the King figure on Cromwell's list of 'desperat bills', not the last occasion on which the friendly minister had to deal with his protégé's chaotic finances.[4] In 1533, if not before, Wyatt was back at court. He served as chief ewer in place of his father at Anne's coronation on Whit Monday, 1 June. His feelings on this occasion can be left to the imagination, but the coronation itself is worth dwelling upon. For it is exactly what it was intended to be, one universal paean of praise, one great love song for a great lady. The curtain falls on the court mistress, if only temporarily.

From the Tower the Queen progressed through the city to Westminster. At Cornhill a spring, by which three Graces sat, ran wine.

[1] LP, iv. 6751 (24).   [2] LP, v. 838 (13).
[3] LP, v. 798 and 1309.   [4] LP, v. 1285.

'Afore the fountain satte a Poete declaring the properties of euery grace.' Further on, 'on the ledes of sainct Martyns Churche stode a goodly quere of singyng men and children whiche sang newe balades made in praise of her'. And, again, from turrets erected in Fleet Street, Virtues spoke, promising the Queen never to leave her, while, 'an heauenly noyse' of 'solempne instrumentes' provided a background.[1] Halle's account gives no names, but Nicholas Udall and John Leland were, in fact, the poets ordered to provide the 'verses and dities made at the coronation of Quene Anne'.[2] Poetry was like music and allegory, an essential part of a great court occasion. Praise, honour, and virtue were its themes. This was, in fact, a kind of *public* love poetry. Finally, at Westminster, a vast crowd of courtiers attended the coronation dinner, all with ceremonial offices: some to bear the canopy over the Queen, some to carve before her, some to present a towel or cup, Wyatt, as chief ewer, to pour scented water over her hands. Knights of the Bath were created to mark the occasion. Truly Anne was the great lady, to whom all did obeisance, all tendered service.

The kaleidoscope then shifts again. After the coronation men returned soberly to their permanent posts, while more informal gaieties continued among the royal intimates at court—a group which had probably now readmitted Wyatt. A fresh aspect of 'courtly' love, its superficial flirtatiousness, comes into view. Only nine days after the coronation, Sir Edward Baynton her vice-chamberlain wrote to the Queen's brother, George Boleyn, Viscount Rochford, on court business, and included a lighthearted, man-of-the-world's aside:

> And as for pastime in the Queen's chamber was never more. If any of you that be now departed have any ladies that they thought favoured you, and somewhat would mourn at parting of their servants, I can no whit perceive the same by their dancing and pastime they do use here.[3]

'Pastime in the Queen's chamber' is the appropriate background to the courtly love lyric, of which (in reference to one of Wyatt's) C. S. Lewis has remarked: 'It has little meaning until it is sung in a room with many ladies present. The whole scene comes before us. . . . We are having a little music after supper.'[4] The social uses of the 'practical love-lyric' are also emphasized by John Stevens. And these two authorities differ only on one point: the connection of words and

[1] Halle, *Chronicle*, ed. cit., pp. 801–2. [2] LP, vi. 564. [3] LP, vi. 613.
[4] *English Literature in the Sixteenth Century* (Oxford, 1954), p. 230.

music. Stevens undermines Lewis's assumption that music and the prospect of performance were the mainspring of the courtly lyrist's inspiration. Henry VIII, expert on the organ, lute, and virginals, was 'the only noble person who could lay claim to be considered a latter-day troubadour, poet and musician in one'.[1] The royal household was well staffed with professional musicians, ranking rather below the gentlemen, though not with the menial, servants, and these could invent, or supply from their repertoire, tunes for the courtly makers' verses. However, in view of Stevens's researches, the musicians and poets are perhaps best left in two camps. A distinction between the gentlemen-poets and the household poets is also to be made. John Skelton had celebrated Flodden Field, and John Leland wrote ditties for Anne's coronation. Both were respected as royal servants, but neither ranks with the gentlemen-poets, whose work was for private, not public, occasions. They do not, in fact, belong with the 'pastime in the Queen's chamber'. Of those who did, besides the King and Wyatt, are to be reckoned 'sweet-tongu'd' Brian,[2] and Rochford, who 'clambe the stately Throne, / Which *Muses* holde, in *Hellicone*'.[3] Brian 'had a share' in Tottel's *Miscellany*,[4] but his poems have not been identified. Rochford's have either not survived or not been identified, and undoubtedly other of Henry's friends have suffered a similar eclipse. The possibility of rivalry among these amateur chamber-poets will be raised in due course.

Meanwhile, I return briefly to Wyatt's life during the three-year reign of Anne. Early in May 1534 'there was a great affray between Mr Wyatte and the serjeants of London, in which one of the serjeants was slain. For this Mr Wyatt is committed to the Fleet.'[5] Any displeasure under which he suffered was short-lived. In June a grant was made to Thomas Wyatt 'esquire of the Royal Body' to command 'all men able for war' in various parts of Kent, 'with licence to have twenty men in his livery'.[6] A further mark of favour came in February 1535 when he was the King's nominee for the High Stewardship of West Malling, and, to the Abbess's fury, three other applicants were invited to give

[1] *Music and Poetry in the Early Tudor Court* (London, 1961), pp. 112–3.

[2] Michael Drayton, 'Henry Howard, Earle of Surrey to the Lady Geraldine' (1598), line 153: see *Poems*, ed. John Buxton (London, 1953), ii. 475.

[3] Richard Smith's verses, prefaced to George Gascoigne's *Posies* (London, 1575).

[4] Drayton, 'To My Most Dearely-loved Friend Henery Reynolds Esquire' 1627), line 67: see *ed. cit.*, i. 152.

[5] LP, vii. 674.   [6] LP, vii. 922.

way.[1] In July he received the grant of a lease for eighty years on Aryngden Park in Yorkshire.[2] And, finally, Wyatt, in all probability, was knighted, not, as formerly supposed in 1536 or 1537, but on Easter Day, 28 March 1535.[3] At the same time he had opened negotiations to buy the office of High Marshal of Calais from the incumbent, Sir Richard Grainfield.[4] Wyatt's affairs were still flourishing tolerably well, with the King and Cromwell apparently friendly, when, on 5 May 1536, he was suddenly thrown into the Tower. He was, in fact, again implicated in the affairs of Anne Boleyn, this time in those leading to her fall. The event will be studied in some detail, before Wyatt's part in it is taken up.

Having reigned for twenty-seven years and been twice married, Henry, in 1536, was still impatiently awaiting a male heir. Anne's miscarriage of a boy on 28 January did not improve his state of mind. He became anxious to rid himself of his Queen, and of the Boleyn–Howard faction at court. Brian obligingly quarrelled with Rochford, thus enabling Henry to take his favourite's side and break with his brother-in-law. On 24 April he appointed a commission to inquire into all kinds of treason. This was at the instigation of Cromwell, who had now recognized the necessity of contriving Anne's fall. On 30 April he invited a certain Mark Smeaton to a meal, but, instead of feeding him, persuaded him, under threat of torture, to implicate himself and other courtiers in the charge of treasonous adultery with the Queen. He sent Smeaton to the Tower, and the names of the supposed adulterers to the King.

On May Day 1536 the usual jousts, with Rochford as challenger and Henry Norris as defender, took place at Greenwich. Anne, legend has it, dropped a handkerchief to a lover, and the King departed in rage. He is said, more credibly, immediately to have informed several courtiers that they were suspected of adultery with the Queen. Henry Norris was despatched to the Tower on that very day. Anne and Rochford, under suspicion of incest, followed on 2 May, while Francis Weston and William Brereton brought up the rear on the 4th.

Cromwell gathered evidence. Sir William Kingston, Constable of the Tower, kept him minutely informed of Anne's conversation. Due

---

[1] *V.C.H. Kent*, ii. 148, and LP, viii. 249, 275, and 349.

[2] LP, viii. 1158 (16).

[3] See William H. Wiatt, 'On the Date of Sir Thomas Wyatt's Knighthood', *J.E.G.P.*, lx (1961), 268–72.

[4] LP Addenda, i (i), 1070.

allowance must be made for the prisoner's inclination to conceal the worst and throw blame on others, as well as for the Constable's inclination to provide information. Otherwise Kingston's letters to Cromwell provide the best guide as to what had gone on between Anne and her 'lovers'. Unfortunately they have been mutilated, but, with the help of John Strype,[1] who saw them intact, some sense can be made out.

Anne arrived at the Tower with tears and laughter, and her hysteria did not wear off in the ensuing days. She was distressed to hear of her 'sweet broder's' arrival a few hours before her own, but at no time said anything to incriminate him. Only his official judges proclaimed Rochford guilty of incest. The Spanish chronicler is silent, and except for bigoted Catholics like Nicholas Sander, later historians have not taken the inherently improbable charge seriously.

On the first night Anne also heard of Norris's arrest. 'O, No[res],' she exclaimed, 'hast thow accused me? Thow ar in the Towre with me [and thow and I shall] dy together.' Next day she declared that he had sworn to her innocence. When asked why such a matter should have been under discussion at all, she replied that it was at her own wish: 'I bad hym do so.' Apparently Weston declared that 'Norris came more unto her chamber for her than he did for Mage'. She therefore asked Norris about the delay in his marriage, and asked if he did 'loke for ded men's showys', for if the King were to die, he might 'loke to have' Anne.[2] Even taken as what it probably was, a joke, this conversation is compromising, and indecorously familiar. The Spanish chronicler suspects that Anne's and Norris's familiarity went as far as adultery. History records only his close friendship with her and the King. He is supposed to have been one of the three witnesses to their private marriage. In 1536 the Spanish ambassador Eustace Chapuys referred to him as 'the most private and familiar *somelier de corps* of the king'. But Chapuys at first reckoned Norris's imprisonment the result, not of his own misdoings, but of his failure to reveal Mark Smeaton's.[3]

Shortly afterwards, Anne spoke in the Tower of Francis Weston, and this probably led to his arrest. She alluded to his not loving his wife, and to her inquiring whom, then, he did love. 'It ys yourself,' was the reply.[4] Again, the conversation appears improper, and Anne's hunger for romantic admiration is more than usually evident. Weston,

---

[1] *Ecclesiastical Memorials* (written in 1721) (Oxford, 1822), I (i), 431–6.
[2] LP, x. 793.   [3] LP, x. 782.   [4] LP, x. 793.

one of the youngest of the group, was a very popular courtier, an excellent sportsman, who often played tennis and bowls with the King. On the other hand, if friendly, he was far from being a member of Anne's faction. His family was against the Boleyns, and it was thought that their intercession for him, backed by the French ambassador's, would succeed: 'some say, Weston shall scape'.[1] Furthermore, the Spanish chronicler does not mention him among Anne's nocturnal visitors, or, indeed, in any connection with her.

The case against William Brereton is even weaker. Anne 'made very gud contenans' when Kingston told her he had been brought to the Tower with Weston.[2] She said nothing to imply that he loved her. This gentleman of the Privy Chamber, though known to Rochford,[3] seems to have been little in the public eye.

Mark Smeaton suffered most, both as lover and suspect. He was a court musician and the humblest of Anne's 'lovers'. Chapuys's account refers to him as a nameless 'player on the spinnet',[4] and the English ones, familiarly, as 'Mark'. In the Tower Anne naturally protested that he was never in her chamber, except when she called him in to play on the virginals. She did, however, on the Saturday before the fatal May Day, find him standing at her window, the very picture of the melancholy lover. She asked him why he was so sad, to which he replied 'Now mater' (No matter). Anne then reminded him that he was an inferior, implying, clearly, that he must not take the liberties permitted to her gentlemen-henchmen. 'No, no, madam, a loke sufficed me,' exclaimed poor Mark.[5] The Spanish chronicler adds lurid details. Anne, he says, early in 1536, took up Mark, the son of a carpenter but 'one of the prettiest monochord players and deftest dancers in the land'.[6] She ordered him to play, while she danced with Norris. The context, in fact, is 'pastime in the Queen's chamber'. Anne soon fell in love with Mark, and an old woman brought him to her at night. The chronicler also suspects that Norris and Brereton were in the habit of sleeping with Anne and became jealous: a point repeated in the official report of Anne's trial.

The evidence suggests that Anne, with Mark, Norris, and, to a lesser extent, Weston, had conducted herself badly, encouraging compliments and attentions, and delving too deeply in their private lives. In fact she provided Henry with his opportunity. On the other hand,

---

[1] LP, x. 865.
[2] LP, x. 798.
[3] LP, vi. 613.
[4] LP, x. 782.
[5] LP, x. 798.
[6] *Chronicle of Henry VIII*, ed. cit., p. 55.

D

adultery is not proved in a single case, for Mark's confession was secured under duresse.

While the lovers were in the Tower, the Blatant Beast was rampaging in London:

> if all the books and chronicles were totally revolved, and to the uttermost persecuted and tried, which against women have been penned, contrived, and written in since Adam and Eve, those same were, I think, verily nothing in comparison of that which hath been done and committed by Anne the Queen.[1]

John Husee was bewildered by sensational rumours.

The trial of Norris, Weston, Brereton, and Mark took place on 12 May. All, except, of course, Mark, declared their innocence, which they maintained till death. So did Anne and Rochford, who were brought to trial before their uncle Norfolk, the Lord High Steward, on the 15th. Witnesses declared on oath that the Queen 'following daily her frail and carnal lust, did . . . procure . . . diverse of the King's daily and familiar servants to be her adulterers'.[2] Their peers unanimously found Anne and Rochford guilty. The men were executed on 17 May and Anne on the 19th.

The Spanish ambassador was decidedly more level-headed than John Husee. He wrote home on the very day of Anne's execution, to express his joy at the fall of the 'putain' or 'concubine'. He nevertheless perceived that no case had been made out against Rochford and the others. Only the *valet de chambre*, he remarked, had confessed. The suspicion was, notwithstanding, that many more would fall 'because the king has said that more than 100 had to do with' Anne. 'You never saw prince nor man,' the sceptical observer added, 'who made greater show of his horns or bore them more pleasantly.' Obviously Chapuys thought that Henry's whim was behind the whole affair, describing his recent banqueting thus:

> Most part of the time he was accompanied by various musical instruments, and, on the other hand, by the singers of his chamber, which many interpret as showing his delight at getting rid of a 'maigre vieille et mechante bague', with hope of change, which is a thing specially agreeable to this King.[3]

This 'interpretation' is hardly mistaken. Sir Francis Brian had rushed with the news of Anne's conviction to Jane Seymour on 15 May. On the 30th she was to be married to the King.

[1] LP, x. 866.   [2] LP, x. 876.   [3] LP, x. 908.

On 19 May Chapuys also wrote that there were 'still two English gentlemen detained on her [Anne's] account'.[1] Though he gave no names, one was Wyatt.

According to the Spanish chronicler, Wyatt, than whom was 'no prettier man at Court', did 'better than anybody' at the May Day joust. The King, he continues, ordered his arrest immediately afterwards.[2] In fact, the order was not put into effect till 5 May, that is, one day after the last of the 'guilty' men. This is either an odd coincidence, or a sign that he was under the same suspicion. That is, he was suspect either of having to do with Anne himself, or of failing to reveal the doings of others. Objections to this interpretation have been raised, the chief being Wyatt's imputing of his imprisonment, not to the King's suspicions, but to Suffolk's 'vndeservyd evyll will'.[3] That was part of his Defence', in 1541, against the charge of treason. He was sufficiently daring to attack Suffolk. But Wyatt would at no time or place—least of all before the council of 1541—be so foolhardy as to speak of the *King*'s evil will. Counsellors often, and conveniently, took the blame for royal errors of judgement. In this case Suffolk probably deserved to. As one who knew of Wyatt's youthful love for Anne and had officiously abused that knowledge, who nursed a grudge against him, and who, moreover, was a member of the new treason commission, he may well have egged Henry on to the arrest. He may well, in fact, have acted as the King's *alter ego*, playing on his habitual fear of treason. Certainly had his quarrel with Wyatt been purely private, the prisoner would have been sent, not to the Tower, but to the Fleet as in 1534.

Sir Henry Wyatt, at Allington, received the news of his son's arrest in the dead of night. 'If he be a true man, as I trust he is, his truth will him deliver,' exclaimed the old man, and promptly fell asleep.[4] On 7 May he wrote his son a vague letter about the dangerous time the King endured with traitors, expressing the hope that they would 'be punished according to justice to the example of others'.[5] There are no anxieties for Wyatt here, but if Sir Henry did entertain any, it would have been folly to put them in writing. The Spanish chronicler then takes up the tale. Cromwell cross-questioned Wyatt, who was 'astounded' at the suspicion that he had committed adultery with the Queen, declaring himself 'stainless' and reminding Cromwell of his earlier warning: 'The

---

[1] LP, x. 909.   [2] *Chronicle of Henry VIII, ed. cit.,* p. 63.
[3] Letter no. 37, p. 201.
[4] Wyatt MSS, no. 29. f. 37ʳ.   [5] LP, x. 819.

king well knows what I told him before he was married.'[1] The reminder he repeated in a letter to the King written on the night of the lovers' execution. The old woman who used to bring Anne's lovers to her bed-chamber also exonerated Wyatt. 'She said she had never even seen him speak to the Queen privately, but always openly, whereupon Secretary Cromwell was glad, for he was very fond of Master Wyatt.'[2] The state papers continue the story. By 11 May Cromwell had informed Sir Henry that his son's life would be spared. He received thanks for the 'comfortable articles'. Sir Henry wanted Wyatt to realize that 'this punishment that he hath for this matter is more for the displeasure that he hath done to God otherwise', a reference either to his youthful sins in general, or to his old love for Anne in particular. Suffolk is not mentioned. Sir Henry asked Cromwell when it would be the *King's* pleasure to release Thomas.[3] But he remained for the time being in the Tower. The rumour got round. Husee, by 12 May, had heard that Wyatt was there but 'without danger of life'.[4] The next day, however, it was said that he was 'as like to suffer as the others'.[5]

Meanwhile Kingston told Anne of Wyatt's presence in the Tower. Unfortunately, Strype did not describe the record, and her reply is beyond recovery: 'then she said he ha . . .'. A fascinating conversation follows shortly. Anne, reports Kingston, and the reference is undoubtedly to her fellow-prisoners, 'hathe asked my wyf whether hony body makes thayr beddes, [and m]y wyf ansured and sayd, Nay, I warrant you; then she say[d tha]y myght make balettes well now, bot ther ys non bot . . . de that can do it. Yese, sayd my wyf, Master Wyett by . . . sayd trew'.[6] 'Thay myght make balettes well now' is surely Anne's bitterly ironic comment on the present situation. Successful courtiers had sung of the triumphant Queen. Their fall, as well as hers, provided fresh copy and leisure for lamentations more desperate than those of the disdained lover. Anne had had the opportunity to be something of a connoisseur. The possibility distinctly arises that, for her, Wyatt was the master-poet, the only one 'that can do it'.

> The daise delectable: the violett wan and blo,
> Ye ar not varyable: I love you and no mo.[7]

Sung by three voices to his own tune, Henry's song by no means lacks charm. Yet the bare words are more inane than those of most 'balettes',

---

[1] *Chronicle of Henry VIII*, ed. cit., p. 63.   [2] *Ibid.*, p. 66.
[3] LP, x. 840.   [4] LP, x. 855.   [5] LP, x. 865.
[6] LP, x. 798.   [7] Henry VIII, *Songs*, ed. cit., no. 12.

certainly than Wyatt's. That courtly balladry might have occasioned
rivalry, or at least derision of the King's comparatively weak efforts, is
hinted by Chapuys. On 19 May he described a recent dinner at which
the King was entertained by the Bishop of Carlisle, who next day reported to him. Henry, it seems, told the Bishop that he had long
expected the present issue of events, and had composed a 'tragedy'
upon it. He then produced a little book, written in his own hand, but
the Bishop did not read it. 'It may have been,' conjectures Chapuys,
'certain ballads that the King has composed, at which the *putain* and
her brother laughed as foolish things, which was objected to them as a
great crime.'[1] No one, of course, will believe that poetry brought about
the Boleyns' fall. But this is a shrewd comment on their tactless gaiety,
the King's touchy vanity, and the mistrust bred by 'pastime in the
Queen's chamber'.

One further link between Wyatt and two other of Anne's ballad-
makers remains to be discussed. The Royal MS 20 B xxi, in the British
Museum, provides not only the most intriguing piece of evidence, but
the most difficult to assess. Its placing with the events of 1536, and my
other suggestions about it, must be taken only as conjectures. The
manuscript is a fifteenth-century book of French poetry, containing
Jean Le Fèvre's 'Les Lamentations de Matheolus' and 'Le Livre de
Leesce'. The former is a translation of a satire on women and marriage,
the latter an original poem with the alternative title 'Le Resolu en
Mariage'—reading-matter, incidentally, of some interest to Anne's
group.

This book, like the Devonshire MS, was evidently handed round,
most likely at a time or times between 1526 and 1536. And, in due
course, its front and back fly-leaves acquired a variety of scribbles,
cryptic statements and names. Those at the front (ff. 1^v and 2^r) are well
nigh incomprehensible. The name 'Chapman' is appended to some
illegible writing, 'Here I set Myselfe' and 'ALYS' are clearly distin-
guishable, while 'Thys indenture made' is followed by an illegible date.
Only the one clue to a connection with Anne's friends is tantalizingly
suggested in a line of writing which, starting in illegible Latin, breaks
into legible English with the words 'Spanish Kathryn' followed by the
signature 'Jhone S[luessel?]'. Whatever this may mean, it does not
sound complimentary to Catherine of Aragon.

Proceeding forwards, we find clearer clues. Rochford, who probably
acquired the book on one of his many visits to France, has inscribed

[1] LP, x. 908.

'Thys boke ys myn George Boleyn 1526' before the text (f. 2ᵛ). We may conjecture that he either gave or lent it to Smeaton, who has written 'A moy m marc S' at the end of the text (f. 98ʳ). If the Spanish chronicler is right in assigning Smeaton's appearance at court to early 1536, this must have occurred between January and May of that year. The book may even have been passed round while both men were in the Tower, with Wyatt.

His name is the last to crop up, but here, unfortunately, there is no date to help us. 'Wyat', 'Wyoto', and 'Wyot' are scribbled on the back fly-leaves (ff. 99ᵛ and 100ʳ), and these also bear a variety of mottos and proverbs in Latin, French, Spanish, and Italian. A number of hands seem to have been employed, though even this is difficult to determine, for some words are printed, others neatly italicized, and others scribbled. Wyatt's hand is not clearly discernible, and, as he usually spelled his name 'Wiat', he cannot be labelled with certainty as the writer, or one of the writers. Nevertheless, the presence of his name here, and his acquaintance with the languages used, make it legitimate to connect him closely with these writings. Possibly he inherited the book. The proverbs certainly match his mood in and after 1536.

The presence of the proverbs occasions, in itself, no surprise. The habit of inscribing them on the fly-leaves of books was well established by the fifteenth century. And, of course, in the early sixteenth century, proverbs themselves were still at the height of their popularity. The numerous 'flowers' and 'gardens' of wisdom, culled from the ancients or from Erasmus's *Adagia* bear witness, while John Heywood, in the preface to his *Proverbes* (1546), claims that even the 'bare and rude' native ones are of 'fine and fruitfull effect'. Wyatt, too, to judge by his Plutarch translation, his 'Defence' and his poems, was as fond as any man of what he calls 'a proverbe notable'.

The first back fly-leaf in the Royal MS bears the name 'Wyat', then, 'presto para seruir' with 'forse' three times in its neighbourhood. ('Perhaps' is maybe an amused or cynical comment on 'ready to serve'.) On the second leaf appears 'LAUDA, FINEM', neatly printed alongside the latinized 'Wyoto'. There is also 'Rien que detre', and

> auditori mei notate questo argumento
> che il nouo cassa il vechio pensamento.

(*i.e.* the new thought drives out the old). Mottos and proverbs by nature fit most cases, so that this key will turn with suspicious easiness in the lock of Wyatt's and his friends' experience. Service to state or mistress was familiar to them, while Phillis drove out the thought of Brunet, and the Tower the thought of love, &c.

There is just the one item, upon f. 100ʳ, which might well refer explicitly to Anne Boleyn's brief reign and its catastrophic end:

> qui asne est et cerff cuyde bien estre
> a sallir une fosse on le puyt bien cognostre.

This is a French version, I believe the first known, of a common sixteenth-century Italian proverb:

> Chi asino è & ceruo esser si crede,
> al saltar della fossa se n'auuede.[1]

(*i.e.* He/she who is an ass, and thinks him/herself a hind, on leaping the ditch will realize the truth). The proverbial ass, well known to readers of Aesop, Wireker, or Erasmus, needed no gloss. The drift, therefore, would be quickly understood by any sixteenth-century reader. But what of the exclusive group of readers of the Royal MS? For what it is worth, I suggest that the following interpretation would prove valid for the inner circle of Wyatt's friends in 1536: 'Asne' is Anne, who thought herself, and was thought to be, a hind. As such she had appeared in Wyatt's 'Who so list to hount, I knowe where is an hynde.' At that time, *c.* 1527, she had been elevated by Caesar-Henry. Now, in due course, she has fallen. The illusion is shattered. Anne is, in the long run, no hind, but—true to her name—'asne'. Such would be the epitaph of Wyatt, or of one of his friends, on his old idol. Given the habits of punning and covert allusion, and of projecting ideas in proverb-form, the meaning would be clear to those who knew his history. But it is best now to leave what may be a mere house of cards, and return to facts of solid foundation.

On 17 May 1536 Wyatt watched the execution of Rochford, Norris, Weston, Brereton, and Mark 'from a window of the Tower, and all the people thought that he also was to be brought out and executed'.[2] Rochford, on the scaffold, confirmed, from bitter experience, the traditional truisms about court life:

> I pray yow take hede by me, and especially my lords and gentlemen of the cowrte, the whiche I have bene amonge, take hede by me, and

---

[1] John Florio, *Giardino di Ricreatione* (London, 1591), p. 40. Cp. Charles Merbury, *Prouerbi Vulgari* (London, 1581), p. 8.

[2] *Chronicle of Henry VIII*, ed. cit., p. 68.

beware of suche a fall, and I pray . . . that my deathe may be an example unto yow all, and beware, truste not in the vanitie of the worlde, and especially in the flateringe of the cowrte.[1]

No one dared affirm publicly that the traitors' deaths were undeserved. But a spokesman for 'we that now in court dothe led our lyffe' has defied the opinion that they should not be mourned. The elegy is in the Blage MS recently brought to light by Kenneth Muir. Muir suggests Wyatt as author, and though the style is unlike his and cruder than his, he might, at any rate, have shared these sentiments.

> Some say: 'Rochefford, hadyst thou benne not so prowde,
> For thy gryt wytte eche man wold the be mone;
> Syns as yt ys so, many cry alowde:
> Yt ys great losse that thow art dead and gonne.' (Blage no. xxvii)

Norris 'ys bewaylyd in court of euery side', as is Weston 'that pleasant was and yonge', and who excelled in 'actyve thynges'. Brereton, though 'one that lest I knewe', is lamented, and even Mark, though 'best' deserving death and one of 'poore degre', is not left out.

The shock to Wyatt, who remained, innocent yet friendless, in the Tower, is recorded in a poem headed 'V. Innocentia Veritas Viat Fides, Circumdederunt me inimici mei':

> These blodye dayes haue brokyn my hart;
> My lust, my youth dyd then departe,
> And blynd desyre of astate;
> Who hastis to clyme sekes to reuerte:
> Of truthe, *circa Regna tonat*.
>
> The bell towre showed me suche syght
> That in my hed stekys day and nyght;
> Ther dyd I lerne out of a grate,
> Ffor all vauore, glory or myght,
> That yet *circa Regna tonat*. (Blage no. xliii)

The disillusion with court accords with Rochford's. The old axioms about court life are, in fact, 'proved upon the pulses'. To suppose that Wyatt's youth did indeed 'departe' in the 'blodye dayes' of May 1536, when his gay, courtly companions fell before his eyes, is far from fanciful.

[1] *The Chronicle of Calais in the Reigns of Henry VII and Henry VIII*, ed. J. G. Nichols. Camden Society (London, 1846), p. 46.

'Wyat grudged at his fyrst puttinge in the tower,' said Bishop Bonner, and he admitted, at least, to 'complayninge' and 'moninge'.[1] There he was still when Anne went to the scaffold, attended, it is supposed, by his sister Margaret. He was not brought to trial, and by 14 June he had been released and sent to Allington, to learn, under his father's supervision, 'to address himself better'.[2] Sir Henry wrote to thank the King for not chastising his son extremely.[3] Thus the fiction that royal punishment is always just was kept up. Victims merely pleaded, as Cromwell did later, for 'mercy, mercy, mercy'. Hence Wyatt's prudence in alluding only to Suffolk's private tyranny. The Spanish chronicler's belief that Henry apologized to Wyatt is naïve, though the corollary that he grew to trust him more after 1536 contains truth. Sir Henry's letters make it clear that Wyatt was by no means utterly disgraced either in the King's or Cromwell's eyes.

Wyatt later boasted of the King's immediate proofs of trust. In the autumn of 1536 Henry met his greatest challenge, the northern rebellion known as the Pilgrimage of Grace. Lincolnshire rose first, to be followed by Yorkshire and Lancashire, and the crisis was not over till December. Wyatt was made Steward of Conisborough Castle in South Yorkshire in September, and in October raised three hundred and fifty men of Kent for service. All available men were mustered on this occasion, and perhaps a more singular proof that Wyatt was considered trustworthy is his appointment as Sheriff of Kent for 1536–7.

The northern service apart, Wyatt remained in Kent from June 1536 to March 1537. His father died on 10 November 1536, leaving him master of Allington and other properties, and head of the family. At about the same time, Thomas Wyatt the younger was married to Jane Hawte, the daughter and co-heiress of Sir William Hawte of Bourne, while Wyatt himself prepared to repudiate finally his own wife, who repaired penniless to her brother at Cobham in March.

A turning-point in Wyatt's inner and outer life came in 1536–7. His youth departed. The early court years were decisively over. If his courtly life begins with a love song, it ends with a satire. 'These blodye dayes haue brokyn my hart.' 'Truste not . . . in the flateringe of the cowrte.' Wyatt had assimilated his own and Rochford's experience. As before, he adapted an Italian model to his own circumstances. The tenth satire of the proud, indignant, Florentine exile, Luigi Alamanni, supplies the basis for Wyatt's first satire. Addressed to John Poynz, his

---

[1] The 'Defence': see Letters, no. 37, p. 200.
[2] LP, x. 1131.   [3] LP, xi. 1492.

inconspicuous courtier friend, it boasts of his freedom from commit-
ment to a vicious court life:

> homeward I me drawe,
> And fle the presse of courtes wher soo they goo, . . .
> To will and lust lerning to set a lawe . . .
> In lusty lees at libertie I walke . . .
> Sauf that a clogg doeth hang yet at my hele.
>   (no. 196, lines, 2–3, 6, 84, 86)

While proudly insisting that his exile is voluntary, Wyatt does, here,
seem to refer to the required amendment of his conduct, and to the
limits imposed on his freedom in June 1536. He does not, he affirms,
flee 'the presse of courtes' because he denies

> The powar of them, to whome fortune hath lent
> Charge over vs, of Right, to strike the stroke.   (lines 8–9)

In other words he loyally accepts the King's 'stroke'. But he does im-
pute the main cause of his withdrawal homeward to hatred of the
'flateringe of the cowrte'. 'I cannot frame me tune to fayne,' he declares,
cannot praise Favell (Flattery), cannot honour fools and drunkards, or
'call crafft counsell'. Suffolk certainly epitomizes these vices, but it is
rather the whole temper of court life that Wyatt rejects. He does so
again in the third satire which attacks the same vices by ironically
defending them:

> Thou knowst well first who so can seke to plese
> Shall pourchase frendes where trowght shall but offend.
> Ffle therefore trueth: it is boeth welth and ese.   (no. 198, lines 32–4)

This satire is in the form of a dialogue between the home-loving Wyatt
and Sir Francis Brian, who 'trottes still vp and downe' on royal business. It could imply, as has been suggested, a reproof of the friend who
was so clever at keeping in with all parties. (I do not myself think that
Wyatt's irony extends that far.) It could also mock Wyatt's own trot-
tings up and down 'Ffrom Reaulme to Reaulme': that is, his diplomatic
activities in foreign courts, to which I turn shortly. The satires have
been included here, in proximity to Wyatt's experience at Henry's and
Anne's court. He knew other courts, however, and other aspects of
court life than the purely social. The satires, which are his most mature
poems, reflect not only the shock of a courtier's disillusion, but the
studied criticisms of an experienced Tudor 'governor'.

In March 1537 Wyatt was appointed ambassador to Spain. Beyond doubt he was now fully restored to royal favour, for this was the most important public responsibility of his life. New responsibilities, public and private, increase the emphasis on this period as a turning-point in his life. There is little to suggest that his sombre mood was quick to lift. On 15 April he was in Paris, whence he wrote, in an appropriate strain of moral gravity, one of the letters of advice to his son.

CHAPTER III
Courtly Wisdom

And tho the smalnesse of the present be great / in respecte of that / that accordeth to your excellence / the sentence parauenture shall nat be moche vnacceptable / if it greue nat your grace to marke it after *your accustomed wysdome*. (Wyatt's dedication of Plutarch's *Quyete of Mynde* to Catherine of Aragon; the prefatory letter, 31 December 1527: sig. a 2ᵛ, with my italics.)

Your parte shalbe nowe like a *good Oratour*, bothe to setfurthe the princely nature and inclynacion of his highnes with all *dexteritie*, and soo to *obserue* Themperours answers to the said Ouerture and to the rest of the pointes in the same letteres expressed, as you may therby *fishe out the botom of his stomake*, and aduertise his Maieste howe he standethe disposed towards him, and to the contynuance of thamytie betwene them. . . . Contynue *vigilant* nowe in thenserching out of thinges mete to be knowen . . . Gentle Maister Wiat nowe vse all *your wisedome*. (Thomas Cromwell's instructions to Sir Thomas Wyatt, ambassador at the Imperial court, from a letter of 10 October 1537: Merriman no. 222, with my italics. Cp. LP, xii (ii), 870.)

T wo kinds of 'wisdom' were idealized at the court of Henry VIII, one represented by Catherine of Aragon, the other by Thomas Cromwell, one moral, the other political. Both were enhanced by education, learning, even by solid scholarship. Few things divide us so sharply from our ancestors of the Renaissance as their belief that study benefits man's moral and worldly welfare. True, the Italian observer of 1500 remarked that, while the English are clever, few 'excepting the clergy, are addicted to the study of letters'.[1] Yet, as the century advanced, the idea that learning was for 'clodhoppers' and the 'gentleman's calling' 'to blow the horn, to hunt and hawk'[2] receded. Henry VIII himself, educated by that formidable scholar John Skelton, acquired skill in scholastic Latin, modern languages, and theological controversy. His destruction of Thomas More and John Fisher argues no animosity to their learning as such. He was ready enough to encourage obedient scholars, like his antiquary John Leland, and to accept from others, like Lord Morley, gifts in the form of translations from the classics. Moreover, in these matters he was encouraged by his first Queen.

Catherine of Aragon's reign (1509–32) was the longest of any of Henry's Queens. From 1527 her power was on the wane, but during the eighteen years before, she gave valuable service to English classical and humanistic learning. She had herself enjoyed an Italian and humanistic education under the brothers Antonio and Alessandro Geraldini. Her mother, Queen Isabella, was an earnest promoter of the Spanish Renaissance, and of women's part in it. Catherine's Latin, which startled several ambassadors and made Erasmus admire her as a miracle of feminine learning, was superior to and more modern than Henry's. Her patronage of scholarship, though not flamboyant, was sensible and consistent. She drew her countryman Juan Luis Vives to England, and also tried to detain the itinerant Erasmus. Vives, with Thomas Linacre, was tutor to the Princess Mary, whose Latin exercises Catherine herself corrected. Mary's reading list, drawn up by Vives and presented to Catherine, included, in an array of Latin works, some by Erasmus and the *Utopia* of More. The love of learning and virtue, always connected in the Humanist mind, was as familiar to Catherine as it was ultimately to prove alien to Henry.

But Renaissance Humanism connects learning, not only with moral, but with political wisdom. More's Utopian government was, in fact, sustained by learning allied to virtue. 'Good literature and learning' produces reasonable social opinions, such as contempt for riches. The authorities spot those children in whom they perceive 'a singular towardnes, a fyne witte, and a minde apte to good learning'.[3] They are the future 'governors', in the phrase made famous by Thomas Elyot's book.[4] Yet how easily More's noble statecraft could be twisted so that learning acquired a solely utilitarian purpose. And precisely such a

[1] *A Relation of England*, ed. cit., p. 22. [2] LP, ii (ii), 3765.
[3] *Utopia* (1516), trans. Richard Robinson. Everyman ed., p. 71.
[4] *The Boke named the Governour* (London, 1531).

twist Henry, with Wolsey, gave to the Humanist ideal—and so prepared the way for the emergence of Cromwellian 'wisdom'.

The foundation of St John's College, Cambridge, was an act of pure piety on the part of Henry's grandmother, Lady Margaret Beaufort, and her chaplain John Fisher. By contrast, Wolsey's foundation of the Cardinal's College at Oxford exemplifies not so much his love of learning as his government's need of learned men. The fact that ambassadors were called 'orators' draws attention to a *sine qua non*. They must be capable of expressing themselves properly in Latin and modern languages. English being but little spoken outside these islands, the day of the national blockhead, unskilled in any language but his own, was yet to dawn. If the ambassador's services extended no further than a well-bred speech of compliment to the Emperor Charles V or King Francis I of France, he was still of value. Many embassies were of a complimentary kind. Others, however, involved negotiations, sounding of foreign feeling, or gleaning of intelligence. And here informed, experienced, clever men were needed.

An academic training, supported by travel, and followed by secretarial assistance to an ambassador, seems to have been the Tudor formula of training for the royal service abroad. This is observable in the career of John Mason (1503–66), who is of the more interest in the present context because he was not only exactly of an age with Wyatt, but also his close friend and colleague at the Imperial court. Mason, said to have been the son of a cowherd, was of much humbler birth than Wyatt. But he was sent to Oxford, graduating B.A. in 1521 and M.A. in 1525. His gifts must eventually have attracted attention in high quarters, for, from 1530, supposedly on More's recommendation, Mason was King's Scholar in Paris. In 1532 he was present at the meeting in Calais of Henry VIII and Francis I. Not long after, he was sent on a training tour, planned with a view to his entry into the diplomatic service. He travelled in France, Spain, and Italy, with instructions to keep in touch with the King and Council. In 1537 he became secretary to Wyatt. There we must leave him, though it is impossible to refrain from adding a note on Mason's truly diplomatic character. According to an anecdotal biographer of the next century, he survived all revolutions under four sovereigns, ending as Privy Councillor and Chancellor of Oxford, by the following means: He was 'always intimate with the exactest Lawyer, and ablest Favourite'. He 'spake little, and writ less'. He was 'so moderate, that all thought him their own'. 'Do, and say nothing' was Mason's motto, while 'Secresie' and 'Timing' were his means of promoting any business.[1] Maybe there is too much pliability here, but the implied comment on the Tudor governor is important. Native wit, as well as learning and experience, was at a high premium.

While in Padua, in July 1534, Mason visited the household of Reginald Pole (1500–58), the importance of which, as an academic training ground for government servants, has been fascinatingly described by W. G. Zeeveld.[2] The aristocratic Pole had his education partly at the King's expense. In 1519 he settled in Padua, where, until in 1536 he suddenly showed himself the enemy of the royal supremacy, he served the English government faithfully. Thomas Starkey, Richard Morison, and Thomas Lupset were among those who joined Pole in the study of Greek and Roman classics which made his house a famous resort of learning. The studious impulse was humanistic in that the general aim of the English Paduans was to make their knowledge useful to the state. Thomas Cromwell was quick to take advantage of it. During his rise to power, following the fall of his master Wolsey in 1529, he learned to rely even more than Wolsey had done on men of wit and learning. Accordingly he used the Paduans as propagandists for the royal supremacy. Starkey offered his services in 1534. Speaking for the King and Cromwell, he urged Pole to give an opinion on the royal divorce. His *Exhortation to Unity and Obedience*, written in 1535 and published by the King's printer in 1536, is the first statement of the English *via media*. But Starkey staked too much on Pole's supporting the King, was wrong, and so, having outlived his uses, declined into obscurity—a Tudor pattern as relentless as it is familiar. Richard Morison, a zestful classical and Italian scholar, was more successful because he capitalized Pole's fall from grace. He addressed his first appeal for advancement to Starkey, offering to return to England if his learning could be used. In 1536 Cromwell invited him home, to write tracts in support of the royal policy, and invectives against 'the great detestable vice, treason'. Cromwell had not only Pole's desertion to Rome to contend with at this time. The horror in Europe following the execution of More and Fisher in 1535, largely Cromwell's work, made it the more necessary to have such useful propagandists as Morison.

Their usefulness characterizes all Cromwell's Men. Anthony St Leger, educated in France, Italy, Cambridge, Gray's Inn, and the court, was an active agent in the dissolution of the monasteries, and, in 1537, headed a highly successful commission on Irish affairs. Christopher

[1] David Lloyd, *State-Worthies* (London, 2nd ed. 1670), pp. 212, 214–15.
[2] *Foundations of Tudor Policy* (Cambridge, Mass., 1948).

Mont (or Mundt) was a native of Cologne, a doctor of laws, who, in 1531, became a denizen of England and one of Cromwell's team. The year 1533 finds him in Germany, reporting on the situation, 1534 stirring up the German princes against the Pope, and 1535 in France, counteracting the French influence on Germany. Mont was one of many foreign agents on whom Cromwell depended for information, and whose letters are simply the sixteenth-century's equivalent of newspapers.

Cromwell's letters to his agents give yet more insight into what were regarded as the chief diplomatic virtues. Notice the italicized words in his letter to 'Gentle Maister Wiat': '*obserue*', '*dexteritie*', '*fishe oute the botom of his stomake*', '*vigilant*', and, above all, '*wisdome*'. 'Felowe Christofer' (Mont) and the rest were treated to the same advice. 'Contynuel vigilancy', 'wisedome and dexteritie', are Cromwell's recurrent general themes. He also descends to particulars. His agents must use caution in communicating news bound to be unpalatable abroad, like the deaths of More and Fisher. They must learn to be more or less cordial according to the changes in the European balance of power. They must 'inculcate and persuade' ideas and men. For instance the Emperor's and Pope's malice must be insinuated into Germans. When, therefore, Cromwell said 'vse all your wisedome', his advice by no means carried Catherine of Aragon's meaning. Cromwell's 'wisdom', like his 'dexterity', is, in fact, a Machiavellian term.

Morison's tracts contain references to Machiavelli, and these would not be lost on Cromwell. The devotion to Machiavellianism, popularly imputed to him, is not a myth, but the term must be properly understood. Cromwell was not 'determined to prove a villain' like the Elizabethan stage version—a ridiculous travesty—of the 'cunning Machiavel'. He was, in the first place, a student of Italian, found, for example, lending out his copies of Petrarch's *Triumphs* and Castiglione's *Courtier*.[1] The study of Machiavelli was not necessarily more sinister than the study of these noble classics. Throughout the sixteenth century, students of statecraft saw his value, remarking on how he 'doth seeme greatly to follow the truth, and setteth forth rather the causes and effects of everie action, then overmuch extoll or disgrace the persons of whome the storie entreateth'.[2] How childish, in comparison

---

[1] LP, iv (iii), 6346.

[2] Thomas Bedingfeld's dedication, to Sir Christopher Hatton, of Machiavelli's *The Florentine Historie* (1595): see Tudor Translations, no. 40 (London, 1905), pp. 4–5.

with his *Florentine Historie*, appears Halle's *Chronicle*, not only for its endless pageantry, but for its crudely melodramatic distinctions between heroes and traitors. Machiavelli was different because he repudiated the roles of moralist and idealist, and claimed only to observe and analyse. Deeply perturbed at the disunity which weakened sixteenth-century Florence, he preached strong, efficient, successful government.

The famous report by Reginald Pole, to the effect that Cromwell had pronounced Machiavelli's political ideas more up to date than Plato's, was not, after all, so very sensational. Lord Morley would hardly have thought so, for he actually presented *Istorie Fiorentine* and *Il Principe* to Cromwell, pointing out that the latter, particularly, was 'surely a good thing for your Lordship and for our Sovereign Lord in Council'.[1] So it was. The lesson of 'prudenzia'—Cromwell's 'wisdom' and, in the Elizabethan translation, frequently rendered 'discreation'[2]—is on every page. The state's need of money, military strength, profitable alliances, and gifted men is clearly demonstrated. The prince should encourage all men who can benefit the state. His choice of ministers reflects his own 'prudenzia'. He should honour them, but keep them dependent. Such ideas, though susceptible to a sinister emphasis, do not demand it.

While Pole found the antithesis of *The Prince* in Plato's *Republic*, the modern mind usually finds it in Baldassare Castiglione's *Il Cortegiano* (1528), a book also on Cromwell's shelves. This antithesis, too, is misleading. Writing more from the servant's than the prince's point of view, Castiglione is far from ignoring his desire for 'favour and promotion'. His courtier must 'helpe himselfe with wit and arte'.[3] He must be 'pliable' to please his prince, though without flattering. He must show worldly wisdom in the choice of friends, lest disreputable ones discredit him. This most influential of courtier's manuals may have owed its popularity to its practicality, as well as to its idealism.

Ascham said that the *Courtier* 'aduisedlie read, and diligentlie folowed, but one yeare at home in England, would do a yong ientleman more good ... then three yeares trauell abrode spent in *Italie*'.[4] It is well, perhaps, that the grand tourists thought otherwise. Yet he spoke for Reformation England. Cromwell's decade (1530–40) rapidly

---

[1] LP, xiv (i), 285.

[2] *The Prince: An Elizabethan Translation*, ed. H. Craig (Chapel Hill, 1944), *passim*.

[3] *The Book of the Courtier*, trans. Thomas Hoby, Everyman edition, p. 123.

[4] *The Scholemaster*, ed. cit., p. 66.

E

enhanced the characteristically English ambivalence of feeling about Italy: the love of its art and poetry combined with the hatred of its factiousness and vice. Cromwell's Men were imbued with a regard for Italian ideas, combined with a distrust for the country of their origin. All, moreover, looked for 'favour and promotion'.

'I am a graft of your Lordship's own setting, and will stand in no other's ground.'[1] Morison's words, with his actions, convict him of sycophancy in Cromwell's service, yet many of that team were neither 'grafts' nor sycophants. Thomas Wriothesley was a clerk, under Cromwell, in the Privy Council office, intimate with his secrets, constantly employed to send or back his instructions to agents abroad. He was regarded as his dependant, but at heart he was a conservative, that is, of the Howard persuasion. At Cromwell's arrest on 10 June 1540, while the Duke of Norfolk snatched the George from his neck, Wriothesley seized the Garter. Before Wriothesley is condemned for disloyalty, it should be remembered that he would regard himself as a state official *under* Cromwell, rather than a feudal retainer *of* Cromwell. All Cromwell's Men, even the trustiest, survived his fall, just as Cromwell himself had survived Wolsey's. The master–servant link, had, in fact, lost much of its feudal strength. At most the master represented an intermediate loyalty between servant and state. There was room for benevolence and devotion in this relationship, but, in a last resort, the King conquered all private sentiments. That the successful prince must keep all men dependent on him is a Machiavellian doctrine. Henry followed Machiavelli, too, in not making an unnecessary sacrifice of his minister's well-trained team. Morison had been closely associated with Cromwell's policies, but he lived to serve as ambassador. St Leger had escorted Anne of Cleves to England in 1539, so that he was connected with that part of Cromwell's policy that precipitated his fall. Yet on 7 July 1540, less than a month after the arrest, he was appointed to use his Irish experience as Lord Deputy. Mont, who had also helped with the Cleves marriage, merely had to undertake the tricky task of explaining Henry's conduct to Anne in Germany.

Thomas Wyatt encountered both Catherine of Aragon's wisdom and Cromwell's. 'Pastime in the Queen's chamber' was, after all, not his chief occupation in life. And he had in his father a notable example of both piety and service. Sir Henry would have valued Catherine's wisdom and understood Cromwell's. Though his own 'feudal' loyalty to Henry Tudor smacks of archaism, he kept abreast of the times. His

[1] LP, xi. 1481.

letters insist on service to the King as his son's chief duty, while Cromwell is to be regarded as his second father. This yields as good an example as any of the Tudor servant's ultimate and intermediate loyalties.

At the beginning of Wyatt's diplomatic career, in March 1526, the situation in Europe was, briefly, as follows. France, whose crown Henry had long entertained hopes of winning, was at her lowest ebb, while the Empire, England's traditional ally, was at her height. Francis I met disaster at the Battle of Pavia (1525). He was captured by the Emperor, not to be released until March 1526, and then under the onerous terms of the Treaty of Madrid. Henry and Wolsey, if momentarily tempted to join the Emperor in the dismemberment of France, soon realized that he was far too strong. So did other powers. Pope Clement VII absolved Francis from his obligation to observe the Treaty of Madrid, and prepared to join France, Florence, Venice, and Milan in the League of Cognac. This was intended to resist the Emperor's designs, especially in Italy. Henry was named as protector of the league. Accordingly, in March 1526, Sir Thomas Cheney was sent to France to promote a new policy: to cement a French alliance, frustrate the Emperor, and arrange Henry's part in the League of Cognac. Wyatt accompanied him.

Sir Thomas Cheney (1485–1558), nephew of the Sir John Cheney who fought hand to hand with Richard III at Bosworth, was a 'spriteful Gentleman' of Kent.[1] This is sufficient to explain his patronage of Sir Henry Wyatt's son. He was also an experienced ambassador, with a good knowledge of French. He arrived in Bordeaux on 6 April 1526, 'very weary with the great haste he had made'.[2] On the 9th he was graciously received by Francis, who expressed gratitude to Henry and spoke of the horrors of captivity in Spain, and of the fact that his promises to the Emperor had been obtained through fear.[3] Other audiences followed. Cheney presented the towel at Francis's *levée* and rode to mass with him before the King left for Cognac on 22 April.[4] The English embassy followed for further audiences, and on 1 May, Wyatt was sent home with despatches: 'We send Wyatt with this, because the matter is important, and requires great haste.'[5] The compliment is amplified: 'he hath been at the court with us from time to (time), and,

---

[1] Thomas Fuller, *The History of the Worthies of England* (1662), ed. J. Nichols (London, 1811), i. 525.
[2] LP, iv (i), 2075 and 2079.   [3] LP, iv (i), 2091.
[4] LP, iv (i), 2092 and 2115.   [5] LP, iv (i), 2136.

as we think, hath as much wit to mark and remember everything he saith as any young man in England'.[1] Wyatt was back in Cognac by 21 May and Francis, when informed, said he would rejoice to hear from his brother Henry. Cheney therefore presented Wyatt, who, with good and discreet behaviour, uttered Henry's compliments to the same effect.[2] The League of Cognac was sealed on 22 May, and Cheney's embassy, bearing Francis's oath to Henry left on the 27th. It was felt to have been a success.

For Wyatt this visit afforded his first opportunity of meeting French men of letters. To save any misunderstanding, it may be said at the outset that, from all Wyatt's foreign travels, no record survives of meetings with foreign scholars and poets. Consequently, the modern student can speak only of opportunities and likelihoods, not of established facts. Thus in 1526 Wyatt may have met the Humanist scholar Guillaume Budé (1468–1540), who was Francis I's librarian, and whose Latin version of Plutarch's *De Tranquillitate & Securitate Animi* (c. 1505) he was to translate in the following year. As for his contacts with foreign poets, a further point needs first to be made: Wyatt's French and Spanish contacts are distinctly subordinate to his Italian ones, or, rather, they serve to reinforce the importance of the Italian. For example, at the French court in 1526, he encountered an Italianate monarch, surrounded by Italianate protégés. Francis, though less the Italian scholar than his sister Marguerite de Navarre, was well versed in the language—Benvenuto Cellini described his fluency—and a lover of the poetry—Luigi Alamanni read Dante to him. At the time of Wyatt's visit Mellin de Saint-Gelais (1487–1558) was the leading French court poet, with Clément Marot (1492–1549) as his friendly rival. Saint-Gelais, after nine years in Italy, had returned in 1518 to spread the knowledge of Petrarch and Serafino, notably to Marot. In order to keep him at court, Francis made him, in 1525, the Dauphin's almoner, so that Wyatt would see him at the height of his credit, and at a time when one of his occupations was to correct the King's verses. There is rather less likelihood of his meeting Marot, who, on Francis's intercession, was released from prison on 1 May 1526. But if Marot's and Wyatt's paths did not cross in 1526, they probably did so on two future occasions. Wyatt was to be present at the meetings of Francis and Charles at Nice and Aigues Mortes in 1538, and in Paris in 1540: events which Marot was charged to celebrate in verse. Meanwhile, any minor poets whom he met in 1526 would serve to reinforce the Italianate-French

[1] LP, iv (i), 2135. [2] LP, iv (i), 2194.

impression on him. For example, two *poétes marotiques*, Victor Brodeau (*c.* 1502–40) and Hugues Salel (1504–53), men of his own generation, and both *valets de chambre* at court, were much addicted to such Italianate forms as the epigram. The arts and graces of Francis's court were not unlike those of Henry's. Saint-Gelais, an expert player on the lute, and Brodeau used to entertain the ladies with gallant love songs. It is not necessary, therefore, to suppose that foreign travel revolutionized Wyatt's courtly habits. But certainly, wherever he went, between 1526 and 1540, the Italian influence was paramount.

The League of Cognac soon proved helpless. Francis, an uncaged bird, was given over to amusement. The Emperor did better than ever in Italy. Sforza yielded Milan in July 1526, and in September the Imperialist troops, with Cardinal Colonna's, occupied Rome. Only in Naples had the Pope the advantage. Everywhere else was manifest that disunity and weakness that made Italy Europe's battle-ground and so impassioned Machiavelli. Thus the Duke of Ferrara was actually supplying money and food to the Imperialist troops. During the bad weather of the winter of 1526–7, they were not, though threatening, doing so very well. The Duke of Urbino could have tackled them, but he did nothing. Florence appealed to the Pope to come to terms with the Imperialist generals: Machiavelli's city was trembling at the nearness of the Constable Bourbon's troops, bivouacked near Bologna. Venice wanted to prevent an armistice, but was not prompt in providing the means. The Pope, assailed on all sides, was in despair. He sent out pitiful appeals for money, and Henry promised 30,000 ducats.

Sir John Russell (1486?–1555), a highly respected diplomat and the future Earl of Bedford, was sent with the money and the hope of building up Clement's morale. On his way down the Thames he met Wyatt, who asked whither he went. 'To Italy, sent by the Kinge.' 'And I,' said Wyatt, 'if yow please, wil aske leave, get mony, and goe with yow.' 'No man more welcome,' replied Russell.[1] The episode is not without importance. Distinct from his later diplomatic missions, the Italian one was undertaken of Wyatt's own volition. The influence of Italy, as his poems bear witness, outweighs all others except the native English. Perhaps he himself was to become an Italianate type, the diplomat who was also a poet and scholar, and of which the Italy of 1527 provided many examples. Yet his Englishness is also apparent. His attitude to Italy expresses an ambivalence similar to Ascham's. A love for Italian culture mingles with a scorn of Italian behaviour.

[1] Wyatt MSS, no. 18 f. 3ᵛ.

The embassy set off on 7 January 1527, and travelled by Paris, Lyons, Chambéry, and Savona, arriving in Civitavecchia on 4 February. Fortunately for the travellers an eight-day truce in the Italian war had been arranged on 28 January, and the Pope's optimism had temporarily revived on the arrival of the Count de Vaudemont from France with another 30,000 ducats. Twelve miles from Rome Papal officials met them bringing Turkish horses for Russell and Wyatt and hacks for the other members of the ambassadorial suite.[1] A little further on they were met by Sir Gregory Casale, resident English ambassador in the Vatican, who took them home for the night. The Pope's offer of hospitality was equally pressing, but Russell feared to cause jealousy among the many other foreign visitors. Soon, however, he was living in the Vatican Palace at the Pope's expense. Indeed, the courtesies were numerous, though the crowning one is difficult to credit. A papal official brought two of the choicest courtesans to his English visitors, with 'a plenary dispensation verbal', an event which Wyatt took as 'an Italian scorne and a kinde of pronostike of the event of their successe'.[2]

The outlook was not, indeed, promising, nor was Clement's demeanour such as to command respect. A polite, futile, nervy man, he was, at this time, swamped with advice, to which he responded with an endless patter of 'if', 'but', 'perhaps', 'then', and 'nevertheless':

> Un papato composto di rispetti,
> Di considerazioni e di discorsi,
> Di pur, di poi, di ma, di se, di forsi,
> Di pur assai parole senza effetti . . .
> Con audienze, risposte e bei detti.[3]

The satiric description is by Francesco Berni (*c.* 1477–1535), secretary to the papal *dattario*, Matteo Giberti. There can be little doubt that Wyatt, in the confined Vatican society, met both. Giberti was the statesman and patron of the arts, Berni the diplomat, poet, and scholar. Berni's wit, directed not only at governmental weaknesses, but at those of current literary schools, notably the Petrarchan, makes him most memorable. How, one wonders, was Wyatt impressed?

The brief respite from fighting had been arranged as a prelude to a

[1] LP, iv (ii), 2875.   [2] Wyatt MSS, no. 18 f. 3ᵛ.
[3] Berni, *Poesie e Prose*, ed. Ezio Chiòrboli (Geneva and Florence, 1934), Rime, no. xx.

possible armistice, and this was the matter so agonizingly debated in the Vatican in the early days of Russell's embassy. It was, in fact, Russell who insisted that before the Pope succumbed ignominiously to the Imperial will, Venice should be heard. His offer to go there was accepted, he left on 12 February but suffered a fall which forced him to send Wyatt on alone. In Venice, Wyatt joined forces with the English ambassador, Giovanni Casale, Sir Gregory's brother. The two attended audiences before the Signory on 2 and 3 March.[1] The Lords were slow to reply to their pleas, but agreed to allow the Pope troops and money. Casale then turned his attention to Ferrara, travelling there, probably with Wyatt, on the 6th and with the object of inducing the Duke to join the anti-Imperialist league.[2] On the 11th he returned with the news that Alfonso felt obliged to keep his prior promises to the Emperor.[3] Meanwhile the Pope lost his last shred of confidence. On 15 March, without awaiting the Venetian reply, he agreed to an armistice of eight months. When the news arrived in Venice there was keen disappointment. But this was not the only trouble, for while Lannoy, the Imperialist general, was certainly sincere in his intention to keep the new peace, the Imperialist troops would have none of it. They were cold, starving, penniless, and quite out of control, and by the end of March left their base at Bologna to move ominously south.

Wyatt, meanwhile, was 'desirous to see the country', which implies, no doubt, also to meet its denizens. Unfortunately, as before, there is no record of whom he actually did meet. Baldassare Castiglione and Andrea Navagero, whom Miss Foxwell says he met in Venice, were both absent on state service in Spain. Castiglione's work, certainly, might be known to Wyatt even as early as this: *Il Cortegiano* was circulating in manuscript in Venice prior to its publication in 1528. Cardinal Pietro Bembo (1470–1547), Italy's leading Petrarchan, who from the neighbouring city of Padua ruled the cultural life of Venice, was available. Padua lay not far off Wyatt's route back to Rome, and, after it, Ferrara, 'the first really modern city in Europe',[4] ruled by an enlightened Duke. Alfonso I was well-educated, had travelled studiously in England, France, and the Netherlands, and now exercised a generous patronage of the university and the arts in Ferrara. He is a perfect example of the Italian *magnifico*, and it is to be hoped that Wyatt's contact with him consisted in more than the obtaining of his safe-conduct.

---

[1] *C.S.P. Venetian*, iv. 53 and 55.   [2] *Ibid.*, iv. 59.   [3] *Ibid.*, iv. 63.
[4] Jacob Burckhardt, *The Civilization of the Renaissance in Italy* (1860), Phaidon edition, p. 31.

But Ferrara's chief pride was Lodovico Ariosto (1474–1533), who, almost uniquely, had realized a favourite dream of sixteenth-century diplomats. Like Berni, he had longed to be free of state duties, to devote himself to letters. And, unlike Berni, he had succeeded. In 1527 Ariosto was contentedly living in retirement in Ferrara, and working upon the third edition of *Orlando Furioso*.

Wyatt continued his journey via Bologna. Notwithstanding Alfonso's safe-conduct, he was captured by the mutinous Imperialist troops, and, for all Russell's protestations, held for ransom at 3000 ducats. Russell reports that he escaped,[1] which piece of 'adroitness' has attracted Wyatt's biographers. However, he merely means that Wyatt was liberated through the intervention of Giovanni Casale and the Duke of Ferrara.[2] He then went on to Florence, a city of fears, for it lay on the Imperial route from Bologna to Rome, and was saved only by luck when the army unexpectedly decided to pass it by. Florence was ruled by Pope Clement's representatives, the Medici, hardly more popular than he was. The Republicans were in disgrace. Luigi Alamanni (1495–1556) had fled to France, and Wyatt's contact with his work belongs to later years. Niccolò Machiavelli (1469–June 1527) was, however, present in Florence. *Il Principe* and *Istorie Fiorentine* were complete, though not yet published. And these works, with their urgent pleas for unified government, form the best of comments on Italy in the year of Wyatt's visit. If he did not read their pages, he saw their message in the scene before him. Rome was a beleaguered city when he re-entered it some time in April, in which month Wolsey also wrote to recall Russell's embassy.

'Wo to us, wo to the Emperor, if these Germans and Spaniards get the upper hand.' A joint letter to Wolsey, of 26 April, by Russell and Gregory Casale describes the atrocities of war, as the Imperialist troops under Bourbon drew near to Rome. Spanish soldiers, they reported, were burning houses, ordering monks to violate nuns, and casting the blessed sacrament into the river.[3] The embassy left shortly afterwards —it had reached Civitavecchia by 2 May—escaping only just in the nick of time. Bourbon arrived before Rome on the 4th, with a hungry and desperate army of looters. The Pope, to Russell's despair, had realized too late that the armistice was an illusion. The sack of Rome on 6 May 1527 shocked Europe none the less because it was half expected. By the time the English embassy was safe at home, the Pope was virtually the Emperor's prisoner in Castel Sant'Angelo, no masses

[1] LP, iv (ii), 3011.   [2] LP, iv (ii), 2982 and 3023.   [3] LP, iv (ii), 3066.

were said in Rome, and Benvenuto Cellini was pathetically melting down tiaras. Wyatt, first and last impressed by the scorn with which the embassy was treated, had left behind him a sketch of a triple-crowned minotaur lost in a maze. It bore the legend 'Laqueus contritus est et nos liberati sumus'.[1] Henry VIII and Russell were amused, Clement VII simply puzzled. The traveller's critical mind also seized on a contrasting example of strength and virtue. Sir John Russell had won a permanent admirer in Wyatt, who set him up as an example his son would do well to bear in mind.[2]

Wyatt returned to court, in the early summer of 1527, to encounter news of the royal divorce. The antithesis between Anne Boleyn and Catherine of Aragon is expressed in his life as a young courtier. For, while he wrote love poetry about the one, to the other he dedicated his translation of Plutarch's moral essay, *De Tranquillitate & Securitate Animi*. 'Even for a courtier, the study of moral laws in Greek philosophy was as much a part of the Renaissance ideal as was the cult of love.'[3] C. R. Baskervill's comment is not only true in general, but also, in particular, helps to complete Wyatt's portrait. He was more serious, pious, and scholarly than the affair with Anne, taken in isolation, suggests. His experience of the court included experience of Catherine's 'acknowledged wisdom'. Wyatt arrived at court in time to catch only the tail-end of the patronage of her best years. He was eighteen years—in Tudor reckoning a generation—her junior. There could be little comparison between Catherine and his contemporary Anne, whose culture was French and who was not, as Queen, to encourage piety and learning. But it is quite possible that, coming at this moment, Wyatt's learned offering marks his swift revulsion of feeling against Anne's values and in favour of those for which Catherine stood.

Wyatt's *Quyete of Mynde* was, fairly certainly, written after his return from Italy, in the latter part of 1527. The Queen commanded him to translate Petrarch's 'remedy of yll fortune', that is, Book II of *De Remediis Utriusque Fortunae*. He began upon this formidable task, and completed nine or ten of the one hundred and thirty-two dialogues, before deciding to substitute Plutarch's short essay on the same theme. He presented this to Catherine, a New Year's gift of a kind familiar to Tudor courtiers. The dedicatory epistle is signed by Wyatt, then at Allington, and dated 'the last day of Decembre. M. D. XXVII'. It was printed by the King's printer Richard Pynson, almost certainly in 1528.

[1] Wyatt MSS, no. 18 f. 3ᵛ.　　　　　　　　[2] Letter no. 1.
[3] *Quyete of Mynde, ed. cit.*, Introd., p. xv.

This was indeed a poignant moment in Catherine's life, to which both the work she commissioned of Wyatt and the one she got are appropriate. The year 1527 marks the beginning of her 'yll fortune' and her endurance of it fell little short of the ideal of Stoic fortitude that Petrarch and Plutarch hold in common. Though Henry put before Catherine his religious scruples concerning the validity of their marriage, she, with others, believed Wolsey responsible for the divorce project. Being committed to a French alliance, Wolsey really wanted Henry to marry a French princess. From Catherine's Spanish point of view, his foreign policy was wicked, as he was himself in his dealings with her. Wolsey made spies of her women, opened her letters, tried to prevent her seeing the Spanish ambassador. Nevertheless, during the winter of 1527–8 Catherine went about her duties with her usual conscientiousness and serenity. Hers is a side of court life that has more to do with the 'study of moral laws' than with the 'cult of love'.

Wyatt's contact with Catherine, though momentary, was real. She gave a task to her 'humble subiect and slaue', as he, conventionally enough, described himself. Furthermore he declared that the work, with her encouragement, might lead 'this hande / towarde better entprises'.[1] Had Catherine not lost her influence at court in 1527, the direction of his future career might have been different. It may be fanciful to suppose that Catherine would have held Wyatt to scholarship. His own tastes must obviously have had most weight in determining his literary choices, and, evidently, he was ready enough to convert her 'commaundement' into something more suited to himself. Yet, if Wyatt did not become a replica of Lord Morley, he was to win his own reputation for gravity. Catherine of Aragon, like Sir Henry Wyatt and Sir John Russell, brought out that aspect of his character. Many later experiences, imprisonment among them, sharpened it further.

When, after the years in Calais and at Anne Boleyn's court, Wyatt resumed his diplomatic career, the situation in Europe had changed. During those ten years (1527–37) Henry, backed by Cromwell, showed himself supreme at home. Abroad there were some awkward situations. The Emperor made his peace with the Pope on 29 June 1529, and, six weeks later, by the Peace of Cambrai, came to terms with Francis. Clement VII at last declared for Catherine of Aragon in March 1534, not long before his death. Paul III proved a stronger Pope, fired with zeal to reunite Christendom. In May 1535 he bestowed a red hat on

[1] *Quyete of Mynde*, sig. a 2ᵛ.

John Fisher. The execution of the new cardinal in June, and of More in July, did not improve Henry's standing in Europe. The bull of ex-communication was issued in August, though the order to execute it was delayed till 1538. In 1536 Reginald Pole became 'traitor Pole' and a cardinal. Still, there was hope in this year, for in March Francis invaded Savoy, thus renewing his war with the Emperor. Moreover, the death of Catherine in January 1536 removed a bone of contention between Henry and the Catholic powers, especially her nephew the Emperor. Henry wished to improve relations with Charles and prevent his recon-ciliation with Francis. On 12 March 1537 he issued his instructions[1] to Sir Thomas Wyatt, newly appointed ambassador to the Imperial court in Spain. He dictated an explanation of the law concerning the illegi-timization of Mary, in case Charles should appear aggrieved at it. She could succeed to the throne only if Henry had no legitimate child. If Charles could accept this, then Henry might consider the projected match between Mary and the Infant of Portugal. And so on. But behind all Henry's *minutiae* is the determination to persuade Charles that his religious reforms were just, and to prevent the peace which might lead to the formation of a Catholic league against England. And if per-chance a truce did come to pass, Henry was not to be left out. Ere long Wyatt was in fact instructed to arrange for him to mediate between Charles and Francis.[2] Certainly a man of 'wisdom and dexterity' was needed in Spain, not to mention one of superhuman patience. Through-out his embassy Wyatt was to be frustrated by the impossibility of dis-suading the Emperor from allegiance to Rome, by the absurdity of getting the Catholic powers to make Henry 'third contrahent' in any pact, and by the futility of discussing the Anglo-Spanish negotiations, half-hearted on both sides, for Mary's Portuguese marriage. He began his task with fair hopes and ended it in near despair. Thus he describes his impotence to exploit the golden opportunities that seemed his:

> Off Cartage he, that worthie warier
> Could ouercome but cowld not vse his chaunce;
> And I like wise off all my long indeuer,
> The sherpe conquest, tho fortune did avaunce,
> Cowld not it vse: the hold that is gyvin ouer
> I vnpossest. So hangith in balaunce
> Off warr, my pees, reward of all my payne;
> At Mountzon thus I restles rest in Spayne. (no. 81)

---

[1] LP, xii (i), 637.   [2] Merriman, no. 244.

Wyatt left England in April and travelled by Paris, Lyons, Avignon, Barcelona, and Saragossa. Thence, after a row with the rapacious Aragonian customs officials,[1] he proceeded to Valladolid, and was well received at the Imperial court in June. At first he was somewhat 'slak and negligent' in writing to Cromwell, used illegible cipher, delayed in delivering Princess Mary's letters, and actually left his signature off a letter to the King.[2] Nevertheless his first letters pleased Henry 'marvellously well', and Cromwell and Wriothesley, both his friends, covered up his mistakes. In Spain the indispensable John Mason, fluent in Spanish, was equally co-operative. Wyatt threw himself into his new task vigorously. On 4 November 1537 a shocked Italian observer reported that the new English ambassador was encouraging people to read *libretti* full of heresies.[3] At an audience with Charles on 17 January 1538 Wyatt actually tried to persuade him that the authority of the Holy See was unjustly acquired and pressed 'writings' on him. Charles, whose account reveals that Wyatt was up against a brick wall, blandly bad him keep such 'literary matters' for his chancellor, Cardinal Grandvela.[4] Wyatt later recorded that, in Spain, he was in hazard with the Inquisition, and that the Emperor had 'myche a doe to save' him.[5]

An early duty was to communicate the joyous news of Prince Edward's birth in October 1537. Sir John Dudley, arriving in November to make the official announcement, joined Wyatt in an audience with the Emperor. Wyatt's memorandum[6] itemizing the points raised contains some appropriately cheerful notes. The Emperor, rejoicing at the birth of Henry's son and heir, thought Mary 'delyuerd of a gret bourden'. And it is true that her position was now much simplified. On the other hand, had her stock in the marriage market sunk? The question was not raised at so early a juncture, the ambassadors' conversation turning to Charles's truce with France and his proposal— received politely but sceptically by Wyatt and Dudley—to reconcile England and Rome.

Edward's birth was quickly followed by his mother's death, which at once raised the question of the next English Queen. Henceforward, Charles's favourite marriage scheme comes up with a corollary. Mary, endowed with 300,000 crowns from Henry, is still to marry the Infant of Portugal, on whom Charles will bestow Milan, and, meanwhile, Henry is to marry the Duchess of Milan. The Duchess, to whom

[1] LP, xii (ii), 131.
[2] LP, xii (ii), 871 and Merriman, no. 189.
[3] LP, xii (ii), 1031.
[4] LP, xiii (i), 100.
[5] 'Defence': Letters, no. 37.
[6] Letters, no. 4.

legend imputes the remark that she had but one head to lose, was not at all keen. Henry, though he went so far as to commission her portrait, was simultaneously found toying with the alternative idea of a French bride. Wyatt thought his master would gain little and incur much expense by falling in with Charles's plan. Nevertheless he dutifully proceeded with the courtly discussions about the Duchess of Milan's qualifications. Pointless as this was, it was not the biggest of his worries during the winter of 1537–8.

Though Wyatt had succeeded in establishing good personal relations with the Emperor, the main purpose of his embassy was hardly flourishing. By the spring of 1538 the dreaded alliance between Pope, Emperor, and King of France was pretty well a reality. To set the seal upon it, Paul III arranged their meeting at Nice for May and June. Still, Henry's nerve did not break, and, with the object of influencing the Emperor against his allies, he sent out two special ambassadors, both officers of his church, to help Wyatt.

So it was Wyatt's misfortune to be joined by Edmund Bonner and Simon Heynes, the former apparently with Cromwell's instructions to keep an eye on him. Bonner, who has come down in history as a man of caustic temper and flexible religious opinions, was a tactless, rude ambassador. Heynes was a cipher, a man who wanted at all costs to avoid 'contention and brabling'.[1] They were already in Nice when Wyatt arrived on 9 May with the Imperial fleet. He conducted them to Villefranche, about a mile from Nice, 'the Toune beinge full of the Courte of Rome'.[2] The place was buzzing with activity. The Pope arrived on 17 May and next day held the first of several meetings with the Emperor. Wyatt 'trotted contynually vp and downe', like the Brian of his third satire. He was not only looking after his guests, but trying desperately to glean intelligence. He justly feared that Charles and Francis (who was still on his way to Nice) would 'conclude amonge them selves and leave vs owte'.[3] Therefore, one evening, when alone with Bonner, Heynes, and Mason, he suggested that the latter should insinuate himself into the confidence of Cardinal Pole 'to loke yf he culde sucke owte any thynge of hym that were worthe the kynges knowledge'.[4] Wyatt was taking advantage both of Pole's presence and of the fact that Mason knew him from the old days at Padua. Mason

[1] Bonner's description: see Letters, p. 68.
[2] Wyatt's 'Declaration': see Letters, no. 36.
[3] Wyatt's 'Defence': see Letters, no. 37, p. 198.
[4] Ibid., pp. 191–2.

tried, failed, and wrote a full explanation to Cromwell, events which occurred during Wyatt's absence on leave.

Wyatt's leave, though it afforded the opportunity to talk with the King and visit Elizabeth Darrell, was strangely timed. And this arouses the suspicion that it was Charles's ruse to be rid of the English ambassador before the arrival of Francis on 28 May. At any rate he granted Wyatt twenty-five days leave that he might carry the imperial marriage proposals to Henry, and graciously promised that no treaty would be concluded in Nice during that time. Wyatt must have left about the 24th, for he arrived in England, after what was described as a ten-day journey, on 3 June. Henry and Cromwell realized that he could hardly return within the stipulated period, and his excuses were sent back to Nice. During his absence things moved rapidly. The King and Queen of France arrived, and numerous meetings took place between the three main Catholic parties, before, on 20 June, their ten-year truce was signed and sealed. The treaty gave no special mention to Henry, who on that very day despatched Wyatt. The twenty-five days had but just expired, so that the subtle Emperor had kept his promise to the letter.

By the time Wyatt caught up with the Imperial court on 13 July, it was afloat and bound for Aigues Mortes in answer to a hospitable invitation from Francis. Charles and Francis had not, it appears, actually met in Nice, and from 14 to 16 July they made up for it. Though they announced that the meeting at Aigues Mortes was not for political talks but for good cheer, the English were bound to suspect their motives. Wyatt, in fact, wanted to prevent their personal encounter, 'but I cam to late to breke anye thynge'.[1] Brian, who was also trotting round at Aigues Mortes, had no more success. Bonner and Heynes, still at the Imperial court, merely hung on. They even returned with it to Barcelona, where the fleet arrived on 20 July. It was not till August that Wyatt was rid of these colleagues, and not till September that Bonner formulated his malicious account of the English embassy.

Bonner wrote to Cromwell from Blois on 2 September, priggishly pretending to do his duty, and more in sorrow than anger at Wyatt's misdoings.[2] How much he admired Wyatt's 'many good qualitees' he could hardly express. 'Wittie he is, and pleasant amongs companye, contented to make and kepe chere.' Unhappily he regarded 'his own

---

[1] 'Declaration': Letters, no. 36.

[2] See John Bruce, 'Recovery of the Lost Accusation of Sir Thomas Wyatt, the Poet, by Bishop Bonner,' *Gentleman's Magazine*, xxxiii (1850), 563–70. Cp. Letters, pp. 64–9.

glorie' more than the King's, and was corrupted by that 'unthriftie bodye' Mason, who was nothing but a rank 'harlot' and 'papiste'. Not that Bonner's 'mislikings' do not smack a little of the truth, but they are the exaggerations of a vain, touchy man. 'Mr Wyat and Mason aloon woold doo all thymself, not making Mr Heynes and me pryve.' Wyatt discouraged them, saying, 'Ye shall doo noo good with themperour, I knowe it.' He was inhospitable. He grumbled bitterly about his imprisonment in 1536: 'Goddes bludde! was not that a prety sending of me ambassadour . . . first to put me into the Tower.' His legitimate fear that Charles and Francis would 'leave us out' becomes, in Bonner's account, high treason: 'By goddes bludde, ye shall see the kinge our maister cast out at the carts tail. . . . By godds bodie, I woold he might be soo serued, and then were he well serued.' He put everything on his expense account, 'spending vnthriftely apon nunnes'. Indeed, Wyatt's honest servants were lamenting that he would come 'to nought'. A month later, Bonner had cold feet, and wrote saying that since Wyatt had credit with the Emperor, there was no man 'so meet to fill that room'. 'Yet,' he added, 'if some things were reformed in him he could do better.'[1]

Cromwell reacted with typical caution. In October he told Wyatt that Mason, actually detained in England for examination on Bonner's charges, was too sick to return to Spain. In November he congratulated him on the King's favour and his 'accoustumed dexterite'.[2] But the same letter also contains news of the arrest of Lord Montague and the Marquis of Exeter, and, since Elizabeth Darrell had served the latter, Wyatt may well have been alarmed. Moreover, he certainly got wind of Bonner's charges. Grandvela told him of Mason's detention, and, though he professed to 'take it light', from this moment he became more and more 'restles . . . in Spayne'. Meanwhile the fruitlessness of his renewed efforts at diplomacy merely served to increase his desire to get home.

For though the witty English ambassador had 'credit' with the Emperor, he had also met his diplomatic match. After an interview with Wyatt in July, Grandvela told his master that the English were 'only aiming at getting as much profit as possible out of Your Majesty's reconciliation with the king of France'.[3] Brian simultaneously aroused imperial suspicions in France, failing to conceal the fact that Henry was trying to cause 'jealousy' between the allies.[4] They were so little

[1] LP, xiii (ii), 615.
[2] Merriman, no. 281.
[3] C.S.P. Spanish, vi (i), 2.
[4] Ibid., vi (i), 4.

affected by the English 'diplomacy' that in January 1539 an even closer
tie was knit: the Treaty of Toledo provided that Charles and Francis
should make no new alliance without the other's consent.

Wyatt's enterprise did not give way, though there are signs of his
desperation. Cromwell had agreed to get him recalled in March 1539,
but on 2 January he broke out 'I ame at the wall. I ame not able to
endure to March.'[1] In February, Cardinal Pole arrived at the Imperial
court, and Wyatt reported his movements to Cromwell. His cipher
letter betokens considerable agitation:

> I have promised not to open by writinge to the Kinge a practise that is
> offerd me for Italy, to kendle there a fier, but by mowth only, nowe at
> my comminge home; and then shal be tyme ynoughe, for abowte the
> same tyme the partie doth returne thider; it is of importaunce.[2]

It seems likely that this top-secret, Machiavellian 'practise' was nothing
less than a plot to assassinate Pole on his return to Rome. Pole himself
heard that Wyatt, once free of his embassy, would pledge his posses-
sions to procure it. 'Temere et impie dicta a furioso juvene' the plot
might be, but the Cardinal was obviously in some fear.[3] 'Me thinketh
my hed is with child,' declared Wyatt in his letter to Cromwell. His
plot was, however, an abortion, for Henry and Cromwell did not take
it up. Wyatt expressly repudiated the notion that the plot was devised
'because I wold come away'. It was probably, therefore, a serious
scheme, produced by his violent anti-Catholic zeal and desire to prove
his loyalty.

Wyatt's successor did not arrive till June, when at last he could say:

> Tagus, fare well, that westward with thy stremes
>   Torns vp the grayns off gold alredy tryd:
> With spurr and sayle for I go seke the Tems
>   Gaynward the sonne that shewth her welthi pryd
> And to the town which Brutus sowght by drems
>   Like bendyd mone doth lend her lusty syd.
> My Kyng, my Contry alone for whome I lyve,
> Of myghty love the winges for this me gyve.   (no. 97)

Wyatt thus saw Spain for the last time. What, diplomacy apart, had
been his life there? The Emperor liked him, and he had also formed
two of his greatest friendships. Wyatt loved John Mason for his learning—'Doctrinæ titulo gratus Masonius albo'—and George Blage for

---

[1] Letter no 11.   [2] Letter no. 14.   [3] LP, xiv (ii), 212.

his wit—'Ingenio Blagi delectabatur acuto.'[1] Blage probably started his collection of Wyatt's poems, but, unfortunately, no record exists of which were actually written at this time. One exception is 'Off Cartage he' (quoted above), a free version of Petrarch's 'Vinse Anibàl', and written, evidently, during a visit to Monzón. Another, no less unhappy, is 'So feble is the thred', bearing Wyatt's title 'In Spayne':

> Eche place doth bryng me grieff where I do not behold
> Those lyvely Iyes wich off my thowghtes were wont the kays to hold.
> (no. 96, lines 29–30)

Here, most likely, Wyatt describes his nostalgia for Elizabeth Darrell. If so, he has again tuned his own thoughts to Petrarch's notes. 'Si è debile il filo', composed at a time when mountains and seas separated Petrarch and Laura, is his source. This is evidence that the memory of Italy had not faded from Wyatt's mind, and that the study of Petrarch was not merely a youthful phase. At the Imperial court he mixed with Italian diplomats. In his 'Defence' (1541) he recalled his polite visits to the nuns of Barcelona, in company, not with ruffians, as Bonner alleged, but with courtiers, including his fellow-ambassadors of Ferrara, Mantua, and Venice. Meanwhile, his enmity towards the Inquisition would cut Wyatt off from sympathy with Spanish learning, and any he had for Spanish poetry is likely to have strengthened his love for Italy. Spanish poets and poetry at this time were, in fact, highly Italianate. Benedetto Gareth (1450?–1520) had dropped his Catalan name, assumed the Italian 'Cariteo', and become a leading Italian Petrarchan. Garcilaso de la Vega (1501?–36), the courtier-poet, was the friend of Bembo and an experimenter with Petrarchan forms in Spanish. To this task he was encouraged by Boscán, whom, in turn, he persuaded to translate Castiglione's *Courtier*. Juan Boscán (1493?–1542) himself, as an aristocrat-poet attached to Charles's court, may well have been personally known to Wyatt. As Italianate poets, the two are strikingly alike. At a famous meeting in Granada in 1526, Boscán was persuaded by the Venetian ambassador, Andrea Navagero, to try out Italian poetic forms. Thereafter he introduced into Spain the Italian sonnet, octave, canzone, and tercet. Wyatt performed the same service for England.

Wyatt's journeyings through France would also strengthen this Italian influence. Avignon was on his route home, a place of pilgrimage for all good Petrarchans, since, in 1533, Scève had discovered Laura's

---

[1] Leland, *Naeniae, ed. cit.*, sig. A 3ʳ.

tomb there, and Francis I had paid homage. Lyons, again on the route, was a half-Italian town. Italian merchants had settled there in the fifteenth century, and up to 1535 Lyons was governed by the Milanese family of Trivulzi. Cardinal de Tournon, who then took over, continued their liberal patronage of men of letters. Italian books were issued from the Lyons press, the most important, for Wyatt, being the *Opere Toscane* (1532–3) of Luigi Alamanni. On the fall of the Medici in Florence in 1527, Alamanni had returned home, but the Republican interlude was short, and in 1530 he was again an exile in France. When he was not at court, he made his home in Provence, and his friends were Florentine businessmen and political exiles in Lyons. Also living there, in Wyatt's time, was a powerful group of Italianate-French poets: Maurice Scève (*c.* 1510–64), Antoine Héroët (d. *c.* 1568), and Louise Labé (*c.* 1520–66), the leader of the *École Lyonnaise*, and a woman remarkable for her skill in music, Latin, Italian, and Spanish.

To return to Wyatt's career: On his return home, Cromwell cleared him on Bonner's charges, and he repaired to Allington to rejoin Elizabeth Darrell, and see to his wretched finances. 'How slenderly Mr Wyatt's matters have been handled here, and how few friends he has.'[1] Wyatt had owed the King 'no small sum'[2] on his departure for Spain, and though Sir Henry's will had been proved in February 1538, his agents were negligent. Wriothesley had done what he could to help. Cromwell had been even more friendly, procuring an increase in Wyatt's ambassadorial 'diets', rebuking him for over-generous loans, and always wringing fatherly hands. 'In dede you had nede of Freendeship, for I haue not seen a wise man leave his thinges soo rawlye, as yours be left.'[3] 'I thinke your gentil franck hert doth moche empovrishe you.'[4]

Wyatt probably remained at Allington from June to November 1539, and during this time his patron was still apparently at the height of his power. Cromwell was to be created Earl of Essex and Lord Chamberlain the following April. But he had already set his foot on the downward path. Distrusting Henry's neutrality policy, fearful of a Catholic league, and anxious for an ally, he was arranging the Protestant match between Henry and Anne of Cleves. Wyatt shared his Protestant sympathies. Yet he was not directly associated with Cromwell's foreign policy at this time, but with the King's. In November he was ordered to apply his experience to Henry's favourite project. He was

---

[1] LP, xii (ii), 1135.   [2] LP, xii (ii), 1048.
[3] Merriman, no. 229.   [4] Merriman, no. 285.

instructed to express Henry's joy at the amity between Charles and Francis at their meeting in France. In other words, he was to foment discord between them. This signifies that the King thought him a successful diplomat, good at handling the Emperor. And Wyatt's only stroke of bad luck, at this stage, was in again having Bonner, now Bishop of London and resident ambassador in France, as a colleague.

Wyatt applied round-about methods to his task, and his descriptions of them are among his liveliest. Once arrived in France he set about obtaining the extradition of Robert Brancetour, a Welsh 'rebel' in the Emperor's train, a henchman of Pole, and one who had already excited his hostility in Spain. Francis agreed in a most friendly way, and Wyatt arrested his victim on 3 January 1540. A day or so later, Charles, who had heard from Francis, asked Wyatt who the rebel in question was, and when told Brancetour, ' "Ah," quod he, "Robert ",' and began to discourse of his services. The arrest, he told Wyatt, 'was evill done of yow (I must say plainly to you) withowt aduertising me theroff afore'. 'We aske here off the kyng that is owner of the terytory,' replied Wyatt, and they then launched into a sharp argument about many controversial issues, the Inquisition, 'the primacy of the bishopp of Rome', and so on. Wyatt had never seen Charles, who procured Brancetour's release immediately, so vehement, intractable, and imperious.[1] Bonner rudely remonstrated with Francis for permitting the release, and so disgraced himself that he had to be recalled to England and replaced by Sir John Wallop. This cannot have improved his feelings towards his rival. Wyatt, meanwhile, had pursued Charles into Flanders. He, too, has been judged a bungler in this affair, and certainly Brancetour had the laugh on him.[2] He, too, was rude, though perhaps to more effect than Bonner. At any rate, without Bonner, he went ahead in the role of gadfly. He saw that it was useless to blame Francis for submitting to his imperial guest's wishes, and elected to quarrel instead with Charles. He proceeded to insinuate that he had shown 'Ingratitude' to Henry. The term infuriated Charles. 'The inferyour,' he declared, 'may be Ingrate to the greter', but for a mere king to accuse an emperor of ingratitude was out of place.[3] Wyatt's evidence that Charles considered himself peerless was passed to Henry and

[1] Letter no. 20.
[2] See J. J. Scarisbrick's account of Brancetour's career in 'The First Englishman Round the Cape of Good Hope?', *Bull. Inst. Hist. Res.*, xxxiv (1961), 165–177.
[3] Letter no. 22.

thence to the Duke of Norfolk, who, having come out to France, set about using it to make Francis distrust his ally. By 15 February, after an interview with Francis, Norfolk 'dyd conjecte He was not content with thEmperors wordes'.[1] This rather optimistic conjecture was the only positive gain from the present mission. Francis was more indifferent than discontent, and when he quarrelled again with the Emperor it was largely for other reasons.

When Wyatt returned to England early in May, he was rewarded with 'landes above my deservinge'.[2] He refers to a profitable exchange with the King, by which he acquired two suppressed monastic properties, Boxley Abbey in Kent and the Priory of the Crutched Friars in London. More to his eventual advantage was his recent association with Norfolk's mission. To work for the breach of the Catholic powers was to imply that the Protestant Cleves alliance might prove unnecessary. Hence, ironically, Wyatt's efforts were efforts to discredit his master Cromwell. It must therefore have been with grim feelings that he witnessed the changed scene in England on his return. On 10 June Norfolk gleefully arrested Cromwell. On 12 July the Cleves marriage was annulled. On 28 July Henry married Catherine Howard. And on that very day Wyatt witnessed Cromwell's execution at Tyburn. 'Oh, gentle Wyatt, good-bye, and pray to God for me. . . . Oh, Wyatt, do not weep.'[3] Wyatt's tears for Cromwell also flow in his adaptation of Petrarch's 'Rotta è l'alta colonna':

> The piller pearisht is whearto I lent,
>   The strongest staye of myne vnquyet mynde; . . .
>   What can I more but have a wofull hart,
>   My penne in playnt, my voyce in carefull crye,
> My mynde in woe, my bodye full of smart,
>   And I my self, my self alwayes to hate,
>   Till dreadfull death do ease my dolefull state?   (no. 173)

The mortification of the last lines is Wyatt's own contribution to Petrarch's lament for his patron, Cardinal Colonna. Another phase in his life closes, and it may be that his thoughts took an even graver turn than they had done in 1536: the translation of the Penitential Psalms is assigned, by most authorities, to the latter part of 1540, when Wyatt had again withdrawn to Allington and Elizabeth Darrell.

[1] *State Papers: Henry VIII* (London, 1830–52), viii. 562.
[2] 'Defence': Letter no. 37, p. 208.
[3] *Chronicle of Henry VIII*, ed. cit., p. 104.

He can hardly have considered himself in disgrace, and by the new year he was living in his new house in London, and frequenting the court. Yet, though Henry had not pounced on Cromwell's followers, Wyatt was weakened by the fall of his pillar, because it made him vulnerable to his old enemies. Cromwell's papers were raked over, and through the Privy Council, which included Suffolk, Bonner's old charges were raised against Wyatt. Suffolk was even more powerful than he had been in 1536, for he was now Great Master of the Household and Lord President. Wyatt was warned that trouble was brewing. At Hampton Court, on 16 January 1541, he asked Suffolk to 'remit' his old ill-will. Next day he was seized, bound, and conveyed to the Tower. Mason was recalled *en route* for Spain and joined Wyatt in the Tower, while his coffers, which had been sent to Allington, were searched. It can be no coincidence that Sir John Wallop, hardly a Cromwellian but certainly a rival of Bonner's, was soon after revoked from his French embassy and also charged with treason. Meanwhile Wyatt's danger was much greater than it had been in 1536. On 20 January the order to confiscate his property and discharge his servants and family, including his daughter-in-law and Lady Poynings, was sent down to Allington. The only sign of mercy was the provision made for Elizabeth Darrell, in case of danger to her unborn child.[1] The fearful atmosphere is communicated by the French ambassador, who thought it would be difficult to learn the 'true cause' of Wyatt's imprisonment, for the English 'condemn people without hearing them; and when a man is prisoner in the Tower none dare meddle with his affairs, unless to speak ill of him, for fear of being suspected of the same crime'.[2] 'It may be the relics of Cromwell,' he added. Marillac saw Wyatt's arrest, with Mason's and Wallop's, as part of the faction warfare at court: Cromwell's 'minion' had for enemy all who had 'leagued against' the fallen minister.[3] Wyatt, in fact, was hardly heard, though he sent a 'Declaration' to the Council, and prepared a longer 'Defence' for a trial which does not seem to have taken place. Both, and particularly the latter, are brilliant expressions of his genius and courage.

'Syghes ar my foode, drynke are my teares' (no. 168): if Wyatt thus poetically addressed Brian from prison, nothing of the same lamentation, only a robust common sense and laughter, emerge from the prose of the 'Defence'.[4] His common sense can be challenged only on one point: his belief that the King was 'no tyrant'. This at a time when

---

[1] LP, xvi, 470. [2] LP, xvi. 466.
[3] LP, xvi. 467. [4] See Letters, no. 37.

Henry, discarding wives and favourites at will, was basking in the noon of Tudor despotism, seems, if not hypocritical, downright absurd. Yet when Wyatt adds that Henry 'will but his lawes', he is reasonable. He merely omits to mention the obvious: that the King makes the law, since Parliament exists only to register his decrees. Wyatt appeals to the law throughout. He is not a double-thinker or hypocrite, for he simply expresses the faith of any Tudor servant, say of Sir Henry Wyatt, in one who has 'Charge over vs, of Right, to strike the stroke'. Not one of his victims, however innocent, denied Henry's legal right to strike at his property or head. Wyatt, of course, shows prudence, but that is a matter apart from hypocrisy. He does not mention the King in connection with the 1536 imprisonment, except to show that he employed him afterwards. He is silent as to his plot to assassinate Pole, which evidently won no official blessing, though ready to use this traitor as a foil to himself, the loyal patriot. For the rest, Wyatt's 'Defence' consists in a display of evidence, chiefly of his conduct in the Imperial court, which need not be recapitulated here. 'My Kynge, my Contry alone for whome I lyve': his patriotism, too, needs no further emphasis. Wyatt's pride and his loyalty to his old master are yet more pleasing qualities. He himself, he asserts, never sought the honours bestowed on him. Cromwell's use of Bonner as 'spye ouer me' was no sinister design, 'but to fynd whether yt were trewe that I dyd so good service as was reported'. With the same fearlessness Wyatt mentions that the fallen Cromwell had cleared him in 1538–9, and acknowledges the powerful Suffolk as his personal enemy. Bonner and Heynes, on the other hand, are simply mocked as fools and flirts:

> your carvinge to Madona, your drynkynge to her, and your playinge vnder the table. Aske Masone, aske Blage. . . . Theie cane tell howe the gentelmen marked yt and tawlked of yt. Yt was a playe to them . . . that 'the lyttel fatt prest were a iollye morsell for the signora'. This was there tawlke. Yt is not my devyse. Aske other whether I do lye.

'Innocencie is all the hope I have' declares the poem to Brian, and his grandson's belief that the innocence so courageously proved in the 'Defence' saved Wyatt has persisted. Maybe it helped, but, in itself, it is not a good enough reason for his pardon. Henry neither regarded innocence, nor, necessarily, rewarded service. It was convenient to show mercy to a useful servant. Henry, moreover, was infatuated with his new Queen, Catherine Howard. According to the official record, Wyatt, like Wallop, was saved by the intercession of the Queen, which

means of her family, then enjoying the brief heyday which followed
the fall of Cromwell and Anne of Cleves. For all his enmity to Cromwell, Norfolk had no personal grudge against Wyatt, with whose
family the Howards had friendly links, and whose co-operation in
recent diplomacy deserved recognition. It is also suggested that Surrey,
Norfolk's son, interceded for his fellow-poet. Being fourteen years older,
in a different political camp, and frequently abroad, Wyatt cannot have
known Surrey early. Their friendship must belong to 1540–2. Surrey
not only claimed to know what he 'harbourd' in his head, but, in all
three of his elegies on Wyatt, held forth, with generous resentment, on
the envy and malice of his enemies. Thus Wyatt was saved by the
Howards, the ruling powers, mightier at that moment even than
Suffolk. In March 1541 he

> confessed uppon his examynation, all the thinges objected unto him, in
> a like lamentable and pitifull sorte as Wallop did ... yelding himself
> only to His Majesties marcy ... At the contemplation of which sub-
> mission, and at the greate and contynual sute of the Quenes Majestie,
> His Highnes, being of his oune most godly nature enclyned to pitie and
> mercy, hathe given hem his pardon.[1]

Wallop's conduct exactly matched Wyatt's, and neither is exceptional.
He 'at first stood very stiffly to his truth', afterwards half-heartedly
confessed and 'cried for mercy'. It is a common Tudor pattern, the
work less of brain-washing than of expediency. Tudor confessions are
often mere words of course, practically meaningless. In this case the
two reprieved men were immediately sent for by the King, who was at
Dover in military mood. Wyatt was sent to help defend Calais, while
Wallop was made Captain of Guisnes.

The last and most serious crisis of Wyatt's life was over, and he
served with credit for the brief remainder of it. In 1542 he sat as M.P.
for Kent, was made captain of a galley in the King's new fleet, and obtained various grants of land. In August 1542 war with France was
imminent, and the alacrity with which 'certayn Gentyll men in this
Countye of Kent' responded much impressed Thomas Becon. Among
the Kentish patriots was Wyatt, to whom he dedicated *The New
Pollecye of Warre* (1542), valuing him for his

> moost goodly qualities, worthy the renowne of worshyp, & apte for the
> godly administracion of the publique weale no less in the perfecte knowe-
> ledge of the diuersite of Languages, than in the actiuite of martiall

[1] *State Papers, ed. cit.,* viii. 668.

affaires, & also for as much as ye haue euer hytherto earnestely em-
brased not only the studies of humayne letters, but also the graue
exercises of diuine litterature.[1]

Appropriately, Wyatt, in the last year of his life, figures as the all-
round man of the Renaissance—governor, soldier, linguist, scholar,
versed alike in human and divine studies. Informing all these activities
is a patriotism corresponding to Becon's own. Becon's dedicatory
epistle lauds 'the det, wherwith we are obliged to oure contre' and
explains how 'vnspeakable louing affeccion toward his contre' is felt
by all men, except those, like Pole, who are of 'pestiferous and poy-
soned nature'. Love of country teaches 'vnfayned obedience toward
our superious'. 'It tylleth our hartes wyth the plough of paynful diligence', sowing all other virtues—gravity, patience, fortitude, prudence,
learning, wisdom, &c.[2] True, in the pamphlet itself, Becon can also
weep 'salte teares' over England, as he exhorts her to bestir herself, to
prepare weapons, fortifications, and 'innumerable thousandes of
stronge and valeaunt warryours', while at the same time acknowledging
that 'God alone is the myghtye helper'.[3] He is not far, in fact, from Milton's belief that God reveals Himself first to His Englishmen. Naïve as
the identification of religious, moral, and political motives appears to
the twentieth-century mind, *The New Pollecye* is wholly in harmony
with the national temper of 1542. It also reflects Wyatt's principles and
practice as his father's heir and himself the best of patriots. Becon's
dedication is, as it were, the first of his epitaphs, showing in what light
his contemporaries valued him.

On 3 October 1542, shortly after the new Spanish ambassador, De
Corrierez, had landed at Falmouth, Wyatt was sent in haste to meet
him. He rode too hard, caught a fever, and died. He was buried in
Sherborne Church on 11 October. His son inherited not only his
properties, but those strong anti-Catholic and anti-Spanish feelings
which were to lead to the disaster of 'Wyatt's Rebellion'.

The official elegy, by the King's antiquary John Leland, was in print
before the end of the year, with a dedication to Surrey. Surrey's *An
Excellent Epitaffe of Syr Thomas Wyat* was anonymously published,
also in 1542, while the elegies by Sir Anthony St Leger and Sir Thomas
Challoner remained for many years in manuscript. If allowance is made
for the usual lapidary exaggeration of a dead man's 'heauenly giftes', a
fair guide to Wyatt's character will be found in Surrey's tribute,[4]

---

[1] *Op. cit.*, sig. B 5ᵛ.   [2] *Ibid.*, sigs. A 2ʳ-ᵛ, A 4ᵛ.
[3] *Ibid.*, sigs. D 6ʳ, D 8ᵛ, F 3ᵛ.   [4] Padelford, no. 46.

and it is of interest that his points are repeated by Challoner.[1] Both remark on the fact that Wyatt was a victim of envy. And Surrey's claim that his virtues, of which the chief is surely courage, were brought out in the face of enmity, is on the mark: 'Such profit he by enuy could obtain.' Both confirm his patriotism. For Challoner he is 'so great a proppe of countries good', while Surrey remarks on his striving to turn all 'to Britaines gayn'. Surrey's opinion that Wyatt's 'iudgement none affect could blinde' is more open to question in the light of history. Even the Brancetour affair, product of his mature years, shows more enthusiasm than judgement. He never learned Mason's lesson, 'Do, and say nothing.' At the same time we may be sure that Cromwell would never have used a stupid or irresponsible man and allow that in judging such matters as the Milan marriage or Bonner's diplomacy Wyatt was shrewd.

Challoner, like Surrey, praised Wyatt's 'comely corpes'; and this is still before us in Holbein's fine portrait, a portrait which makes it easy to believe in the great charm with which all contemporaries accredited him. Wyatt's 'courteous talke' is mentioned not only by Surrey but by David Lloyd, who reports that, even when opposing another, he would politely yield an 'It may be so.'[2] Certainly even Bonner would grant him social success and gracious manners. Nevertheless his hospitality and generosity, as so often happens, went with a careless disregard for detail, and, sometimes, for prudence. Wyatt could also speak with vigorous bluntness. Lloyd describes him as 'often jesting, but never jearing'. But there was much contempt in his nature, and at men beneath him, like Bonner, he did jeer. The 'decorum' Lloyd admires and the 'wisdom' Surrey acclaims are, furthermore, not uniformly apparent: they belong chiefly to his later years, after the chastening of 1536.

Wyatt's 'wisdom' is that of the Tudor governor. He was learned, but, in the long run, more the student of life than of books. 'My head is with child.' And that head conceived not only noble notions, but the brutal, if patriotic, plot against Pole. Yet if the vehemence of More's attacks on Tyndale be recalled, Wyatt's behaviour will not, even here, appear incompatible with a Tudor idea of nobility. Miss Foxwell idealizes his conduct somewhat, but is surely right to stress his 'deeply rooted love of truth'.[3] And it is likely that Wyatt's love of truth would dictate a hatred of Pole, as representative of Romish falsehood.

[1] See the English translation of Challoner's Latin elegy, done by the minister of Boxley and dedicated to George Wyatt: Wyatt MSS, no. 11.
[2] *State-Worthies*, ed. cit., p. 80.   [3] Foxwell, ii. p. xv.

The Renaissance courtly character has violence as well as refinement. Hamlet, if on the one hand a 'sweet prince', on the other is the slayer of Polonius, nor is he squeamish in dealing with Rosencrantz and Guildenstern. Wyatt's nobility is of the same order. He was an 'accomplish'd gentleman', and loved by Cromwell for his 'gentle heart'. In Renaissance terms these graces were not incompatible with the violence and vehemence he quite frequently displayed.

The man who 'professed not chastity' was, obviously, not superior to the generality of erring mortals. Wyatt is best summed up in Lloyd's words as 'neither too severe for King *Henry* the eighth's time, nor too loose for *Henry* the seventh's; neither all honey nor all gall'.[1]

[1] *State-Worthies, ed. cit.,* p. 78.

PART TWO
Wyatt's Poetry and Prose

CHAPTER IV

Classical Philosophy and English Humanism

P<small>RACTICALLY</small> all[1] Wyatt's translations from Latin originals have to do with peace of mind, the 'remedies' against Fortune's blows that the wise man will seek. This is a traditional theme, common to classical, medieval, and Renaissance philosophizing. Plutarch, Seneca, Boethius, and Petrarch—all sources of Wyatt's—give it great prominence. They are also alike in promoting the wisdom of inner strength. Pagan fortitude matches Christian patience, and, long before Wyatt, the lesson of ancient philosophy was being assimilated into Christian philosophy. The Boethian commentators of the Middle Ages, and, later, Petrarch assisted the process.

The process continues with Erasmus, that most influential of early visitors to Henry VIII's England. If the Erasmian Humanists gave a new emphasis to the value of classical writing, their aims were essentially those of their most enlightened predecessors. Erasmus himself admired 'Good Letters', but he shared Roger Bacon's belief that the ancients as sources of wisdom were more important than the ancients as models of style. His wish was to make that wisdom more and more accessible, in all its richness and variety. When Erasmus and his friend Guillaume Budé translated Plutarch's moral essays into Latin, and Wyatt put one of them into English, they did a new thing, yet without flouting medieval feeling as to the proper—that is, the moral—use of the ancient classics.

---

[1] An insignificant exception is no. 100.

79

To group Wyatt's classical works together is a convenient way of mapping his mind. He was not consciously being modern, or aligning his thoughts to different schools. Aware only of the most obvious differences, he moved calmly from Petrarch to Plutarch, while Seneca and Boethius yielded him much the same treasure of wisdom. He was an early Humanist, that is, he retained the medieval love of ancient wisdom, and, with a few intriguing exceptions, did not attempt the imitation of ancient forms and style which was to characterize the ater phase of Renaissance Humanism. Thus the ancient teaching aboutl peace of mind, fortitude and Fortune served to enrich, not to alter, the content of his mind. Through it Wyatt learned to understand what experience also taught him: that ideals of conduct are to be found in purely human things, that Man, if ultimately dependent on grace, also has his own natural dignity to sustain him in adversity.

Wyatt's dedicatory epistle to *Quyete of Mynde*, addressed to Catherine of Aragon, describes the preceding attempt, the results of which are lost, to translate Book II of Petrarch's *De Remediis Utriusque Fortunae*. It also draws attention to the importance of the year 1527 in his career. For this is not only the year in which the waning Queen commanded him to translate a moral treatise, but also the one in which, as George Puttenham puts it, he 'trauailed into Italie, and there tasted the sweete and stately measures and stile of the Italian Poesie'.[1] Petrarch is the link between the two. The mention of his name at the very beginning of Wyatt's dedicatory epistle itself lends colour to the idea that it was during 1527 that he fell under the spell of Petrarch's poetry. But however that may be, the vernacular poems to Laura must now give way to the most important Latin treatise of the latter part of Petrarch's life. And, accordingly, the present emphasis falls, not on Wyatt in his familiar guise as courtly love lyrist, but on Wyatt as sober, prosaic translator and minor Humanist; in short, on Catherine of Aragon's Wyatt.

The dedicatory epistle shows that Wyatt had got the gist of Petrarch's *De Remediis*, but that he was bored by it (or at least by the task of translating it) in spite of his admiration for so approved an author:

The boke of Fraunces Petrarch / of the remedy of yll fortune / at the commaundement of your highnesse / I assayd / as my power wolde

[1] *The Arte of English Poesie* (1589), ed. G. D. Willcock and A. Walker (Cambridge, 1936), p. 60.

80

serue me / to make into our englyssh. And after I had made a prose of nyne or ten Dialogues / the labour began to seme tedious / by super-fluous often rehersing of one thyng. which tho parauenture in the latyn shalbe laudable / by plentuous diuersite of the spekyng of it (for I wyll nat that my iugement shall disalowe in any thyng so aproued an auc-tour) yet for lacke of such diuersyte in our tong / it shulde want a great dele of the grace. (sig. a 2ʳ)

Distinctively humanistic is the view that any lack of diversity in style is to be laid at the door of 'our engylyssh' rather than of the 'laudable' Latin. Even Petrarch had set more store by his Latin than his Italian works, while Erasmus and Budé positively scorned the vernaculars as vehicles for serious scholarship and literature. Wyatt also admires Latin for the orthodox humanistic reasons, that is, for its variety, speakability, grace, and 'plenteousness' (*i.e.* 'copiousness'). English is comparatively tedious.

The other cause of tedium, Petrarch's repetitiousness, is by no means exaggerated. His dedication states the main theme of *De Remediis*: 'Nihil ferme fragilius mortalium vita, nihil inquietus inuenio' (f. 1ʳ)—'I finde . . . nothyng almost more fraile, nothyng more vnquiet, then the lyfe of man' (sig. ❡ 3ʳ).[1] It remains for the two hundred and fifty-four dialogues to elaborate. In the first of Book I, Reason reminds Joy that youth is a vain, brief spell, and in the second that beauty is also impermanent. The third, 'De Valetudine Corporis', evokes what is really a confession that Reason has nothing new to say: 'Quicquid de forma modo diximus, repetitum puta' (f. 10ʳ)—'What-soeuer I sayd erewhile concernyng beautie, imagine that it were now agayne repeated' (f. 4ᵛ). Book II, 'of the remedy of yll fortune', com-prises a formidable array of one hundred and thirty-two dialogues, this time between Reason and Sorrow, but following the same pattern as before. The tedium is increased by Sorrow's apparent deafness to the wise interjections of Reason, as he reiterates such laments as 'At aduersa valetudo est . . . inualida valetudo est . . . Mala valetudo cor-poris' (f. 171ᵛ)—'But I am sicklie . . . I am sicklie . . . I am sicke' (f. 165ʳ).

De Remediis is certainly an exhaustive work, whose main theme, Fortune's smiles and frowns, has a strongly medieval flavour: not

[1] The quotations and page references in this section are from Petrarch's *De Remediis* (Venice, 1515) and from the parallel passages in the first English trans-lation of the whole work, Thomas Twyne's *Phisike against Fortune* (London, 1579).

surprisingly it provides one of John Lydgate's authorities in his equally exhaustive *Fall of Princes* (1431–8). For us its interest is that Wyatt read it, and that it is informed with Petrarch's Humanism. He assimilates to a Christian viewpoint the philosophy of the ancients, whom, with his usual breadth of learning, he freely cites. The emphasis on man's reason, integrity and dignity at once links Petrarch with ancient philosophers like Plutarch and Renaissance philosophers like Erasmus. The main message, that good and ill fortune alike must be met with philosophical detachment and self-control, is as Plutarchian as the strongly rational conduct of the argument. Petrarch not only recommends that we suffer misfortune with Christian patience as the will of God, he also argues that the rational man, the true philosopher, will see the good in the evil. For example, 'Sic perdendo pecuniam, duo bona vnum quidque et perstantius amisso, securitatem, et requiem inuenisti' (f. 188^r)—'Thus by loosyng thy money, thou hast founde two good thynges, and both of them better then that whiche thou hast lost, to wit, carelesnesse, & quietnesse' (f. 183^r). The philosophy of this dialogue, 'De Amissa Pecunia', is both Christian and Stoic. If Petrarch calls money one of the devil's snares, he also quotes Seneca to the effect that that man is valiant who uses earthen vessels as silver, and silver as earthen. The true philosopher, whether Christian or pagan, does not reckon money among his goods. The only goods are those of the mind.

When Wyatt turned his attention from Petrarch to Plutarch, he certainly did not think to make literary history. Lord Morley had presented manuscript translations of Plutarch's 'Lives' to various noble persons. Wyatt took up a moral essay, Budé's Latin version of Plutarch's *De Tranquillitate*, and afterwards, no doubt on royal advice, broke into print. Yet as the first published rendering of Plutarch in English, and, Lucian's *Menippus* (trans. *c.* 1520) apart, the first of any Greek author, *Quyete of Mynde* is as much a pioneer work as Wyatt's sonnets, octaves, and tercets. It is an early example of the prose essay, a genre new to the Renaissance, in English.

Moreover, when Wyatt turned his attention from Petrarch to Plutarch, he was by no means confounding the Queen's original purpose:

> this sayde Plutarch hath handsomly gadred togyder / without tedyousnesse of length / contayning the hole effect / of that your hyghnes desyred of Petrarch in his lytell boke / which he wrate to one of his frendes / of the Quiete of mynde / nerawhyt erryng from the purpose of the sayd Petrarch. (sig. a 2^{r-v})

The actual subject matter of the two works, resistance to the blows of Fate, is identical. *De Tranquillitate*, like *De Remediis*, comprises advice to a friend, being a reply to a request for an exposition of 'quiet of mind' (cp. the 'carelesnesse, & quietnesse' of Petrarch's dialogue on money). It, too, is throughly compatible with Erasmian Humanism. Indeed, it is more so. Plutarch, often called the 'tutor' of the Renaissance Humanists, was Erasmus's favourite among ancient philosophers, while More's Utopians 'sette great stoore' by his books.[1]

A Christian Queen could learn as much from Plutarch as from Petrarch. *Quyete of Mynde* not only contains nothing opposed to Christianity, but also, at times, closely approximates to Biblical concepts. In noticing the fault that makes us see other men's vices with 'kytes eyes', while letting pass our own with 'wynkynge owles eyes' (sig. b 3^r), Plutarch is not far from the mote and beam of St Matthew (vii. 3). Likewise the pricks of conscience are as familiar to virtuous heathen as to Christian: 'lyke as botches be in the body / so is a naughty conscience in the soule / as that that leueth repentaunce / busely prickyng and pulling the minde' (sig. d 2^r). How easy such passages make the task of understanding the Humanists' ambition to reconcile ancient and Christian doctrines. Budé encountered more obstacles than Erasmus, but even he, while condemning the ancients for polytheism, believed their philosophy pure.

Quyete of Mynde is Erasmian in that it legislates for philosopher rather than saint, just as it attacks fool rather than sinner; in that it is based on observation, analysis and criticism of life; in that it is no narrowly didactic work; in that it embodies not an ascetic, but a practical ideal. From the start the reader is aware that Plutarch is empirically determining the sanest mode in which to live. He is highly individualistic, for he believes in man's power, by reason and will, to live wisely, and this whatever society, that is 'fools', dictate to the contrary. His critical comments on court life, itself a microcosm of social life as a whole, typify his method, at the same time embodying arguments highly popular with classical philosophers and satirists in general. Quiet of mind, Plutarch begins, has not to do with multitude or scarcity of business, nor will a change of life effect anything but perturbation: 'for these selfe same causes / it repenteth many / of that they haue begon / that with gret labour haue thrust them self in to the courtes of

---

[1] *Utopia* (1516), trans. Richard Robinson. Everyman edition, p. 82.

kynges' (sig. a 6ʳ). Courtly ambition is frequently frustrated but the wise man will reason the good out of this supposed evil:

> Thou art fallen from some rule or authorite / thou shalt lyue in the countre. Aplyeng thy priuate busynesse / with great compasse assayeng to auaunce thy selfe in the princes fauour / thou art refused / thou shalt lyue surely euery where / with no busyness layd vnto thee. (sig. a 8ʳ)

Contrariwise the wise man will see the ill reward of public success, that is, backbiting, slander, envy. He himself will not envy court syco-phants and flatterers, for they are 'constrained to be as parasites to princes' (sig. b 6ᵛ). And just as constraint has to do with perturbation, so freedom is a condition of peace of mind. The wise man therefore retires cheerfully from court, finding that his 'best remedy is with the muses / or in som place of lernyng' (sig. a 8ᵛ). These few critical comments contain the core of the 'classic' case against courtly life—a case which the Renaissance was not slow to adopt as its own.

Plutarch's positive criticism reveals his 'humanistic' appeal on a deeper level. Destructive attacks on society are, in the last resort, futile. Responsibility for his peace of mind rests squarely on the individual. Wisdom is founded on self-knowledge and knowledge of Nature, which is the same as self-knowledge. 'We se nature to tech vs maruey-lusly', for it ordains that some beasts feed on seeds, others on flesh, and likewise that men should have 'dyuers orders of lyueng' (sig. c 2ʳ). A vine does not bear figs nor an olive grapes, yet a fool will labour to achieve the fruits of war, philosophy, finance:

> he that wyll obey the poesy of Appollo / must first knowe him self / and so take aduyse of his owne nature / & as she ledeth to take an order of lyfe / rather than passyng from one to another / to force & constrayn his nature. (sig. c 1ʳ)

Reason is as common a watchword in *Quyete of Mynde* as Nature. Plutarch assents to the common Christian doctrine that Man, wanting 'discourse of reason', is 'a beast, no more'. Thus it is 'beestly' to give way to anger (sig. b 2ʳ). Reason means restraint, and is therefore the foundation of man's inward dignity. 'The apasionate parte of the mynde / wantyng reason' will lead to the loss of the necessary control (sig. a 3ᵛ-4ʳ). 'So the wood affections of the mynde / it is no lytel busy-nesse to order and apese' (sig. a 4ʳ). Striving towards a purely human ideal, the inward balance and sanity that so strongly appealed to Erasmus, Plutarch does not make the effort sound easy. While the futility of opposing Fate is constantly emphasized, there is no crude fatalism in *Quyete of Mynde*. A mariner, however cunning, cannot repress the fury of the waves. But where the foolish or fearful man will allow his ship to be wrecked, the wise man will labour to save it. Plutarch sternly orders us not to blame Fortune or Destiny for what is our own fault, an error caused by 'noughti loue of our self' (sig. b 7ᵛ). The scope of Free Will is defined. 'It can no wyse be sayde / whyle I lyue this I wyll nat suffre . . . but this I may saye whyle I lyue / this I wyll nat do' (sig. d 1ᵛ). Yet for all his severity, life, for Plutarch, is, finally, neither a veil of tears nor a test of endurance. We can have 'inwarde gladnesse', and to 'blame this lyfe / sayeng it is a congregation of ylles' is an 'errour' (sig. d 2ᵛ). With the full emphasis of a noble and civilized Humanism, there emerges from *Quyete of Mynde* the idea of life as an art, a 'tune' that the skilled musician can play: 'the tenour of the hole lyfe / made & gadered with prosperites & aduerstyes / as a certayne accorde / tempred with connyng reason' (sig. c 4ᵛ). Thus the confidence in man that formed the ancient legacy to the Renaissance is no glib optimism, but the strenuously-achieved result of constant vigilance and skill. How much more adult and reasonable all this is than the gloomy tragedies of Fortune in Lydgate's *Fall of Princes*.

As to style, if the Humanists valued Plutarch largely for his critical analyses of life's problems, they also enjoyed—and honoured by copying—his many witty aphorisms and anecdotes of the Greek sages. When Anaxagoras heard of his son's death 'I knewe quoth he / whan I begote him that he shuld dye' (sig. c 5ʳ). Of one who let him down, Plato remarked 'I knew that my frende was a man / that is to say / a lyuely thyng redy of nature to be depraued' (sig. c 5ᵛ). Both illustrate a wisdom and strength rationally based on knowledge of life. More light-hearted is the story illustrating wisdom's ability to extract value from the most 'unhandsome' circumstances. Missing a dog with his stone, a man hit his step-mother: 'It is nat moch amysse quoth he' (sig. a 8ʳ). These certainly underline the point less tediously than Petrarch's lengthy dialogues. And, though dialogue form is congenial to the Humanists, Wyatt's final choice of a lively anecdotal essay is at least equally so. Erasmus's *Adagia* is a collection of proverbs from Greek and Latin, with interpretations, while his *Apopthegmata* comprises anecdotes of great men, with their sayings, the early parts being based largely on Plutarch. More comforted himself in the Tower with old wives' tales, like that of the Ass and Wolf confessing to the

Fox, and attributed to 'Anthony's' nurse.[1] This would not have been too homely for Plutarch, who compares Ulysses stuck between Scylla and Charybdis to one who 'held the wolfe by the eres / as the prouerbe saith' (sig. c 8ʳ). As Wyatt penned the sentence, he cannot have felt far from his own 'proverbs notable'. There was, in fact, no great wrench here from native habits of expression. A delightful new dish of anecdotes and aphorisms from Plutarch is easily assimilated into English. If, for us, they seem meagre, for the sixteenth-century Humanists they were rich didactic fare. Didactic *Quyete of Mynde* certainly is, and it declares its affinity with Erasmian Humanism on every level of its didacticism.

Didacticism is the main impulse behind the early sixteenth-century translations from the Greek classics. While Erasmus's Latin versions enlightened the erudite, the English ones, done less systematically and by lesser men, served a wider public. Perhaps in consequence, theirs is a narrower, more practical didacticism. The ethical bias in the English translations between Caxton and Tottel (*i.e.* between 1477 and 1557) is well brought out by H. B. Lathrop.[2] Works by Lucian, Plutarch, and Aristotle appeared, but the Greek dramatists and lyric poets were neglected. Even Greek history, considered important for its practical lessons, was not so much favoured as 'pure' ethics. The translations from Plutarch illustrate the trend. Thomas North's version of the *Lives of the Noble Grecians and Romanes*, the only complete and the only printed English version of the whole century, did not appear till 1579. The moral essays, by contrast, were tackled early and comparatively frequently. Within the century at least eleven of these were published and there seem to have been a few steady favourites. The essay on peace of mind was translated thrice, by Thomas Wyatt (1527), Thomas Blundeville (1561), and John Clapham (1589). 'On health' appeared twice, in a poor version issued by the printer Robert Wyer (?1530) and a better one by John Hales (1543). 'On education' was done by Sir Thomas Elyot (*c.* 1535) and Edward Grant (1571). The essay on 'how to take profit from your enemies' was anonymously published—the translator is probably Elyot—in about 1535, to be followed by Blundeville's version. All these are short, unpretentious guides to life, designed either to build up 'character' or to settle some practical problem.

[1] In *A Dyalogue of Comforte Agaynste Tribulacyon* (1534).
[2] In *Translations from the Classics into English from Caxton to Chapman, 1477–1620*, University of Wisconsin Studies in Language and Literature, no. 35 (Madison, 1933).

Wyatt sets the tone for the sixteenth-century Plutarchian essay when he says, of *Quyete of Mynde*, that he has been 'seking rather the profite of the sentence than the nature of the wordes' (sig. a 2ᵛ)—a statement of a doggedly didactic and virtually non-literary purpose which must derive from Plutarch's own: 'in such declaration thou sekes nat the delicacy of sayeng / and the piked delight of spech / and thou has consyderatyon onely of some doctryne / to be as helpe for the lyfe to be ordred' (sig. a 3ʳ⁻ᵛ). Elyot's *Of the Education or Bringinge vp of Children*, translated for a 'pastyme without moch studie or trauaile', was presented to his sister in the belief that she would be 'maruaylously instructed . . . in ordrynge and instructynge' of her children (sig. A 2ʳ⁻ᵛ). The instructions cover such matters as physical exercise, the protection of children from bad company, their punishment and nursing. Equally sensible are *The Preceptes . . . for the Preseruacion of Good Healthe* which Hales presented to Lord Audeley, the Lord Chancellor. Like Wyatt's and Elyot's this essay is intended to answer the immediate needs of a particular person, in this case a man in a public position whose health must be preserved, yet not at the expense of his social obligations. For instance, though abstemiousness is ideally best for health, the 'lawes of good felowship' often necessitate feasting. The practical solution is to prepare ourselves against 'ineuitable quaffyng' by refraining beforehand, and so 'reseruyng a place in our bodyes for meates, iunkettes, yea & drunkennesse' (sigs. a 6ʳ, 7ʳ). The English Plutarchian essays make a restricted, down-to-earth—one might almost say *provincial*—contribution to the more ambitious design of Erasmian enlightenment. Plutarch in England between Wyatt and North stands for 'doctryne to be as helpe for the lyfe to be ordred'.

Accordingly classical and humanistic elements are to be expected less in Wyatt's manner than in his matter. Whether they are present in his moralizing in general, reinforcing the sobriety natural to him, is a tricky question, which can best be answered by reference to his only direct statement of his moral message, the two letters of advice to his son written in 1537. In the first place the precedents suggest a negative answer. Wyatt was probably influenced less by his knowledge that classical texts like *Quyete of Mynde* comprised advice to individuals, than by the established habits of English gentlemen. On the eve of his banishment, the Duke of Suffolk (d. 1450) wrote a letter of advice to his son. A Kentish gentleman, Peter Idley (d. 1473 or 4), went so far as to versify *Instructions to his Son*, and his pious, patriotic and humane notions, as well as his learning and experience, are very similar to

Wyatt's. Thus Idley's ideas come to him 'Som by experience and som by writyng' (*i.e.* some from books)(IIA. 31).[1] He quotes 'Senek', but, more frequently, the Bible. He is fond of homely precepts: 'Lete thy tonge not clakke as a mille' (I. 50); and of well-established concepts: 'Trust not to fortune for she is fraylle' (I. 603). He preaches 'diligence', not only in God's cause, but 'for thy kyng and for the Reawmes right' (I. 855–6). His son should not tyrannize over his servants any more than Wyatt's should over his wife. Idley differs from Wyatt only in being, occasionally, rather more worldly: his advice to his son to study law, for which he has a 'witte bothe good and able' (I. 127), has no parallel in the two letters.

Though the argument that the letters represent a purely medieval and English Wyatt is strong, there is also a case for the Humanist. In both letters Wyatt's son, like Polonius's, is submitted to dense lists of practical precepts: 'Beginne therfore betimes, make god and goodnes your fundations. Make your examples of wise and honist men; shote at the mark; be no mokker—mokkes folow them that delite therein' (Letter no. 1). If not the actual product of collections such as the *Adagia*, Wyatt's faith in the efficacy of maxims is decidedly that of his time. To acquire a set of well authenticated 'opinions'—the word is significantly a favourite with Wyatt—is the first step on the ladder of good conduct. The aim declared at the beginning of the first letter is to 'advertise' Wyatt's son 'to take the suer fondations and stablisht opinions, that leadeth to honestye'. And where but from the Stoic philosophers of antiquity should he make his gleanings? 'And it is no smal help to them the good opinion of moral philosophers, among whom I wold Senek were your studye and Epictetus, bicaus it is litel to be euir in your bosome' (Letter no. 2). It is perhaps evidence of Wyatt's practical sense that, as for Catherine of Aragon, so for his son, he should choose 'litel' works. But the chief interest here lies in the claim that the works of Seneca and Epictetus, like Plutarch's *Quyete of Mynde*, are of 'no smal help'. By contrast, wherever Wyatt mentions, as he does constantly, 'god and his grase', it is as the very 'fundation' of every 'goodly thing'. The blending of Christian and pagan doctrine, and the sense of their relative value—the one fundamental, the other practical—accords with that of the Humanists.

There is some suggestion, too, that the experience to make men wise can be found in human things. Sir Henry Wyatt was an example of

[1] *Op. cit.*, ed. Charlotte D'Evelyn. Modern Language Association of America, Monograph Series, no. 6 (Boston and London, 1935).

probity in action, and richer than his lands was his moral legacy: 'that was wisdome, gentlenes, sobrenes, disire to do good, frendlines to get the love of manye, and trougth above all the rest' (Letter no. 1). The first letter, particularly, is suffused with Wyatt's own moral experience, a quality which makes the comparison with Polonius's platitudinous exhortations insignificant, and which springs immediately from life: the recent death of the head of the family with the consequent responsibility devolving on Wyatt, his son's recent marriage with the failure of his own. He appeals, and in a very practical spirit, to imagination and experience. His son is to 'Think and ymagine alwais' that he is in the presence of some honest man he actually knows, such as Sir John Russell, his father-in-law, uncle, or parson. The personal experience of human goodness gives reality and maturity to Wyatt's moralizing. It is in no bookish, platitudinous spirit that he handles 'the chansis of thes troublesome worlde' and 'the danger of sodeyn changes and commotions diuers'. This is the familiar theme of Plutarch, Petrarch, Idley—indeed, it is time-honoured. But for a lesson in endurance and fortitude Wyatt need look no further than his Christian father, who, by God's grace, was not overwhelmed by the rigours of a prison equipped with irons, stocks, and rack. Wyatt, too, had been in prison in 1536, and the juxtaposition of this event with his appointment as ambassador in 1537 provides a striking example of 'sodeyn changes' in the world as he knew it. His own experience authenticates his advice to his son. In his case, he acknowledges, 'prisonments' and other ills have been 'wel deseruid': 'And of myself I may be a nere example unto you of my foly and unthriftnes'. Wyatt's moralizing is peculiarly sombre, anxious, and, often, intensely personal. Such qualities are hardly traceable to philosophic schools or traditions. Nevertheless they can be related to Erasmian qualities. Wisdom can be found in human experience, and it is expressed in moral action. Wyatt, like Erasmus, sets up not an ascetic but a practical ideal. Mysticism is alien to him, as to Erasmus, and he, too, deserts moral symbolism and allegory for the 'nere example' taken from life.

On the other hand, whatever their common faith in maxims and ancient philosophers, it is apparent that Wyatt, at heart, and perhaps also because he is writing for so young a reader, is decidedly more dogmatic, more authoritarian, than the most enlightened of Humanists:

Then too had ye nede to gathir an hepe of good opinions and to get them perfectly as it wer on your fingers ends: Reason not greatly apon

the approuing of them, take them as alreadye approuid bicaus they wer
of honist mens leauings, of them of god ther is no question.

(Letter no. 2)

Erasmus interpreted each of his adages. Wyatt does not invite a critical
understanding of his heap of good opinions. In the letters his appeal is
not to reason, and life is described more as a discipline than an art.
There is a suspicion of narrowness, a rather rigid adherence to precept
and example, a refusal to rationalize and 'philosophize'. Furthermore,
though Wyatt points to examples, he is scarcely anecdotal, much less
witty. In these matters, no debt, specific or general, to either pagan
philosophy or Erasmian Humanism is remotely discernible: these
'sources' sound a note in, but not the whole strain of, Wyatt's moral
music.

The note sounds again, and in the key of classical moral philosophy
rather than of Erasmian Humanism, in Wyatt's few translations of
Latin poems. Comparisons with *Quyete of Mynde* become directly
relevant here, and especially so is Plutarch's valuation of courtly life,
which, it will be recalled, represents views common to classical philosophers and satirists—common, for example, to Seneca, Horace, and
Persius, to name a few whom Wyatt seems to have read. Compositely
built up, their philosophy amounts to this: The wise man seeks inner
peace and is not enslaved to passion and ambition. Particularly, he is
not ambitious of princely favours or the insecure joys of court. He prefers country to court, simplicity to sophistication, private to public
business. He endures misfortune stoically, finding his 'best remedy . . .
with the muses / or in som place of lernyng'.

Professor Muir thinks that Seneca was Wyatt's favourite Latin
author, and, at any rate, his knowledge of his work was fairly wide. A
translation and adaptation come from the plays, while Wyatt evidently
meant his son to read the 'little' moral epistles and dialogues. Among
these, the 'De Tranquillitate Animi' and the 'Ad Helviam' (which gives
brave, dignified comfort to Seneca's mother on the occasion of his
exile from court) match Wyatt's other classical studies. Seneca provides
Wyatt's strongest link with ancient Stoicism, a philosophy highly congenial to him. 'Me dulcis saturet quies.' *Thyestes* (399 ff) provides the
original of Wyatt's most purely Stoic utterance:

Stond who so list vpon the Slipper toppe
  Of courtes estates, and lett me heare reioyce;
And vse me quyet without lett or stoppe,
  Vnknowen in courte, that hath suche brackishe ioyes. (no. 176)

The irreconcilability of inner peace and public ambition is again the theme of a poem which borrows its refrain phrase from a chorus in *Hippolytus* (line 1140). There Seneca develops the idea that Jove, or Fortune, rages not so much in the humble cottage as 'around thrones':

> Quanti casus humana rotant!
> minor in parvis Fortuna furit
> leviusque ferit leviora deus. . .
> circa regna tonat.   (lines 1123–5, 1140)

His meaning came home to the Wyatt of 1536:

> Who lyst his welthe and eas Retayne,
>   Hym selffe let hym vnknowne contayne;
> Presse not to ffast in at that gatte
>   Wher the Retorne standes by desdayne:
> For sure, *circa Regna tonat.*   (Blage, no. xliii)

The poem has already been quoted, in Part I, for its precise reference to Wyatt's distress at witnessing 'out of a grate' in the Tower the execution of Lord Rochford and Anne Boleyn's other 'lovers'. Seneca simply bears out Rochford's dying words and Wyatt's own revolutionized feelings about public life. Literary and personal experience coalesce. The Senecan axioms are proved on Wyatt's pulses. Did he remember that Anne's predecessor as Queen had asked for a 'remedy of yll fortune' and been given it in *Quyete of Mynde?*

The 'remedies' of Fortune form the subject of Boethius's *De Consolatione Philosophiae* Book III, from which Wyatt chose metres 3, 5, and 6 (in that order) as the basis for the following poem:

> If thou wilt mighty be, flee from the rage
>   Of cruell wyll, and see thou kepe thee free
> From the foule yoke of sensuall bondage;
>   For though thy empyre stretche to Indian sea,
>   And for thy feare trembleth the fardest Thylee,
> If thy desire haue ouer thee the power,
> Subiect then art thou and no gouernour.
>
> If to be noble and high thy minde be meued,
>   Consider well thy grounde and thy beginnyng;
> For he that hath eche starre in heauen fixed,
>   And geues the Moone her hornes and her eclipsyng,
>   Alike hath made the noble in his workyng,
> So that wretched no way thou may bee,
> Except foule lust and vice do conquere thee.

> All were it so thou had a flood of golde
> Vnto thy thirst, yet should it not suffice;
> And though with Indian stones, a thousande folde
> More precious then can thy selfe deuise,
> Ycharged were thy backe, thy couitise
> And busye bytyng yet should neuer let
> Thy wretchid life ne do thy death profet.   (no. 195)

Boethius was a curriculum author. That Wyatt read the whole of his very popular work is likely, and that Book III claimed his attention significant. For it is precisely here that Boethius, feeling at last no longer 'unparygal to the strokes of Fortune', asks Philosophy to speak of the 'remedies'.[1] The need to 'withdrawe thy nekke fro the yok of erthely affeccions'—a fundamental idea, which is also developed in Wyatt's first stanza—is immediately and strongly stressed. The ensuing argument is not unlike a Plutarchian argument in that it is founded on Nature and guided by Reason. Thus 'natural entencioun' leads man to the 'verray good', desired by all things, even beasts and plants. Philosophy proves, in turn, that Riches, Honours, Power, Glory, and the Delights of the Senses are false goods. The 'metres' on them, from which Wyatt chose the three on Riches, Power, and Glory, adorn her argument. And this argument is, she adds, like a geometrical proof, 'ferme by resoun'. Then she goes on to reveal, in a splendid climax, her greatest truth, the divine substance, the unmoved mover, controlling the world and Fortune. The beautiful fable of Orpheus, whose turning back is like that of a man who turns from true to false good, brings Book III to an end.

Wyatt chose to translate not the sublime concluding passages of Book III, but those most deeply embedded in its argument, those which embody the Stoic ideal—familiar to him from Seneca and Plutarch—of self-control and detachment, those which invite the reader to behave well and to 'consider well'. It was an ethical, unmystical Wyatt who made this choice. The result, though a faithful rendering of the three metres, suggests the Wyatt who lectured his son more than the Boethius who could mix wonder with his sternness.

'How charming is divine Philosophy!' Did Wyatt ever experience that? There is a sign that he did in his second stanza, rendering Boethius's consolatory reminder of the soul's high origin and man's essential nobility:

---

[1] The quotations, in this section, are from Chaucer's translation, *ed. cit.*

> For he that hath eche starre in heuen fixed,
>   And geues the Moone her hornes and her eclipsyng,
>   Alike hath made the noble in his workyng.

Yet at this point a stern orthodoxy threatens to break the Boethian spell. Wyatt omits Boethius's fifth line which reads 'Hic clausit membris animos celsa sede petitos' (in Chaucer's translation, 'He encloseth with membres the soules that comen from his heye sete'). 'Quid non est verum' warns the gloss in the edition of the *Consolation* once attributed to Aquinas: Boethius, on the pre-existence of the soul, speaks 'more Platonico'.[1] Platonism must give way to Thomism. And, though Boethius was a Christian, he needs the kind of editing that the pagan philosophers need: the *Consolation*, ready with its references to the ancients, does not once mention Christ. Hence Wyatt's omission brings the reminder that the ancients, for him, were guides to conduct, not to belief.

Why did Wyatt deal with Power, Glory, and Riches in that order, instead of following the Boethian Riches, Power, Glory? He preferred, perhaps, to place metre 6, with its speculations on Man's high origin, in the centre. The conclusion afforded by the more ethical metre 3— a warning that death renders riches vain—is more logical, more sombre, more final.

Wyatt's minor omissions, as well as his few alterations of the Boethian material, are dictated by his artistic purposes. Forming a short didactic poem with gleanings from a long work, he aims at a self-contained, consistent, compact, and personal statement. The translation done by his contemporary John Walton in 1525 excludes no detail, and his version of metres 3, 5, and 6 runs to six octaves. Wyatt's, omitting such details as the 'many oxen', and compressed to three stanzas of rhyme royal, is less than half that length. He transposes the whole into the second person, thus making an alarmingly direct attack on the individual reader. He knits up the parts. The precious stones of his last stanza come not, as in the original, from the shores of the Red Sea, but from India—India, which, in the first stanza, has represented the limits of man's empire.

For all the occasional clumsiness in handling the complex Latin sentence-structures, Wyatt's is a mature poetic adaptation. As such it has little enough to do with its supposed source in the wearisome prose of Chaucer's *Boece*.[2] It is Chaucerian in a totally different sense, being

---

[1] *Boetius cum Commento Sancti Thome* (?1490), sig. g 6ᵛ.
[2] See Appendix F.

a literary imitation of a Chaucerian ballade. His model was, quite
probably, the 'Balade de Bon Conseyl':

> Flee fro the prees, and dwelle with sothfastnesse,
> Suffyce unto thy good, though it be smal;
> For hord hath hate, and climbing tikelnesse,
> Prees hath envye, and wele blent overal;
> Savour no more than thee bihove shal;
> Reule wel thyself, that other folk canst rede;
> And trouthe thee shal delivere, it is no drede.

In this poem Chaucer couches Boethian advice in three stanzas of
rhyme royal followed by an envoy, the last line of each stanza serving as
a refrain: that is, he uses a favourite ballade-form of his. In Wyatt's
'If thou wilt mighty be', both refrain and envoy are, admittedly, lacking. Boethius's text did not, perhaps, provide him the wherewithal for
a refrain. As for the envoy, Wyatt certainly knew the 'Balade de Bon
Conseyl' simply as three stanzas of rhyme royal. The envoy, which
appears in only one of the twenty-two extant manuscripts, was not
printed in the major editions, Pynson's (1526) and Thynne's (1532), of
Wyatt's lifetime.

Wyatt resumes the attack on worldliness, and especially on that of
court and town, in his three satires, which form the subject of a later
chapter. 'Welth and ese'—the very phrase from his Senecan lyric recurs
in 'A spending hand' (no. 198), while Plutarchian, Petrarchan, and
Boethian 'remedies' come again to hand. The satires do not fall into a
class apart from Wyatt's other classical poems because they are different in tone: arguably, they are his most distinctively classical, philosophical, and humanistic works. But, unlike the others, they are not
exclusively dependent on classical material, and, moreover, their
classicism has filtered through Italian neo-classicism. At the same time,
in form, they approximate more closely than any other work of Wyatt's
to ancient literary models.

In as much as they are classical imitations, the satires are exceptional
among Wyatt's poems. For the rest he is not an exponent of Imitation
in the sense intended by a critic twelve years his junior. Roger Ascham
(1515–68), while admiring Wyatt for translating the ancients, regrets
that, like Chaucer, he failed to follow the 'best examples' of style.[1]
While George Puttenham links Wyatt's Italian poems with the future,
Ascham links his classical ones with the past. Stylistically they struck

[1] *The Scholemaster, ed. cit.*, p. 145.

the aesthetic neo-classicist as old-fashioned, even Chaucerian. Wyatt's classical poems belong, then, to the early, didactic phase of English Humanism. That is, they belong with *Quyete of Mynde*, and, like it, they also derive from Latin texts. There is no evidence that Wyatt read Greek. His mention of Plato means no more than that he had read of him in Budé's Plutarch, in Boethius, or in Chaucer. An epigram appearing under Plato's name in the Greek anthology is the ultimate source of Wyatt's 'For shamefast harm' (no. 191), but he got it from Ausonius's expanded Latin version. Tottel's title, 'Against hourders of money', sums up the moral of this grim tale of a man, who, losing his gold, commits suicide. Wyatt puts it into the form of the strambotto, learnt from the fifteenth-century Italian poet Serafino, and the fact illustrates the nature and limitations of his classicism. For form and style, where he is not purely English, as in the rhyme royal of the Boethius translation, he looks to Italy.

Negative evidence is provided by the whole body of Wyatt's poetry. Of the three chief contributors to Tottel's 'Miscellany' (1557), only the youngest, Nicholas Grimald (1519?–1562?), cultivates the classics for aesthetic reasons:

> O happy, happy land:
> Where Mars, and Pallas striue to make their glory most to stand
> Yet, land, more is thy blisse: that, in this cruell age,
> A Venus ymp, thou hast brought forth, so stedfast, and so sage.
> Among the Muses nyne, a tenth yf loue would make:
> And to the Graces three, a fourth: her would Apollo take.
>
> (Tottel, no. 128)

This is not the only case in which Grimald constructs a whole passage from classical myths. Surrey is sparing with them, Wyatt even more so. In his poor way, Grimald looks forward to the post-1557 phase in English Humanism, that in which the classics, while retaining their ethical status, also provided 'piked delights'. Grimald's form of dilettantism is not found in the sober Wyatt. Or perhaps it would be fairer to say that, for the delights, for a rest from moralizing, they turned in different directions: Grimald to the classical, Wyatt to the Italian poets.

Yet, leaving aside the stylistic delights, Wyatt's Italian poems are not altogether irrelevant to the subject of doctrine. 1527 was the year in which he not only plodded through Petrarch's *De Remediis* but also, in all probability and certainly with more pleasure, succumbed to the influence of his *Rime*. These works present a contrast so strong as to suggest at first a state of schizophrenia. Courtly love on the one hand,

Christian and classical philosophy on the other, go far to explain the contrast, but Petrarch was also a man divided inwardly. Not only is the one work serious Latin prose, the other amatorious vernacular poetry, but also their basic attitudes appear irreconcilable. Yet, without touching, the two works interlock, and Wyatt probably understood this. On the one hand Petrarch describes the rational ideal, on the other the irrational reality. The Petrarchan lover, without either the Christian or pagan stamina of the Petrarchan philosopher, refuses to be reconciled to those blows of Fortune that come in the form of rebuffs from Laura.

> Mie venture al venir son tarde e pigre,
> La speme incerta, e'l desir monta e cresce. (*Rime*, no. lvii)

> Ever myn happe is slack and slo in commyng,
>   Desir encresing, myn hope vncertain. (no. 30)

Sooner shall the Thames or sun move backwards, continues Wyatt, than he shall 'fynde peace or quyetenes'. Quiet of mind, or rather lack of it, is a constant theme:

> Pace non trovo e non ho da far guerra;
> E temo e spero, et ardo e sono un ghiaccio. (no. cxxxiv)

> I fynde no peace and all my warr is done;
>   I fere and hope, I burne and freise like yse. (no. 26)

The lover does not keep the stiff upper lip of the Stoic, but weeps and wails like the Sorrow of *De Remediis*, and with the same persistent monotony he superfluously and often rehearses the one thing. He is not the master but the victim of circumstances and so of himself, for it is on inner perturbation and weakness of will that Petrarch's highly introspective poetry dwells. And Petrarch the poet is, after all, far from forgetting the lessons of philosophy, for indirectly he states them all the time: 'Morta fra l'onde è la ragion e l'arte' (no. clxxxix), which Wyatt renders even more didactically: 'Drowned is reason that should me consort' (no. 28). The Petrarchan lover is more like Plutarch's fool than his philosopher, yet he has the philosopher's self-knowledge and power to analyze the reasons for his disquiet. When the personalities and attitudes of the Reason and Sorrow of *De Remediis* are combined, there results the Petrarchan lover.

Much of this is carried over into Wyatt's original love poems. His

96

recurrent theme is frustration, that inward fretting at adversity that must keep a man so far from peace of mind:

> Suche cruell chaunce doeth so me threte
> Continuelly inward to fret,
> Then of relesse for to trete
>   What may it availl me? (no. 58)

Like Plutarch's self-loving man he continues to blame 'chance', apparently unendingly, for no poet exploits monotony more successfully than Wyatt:

> Ffortune is deiff vnto my call,
> My torment moveth her not at all.

Considerable tension is caused by the lover's knowledge that freedom from passion could confer on him the power to endure:

> If chaunce assynd   Then were I sure
> Were to my mynde   I myght endure
> By very kynd   The displeasure
>   Of destyne;   Of crueltie,
> Yet would I crave   Where now I plain
> Nought els to have   Alas in vain,
>   But onlye liff and libertie.   Lacking my liff for libertie. (no. 67)

And freedom can in fact be achieved by abandoning love for the lore of the ancient philosophers:

> Ffarewell Love and all thy lawes for ever:
>   Thy bayted hookes shall tangill me no more;
>   Senec and Plato call me from thy lore,
>   To perfaict welth my wit for to endever. (no. 13)

These poems do not demonstrate Wyatt's philosophy coherently or systematically. A man's philosophy is not to be judged from occasional love poems which may involve the adoption of fictional attitudes. Above, for instance, Wyatt writes as a veteran, as the ensuing references to 'yonger hertes' and 'idill youth' show. At other times he is himself the idle youth. These are poetic stances similar to Petrarch's, Donne's, Yeats's. The poems therefore merely indicate the content of Wyatt's mind, the extent to which he was in possession of ideas. A favourite theme is falling out of love, which in itself gives him the opportunity to glance over his shoulder at other 'lore' —Reason, quiet of mind, freedom, the 'perfaict welth' of ancient philosophy. Philosophically, Wyatt's poetry is by no means so rich as Petrarch's, but it is something that the comparison can occur without making Wyatt seem an empty-headed songster.

Wyatt's portrait, even when as the courtly lyrist he is apparently furthest from them, is not complete without his classical philosophy and English Humanism. Not that these, as the letters to his son show, fully account for his famous moral sobriety. The purpose of this account has merely been to show that the classical philosophy and English Humanism are there, in Wyatt's work, as part of the total complex.

Before *Quyete of Mynde* is forgotten, its style deserves consideration, for it provides the earliest, though by no means the best, example of Wyatt's prose. Like his whole approach to the task of translating the classics, his style is thoroughly medieval, traditional, and English.

Fifteenth-century prose is, from one point of view, the battle-ground of matter *versus* words. The clear cut distinction between plain and aureate manners survived into the sixteenth century. Many writers, like Wyatt, appeared self-consciously to choose between the two. *Quyete of Mynde*, written in 1527 and published in 1528, stands firmly in the plain prose tradition. Its diction is simple, its sentence structure loose and, frequently, incoherent. It avoids aureate mannerisms such as multiplication, presenting a strong contrast to, say, Lord Berners's recent translations from Froissart's *Cronycles* (1523 and 1525), with their long passages of easy reading, replete with such redundancies as 'shewe, open, manifest and declare'. Utilitarian, if also rather flat, *Quyete of Mynde* is, rather, comparable with the passages of Latinate prose in Leonard Coxe's *Arte or Crafte of Rhetoryke* (1524):

> This Tarquinus wente for ayde and socour to the kynge of Tus-
> caye / which whan he could by no menes entreat the Romains to receiue
> agayn their kynge / he cam with all his puyssaunce agaynst the
> citye / and there long space besieged the Romaynes by reason wherof /
> great penury of whete was in the citye / and the kynge of Tuscay hadde
> great truste / that continuyinge the siege / he shulde within a lytel lenger
> space compell the Romaynes through famine to yelde them selfe.[1]

Coxe, who was about Wyatt's age, produced this dull, long-winded example of the 'Oration Demonstrative', a speech in which a person or

[1] *Op. cit.*, ed. F. I. Carpenter, University of Chicago Studies, no. 5 (Chicago, 1899), p. 61.

act is praised, to inspire schoolboys. It is part of a lesson in epideictic rhetoric. With such standards current in the 1520s, marvels of fine prose are not to be expected, especially of other young, inexperienced writers, like Wyatt.

Coxe's prose introduces yet another problem of early sixteenth-century English, the problem of how to achieve complexity and avoid the native paratactical manner. A Latin model could help here. Coxe is able to attempt in English a fairly complex pattern of thought and expression. In the above example, his first subordination is, indeed, a failure: the 'which when' leads to incoherence and looseness. But later he manages to express clearly intention ('that') and cause ('by reason whereof').

Wyatt lacked theoretical guidance on English prose style. Coxe's work is, in fact, the first on its subject in English. And it could not have been useful to Wyatt, for Coxe deals only with disposition and invention, not with sentence-structure, the choice of words, their relation to matter or the art of translation. Thus Richard Sherry was perfectly right to describe his *Treatise of Schemes and Tropes* (1550) as a 'new fangle' thing in English. It came too late to influence Wyatt. So did Thomas Wilson's warning against unwieldy sentences in *The Arte of Rhetorique* (1553). So did Roger Ascham's plea, in *The Scholemaster* (1570): 'Ye know not, what hurt ye do to learning, that care not for wordes, but for matter.'[1]

Not that the skilled practitioner of 1528 was incapable, without theoretical guidance, of overcoming the clumsiness inherent in English plain prose. More's *Dialogue concernynge Heresyes & Matters of Religion*, written in that year, is both like and unlike *Quyete of Mynde*. By the third sentence one is lost in a maze of clauses, bored by the rambling tedium, and, at the same time, relieved and refreshed by More's dependence upon spoken English. The experience of reading Wyatt's early prose is much the same. But often More takes a step for which the comparatively immature Wyatt was not ready—a step towards the reconciliation of plain and aureate manners. Witness the fine tissue of repetitions, the balance without tautology, the subdued alliteration, all supporting the *matter*, in the opening of his eighth chapter:

But nowe I praye you let me knowe youre mynde concernyng the burn-ing of the new Testament in Englysh which Tyndal lately translated, &

[1] *Op. cit., ed. cit.*, p. 118.

as men say right well, whiche maketh men muche meruayle of the burnyng. It is quod I to me great meruayle that anye good Christen manne
hauing any drop of witte in his head, would anye thyng meruayle or
complayne of the burnyng of that booke yf he knowe the matter.
Whiche who so calleth the new Testament, calleth it by a wrong name,
excepte they wyll call it Tyndals Testamente or Luthers Testament. For
so hadde Tyndall after Luthers counsayl corrupted and chaunged it
from the good and wholesome doctrine of Christ to the deuelishe
heresyes of their own, that it was cleane a contrarye thyng.[1]

Likewise in Tyndale's *Parable of the Wicked Mammon*, published
in 1528, colloquial plainness is combined with significant rhythm and
repetition:

Iff thou wylt therfore be at peace with God and love him / thou muste
turne to the promyses of God and to the Gospel which is called of Paul
in the place before rehersed to the Corinthians / the mynistracion of
rightwesnes and of the spyryte. For fayth bryngeth pardon and for-
gyvnes frely purchased by Christes bloud and bringeth also the spryte /
the spryte loeseth the bondes of the devyll and setteth vs at lybertye
... Se therfore thou have Godes promyses in thyne herte and that thou
beleve them wythout waveringe.[2]

These examples of English prose in 1528 show what could then be
achieved. Wyatt, as a writer of the traditional plain prose, cannot com-
pete with the greatest of his contemporaries. More and Tyndale,
both his seniors, were much more experienced. Wyatt is not on their
level, but on Coxe's. His prose is limited by his age and environment:
by the lack of valuable theorizing and sufficient practical precedent, by
the early Humanists' scorn for the vernacular, and their disregard for
manner in favour of matter.

Further, circumstances peculiar to Wyatt's enterprise affect his style.
He translated literally a poor model: Guillaume Budé's style is 'pénible',[3] lacking the ease and naturalness of Erasmus's. Wyatt undoubtedly
worked hastily: 1527 was a busy year, Petrarch's long treatise had to
be abandoned for Plutarch's short one, and there was not even time to
put Plutarch's quotations from poems into English verse. (It is, indeed,
odd that a poet like Wyatt should be satisfied with a prose translation

[1] *The English Works of Sir Thomas More*, ed. W. E. Campbell (London and
New York, 1931), ii. 220.
[2] *Op. cit.*, f. 2ᵛ–3ʳ.
[3] Jean Plattard, *Guillaume Budé (1468–1540) et les Origines de l'Humanisme
Français* (Paris, 1923), p. 35.

of poetry.) But the most interesting circumstance—one that deserves a fuller investigation than has yet been afforded it—is Wyatt's deliberate adoption of a hard, short manner. That *Quyete of Mynde* will make difficult reading by the standards of 1528 is explained in the Preface to the Reader:

> It shall seme harde vnto the parauenture gentyll reder / this transla-
> tion / what for shorte maner of speche / and what for dyuers straunge
> names in the storyes. As for the shortnesse aduyse it wele and it shalbe
> the plesaunter / whan thou vnderstandest it. (sig. a 1ᵛ)

The general reader of the sixteenth century, frequently supposed hard of wit, was certainly likely to be daunted by such strange Greek names as Anaxagoras, Carneades, Pyttacus. If he cannot get over this diffi-culty, Wyatt[1] 'wolde he shulde nat rede this boke'. So much is clear. But what is meant by the 'shorte maner' and promise that to master it will enhance the reader's pleasure? Baskervill suggests that Wyatt may have been experimenting, possibly 'trying to achieve the compen-diousness of Latin style through the structure of his English sen-tences'.[2] The experiment was, I believe, carried further. First of all, Wyatt, quite literally, aims at a short manner, that is, at rendering the Latin into the fewest possible words. Comparisons between *Quyete of Mynde* and two other translations will, later, illustrate this point. It is sufficient, for the present, to remark that when Latin sentences are not expanded in English, the result is inevitably 'hard', and that, while Wyatt's sentences are frequently long, they are so packed with mater-ial as to warrant the description 'short'. The term was familiar enough in critical contexts. Wyatt's printer, Richard Pynson, had recently praised Chaucer for his 'shorte / quicke and hye sentences / eschewyng / prolixyte / castynge awaye the chaffe of superfluyte'.[3] *Brevitas* in classical and medieval rhetoric is simply the opposite of *amplificatio*, and, especially in the epistolary form, was considered praiseworthy. Wyatt and Pynson remind their readers of the facts of rhetoric, and the pleasure a well-instructed one will get from it.

Furthermore, even at second hand, through Budé, Wyatt has anti-cipated Amyot's recognition of 'Plutarkes peculiar maner of inditing, which is rather sharpe, learned, and short, than plaine, polished and

---

[1] Baskervill takes the reader's preface as Wyatt's work, but it is, of course, possibly the printer Richard Pynson's.

[2] *Quyete of Mynde*, ed. cit., Introd., p. ix.

[3] 'Proheme' to the *Caunterbury Tales* (London, 1526), sig. A 1ᵛ.

easie'.[1] And he has anticipated later understanding of the genre he is handling, the 'litel' moral epistle, usually called in English the moral essay. William Cornwallis thought the term 'essay' applicable only to apprentice work, and, as he explains his point, he echoes Wyatt:

> I Hould neither *Plutarches*, nor none of these auncient short manner of writings, nor *Montaignes*, nor such of this latter time to be rightly termed Essayes, for though they be short, yet they are strong, and able to endure the sharpest triall.[2]

Thus 'short' in Renaissance terms means 'sharp' and 'strong', in modern terms 'concentrated', even 'cryptic'. Such qualities in prose bring a pleasure which is not the less for being hard won.

The ancient short manner Wyatt was, I suggest, attempting to imitate in English. He was ever alert to new forms and styles and a born experimenter, but, unfortunately, in this case, he worked inexpertly and with unsuitable materials. His assumption that a word for word translation of Budé would achieve the desired result is an inevitable error—the result of the contemporary and deeply-entrenched habit of literal translation. Wyatt could not, of course, realize that English plain prose (in which, at this stage, he was no great master) was not really suited to the ancient short manner. For, though it avoids flowery redundancy, it tends to ramble. Wyatt's ideas cannot be made fully effective with the material to hand. They demand what hardly then existed in English—the pithy density of Bacon's manner in the 'certaine breif notes, sett downe rather significantlye, then curiously, which I have called *Essaies*'. 'The word is late', he explains further, 'but the thing is auncient. For *Senecaes* Epistles to *Lucilius*; yf one marke them well, are but *Essaies*.'[3] And so, he could have added, is Plutarch's *Quyete of Mynde*. Wyatt's is, then, the first English imitation of the pithy classical essay, and must take its humble place with the other forms in which he was the pioneer.

Historical and other reasons—not least Wyatt's habitual zeal for experiment—make the prose style of *Quyete of Mynde* what it is. It remains to illustrate. On pages 104 and 105 are three parallel versions of a passage from Plutarch's *De Tranquillitate*, together with Budé's

---

[1] Plutarch *Lives*, trans. North from Amyot's French. Tudor Translations edition (London, 1895), i. 24.

[2] *A Second Part of Essayes* (London, 1601), sig. Gg 8ᵛ.

[3] See *A Harmony of the Essays*, ed. Edward Arber. English Reprints (London, 1871), p. 158.

Latin. The passage fairly represents Plutarch's method. It starts with
a witty and memorable saying of a Greek sage, then elaborates critically
and philosophically upon it. As to the translators, the passage tests
skill in handling both lively conversation and complicated philosophical
argument.

Immediately obvious in the comparison with his successors is
Wyatt's short manner. Blundeville's translation is one quarter, Holland's one half the length again of Wyatt's. (To be exact, where Budé
uses 153 words, Wyatt uses 218, Blundeville 280, and Holland 315.)
Wyatt's comparative hardness is also obvious on a first reading, especially of his two long, complex sentences. A closer scrutiny will show
that the hardness is partly dependent on the shortness and partly on
Wyatt's syntax and his tendency to follow the order of Budé's clauses
too closely. By contrast, as handled by Holland, the two sentences
make extremely easy reading. But as his text is based primarily on the
Greek original—Holland merely consulted Budé's version of Plutarch
—it is only just to confine attention, for the moment, to the two translators of Budé's Latin.

Take the sentences starting 'For this worlde' (Wyatt) and 'For the
world' (Blundeville). Wyatt adds to the already alarming number of
clauses by turning 'nascendo' into a time clause, 'whan he is borne',
while Blundeville neatly renders it 'at his birth time'. Wyatt introduces
two clauses in succession with the same relative pronoun ('from
whiche'. . . ' whiche'), while Blundeville moves from 'from whence' to
'which things', thus giving both variety and emphasis. Again Blundeville's repetition 'things . . . such things', absent in Wyatt's version,
gives clarity through emphasis. Wyatt's antithesis 'nat to beholde
karuyn ymages . . . but the son' is unemphatic, while Blundeville's
repetition 'not to behold . . . but to beholde' has not only the strength
but the rhetorical balance lacking in Wyatt. The intention of the whole
argument is not well brought out by Wyatt's simple conjunction 'that',
whereas Blundeville's conjunctive phrase 'to the intent that' underlines
the logic strongly. Wyatt's slavery to Budé's order is apparent up to
the last phrase 'ut Plato inquit', 'as Plato saith'. This not only reads as
an afterthought and has, rhetorically, an anti-climactic effect, but also
leaves the reader uncertain whether the whole or only the latter part of
the disquisition on images is Platonic. Blundeville subordinates the
phrase by actually bracketing it, and, more important, shifts it forward.
Consequently it not only bears clearly upon the Platonic doctrine but
introduces the conclusion to the whole sentence, a conclusion which is

Equidem diogenis illud dictum memorabile esse censeo qui cum Lacedemone peregrinum quendam conspicaretur ambitiosisseme se ad diem festum componentem: quid inquit uiro bono nonne dies omnis festus est? nempe si sapimus etiam festiuissimus. Est enim mundus fanum quoddam sanctissimum & maxime deo dignum: in hoc homo fanum nascendo admittitur: non quidem spectatum simulachra fabrefacta ac sensus expertia: sed solem: lunam: sidera a quibus uitæ motusque principia manant: quæ prouidentia nobis uisenda præbuit: ut sensibilia sane sit intelligibilium simulachra atque imitamenta ut Plato inquit. adde flumina nouam semper aquam euehentia: terramque tum stirpium: tum animalium generi pabula proferentem. Huius celebritatis ac spectaculi initiaturam uerissime atque auspicatum uitam nostram: securitatis animi perfusique gaudii plenam esse oportet: nec expectanda nobis saturnalia: bacchanalia: quinquatria: quod plærique faciunt: qui hos aliosque dies festos aduentantes magna expectatione. ineuntesque denique lætitia gestiente: iocoque excipiunt: ut in quibus licentiore laxamento uenali sese risu oblectent: mercedes histrionibus & saltatoribus animi causa pensitantes.

'De Tranquillitate & Securitate Animi Liber', translated by Guillaume Budé, in *Moralia* (n.d. ?1505), sig. e 2^{r-v}.

I reken that worde of Diogines worthy remembraunce / whiche he sayd / whan he sawe a straunger in Lacedemona / curiously pyking hym selfe agayn a holyday. what quoth he / is nat euery day holyday with a good man? yes and if we be wyse most gladsom holiday. For this worlde is a certeyne most holy temple / & most mete for god / in to this temple man is admytted whan he is borne / nat to beholde karuyn ymages wantyng senses / but the son / the mone / & the sterres / from whiche cometh mouyng / & the first principles of lyfe / whiche prouidence hath gyuen vnto vs to beholde / that they shulde be sensyble ymages and folowynges of intelligible thynges / as Plato saith. besydes these / the flodes that bring forthe alwayes newe waters / and the erth producyng fode / bothe vnto trees & vnto all kynde of bestes. with this goodlynesse & prospecte begynnyng truely our lyfe / it must be full of surety and of ouerspred gladsomnesse / nor they are nat to be loked for of vs / Saturnus festes / or Bacchus festes / or Myneruas festes / as may do that receyue these and such other festes with great awaytinge / gladsomnesse and sporte / in whiche they may more lyberally / glad them self with bought laughter gyueng wages vnto mynstrels and tomblers for their minde sake.

Quyete of Mynde, translated by Thomas Wyatt, sig. d 2^{v}-3^{r}.

also a real climax: 'images and examples of those things, which are to be comprehended and vnderstanded by the mind'. Budé obviously provides a poor rhetorical model here, but Blundeville handles the 'pénible' Latin better than Wyatt.

Wyatt also has insufficient regard for the overall logic of the passage. He tends to think paratactically. His last sentence is but limply connected to its predecessor: 'with this goodlynesse . . . our lyfe / it must . . .' Blundeville's 'It behooueth our life *therefore*' makes the reader aware of what is going on. Evidently, too, Wyatt's grammar in such phrases as 'our lyfe / it must' is rather loose. Worse, it soon becomes exceedingly muddled. Wyatt changes confusingly from active to passive voice, and, for a moment, when he says that feasts 'ar nat

Trulie I cannot but iudge this saieng of *Diogenes* most worthy of remembrance, who espieng a stranger on a time in *Lacedæmonia*, gorgiouslie araieng himselfe against a festiual day, said thus, *What* (quoth he) *Is not euerie day to a good man a festiuall day?* Yes trulie (if we consider things well) most festiuall and ioifull. For the world is no other thing but a holie temple, and most meete for God: and into this temple, man at his birth time is admitted, not to behold images made by mans hand, and without sense or feeling: but to beholde the Sunne, the Moone, and the Starres, from whence our life tooke hir first beginning & moouing: which things the prouidence of God gaue vs to behold, to the intent that such things as be subiect to the outwarde senses, might be (as *Plato* saith) images and examples of those things, which are to be comprehended and vnderstanded by the mind. Adde herevnto the flouds continuallie bringing fresh water, and earth which nourisheth both plant and beast. It behooueth our life therefore, that will trulie begin to celebrate this noble feast and goodlie sight, to be full of mirth and quietnesse; and not to tarrie for the feast of *Saturne*, of *Bacchus*, or of *Pallas* (as manie do) which abide these and such other festiuall daies when they approch with great expectation: and finallie, being come, they receiue them, and the plaies celebrated in the same, with much reioicing: and for their pleasures sake, they paie hither also to plaiers of enterludes, to minstrels, and to tumblers, that in those daies they maie delight themselues the more wantonlie with bought mirth.

'The Port of Rest', translated by Thomas Blundeville in 1561, in *Three Morall Treatises* (edition 1580), sig. H 6ʳ–H 7ʳ.

And heere I cannot choose but highly commend that memorable saying of *Diogenes*, who seeing once a certeine stranger at *Lacedæmon* dressing and trimming himselfe very curiously against a feastivall & high day: What meanes all this (quoth he) my good friend? to a good and honest man is not everie day in the yeere a feast and holy day? yes verily, and if we be wise we should thinke all daies double feasts, and most solemne gaudie-daies: for surely this world is a right sacred and holy temple, yea and most divine, beseeming the majestie of God, into which man is inducted and admitted at his nativitie, not to gaze and looke at statues and images cut and made by mans hand, and such as have no motion of their owne, but to behold those works and creatures which that divine spirit and almightie power in woonderfull wisedome and providence bath made and shewed unto us sensible; and yet (as *Plato* saith) representing and resembling intelligible powers, from whence proceed the beginnings of life and mooving, namely the sunne, the moone, the starres; what should I speake of the rivers which continually send out fresh water still; and the earth which bringeth foorth nourishment for all living creatures, and yeeldeth nutriment likewise to every plant? Now if our life be the imitation of so sacred mysteries, and (as it were) a profession & entrance into so holy a religion of all others most perfect, we must needs esteeme it to be full of contentment & continuall joy: neither ought we (as the common multitude doth) attend & wait for the feasts of *Saturne*, *Bacchus*, or *Minerva*, and such other high daies wherein they may solace themselves, make merrie and laugh, buying their mirth and joy for money, giving unto plaiers, jesters, dauncers, & such like their hire and reward for to make them laugh.

'Of the Tranquillity and Contentment of Minde', translated by Philemon Holland, in *The Philosophie commonlie called the Morals* (1603), p. 161.

to be loked for of vs . . . as many do', it is uncertain whether 'feasts', 'we', or 'many' is the grammatical subject. Blundeville, having made 'life' his subject, sticks to it. At last when Wyatt reaches the description of the feasts—a word he repeats four times—he rambles on monotonously from event to event. Blundeville, having easily avoided the useless repetition, first deals with feasts as anticipated by the public; then, introducing the phrase 'and finallie, being come', he effects the transition to feasts as actually enjoyed. Blundeville's sentences are, in fact, planned. By contrast Wyatt seems to start on a sentence without knowing whither it is leading him, so that his become overloaded, unbalanced and obscure. These are common faults in the prose of his day, and they make Ascham's reformative schemes seem less dangerous to the health of native prose than they have sometimes been supposed.

Wyatt's clumsiness and obscurity are increased further by the literalness of parts of his translation. 'Securitatis animi' becomes 'surety' with Wyatt, 'quietnesse' with Blundeville, and 'contentment' with Holland. 'Principia' becomes 'principles'with Wyatt, 'beginning' with Blundeville and 'beginnings' with Holland. The concluding phrase, Budé's 'animi causa pensitantes', presents a difficulty in that its meaning has been anticipated by the earlier description of the public craving for gratification, the willingness to buy laughter &c. Wyatt, having said that the people 'glad them self' &c. rattles off a meaninglessly literal 'for their minde sake'. Blundeville, who also alters the position of the phrase (probably, as before, to give a better climax), gives a meaningful 'for their pleasures sake'. And Holland, who is far from disliking occasional redundancy, having already spoken of solace and mirth, uses the equally meaningful 'for to make them laugh'. But the most cryptic of Wyatt's translations is surely his rendering of 'intelligibilium simulachra atque imitamenta' as 'ymages and folowynges of intelligible thynges'. 'Folowynges' derives from 'follow' in its obsolete meaning 'conform to in likeness' (*N.E.D.*, 8b) and, though obscure to a modern reader, may not have been so to Wyatt's contemporaries. The real difficulty arises from his refusal to expand 'intelligibilium' any further than 'intelligible thynges'.[1] Blundeville's 'images and examples of those things, which are to be comprehended and vnderstanded by the mind'

---

[1] If advised well, 'intelligible', here, means 'capable of being apprehended only by the understanding (not by the senses)' (*N.E.D.* 3). In the *N.E.D.* example, More, typically, brings out the meaning far more clearly than Wyatt: 'The sanctifying of the mysticall sacrifice, and the translacion or chaunging of it from thynges sensible to thynges intelligible' (1534).

brings out the meaning even more fully than Holland's 'works and creatures . . . representing and resembling intelligible powers'. Wyatt therefore sometimes carries literalness and the short manner to ridiculous extremes. The advice to the reader who finds the book hard to advise it well seems more like an invitation to do the work that Wyatt should have done himself. In translation into English, Latin demands the expansion that Blundeville, without being wordy, makes.

But Wyatt's manner has its advantages. 'I reken that worde of Diogines worthy remembraunce' goes straight to the point. This unadorned opening may well be preferred to Blundeville's and Holland's more eloquent 'Trulie I cannot but iudge' and 'I cannot choose but highly commend'. Where Wyatt has a simple 'yes', Blundeville must have 'Yes trulie' and Holland 'yes verily'. And certainly Wyatt's best qualities emerge in the short narrative and conversational section at the beginning. Even later Wyatt's brevity is often a relief from the richness of Elizabethan prose. Admittedly it is unfair to attack Blundeville on this score, for he only once, in 'comprehended and vnderstanded', doubles a word unnecessarily. But Holland's prose presents the sharpest of contrasts to Wyatt's, for it is full of such doublets as 'dressing and trimming', 'attend & wait', 'hire and reward'. A common original is scarcely to be recognized behind Wyatt's flat but simple description of a 'certeyne most holy temple / & most mete for god' and Holland's oratorical one of a 'right sacred and holy temple, yea and most divine, beseeming the majestie of God'. And the advantages are not all on the side of an oratory that can become puffy and bombastic. Wyatt's vocabulary, where he is not influenced by Budé's Latin, is thoroughly English. His 'whan he is borne' avoids the Latinate grandeur of Holland's 'at his nativitie'. Likewise Wyatt's 'loked for' contrasts with Holland's 'attend', 'fode' with 'nutriment', 'reken' with 'commend', 'mete' with 'beseeming', 'glad them self' with 'solace themselves'. The range of Wyatt's vocabulary is comparatively narrow. For example, 'glad them self' catches up the earlier 'gladsom' and 'gladsomnesse' (the latter being twice used). 'Holiday' (Lat. *festum*) is used three times, while Holland has a whole array of elaborate variations like 'feastivall', 'high day', 'feast', 'holy day', and 'gaudie-daies'. Hence, as to diction, Wyatt's prose is neither hard nor unpleasing but represents the best in the tradition of plain prose in England.

If *Quyete of Mynde* adds little to Wyatt's literary reputation, it is a useful pointer. His prose was to remain basically what it had been in

1527, its sentence-structure generally loose and its diction generally good native English. But while he continued a plain prose writer, he shed his short manner, his hardness and his clumsiness. And the foundation of his mature work being laid not in literary Latin but in the realities of his day, it achieves an eloquence that leaves *Quyete of Mynde* far behind:

> My lordis, yf yt were here the lawe as hathe byne in some commen welthes that in all accusations the defendaunte shulde have doble the tyme to saye and defende that th'accusers have in making their accuesementes, and that the defendante myght detayne vnto hym councell as in Fraunce, or where the Civil lawe is vsede, then myght I wel spare some of my leasure to move your lordshippes hartes to be favorable vnto me, then myght I by councell helpe my truthe which by myne owne witt I am not able agaynst suche a prepared thynge. (Letters, no. 37)

The opening of Wyatt's 'Defence', written to be spoken at his indictment in 1541, shows that he learned to manage a long sentence, connecting and balancing his clauses, maintaining his argument clearly. But he is at his most persuasive when, dramatizing the situation between himself, his traitorous associates, and his accusers, he uses all the resources of spoken English:

> Reherse the lawe, declare, my lordes, I beseke you, the meaninge therof. Am I a traytor by cawse I spake with the kinges traytor? No, not for that, for I may byd hym 'avaunte, traytor', or 'defye him, traytor'. No man will tayke this for treasone; but where he is holpen, counceled, advertysed by my worde, there lyethe the treason, there lyethe the treason.

The mature courtier of 1541 was a much more confident person than Catherine of Aragon's 'humble slave' of 1527, and to find him lecturing the Lords of the Council on language is entertaining. 'Reherse here the lawe of wordes . . . yt is a smale thynge in alteringe of one syllable ether with penne or worde that may mayk in the conceavynge of the truthe myche matter or error'. If 'myll horse' is transposed to 'horse myll' what havoc is wrought! Likewise, if Wyatt's 'fere' that the King might suffer is perverted into his 'truste' that he would, 'one smale syllable chaynged . . . makethe a great dyfferaunce'. 'Grudginge', used of Wyatt's dislike of imprisonment, means, simply, 'being sorie or grevinge', without implying any acrimonious desire for 'revenge'.

His 'treasonable' statement that the King might be 'lefte owte of the cartes ars', is merely a 'commen proverbe', used of that which is let slip when gear is packed for carriage.[1] The 'law of words', as practised and preached in the 'Defence', means, simply, that perfect truth is achieved only by perfect accuracy in placing every syllable and determining the associations and nuances of every phrase. The pedantic accuracy of *Quyete of Mynde* has suffered a sea change in which the major part is played by Wyatt's experience of actual communication. If Bonner's misconstructions could endanger his life, no wonder Wyatt cared so passionately about the 'law of words'. Coming from a poet, whose linguistic theories are otherwise unknown, the few comments in the 'Defence' are the more valuable.

Wyatt's own vivid, life-like accuracy was, to his contemporaries, his most attractive verbal gift. 'He always told a story well; . . . representing persons and actions so to the life, that you would think you saw what you but hear.'[2] Wyatt's despatches, in addition to describing personalities, conversations and events, convey a fresh and distinct impression of the 'trotting' ambassador's life. He lumbers after the evasive Emperor 'with much ado apon plow horse in the diep and fowle way' (Letter no. 16). He tries to corner the Constable of France —'we went our sellffes to his chamber dore; but he eskapid vs by a bake dore'—and catches Brancetour in the act of flinging his papers 'bak ward into the fire' (Letter no. 20). But Wyatt's narrative and descriptive powers reach their height when lightened by the humour in which Henry VIII is said to have delighted, as in his famous description of Bonner and Heynes off duty:

Dyd you euer see woman so myche as dyne or suppe at my table? None, but for your pleasure the woman that was in the gallie, which I assure you may be well seen, for before you came nether she nor anye other came above the maste. But be cawse the gentell men toke pleasure to see you intertayne her, therfore theie made her dyne and suppe with you; and theie leked well your lokes, your carvinge to Madona, your drynkynge to her, and your playinge vnder the table. Aske Masone, aske Blage—Rowes is dede. Aske Wolf that was my stuarde. Theie cane tell howe the gentelmen marked yt and tawlked of yt. Yt was a playe to

[1] Wyatt's is the first recorded example of this proverb, but his protest that it was in common use need not be doubted: see M. P. Tilley, *A Dictionary of Proverbs in England in the Sixteenth and Seventeenth Centuries* (Ann Arbor, 1950), c. 105.

[2] David Lloyd, *State-Worthies*, ed. cit., p. 81.

them, the kepinge of your bottels that no mane myghte drynke of but your selffe, and that 'the lytell fatt prest were a iollye morsell for the signora'.

Wyatt's speech of 1541, an example of oratory superior to any in Coxe's schoolroom book, makes *Quyete of Mynde*, too, dwindle into apprentice work.

CHAPTER V

English Lyrics

Can we doubt that if we had *all* the songs sung at court between Chaucer and Wyatt we should be able to shew that every word and phrase used by Wyatt was a commonplace and had been used by many of his predecessors? ... By a little application we could compose a dictionary of conventional phrases which would show that many of these poems of Wyatt's are simply strung together from these phrases into set forms. There is not the slightest trace of poetic activity. The reason, I suggest, is that no poetic activity was attempted. Wyatt, like the other court writers, was merely supplying material for social occasions. Consequently, the study of these poems belongs to sociology rather than to literature. (H. A. Mason, *Humanism and Poetry in the Early Tudor Period*, London, 1959, p. 171.)

The lyrics of Chaucer and Charles of Orleans and Wyatt are on the whole dull—it is no use pretending otherwise ... To sum up, the lyric of courtly love from Chaucer to Wyatt is in its most characteristic form a mere gambit in the 'game of love'—deliberately stylized in language, oblique in purport, idealistic, bantering and abusive by turns. Its full, indeed its essential, significance can never be recovered, only guessed at: its study 'belongs to sociology rather than literature'. (John Stevens, *Music and Poetry in the Early Tudor Court*, London, 1961, pp. 207–8, 224.)

THE assumptions behind Mr Mason's statement must be granted, even extended. For though he confines his comments to the English courtly lyric between Chaucer and Wyatt, the commonplaces he refers to are, in fact, those of all forms of courtly love literature in medieval and Renaissance Europe. They derive originally from classical love poetry, and especially from 'Venus clerk, Ovide', as he is called in Chaucer's *House of Fame* (line 1487). But these commonplaces, together with the set topics they adorn, are generally traced no further back than the Provençal poetry of the twelfth century, and to the relationship of great lady and servant within a feudal society. Some of the common topics are love as captivity, love as sickness, love as service, love as religion, love as law, love as warfare in which wounds are inflicted by the god of love and the chaste or disdainful mistress is a beloved enemy. Love is a state of contrariety, full of sweetness and bitterness, hope and fear, and this is expressed through rhetorical contradictions, paradoxes and antitheses, as between cold and heat. Absence is a peculiar agony, for the heart must be left behind. But the lover is rarely other than agonized. This typical melancholic weeps, sighs and groans, is feverish and cannot sleep. His mistress, if somewhat chilly, is virtuous and beautiful. Her beauties are regularly catalogued and enhanced by comparison with rose or lily, and her eyes glance weal or woe. This is no place to investigate this seminal poetry in detail. Sufficient to observe that from Provence the courtly love conventions spread over Europe. In France itself *Le Roman de la Rose* added greatly to the body of love doctrine, while in Italy its moral and spiritual content was considerably enhanced by the poets of the *dolce stil nuovo*. How the conventions reached England remains something of a mystery. But reach these shores they did. Chaucer himself, as translator of the *Roman* and intensive student of French and Italian courtly literature, undoubtedly did more than any other poet to give currency to what was by the fourteenth century a very large body of conventions.

In the fifteenth and early sixteenth centuries Chaucer's influence was paramount, affecting not only courtly literature but all forms. His reputation steered an unbroken course. Hoccleve, who had known him, was an affectionate pupil, while Lydgate constantly referred to him as 'maister'. James I, Henryson, Dunbar, Hawes—all paid tribute. Chaucer was admired for his learning, his morality, and, above all, for his varied rhetoric. In the *Garlande of Laurell* (1523), Skelton, speaking as poet laureate, calls attention to his 'pullisshyd eloquence'.[1] But his unlearned heroine in *Phyllyp Sparowe* (c. 1508) finds Chaucer's style 'plesaunt, easy, and playne', while Gower's is of 'no value' and Lyd-

[1] *Op. cit.*, line 421: see *The Poetical Works*, ed. Alexander Dyce (Boston, rev. edition 1856).

gate's 'to haute'.[1] Sir Brian Tuke, a man known to Wyatt, gave the most judicious assessment to date in his introduction to William Thynne's edition of Chaucer's *Workes* (1532). Here, having praised his learning, metre, invention, and narrative powers, he comments on his 'sensyble and open style / lackyng neither maieste ne mediocrite'.[2] He is recognized as a master of all 'conuenable' styles, plain as well as aureate. Furthermore, the first two collected editions, Pynson's (1526) and Thynne's (1532), fixed the reputation of the 'English Homer' permanently. And because this happened during Wyatt's adult life, it is perfectly natural that his only reference to native literature should be to Chaucer.

Wyatt's reference is incorporated in an attack on fools who

> Praysse Syr Thopas for a nobyll talle,
> And skorne the story that the knyght tolld.   (no. 196, lines 50–1)

And *The Knight's Tale*, combining 'majesty' and 'mediocrity', is a perfect example of the Chaucerian virtues praised by Tuke.

> O Cupide, out of alle charitee!
> O regne, that wolt no felawe have with thee!   (lines 1623–4)

is a passage of 'high' rhetoric following hard upon a contrasting one of plain, deceptively easy writing:

> And if so be that thou my lady wynne,
> And sle me in this wode ther I am inne,
> Thow mayst we have thy lady as for me.   (lines 1617–9)

Lydgate, a timid line-by-line worker, and over fond of 'haute' phrasing, could have managed the first passage, but not the second, in which Chaucer achieves perfect colloquial, grammatical, and metrical rhythm in a moving three-line sweep.

Matching the rhetoric, the content of *The Knight's Tale* would strike Wyatt as 'noble'. It is based on Boccaccio's *Teseide*. Courtly love is expressed in its ideal form, yet without being too far removed from reality. Chaucer tells of the refining influence of pity upon passion, and in this is strongly influenced by the Italian idea of the *cor gentil*. 'Pitee renneth soone in gentil herte' (line 1761). Hence Duke Theseus yields to the ladies' pleas to have mercy on the lovers. But he can be realistic enough on occasion, and his willingness for the marriage of

---

[1] *Op. cit., ed. cit.*, lines 802, 785, 812, respectively.
[2] *Op. cit.*, sig. A 2ᵛ.

Palamon and Emily is founded not only in romantic sentiment, but in the wish 'To have with certein contrees alliaunce' (line 2973). *The Knight's Tale* is not an English *Vita Nuova*. There is no English equivalent to Dante's account of how his love for Beatrice was reorientated towards Heaven. Chaucer notices any such deviations from the common aims of human passion, and accordingly makes Arcite accuse Palamon of worshipping a transcendental rather than a down-to-earth reality:

> Thyn is affeccioun of hoolynesse,
> And myn is love, as to a creature. (lines 1158–9)

Chaucer's discriminations invariably involve 'creaturely' experience, his knowledge of which constantly reinvigorates the conventions of courtly love. Thus, returning to the 'gentil herte' in *The Squire's Tale*, he insists that its existence is 'preved', 'As wel by werk as by auctoritee' (line 482). 'Lat be thyne olde ensaumples, I the preye': Pandarus's pedantic love talk is rejected by the love-sick Troilus (*Troilus and Criseyde*, i. 760). Throughout *The Canterbury Tales* and *Troilus and Criseyde* 'auctoritee' and 'experience', 'books' and 'kynde' constantly check each other. *The Knight's Tale* displays an expert knowledge of the bookish doctrine of love, but its nobility is a human, not a superhuman, reality.

At the same time *The Knight's Tale* would provide ample stocks for Mr Mason's 'dictionary of conventional phrases'.

> The god of love, a, *benedicite!*
> How myghty and how greet a lord is he! (lines 1785–6)

It is about the religion of love, whose commands must be obeyed, as on May morning:

> For May wole have no slogardie a-nyght.
> The sesoun priketh every gentil herte. (lines 1042–3)

It is about the 'gentil herte', possessing which Palamon and Arcite will 'love and serve' (line 1143); and, on her side, the flower-like Emily will, after many a chaste withdrawal, at last display her 'wommanly pitee' (line 3083). True to form, *The Knight's Tale* tells more of the agonies than of the joys of love. Palamon is 'wounded sore' (line 1115). Arcite declares that he will die unless he wins Emily's 'mercy and hir grace' (line 1120). He finds her glance particularly deadly: 'Ye sleen me with youre eyen, Emelye' (line 1567). Absence produces the stock symptoms of love melancholia. When banished Arcite 'wepeth, way-leth, crieth pitously' (line 1221); and, believing Fortune to favour his rival, plans suicide. He can neither eat nor sleep, is hollow-eyed and pale, and 'solitarie he was and evere allone' (line 1365). Love endures for years—seven pass between Palamon's *innamoramento* and his escape from prison and still the story is far from its end—for courtly lovers are for ever 'so caytyf and so thral' (line 1552). And so on. Every single one of these statements has its parallel in a medieval English courtly love lyric.[1]

As for the opinions of that lyric, expressed by both Mr Mason and Mr Stevens, they are extreme. But, except in the inclusion of Wyatt, they are not revolutionary. The late medieval courtly love lyric in England has been variously attacked, not only as stilted and stylized, but as impersonal, abstract, flattering, idealistic, unrealistic, unpsycho-logical, unanalytical, undramatic, even insincere. Wyatt, on the other hand, has been held to rise superior to this dull norm, to have an affinity with Donne,[2] and a distinctive philosophy, even one tinged with 'Platonic mysticism'.[3] No doubt these views too can be repre-sented extremely. There is, in fact, a good deal to argue about. And it is fortunate that a solid premise is provided by the undisputed fact that we have to do with a medieval Wyatt, author of love lyrics in the main courtly tradition, and a professed admirer of Chaucer. Of course, if his poems were really enjoyed, the fact that his thoughts and feelings flow into old moulds, and that his style may be influenced by Chaucer's, would not matter any more than the Senecan revenge conventions or Kyd's influence matter in *Hamlet*. But this is not so. Mason says that the Devonshire poems are 'put together conventionally from conven-tional materials, without transcending art',[4] concluding his discussion with the remark that the Egerton ones would provide no more than a couple of exceptions to his thesis. Apart from a few anthology pieces, the collection of nearly two hundred Wyatt lyrics is worth no more than Chaucer's dozen. He is no more exciting than the monkish Lyd-gate or Charles d'Orleans, a French aristocrat writing in English, not to mention the crowd of anonymous courtly lyrists of the fourteenth and fifteenth centuries. Such a drastic view provokes curiosity as to

[1] See Appendix G.

[2] E. K. Chambers, *Sir Thomas Wyatt and Some Collected Studies* (London, 1933), p. 130.

[3] J. M. Berdan, *Early Tudor Poetry* (New York, 1920), p. 414.

[4] *Op. cit.*, p. 173.

whether Wyatt's predecessors are all equally uninspired, and, if they are, whether Wyatt joins them.

Mason attacks not only the conventional language of courtly lyrics, but the 'set forms', and for these it is necessary to consult the minor Chaucer and the non-Chaucerian poetic tradition. Chaucer's own genius demands ample forms, and his short lyrics have earned the reputation of being metrically rather than poetically important. The 'balades, roundels, virelayes' which he claims[1] to have written, were all French forms, traditionally associated with the Provençal and Troubadour poets. Ballade is a term loosely applied in English. Chaucer's usually comprise groups, often in threes, of rhyme royal stanzas or *Monk's Tale* octaves, the last line being a refrain, the whole sometimes completed by an envoy. This provides the 'set' pattern for Lydgate's 'Fresshe lusty beaute' in six stanzas of rhyme royal with refrain and envoy (SL, no. 131). If, as frequently, the envoy is omitted, then such results as 'A dere god!' (SL, no. 134) and 'Have all my hert' (SL, no. 135) are obtained. These use the *Monk's Tale* stanza, which, though well-known, was not quite so popular as the rhyme royal. The small group of rhyme royal stanzas, often without the ballade's refrain, became, following Chaucer, an extremely popular form, appropriate to a love complaint, compliment, moralization, or any passing occasion. It provides a medieval equivalent to the Renaissance sonnet—an equivalence to which some colour is lent by the 'Canticus Troili', Chaucer's translation, in three stanzas of rhyme royal, of a sonnet by Petrarch. The Duke of Suffolk's 'O thou, ffortune' (SL, no. 187) employs rhyme royal with the refrain, his 'Myn hert ys set' (SL, no. 188) rhyme royal without the refrain.

The Chaucerian roundel, though less important, also provides an imitable formula. This form is defined by its repetition of whole lines, particularly at the beginning and end, and, if not the origin of the later rondeau, is constructed on the identical circular principle. Charles d'Orleans follows Chaucer in using it. Of Chaucer's virelais it is much to be regretted that no examples survive, for, as contrasted with his heavy, decasyllabic ballades and roundel, this form insists on feathery lightness. It is a short lyric, with short lines, arranged in stanzas of two rhymes only, the tail rhyme of one becoming the chief rhyme of the next (*e.g.* SL, no. 173). This gap in the Chaucer canon is not otherwise filled for he makes no excursions into the lighter and simpler

[1] Through Alceste in the Prologue to *The Legend of Good Women*, line 423 (Text F).

forms deriving from the native tradition. Of these, however, there is no lack of non-Chaucerian examples. Five and six lines stanzas are frequently found in medieval courtly lyric, but the ever-popular form is the quatrain: the interwoven (abab), the carol (aaab), the monorhyme (aaaa), the couplet (aabb), and, though this is comparatively rare, the enclosed quatrain (abba). These, then, are some of the chief set forms, and obviously there can be little objection to them in themselves. Where, indeed, would English poetry be without rhyme royal or the ubiquitous quatrain? Still, a bare list, such as is given above, yields no clue to the presence or absence of the 'poetic activity' Mr Mason so rightly demands. And it is therefore important to observe the content and style of the courtly lyric before Wyatt.

Chaucer is unable to transfer his richest statements of courtly love into the short love lyric. In humorous vein he is certainly delightful, as when, the lover of Rosemounde, he likens himself to a 'pyk walwed in galauntyne', or when he parodies the love-complaint in one to his empty purse: 'Beth hevy ageyn, or elles mot I dye!' The triple roundel 'Merciles Beaute' gains from the contrast of the Arcite-like first part,

> Your yen two wol slee me sodenly;
> I may the beautee of hem not sustene
> So woundeth hit thourghout my herte kene,

and the rebellious last part:

> Sin I fro Love escaped am so fat,
> I never thenk to ben in his prison lene;
> Sin I am free, I counte him not a bene.

The transition from formal to colloquial statement is refreshing, though in substance the one is equally as conventional as the other. Bondage and freedom are stock subjects for debate. William Dunbar's 'Tretis of the Tua Mariit Wemen and the Wedo'[1] ends a lively flyting by coming down decisively on freedom's side. Lovers can wait, like the old hero of Gower's *Confessio Amantis*, to be formally absolved from loving. Or they can rebel outright. The religion of love produced its heretics, as well as its saints and martyrs. When Chaucer rebels, he is, like the Shakespeare of the over-praised Dark Lady sonnets, simply practising a form of conventional unconventionality.

His manner is generally that of the orthodox servant of love trained in the French school. His diction is as dignified as his forms, the

---

[1] *The Poems*, ed. W. Mackay Mackenzie (London, 1932), no. 47.

foundations of the fifteenth-century aureate manner being laid in such elaborate lists of virtues as

> Humblest of herte, highest of reverence,
> Benygne flour, coroune of vertues alle,

and

> Auctour of norture, lady of plesaunce,
> Soveraigne of beautee, flour of wommanhede.

The poems from which these lines come are indistinguishable, alike using Palamon's and Arcite's commonplaces. 'The Complaint unto Pity' attacks the 'crueltee and tirannye' of Love, pleading for mercy, though promising, even without it, to remain 'youres evere'. 'Womanly Noblesse' follows suit with more about Chaucer's service and 'woful herte', and his lady's grace, 'gentilnesse' and beauty.

'A Complaint to his Lady' describes a sleepless Chaucer, who can find 'neither pitee, mercy, neither grace', and whose pain can be relieved only by death:

> Thus am I slayn with Loves fyry dart.
> I can but love hir best, my swete fo.

'Swete fo' is soon varied to 'best beloved fo', our first English examples of the traditional oxymoron. Chaucer was familiar with the lover's ambivalent feelings, with Love's own contrarieties, and especially with its exquisite anguish of pleasure and pain. Criseyde, on the brink of loving Troilus, feels 'Now hoot, now cold' (*Troilus and Criseyde*, ii. 811). But here the conventional terms are harnessed to Chaucerian psychology, and long after we have forgotten them we remember his insight into his heroine's conflict. Perfunctorily used, all the contradiction devices fail to express the complexity of experience for which they were originally designed. Dunbar addresses 'Quhone he list to feyne' to a 'swete assured fo' (*ed. cit.*, no. 50). Skelton alludes to 'pleasaunt paine' and 'glad distres' in the *Garlande of Laurell* (*ed. cit.*, line 1391). And 'gladfull sory chere' is a common item in lover's complaints (*e.g.* SL, no. 159). Here words have become the 'tombs of ideas'.[1] Where is the bitter-sweet anguish of love? I reach here a point of strong agreement with Mr Mason.

Lydgate takes up the Chaucerian ballade, piling in the French and

---

[1] George Santayana, *Interpretations of Poetry and Religion* (New York, 1924), p. 119.

Latin terms, shortening the phrasing and destroying the over-all flow that rhyme royal can have:

> Ffresshe lusty beaute Ioyned with gentylesse,
>> Demure, appert, glad chere with gouuernaunce,
> Yche thing demenid by avysinesse,
>> Prudent of speeche, wisdam of dalyaunce,
>> Gentylesse with wommanly plesaunce,
>>> Hevenly eyeghen, aungellyk of vysage—
>>> Al this hathe nature sette in youre ymage!   (SL, no. 131)

His too-lavish praise then expands into a list of 'olde ensaumples' worthy of Pandarus or Gower. 'She' is like Penelope, Griselda, Niobe, Judith &c., only her lack of 'mercy and pytee' for her servant threatening to mar an absolute perfection. The effect is as of cataloguing, and the refrain line hardly succeeds in binding the separate items together.

The catalogue of beauties and virtues is, in fact, the favourite medieval mode of description:

> The smylyng mouth, and laughyng eyen gray,
>> The brestis rounde, and long smal armys twayn,
>> The hondis smothe, the sidis streight & playne,
> yowre fetis lite—what shulde y ferther say?   (SL, no. 184)

What indeed? The trouble with Charles d'Orleans's roundel describing his mistress is that it says both too little and too much. It is far too literal and naturalistic. The absurdity of detailing 'armys *twayn*' (compare Chaucer's 'yen two') is as obvious as the failure to give a total impression, or an equivalent from our general aesthetic or human experience:

> O thou art fairer then the euening aire,
> Clad in the beauty of a thousand starres.
>> (*Doctor Faustus*, lines 1341–2)

Helen's beauty is not distinctly visualized, rather experienced through its effect on Marlowe's hero, whose hellish fears it momentarily stilled. The medieval lover-poet frequently peers myopically at the separate stitches of his now-faded canvas, and, as his addresses to mistresses who are 'of womanhede the floure' are equally frequent, boredom is inevitable. Mr Mason's case again receives support.

Still, Charles d'Orleans can give pleasure. Treating the religion of love as a joke, he confesses to his 'gostly fadir' to stealing a kiss 'of gret

swetnes', vowing to return it (SL, no. 185). Or he sends forth his heart
to his lady:

> I most as a hertles body
> A-byde alone in heuynes.   (SL, no. 183)

It is not originality that pleases here. Gower has already made his love
confession, and the absent lover is traditionally 'lyke to a fygure wyche
that ys hertlees' (SL, no. 169). Naughty humour and light gallantry
simply provide a refreshing change from solemn panegyric.

Again, not all panegyrics are heavy catalogues. The Duke of Suffolk,
having lamented 'noble chaucer' and implored his successor the 'monke
of bury' to 'enlumyne' his pen, devotes some rhyme royal to a 'flour'
—it is suggested to Marguerite, Henry VI's Queen. For all his literary
modesty, his lines compare well with his master Lydgate's, being
simpler and more flowing—

> Myn hert ys set, and all myn hole entent,
>   To serue this flour in my most humble wyse
> As faythfully as can be thought or ment,
>   Wyth-out feynyng or slouthe in my seruyse;
>   For wytt the wele, yt ys a paradyse
>   To se this floure when yt begyn to sprede,
>   Wyth colours fressh ennewyd, white and rede.

and more colloquial and vigorous:

> A fye! for schame! O thou envyous man!
>   Thynk whens thou came and whider to repayr.
> Hastow not sayd eke that these women can
>   Laugh and loue nat? Parde, yt is not fair!   (SL, no. 188)

Suffolk has something of the *sprezzatura* of the genuine insider at
court, a quality which Lydgate could hardly be expected to share but
which is found occasionally in Charles d'Orleans. Suffolk's is among
the most polished writing in the Chaucerian lyric school of the fifteenth
century. This is very far from declaring it original, however. Indeed,
arguably, his love and service, tendered to the lady who married his
King, is of the most conservative, feudal kind. The feelings he displays
are rather of respect than desire. He dismisses, in fact, 'dotage', and
speaks as the man who 'louyth wele all vertu'. This is an example of the
courtly love poetry usually criticized as so much insipid flattery. Its
justification is that it is intended as gallant compliment.

Clearly the terms of courtly love are adaptable to a fairly wide range of relationships, from that of patroness and protégé, to that of husband and wife,[1] to that of lover (or would-be lover) and mistress. This last naturally predominates. The vast majority of the poems are wooing songs, concealing sparks of hope under their ashen despair. The wooing *motif* exists, subterraneously, in many of the aureate, Chaucerian lyrics, but, in illustrating it now, I turn to the simpler form of courtly lyric.

By contrast with Suffolk's public and chivalric address, is a more intimate and erotic one, like it only in being addressed to a 'delectable daysye' and in the use of some common terms. In 'As I my-selfe' the absent lover describes a joyful wish-fulfilment dream and its shattering:

> And I lay styll my-selfe alone,
> & yn no wyse my sorow cowld slake,
> but euer styll mournyng with full great mone
> vnto the tyme that I dyd wake.   (SL, no. 200)

The hard facts flood back, her broken promise to be true, his frustrated desire to be 'receyvyd yn-to your grace':

> I haue pryntyd yow yn my harte soo depe—
> wold to god I were able your seruaunt to be,
> Euery nyght yn your armes that I myght slepe;
> rewarde me with your loue: I aske non oder fee.

Here the idea of 'service', with 'grace' and 'reward', obviously retains no feudal quality, meaning simply the dog-like devotion which, like Troilus's, earns its 'fee' in bed. The polite words, though presumably better understood between Chaucer and Wyatt than now, often muffle the basically erotic ideas of courtly love lyric. They sometimes obscure the fact that the lover has in mind a bargain in which the mistress too must take part: 'Onys ye promysyde me for to be trew.' 'As I my-selfe' proves, however, that this poetry is not, as sometimes maintained, entirely occupied with remote adoration, passive mistresses, or chaste ideals. The idea of 'pity' contained in it is, compared with Duke Theseus's, barbarous, for it simply means yielding to a lover's pressure. Its worship is generally bodily worship, and it has nothing to say of the marriage of minds. The equally common opinion that this poetry is insincere, though also misleading, is more comprehensible. The courtly servant's willingness to behave as a humble worm, while

---

[1] Emily, after her marriage, loves Palamon 'tendrely', 'And he hire serveth al so gentilly' (*Knight's Tale*, line 3104).

entertaining the thoughts of an aggressive male, is hypocritical or civilized according to one's point of view. Courtliness can certainly be a matter of manners rather than morals, and, in this respect, there are differences as great between Dante and the anonymous English lyrist, as between, say, Spenser and Suckling. Donne dropped the polite manner—or, rather, reserved it archaically for his wealthy patronesses—and this is why his love poetry is felt to be more sincere than the traditional courtly poetry.

'As I my-selfe' is, perhaps, unusual in its absence of vagueness and equivocation. In other respects it illustrates typical qualities of the non-Chaucerian lyric. It is simple in diction and metrical form. For its total form or shape it depends upon the simplest medieval structural formula—the semi-narrative. This proves useful, for the non-narrative love pleas are, all too frequently, static or wandering. The poem, therefore, represents much that is valuable in the non-Chaucerian courtly lyric. At the same time it illustrates the opposite faults. For, instead of distorted Lydgatian phrasing, there is distorted chit-chat, as in the clumsy and inane conclusion:

> no more to yow I can now saye,
>   but Iesus kepe yow wher-so-euer ye goo;
> thys to yow I wryte, & also saye,
>   that partyng ys the gronde of my woo.

Descriptions of dreams and day dreams are often a routine way of saying 'would that my love were in my arms'. Medieval psychology easily grasped the idea that fantasies express inner needs, and so these descriptions also provide a good test of the poet's own psychological powers. 'The pasaunte Goodnes', an elaborate rhyme royal lyric, attempts a rudimentary analysis both of experience,

> Whan Reste And slepe y shulde haue noxiall,
>   As Requereth bothe nature and kynde,
> than trobled are my wittes all;
>   so sodeynly Renyth in my mynde
>   youre grete bewte; . . .

and of a mind obsessed and baffled:

> for than me thynkithe y see youre likenes,
>   hit is nat so: it is fantasticall.   (SL, no. 190)

This last line is good in itself, but the whole description is over-ambitious, and this throws its crudity into relief. The mention of man's need for sleep is pedantic and humourless. The poet cannot take leave of facts, or mentally bridge the gap between the truth of fact and the truth of fantasy. Contrast

> My Dreame thou brok'st not, but continued'st it,
> Thou art so truth, that thoughts of thee suffice,
> To make dreames truths.

Donne's 'The Dreame'[1] affords too rigorous a test of the medieval poet, who is neither sufficient of a psychologist nor sufficient of a rhetorician to cope with the difficult task he has set himself. There is a good deal in the view that courtly lyric, at its worst, is unpsychological and un-analytical. It does not make enough of its chief subject matter, personal experience.

The subject matter of courtly lyric is also inherently of psychological interest in that tension is created by the failure of reality to match the ideal. While pity is womanly, the fact remains that many women are pitiless. Hence medieval abuse of women is as extreme as eulogy, and, usually, equally ponderous:

> O wicket wemen, wilfull, and variable,
>   richt fals, feckle, fell, and frivolus,
> Dowgit, dispytfull, dour, and dissavable,
>   Vnkynd, crewall, curst, and covettus. (SL, no. 212)

Thus, even if women's failure to live up to an ideal is a reality, it is so far exaggerated that it becomes itself unreal. Between the extremes or eulogy and abuse Chaucer's interplay between authority and experi-ence is lost. The poets, if they do embrace the extremes within one poem, do so in the debate form, as when Clerk and Nightingale argue academically for and against women (SL, nos. 179 and 180). Aiming at clarity of exposition and antiphonal contrast, these poems are not meant to focus on what is of most *psychological* interest—the process of disillusion as experienced by one frustrated idealist. There are but a few, very simple, attempts to describe revolutions of feeling. An ortho-dox lover can become heterodox. Having complained of 'grevous hevynesse' caused by a 'merseles' lady, one such stages an abrupt *volte face*: 'do as ye list—I hold me content!' (SL, no. 154).

The most promising line of development here is probably not, after

---

[1] *Complete Poetry and Selected Prose*, ed. John Hayward (London, 1941), p. 26.

all, in the direction of psychological analysis of a complex or serious kind, but in that of wordly sophistication. The light rhythm of

> O Mestres, whye
> Owtecaste am I
> all vtterly
>> from your pleausance?

is matched by a light conclusion to the effect that the lover considers himself free to seek better luck elsewhere:

> I truste, percase,
> to fynde some grace
> to haue free chayse,
>> & spede as welle!   (SL, no. 137)

The conventional ideals are not taken too seriously, nor does harsh reality bring on an attack of mud-slinging. Given such gay heterodoxy, superficiality becomes a positive virtue.

Contrast with this the lugubrious farewell song 'Excellent soueraine'. This, too, pinpoints the moment at which the last straw breaks the lover's back. The poet, after a fair start upon a love plea, comes upon the idea that fortune is against him, and thenceforward can only reiterate:

> ffarewell ladi of grete pris,
>> ffarewell wys, both fair & free,
> ffarewell freefull flourdelys,
>> ffarewell burell bright of ble.   (SL, no. 205)

And so on for another twelve quatrains. The author seems spellbound, and, unless it be in terms of trauma, it is useless and boring to discuss his state of mind. The spell is a purely verbal one, and hollow, heavy rhetoric was never better illustrated. The effect of so much repetition on the structure is also disastrous. It is to be noted, too, that, for all its dealing in a particular 'moment', so formal and long-drawn-out a poem cannot supply drama.

Since by definition no lyric can be fully dramatic, drama in lyric is best conceived as 'the individual immediacy of an occasion':

The individual immediacy of an occasion is the final unity of subjective form, which is the occasion as an absolute reality. This immediacy is its moment of sheer individuality, bounded on either side by essential relativity. The occasion arises from relevant objects, and perishes into the status of an object for other occasions. But it enjoys its decisive moment of absolute self-attainment as emotional unity.[1]

Though this form of intense subjectivity has too little place in the courtly love lyric before Wyatt, there are approximations to it:

> A dere god! haue I deservyd this—
> This dere destyny to drede,
> That thus my swete I schall myse
> Thus wondurfully, & wott neuer why?   (SL, no. 134)

A plunge *in medias res*, always arresting, is a positive relief from such ceremonial openings as 'O bewtie pereles, and right so womanhod' (SL, no. 201). Curiosity is provoked by the angry vociferousness and mysterious mention of 'this'. The author of the ballade soon reveals the events relative to the occasion—some muddle, a misunderstanding by which he has been wronged, perhaps by a backbiting rival:

> Yfe anny man haue for envy
> Witt weked wordes made her wrathe,
> ffull mekely nowe I haske mercy—

But his protesting tone belies that meekness, as does the vigorous self-justification that follows, and, even more, his threat:

> Yfe so hit be that I be fore-sake,
>   And youre hert sett at youre dewys,
> More wrathe ye may well take
>   And of wytte be ware & wyse.

In other words, 'she' may not, after all, relish being quit of him. Here is a more complicated situation than is usual to the love complaint, and this, with the colloquial tone, does much to give the poem's 'occasion' dramatic vitality.

The hint that the love affair is not unilateral, that the lover can bargain emotionally with his mistress, is in itself intriguing. Anger has brought to light one of the basic, but usually subdued, courtly love themes. Love is a bargain that must be mutually kept, and, their polite defences down, some lovers will go so far as to behave no longer as worms but as men.

---

[1] A. N. Whitehead, *Adventures of Ideas* (Cambridge, 1933), p. 227.

A rather similar ballade opens

> Have all my hert & be in peys,
> And think I lowfe yow ferwently;
> ffor in good fayth, hit ys no lese,
> I wold ye wyst as well as I.   (SL, no. 135)

Here the immediate occasion is the helpless irritation caused by a beloved, but too-demanding mistress. She has evidently been made
jealous and must be pacified with much lover-like rant:

> Therefore I sweyre, as mot I thye,
> Yf I sayd owght when ye bade pees,
> I wyll full mekely aske mercye—
> Have all my hart and be in peyse.

To remember, too, how far these lover's squabbles are from
Chaucer's complaints or Suffolk's compliments is to acknowledge a
certain amount of variety within the courtly love lyric before Wyatt.

All this provides Wyatt's English background, a background not
wholly devoid of variety and interest, but stronger on the narrative
than on the lyric side. Evaluation of his own 'English' lyrics must be
largely concerned with his skill or ineptitude in handling the medieval
love formulas.

The first question to arise is whether any of the medieval narrative
strength is absorbed into Wyatt's lyric. That is, did any literary osmosis
take place in the mind of a Tudor courtly lover who admired Chaucer
and himself wrote love poetry? For Wyatt, *The Knight's Tale* is an
English classic which, in two poems, he echoes verbally. The borrowing of phrases, though an essential guide to the student, is, however,
unimportant compared with the possible borrowing of attitudes and
styles. Possibilities cannot be transformed into certainties, and, in my
opinion, the relationship of Wyatt to Chaucer is best stated in terms of
affinity and guidance. Their relationship may, indeed, fall outside the
legitimate sphere of literary debts and influences. Wyatt's few biographical poems show that, at least sometimes, his chief source was
life, not books, and this is likewise true of Chaucer, as it is of any good
poet. I would suggest, nevertheless, that Wyatt was guided in his use
of experience, not only by experience itself, but by the Chaucerian
precedent. In particular, he is a Chaucerian student of the relation between experience and conventional behaviour or doctrine.

The biographical poem describing Wyatt's ill May days asks what *does* happen to one individual as distinct from what is supposed to happen or what happens to people in general. The sonnet is, in many ways, a synthesis characteristic of the best of Wyatt. For, while its mainspring is personal experience and its form Italian, its diction is Chaucerian: so, too, are the conventional terms that go with that diction.

> Arrise for shame! Do away your sluggardie!
> Arise, I say, do May some obseruance!   (no. 92)

echoes, probably deliberately, the conventional romantic types, Emily, who, early on May morning

> was arisen and al redy dight;
> For May wole have no slogardie a-nyght.
> The sesoun priketh every gentil herte.
> > *(Knight's Tale*, lines 1041–3)

Arcite, who

> Is risen and looketh on the myrie day.
> And for to doon his observaunce to May,
> > *(Ibid.,* lines 1499–1500)

and Pandarus, who exhorts Criseyde

> Do wey youre book, rys up, and lat us daunce,
> And lat us don to May som observaunce.
> > *(Troilus and Criseyde,* ii. 111–2)

But Wyatt himself, having not a gentle but simply a very sore heart, dismisses others to the traditional joys he cannot share:

> Let me in bed lye dreming in mischaunce;
> > Let me remembre the happs most vnhappy
> > That me betide in May most comonly,
> As oon whome love list litil to avaunce. . . .
> Reioyse! Let me dreme of your felicitie.

Not that Wyatt regards himself as under some new dispensation. The old one is simply his bane, and his knowledge of this feeds his sense of irony. He explicitly acknowledges that his destiny, too, is ruled by love, while his 'dreming in mischaunce' is thoroughly familiar to courtly lovers. Wyatt's effect of independence and irony is obtained because the stock ideas and phrases in this poem are not merely 'strung together'. He uses a selection of them for contrast, the wakeful and dreaming lovers, the happy and the unhappy. The major contrast is between the conventional happiness of May day and the reality of his own unhappiness. It is this that suggests Chaucer's guidance, or, at least, Wyatt's affinity with Chaucer. Having described Arcite's 'obser- vances' Chaucer says that he fell into a 'studie', 'As doon thise loveres in hir queynte geres' (*Knight's Tale*, line 1531). Wyatt is less amused than wry, but has the same alertness to quaint lovers' rituals. Chaucer's is the detached comment of an omniscient narrator, Wyatt's the in- volved one of a personal lyrist.

The other poem echoing *The Knight's Tale* illustrates the same affinity, as well as raising a fresh possibility: that Wyatt shared Tuke's appreciation of Chaucer's majesty and mediocrity, and could himself use these styles in the 'conuenable' Chaucerian way, that is, use them to answer the needs of his story. 'Story' is not too big a term for the poem in question, for Wyatt is recounting his inner history in the course of a disappointing love affair.

> Allas, thou felle Mars! allas, Juno! . . .
> Love hath his firy dart so brennyngly
> Ystiked thurgh my trewe, careful herte,
> That shapen was my deeth erst than my sherte.
> (*Knight's Tale*, lines 1559, 1564–6)

is echoed in Wyatt's opening

> Alas the greiff and dedly wofull smert!
> The carefull chaunce shapen afore my shert.   (no. 5)

This 'majestic' rhetoric is both easy and stock. It is not unlike the breast-beating, line-by-line apostrophizing of the 'O Cupide' passage quoted above from *The Knight's Tale*. Wyatt keeps it up for some time:

> O lost seruis! O payne ill rewarded!
> O pitifull hert, with payn enlarged!
> O faithfull mynde, too sodenly assented!

And, just before it gets wearisome, comes a change of tone, signifi- cantly accompanied by a change from present to past tense, by Chau- cerian talk of 'proof' as distinct from doctrine, and by the unorthodox suggestion that, in practice, a lover's faithfulness can be overdone. By the end of the third stanza, Wyatt is distancing the excruciating experi- ence which gave rise to his outburst:

> Perdy you knowe—the thing was not so straunge
> By former prouff—to muche my faithfulnes.

Imputing his disappointment now to himself, recognizing that it is not so exceptional as he at first imagined, Wyatt has stopped shouting and feeling, to begin talking and thinking. He does so haltingly, however, as the incomplete, disjointed phrasing denotes. By the fourth stanza he believes himself capable of a summing-up:

> I have wailed thus, weping in nyghtly payn;
> In sobbes and sighes, Alas! and all in vayn;
>   In inward plaint and hertes wofull torment.

The retrospective view makes the earlier rhetoric acceptable. That rhetoric was, in itself, stylized and unspecific. Wyatt, it now appears, intends it so, that is, intends it as a typical lover's plaint, one utterance expressing the synthesized emotion of many nightly wailings: 'I have wailed thus'. Nor has he left wailing behind for good. The renewed 'Alas!' is a sign of emotional relapse, of the kind that attends the sessions of silent thought. For retrospection in natures incapable of perfect 'recollection in tranquillity' is always likely to land the sufferer back in his 'fore-bemoaned moans'. Here is the cue for the courtly lover's habitual self-pity. Accordingly Wyatt breaks out again:

> And yet, Alas, lo, crueltie and disdayn
>   Have set at noght a faithful true intent,

Hence the solution—to quit, in spite of his continued torment, the whole enterprise—emerges in the last stanza, which moves firmly into the future tense:

> But though I sterve and to my deth still morne,
> And pece mele in peces though I be torne,
>   And though I dye yelding my weried gooste,
> Shall never thing again make me retorne.

Wyatt's manner has now turned decisively from majesty to mediocrity. Most noticeable are his choice of simple words and his control of a fairly complex grammatical structure, without loss of coherence or rhythm—a technique learned rather from Chaucer than from Lydgate. In the poem as a whole Chaucer's influence is suggested by the combination of contrasting styles, with the feeling for the 'conuenable'. There is, of course, no slavery to the master here. Wyatt's concentrated lyric of five stanzas is obviously no copy of the 'noble tale' he admired. It is his own attempt to unfold the lover's state of mind at various time-stages. Though it is by no means one of his greatest poems, it compares well with the run-of-the-mill 'psychological' lyric of the Middle Ages. There is no naïve talk of the lover's 'troubled wits', &c. Wyatt repeats himself enough to suggest the courtly lover's usual emotional stasis, but avoids getting deadlocked in endless wailing or long farewells. The shifting back and forth in time helps a lot here, and the whole effect is strengthened by the Chaucerian rhetoric.

In its other features, Wyatt's lyric writing is non-Chaucerian. Though he uses some 'haute' rhetoric, his vocabulary is always plain, and this, with his exploitation of the simpler stanza forms, cuts him off from the lyrical Chaucer as from the other aureate lyrists, like Lydgate. The resemblance between Wyatt's and Chaucer's love complaints, for instance, is simply generic. True, the group of three rhyme royal stanzas constitutes a form in which Wyatt is highly skilled. But the lovely, flowing 'Resound my voyse' (no. 22), a complaint against his mistress's 'stony hert', is inspired not by Chaucer but by Serafino. Wyatt's best known contribution to this form, 'They fle from me' (no. 37), could hardly be less like Chaucer's decorous laments. What place has this mistress, gown falling from shoulder, 'stalking in my chambre', in a Chaucerian ballade? If there be any Chaucerian influence here—and there are no verbal echoes to substantiate the idea—it would rather derive from some narrative passage in *Troilus and Criseyde*, and by a process of assimilation beyond the reach of our knowledge.

The aureate speciality, the description of a mistress's beauty and virtue, is almost entirely lacking in Wyatt, who, on the other hand, talks more of his own feelings than the Chaucerians do. In any case, he knows no flowers of womanhood, being aware, rather, of the serpent in the garden. Wyatt rarely admires those he loves, and to this extent is in sympathy more with medieval abusers than with eulogizers of women. It is his older contemporary Skelton who carries forward into the sixteenth century the aureate eulogy of the fifteenth.

Wyatt would certainly join in Chaucer's blunt outbreak against love, or Charles d'Orleans's confession to kissing. But, in general, his humour—for he is often ironical, sardonic, witty, or frivolous—is non-Chaucerian. He is no parodist and wallows in his own feelings too seriously to paint so gay and ridiculous a self-portrait as the pike in galantine.

Wyatt, a much more voluminous lyrist than Chaucer, also tries a greater variety of forms. He does not, of course, ignore the Chaucerian ones. Being skilled not only in rhyme royal but in the refrain, he takes easily to the ballade form. The *Monk's Tale* octave is not popular with him, and he prefers his newly discovered Italian ottava rima. The roundel reappears as the rondeau, but Wyatt is committed to his own fifteen-line version of it, and there is never more than a generic connection with 'Merciles Beaute'. Meanwhile his non-Chaucerian forms cannot be overlooked. The interwoven quatrain is as popular with him as with his predecessors, the carol and monorhyme forms hardly less so. On the other hand, the enclosed quatrain remains with him an un-English form, used in the quatrains of Italianate sonnets and deriving from Petrarch. Wyatt exceeds all his lyrical predecessors in metrical variety, and this is brought out, for example, by his use of four different versions of the six-line stanza.

These considerations do not eliminate the possibility of a debt to Chaucer on the lines suggested above. Negatively they perhaps even strengthen the case for a Wyatt mindful of the narrative but careless of the lyrical Chaucer. But though, in what follows, Chaucer need not be forgotten, it is best now to concentrate, first, on Wyatt's plainness and, next, on his general handling of the courtly conventions.

The exclusion of the mythological paraphernalia of Love, the 'olde ensaumples', and the set descriptions of women or nature, is, as already suggested, a clear sign of Wyatt's alignment with the plain lyric tradition. Like Robert Henryson's hero, he is Venus's 'awin trew knycht'.[1] Yet Venus, on her very few appearances in his poems, is no classical goddess but an astrological influence, and not strongly personified. The unnamed 'ruler of the May' in the May day sonnet becomes simply 'that that governth me' in the Ptolemaic account of the heavens called 'Jopas' Song' (no. 101). Venus's mysterious potency, as an inwardly-working ally of Fate, is hereby strengthened. Wyatt's most elaborate description of her, and of himself as her servant, comes in a parting prayer, as he sets sail, to his guiding star:

> Though this the port and I thy seruaunt true,
>   And thou thy self doist cast thy bemes from hye
> From thy chieff howse, promising to renew
>   Boeth joye and eke delite, behold yet how that I,
>   Bannysshed from my blisse, carefully do crye,
> 'Helpe now, Citherea, my lady dere,
> My ferefull trust, en vogant la galere.'   (no. 78)

There is really no 'classical allusion', properly so called, in Wyatt.

---

[1] 'Orpheus and Eurydice', line 206, in *Poems and Fables*, ed. H. Harvey Wood (Edinburgh and London, rev. edition 1958).

'But no sooner had he made it clear to himself and his friends that she had hardly a good feature in her face, than he began to find it was rendered uncommonly intelligent by the beautiful expression of her dark eyes.'[1] Nor does Wyatt ever catalogue beauties, preferring, with Jane Austen, to describe the effect of beauty on the unwary:

> So vnwarely was never no man cawght
> With stedefast loke apon a goodly face
> As I of late: for sodenly, me thowght,
>   My hart was torne owte of hys place.   (no. 122)

The result of this plain technique is obvious. Weight is thrown not on to what Wyatt sees but on to what he feels about what he sees. The whole of this poem remains entirely self-centred. Description of nature is also harnessed to Wyatt's state of mind. It merely serves as illustration:

> Then was I like the strawe, when that the flame
> Ys drevyn therin by force and rage off wynd.

Nature for Wyatt is never a static backcloth. He paints no scenery. But to express his helplessness he will use its mobile, variable, and uncontrollable forces, such as 'wether and wynd' (no. 111).

> The Rokkes do not so cruelly
> Repulse the waves continuelly,
>   As she my suyte and affection.   (no. 66)

> Save of your grace only to stay my liff,
>   That fleith as fast as clowd afore the wynde.   (no. 73)

> Light in the wynde
>   Doth fle all my delight.   (no. 84)

> Eche westerne winde
> Hathe turnid her minde
> And blowen it clene awaye.   (no. 123)

No one will claim that nature images, among the oldest in literary stock, are original, but the relevance and economy with which Wyatt uses them are marks of artistry. Their relevance is to himself. Wyatt's plainness has to do with his subjectivity.

When it has not, or when Wyatt has nothing to express, then he is occasionally liable to the inanity and flatness of plain lyric at its worst:

> Prayeng you all that this doo rede
> To truste yt as you doo your crede.   (no. 167)

---

[1] *Pride and Prejudice*, ch. vi.

But such examples are comparatively rare, especially in the Egerton poems.

To turn to Wyatt's handling of the conventions, or rather to return to it, for, inevitably, this subject has been anticipated: In the foregoing discussion of his Chaucerian and a few other poems, the scales have been weighted against the Mason–Stevens case. Thus, Wyatt's poems have not so far seemed merely strings of clichés, with no trace of 'poetic activity'. Conventional, yes, but not dully so. That, at least, is my argument. But before a reinforcement of it is attempted, the balance must be fairly redressed. For example, any reader, however partisan, is bound to admit that Wyatt's complaints—that is, a large body of his poems—do fall within range of the Mason–Stevens gunfire.

Wyatt dramatizes himself as the melancholy lover. He is often solitary:

> Alas, lo, I go,
> And wot not where.   (no. 84)

Only his 'faithfull lute' hears this complaint, uttered simply to relieve his pain:

> I seke nothing
> But thus for to discharge
> My hert of sore sighing,
> To plaine at large.

Though I can think of no earlier English poet who uses the lute as part of his melancholy *mise en scène*, I am bound to admit that Wyatt is not here doing or saying anything particularly fresh.

'Bantering and abusive by turns': Stevens's summary description of the courtly love lyric does cover a good deal of Wyatt's. There is humorous defiance and heterodoxy in

> Trow ye I dote withoute ending?
> What, no perdy!   (no. 45)

while he can also break out into the vulgar abuse of the satiric, anti-feminine tradition:

> Ye old mule, that thinck yourself so fayre,
> Leve of with craft your beautie to repaire,
>   For it is time withoute any fable:
>   No man setteth now by riding in your saddell;
> To muche travaill so do your train apaire,
>   Ye old mule!   (no. 35)

Wyatt's mistress is generally true to type, though he sharpens the ferocity of the cruel fair in depicting a sadist:

> Syns ye delite to knowe
> That my torment and woo
> Should still encrese ... (no. 72)

He increases love's agony by loving a thoroughly disagreeable woman. He also does so by never quite taking 'no' for an answer. Thus he can heave the usual 'thousand sighes' and weep the usual 'flod of teres' before playing with the notion that things may improve:

> But yet perchaunce som chaunce
> May chaunce to chaunge my tune. (no. 52)

This draws attention to the persistent, nagging optimism which underlies the courtly lover's expressed despair, and which makes his complaints into wooing songs.

'Ye know my herte, my ladye dere' is a mass of clichés. Wyatt is the 'thrall' who has long and for little 'rewarde', 'serued' a 'cruell ffoo', and is now driven to the extreme of despair:

> But deth shall ryd me redely
> Yf your hard hert do not relent. (no. 41)

The only fresh pleasure to be gained from this poem is in the melancholy swing of the verse, as, for example, in the description of the eternity in which Wyatt has served,

> Howe well, how long,
> How faithefulye,
> And soffred wrong
> How patientlye!

Whatever occasional beauties are found, it must be admitted that Wyatt repeats these ideas to a boring extent. 'Where shall I have at myn owne will' is not substantially different from the foregoing example. The lover, having wept, sighed and plained, works up to a farewell to the mistress who has brought him the usual bitter-sweet experiences of unrequited love—'My gayn, my losse, my salve, my sore'. The hint that death must follow seems automatic:

> Farewell also with you my breth,
> For I ame gone for evermore. (no. 53)

'Hevyn and erth' (no. 73) follows suit. Only his lady's grace can save Wyatt's life, and the last stroke of his emotional blackmail is an allusion to his grave. Here, he even seems aware that he has threatened all this before, for it is, he insists, his 'last complaint'. He is always describing himself as 'oon slain owte right' (no. 72). Yet he takes an unconscionable time dying. One must allow, of course, for the fact that these complaints were probably not meant to be read studiously, and certainly not on end. The relevant point is that Wyatt's perceptions are here under the tyranny of his conceptions, and that these conceptions are stock. The constant repetition proves the reality of that tyranny.

The line of demarcation between the poems in which the conventions master Wyatt and those in which he masters them is bound to shift about in accordance with individual tastes. How, for example, is Wyatt's best known description of his sleeplessness to be judged? He tosses and turns on a bed that seems 'as hard as stone', on which he shakes with 'hete and cold', and from which he rises pale and sick. 'What menys thys?' asks the refrain. Wyatt is obviously relying on the reader's familiarity with the stock symptoms of love melancholia, a familiarity which will supply the answer to his question. Thus the stockness of his behaviour is the point. To judge it harshly is to miss the point. Here, too, fresh pleasure can be won from an old theme through the vivid irritability of Wyatt's description:

> The clothes that on my bedd do ly
> Always methynks they lye awry.   (no. 110)

The picture deserves all the admiration it has earned because, while remaining effective on a purely literal level, it also reflects, metaphorically, the truth about Wyatt's state of mind. These are reasons why the poem is used to introduce the following examples, in which the reader is invited to consider again the idea that a conventional Wyatt is far from being, necessarily, a dull Wyatt.

'In eternum' is dominated by Chaucer's antithesis between convention and experience, or, in Wyatt's own words, 'rule' and 'proofe'. He writes as one who has conscientiously gone through love's mill:

> In eternum I was ons determed
> For to have lovid and my minde affermed,
> That with my herte it shuld be confermed
> In eternum.   (no. 71)

So, much like Pandarus, he has entered 'loves daunce':

> To trase this daunse I put my self in prese;
> Vayne hope ded lede and bad I should not cese
> To serue, to suffer, and still to hold my pease
> In eternum.

But Wyatt's testing of the rules proves that they do not work out where the proper premise is missing:

> It was not long or I by proofe had found
> That feble bilding is on feble grounde;
> For in her herte this worde ded never sounde,
> In eternum.

Where there is no gentle heart or womanly pity, there is, in fact, no groundwork for the courtly love routine. Now in Wyatt's heart 'another thought doeth rest'. Irony is the chief of the effects achieved. Shock is another. Wyatt's dogged, pedantic, emotionless tone does not prepare us for any particular response. It is, working with the irony, mystifying. It also shows, by contrast with such shrill outbursts as 'O lost seruis' &c., that Wyatt could vary his expression of disappointment in love. Again, the narrative formula helps to keep him bound to the facts, the bare bones of his history. The routine he describes is matched by the relentless routine of the carol stanzas (aaa + refrain). These, with the reiterated 'In eternum', also convey the dreadful process of iron entering the soul. For though, as in most comparable medieval lyrics, the lover's change of attitude comes as a *volte face* and is not psychologically analysed, the way has been partly prepared by that grim refrain. Into it all Wyatt's emotion, squeezed out from the narrative part, is allowed to seep. Even so this emotion is expressed obliquely, and the poem is the more impressive for that. It is a poem in monotones, but not, I think, monotonously dull.

Two of Wyatt's ballades serve to illustrate his working with the dramatic formula illustrated above in their medieval counterparts, 'A dere god!' and 'Have all my hert'. In addition they give further evidence of his strong aural imagination. To make vivid a situation Wyatt depends less on visual imagery than on the informal, colloquial opening and various repetition devices, such as the refrain, alliteration, epizeuxis, and thudding monosyllables.

> In faith I wot not well what to say,
> Thy chaunces ben so wonderous. (no. 23)

Wyatt appears to be talking to a tiresome person, an unusual realization of Fortune, as it turns out to be. But, for all this, the poem becomes fairly serious. The translator of Plutarch knows perfectly well the Stoic's reply to Fortune: 'Mens mynds yet may thou not order'. And the lyrist knows perfectly well how to bring his triumph over Fortune to a climax in his refrain: 'Spite of thy hap hap hath well hapt'.

The second ballade is undoubtedly more successful from the dramatic point of view. On the contrasting subject of insecurity, it opens again as it were in the middle of a conversation:

> It may be good, like it who list,
> But I do dowbt: who can me blame?   (no. 21)

'It' turns out to be an unexpected sign of good will, which former experience teaches Wyatt to suspect:

> For oft assured yet have I myst,
> And now again I fere the same.

No precise facts are given, but enough is said of the circumstances relative to this dramatic occasion to show that love is the trouble:

> The wyndy wordes, the Ies quaynt game,
> Of soden chaunge maketh me agast:
> For dred to fall I stond not fast.

The second stanza, with its more formal rhetoric, then projects this experience in terms of the orthodox doctrine of contrariety:

> Alas! I tred an endles maze
> That seketh to accorde two contraries;
> And hope still and nothing hase,
> Imprisoned in libertes.

In the third and last stanza Wyatt gradually slides back into the particular situation and recreates the illusion of conversation. Should he trust in the 'suretie' of a woman proved untrustworthy? 'Nay, sir, in faith it were great foly'. But, whatever the variations of tone, he swings round always to a refrain which sums up, in its firm monosyllables, the meaning of this experience of insecurity: 'For dred to fall I stond not fast'.

'And if an Iye may save or sleye', another and much richer dramatic ballade, also brings out the subtlety of Wyatt, at his best, both in rehandling a conventional *motif* and in psychological analysis. Numerous other poems show that he was well-versed in courtly eye-lore, for example:

> Thorow myn Iye the strock frome hyrs dyd slyde,
> Dyrectly downe vnto my hert ytt ranne.   (no. 122)

In the one under consideration he explicitly draws attention to the orthodox assumptions about lovers' eyes and to what 'men expert' have laid down:

> And if an Iye may save or sleye,
>   And stryke more diepe then wepon longe,
> And if an Iye by subtil play
>   May moue on more thenne any tonge,
>   How can ye say that I do wronge
> Thus to suspecte withoute deserte?
> For the Iye is traitor of the herte.
>
> To frame all wel I ame content
>   That it were done vnwetingly;
> But yet I say, who wol assent,
>   To do but wel, do no thing whie
>   That men shuld deme the contrary.
> For it is said by men expert
> That the Iye is traitor of the hert.   (no. 93)

The basic doctrine that the eye may 'save or sleye', &c., is the premise for Wyatt's argument against his mistress, in the midst of which the poem opens. If she too accepts this premise, then her excuse to the effect that her roving glances mean nothing is illogical. If, on the other hand, Wyatt agrees with her, then he must give up the premise—and hence a love doctrine of proved validity. Throughout he remains divided, reason and inclination at odds. The poem effects a variety of transitions of mood. It is about deception in love, including self-deception, the conventional eye *motif* being Wyatt's means of exploring this subject. The inclination to accept his mistress's excuse is a typical defence mechanism, like Lear's, when he is unable to accept his son-in-law's recalcitrance: 'may be he is not well'. Wyatt has no sooner declared himself 'content' with the excuse than he lapses back into renewed nagging, introducing now a note of real despair:

> But yet, alas, that loke all sowle
>   That I doo clayme of right to haue,
> Shuld not, methinkes, goo seke the scole
>   To please all folke.

The mistress's counter-complaint that he is jealous is then rejected, again on logical grounds:

> For, as ye saye, not only I
> But other moo haue demyd the same.

That proves that he is not imagining things. Yet no sooner has he established the fact, than he again caves in:

> But I your freende shal take it thus,
>   Sins you wol soo, as stroke of chaunce;
> And leve furder for to discus
>   Wither the stroke did sticke or glaunce;
>   But scuse who canne, let him avaunce
> Dissembled lokes; but for my parte
> My Iye must stil bitray my harte.

The refrain has now been varied, the impersonal 'the Iye is traitor of the hert' becoming the personal 'My Iye must stil bitray my harte'. Wyatt thus declares his willingness to delude himself. Furthermore, 'betray', and probably also 'traitor', convey the double meaning[1] of treachery and revelation, applying to both Wyatt and his mistress. For while her eye has revealed the truth, her heart has deceived him. And while his eye has discovered the truth, his heart is ready to deceive him. This poem on deception ends on a serious, rather threatening note, as Wyatt admonishes his mistress to hold fast to truth:

> Cherish him wel, continnewe soo,
> Let him not fro your hart astart;
> Thenne feres not the Iye to shewe the hert.

The vivid actuality of the squabble is such that the reader becomes interested in the participants. Thus he might be tempted to condemn the illogical, flirtatious heroine with 'that loke all sowle', were it not that Wyatt, with his exasperating male self-righteousness, possessiveness, and logic, carries on so tiresomely. The reader cannot, in fact, feel as remotely wise as when reading a medieval, or one of Wyatt's own,[2] set debates. These reactions signify a successful dramatic lyric.

---

[1] *N.E.D.* gives for 'betray', besides the usual meanings such as 'give up', 'prove false', &c., 'reveal against one's will the existence, identity, real character of (a person or thing desired to be kept secret)' (1588).

[2] Nos. 39 and 40 jointly constitute a debate on patience, while no. 91 is an orderly, stanza by stanza argument between Wyatt and his heart.

'Helpe me to seke for I lost it there': the opening, this time, is intentionally mystifying:

> And if that ye have founde it ye that be here
> And seke to convaye it secretely,
> Handell it soft and trete it tenderly.   (no. 17)

Wyatt reveals what 'it' is only in his final stroke of wit:

> It was myn *hert*: I pray you *hertely*
> Helpe me to seke.

So he also reveals that this light, delicately phrased rondeau is a lost heart exercise. The original audience, presumably, would take pleasure in anticipating, or, if not, in recognizing, the revelation of its connection with the popular *motif*. Wyatt, one may be sure, is no more inclined here than elsewhere, and no more inclined than his contemporaries were, to conceal his dependence on 'men expert'; that is a matter in which the Tudors differ from the moderns. Here the point is, then, to ring a new change on an old theme. Wyatt does so by treating the lost heart with witty literalness. The heart is a fragile object accidentally lost, and hence to be sought with fussy, old-womanish concern.

This, in fact, is a subject which, more than once, provokes in Wyatt that kind of witty literalness. The heart is, after all, the physical organ essential to life. Charles d'Orleans, absent from his mistress,

> most as a hertles body
> A-byde alone in heuynes.

But Wyatt's equally slight poem on absence provokes a further thought:

> Hertles, alas, what man
> May long endure? (no. 63)

Again, after exchanging hearts with his mistress, he departs anxious about the likelihood of her remaining faithful. And so continues until struck with the thought that her heartless body will be of no use to anyone:

> I have her hert in my posession,
> And of it self there cannot, perdy,
> By no meanes love an herteles body.   (no. 18)

He associates the lost heart with other conventional love themes in a more rigorous piece of logic. There can be little sense in the following poem for the reader who does not, with Wyatt, recognize these conventions as such. Using his stiffest and most academic manner, he expounds the argument that, in accordance with reason and nature, it is impossible for a man to live without a heart, or in a state of contrariety such as is expressed in the stock heat-cold antithesis:

> To cause accord or to aggre,
> Two contraries in oon degre,
> And in oon poynct, as semeth me,
> To all mans wit it cannot be:
> > It is impossible.
>
> Of hete and cold when I complain
> And say that hete doeth cause my pain,
> When cold doeth shake me every vain
> And boeth at ons, I say again
> > It is impossible.
>
> That man that hath his hert away,
> If lyff lyveth there, as men do say,
> That he hertles should last on day
> Alyve and not to torne to clay,
> > It is impossible.   (no. 77)

Having carefully led his argument this way, Wyatt, by an unexpected stroke of ingenuity, provides a solution to the contradiction between experience and bookish doctrine—a solution the neater in that it gives final authority to the religion of love. There is always an appeal open from the natural to the supernatural. Miracle is Wyatt's solution:

> Yet love that all thing doeth subdue,
> Whose power ther may no liff eschew,
> Hath wrought in me that I may rew
> These miracles to be so true,
> > That are impossible.

Finally, there is the universal favourite, which, fortunately, needs no defence, for it has not been attacked:

> They fle from me that sometyme did me seke
> > With naked fote stalking in my chambre.
> I have sene theim gentill tame and meke
> > That nowe are wyld and do not remember
> > That sometyme they put theimself in daunger
> To take bred at my hand; and nowe they raunge
> Besely seking with a continuell chaunge.

Thancked be fortune, it hath ben othrewise
  Twenty tymes better; but ons in speciall,
In thyn arraye after a pleasaunt gyse,
  When her lose gowne from her shoulders did fall,
  And she me caught in her armes long and small;
Therewithall swetely did me kysse,
And softely saide, *dere hert, howe like you this?*

It was no dreme: I lay brode waking.
  But all is torned thorough my gentilnes
Into a straunge fasshion of forsaking;
  And I have leve to goo of her goodenes,
  And she also to vse new fangilnes.
But syns that I so kyndely ame serued,
I would fain knowe what she hath deserued.   (no. 37)

This is no less courtly and traditional in its terms and ideas than Wyatt's other poems. He combines the effects typical of the moaning complaint and of the satirical attack. His self-pity, decidedly that of the melancholy prototype, takes a sarcastic turn. Wyatt also raises to a high pitch the lively immediacy and artful selectiveness of his favourite descriptive technique. The picture of his erstwhile friends 'stalking' in his chamber could hardly be bettered. So too his bouncing out of day-dreaming—or what might be so considered—into 'brode waking'. (On the other hand, for its inappropriate, lullaby sing-song, Tottel's emendation, 'It was no dreame: for I lay broade awaking', could hardly be worsened). Wyatt is thinking here of the erotic dream of the medieval tradition and expressly destroying the suspicion that he has been indulging in wish-fulfilment fantasies. He is also thinking throughout of the laws of love. The stock adjective 'gentill' has a certain ambiguity in its context. 'Gentill tame and meke', in antithesis with 'wyld', implies not only the courtesy of human beings, but the cupboard love of half-domesticated pets. Hence, though the epithet is one of praise, it already contains a sneer. Besides, in the sublimest courtly demeanour, say, Beatrice's or Duke Theseus's, the gentle is not tame but strong and tender. Wyatt's own 'gentilnes', in the last stanza, is the fine courtly virtue, but it has been taken by his friends as fatuous benevolence, meet to be abused. Wyatt, in his dramatic *persona*, is orthodox, even old-fashioned in his orthodoxy. 'New fangilnes', a term used by Chaucer,[1] is the capital offence against the laws of love. It is

---

[1] *E.g.* in *Anelida and Arcite*, line 141.

inconstancy, the crime that damns Cressida in the pages of Henryson as well as of Chaucer. 'Leve' retains the appropriate legal flavour, but is applied now as part of a new system in which forsaking is duly allowed. 'Syns that I so kyndely ame serued' is topsy-turvy. Wyatt, as the orthodox lover, is presumed to have been serving. He should not have 'been served' in this sense. 'Kyndely' is again ambiguous. It can refer to the law of kind or nature, which, with Wyatt as with Chaucer, does not always match the law of love. Hence Wyatt has been 'served' quite naturally, quite in accordance with the wild, bestial behaviour described in the first stanza. On the other hand, 'kyndely' also has its modern sense, and was read so by Tottel or his editor. His version, 'sins that I vnkyndly so am serued', is ridiculously inept in that it achieves the literally correct meaning at the expense of Wyatt's crowning stoke of ferocious irony. If such a category were recognized, this would be called not a love poem but a hate poem. 'Natural—a little too natural' is the scribbled compliment it receives from the staid compiler of *The Golden Treasury*.[1]

All this presents Wyatt's art in a favourable light, even to the extent of suggesting that the affinity with Donne's is no figment of the critic's imagination. In both we admire the immediacy, the conversational tones, informal openings, sense of situation, wit, logicality, and self-analysis. Not, however, in the same degree. Wyatt is like Donne in his capacity to exercise his wit upon, even to adopt a fresh point of view to, some conventional topic. But, to take the lost heart as an example, Donne's 'The Blossome' goes further than any comparable poem by Wyatt. Throughout this poem Donne rethinks conventional ideas. A flower which 'holds in perfection but a little minute' is the commonest Elizabethan emblem for transitoriness, particularly familiar to us through the sonnets of Shakespeare. Donne does not deny this meaning, but interests himself in the flower's unawareness of it. To come to the lost heart: In the moment of clinging, blossom-like, to happiness, we cannot acknowledge the possibility of loss. It can even be agreed that the lover's impending absence will make no essential difference to the mistress's happiness, especially as he will have left his heart behind. For, as she says, 'If then your body goe, what need you a heart?' A heart without a body is, however, less useful than a body without a heart, and particularly so to a woman herself heartless:

---

[1] Wyatt, *The Poetical Works*. Aldine ed. (1831), British Museum copy (C117 aa 3), 'with copious notes by F. T. Palgrave', p. 32.

> A naked thinking heart, that makes no show,
> Is to a woman, but a kinde of Ghost;
> How shall shee know my heart; or having none,
> > Know thee for one?
> Practise may make her know some other part,
> But take my word, shee doth not know a Heart. (*ed. cit.*, p. 45)

Donne is the more exploratory of the two poets. Wyatt is not averse to explorations, but conducts them with a view more to confirming or denying what is known already than to declaring, with Donne, a new and more complex truth. In this respect Wyatt is closer to Chaucer. 'Ryght true it is, and said full yore agoo' (no. 49). Such affirmations are as typical of Wyatt and Chaucer—both of whom, incidentally, delight in proverbs and 'old saws'—as they are untypical of Donne. For Wyatt a proposition is either true or false according to whether experience confirms it. But with Donne it can be a half-truth. He does not affirm or contradict, but expands, conventional ideas. He is, too, frequently, taken to have repudiated outright the conventional literary idea of love as a union of souls, in which the senses have no part:

> Love's not so pure, and abstract, as they use
> To say, which have no Mistresse but their Muse.

That, however, is not the whole of what he says in 'Loves Growth':

> Love's not so pure, and abstract, as they use
> To say, which have no Mistresse but their Muse,
> But as all else, being elemented too,
> Love sometimes would contemplate, sometimes do.
> > (*ed. cit.*, p. 24)

Love is 'elemented', that is, 'mixt of all stuffes, paining soule, or sense'. The conventional idea is not wrong, only incomplete. Wyatt, therefore, does not stand up to extensive comparison with Donne in one of the most essential points of metaphysical art—complexity.

Furthermore, though his reasoning and analysis are advanced for his time, he remains a more purely descriptive poet. Wyatt's use of the eye *motif* as a means of exploring a situation and elucidating an idea is, indeed, Donne-like. But, more often, his imagery is illustrative, reflective of his feelings. This, at any rate, is true of his 'English' lyrics. With the study of Petrarch, Wyatt did acquire the 'conceptual', metaphysical technique of handling imagery. That subject belongs to the next chapter. What has already been said of Wyatt and Petrarch may, however, also be said of Wyatt and Donne. It is something that the comparison between them can occur without making Wyatt seem inane. Petrarch and Donne are greater love lyrists than Wyatt, but he, in his turn, stands head and shoulders above all his English predecessors.

One question remains unanswered. Has Wyatt a distinctive philosophy of love? Since his poems are not arranged as a sequence, and, in any case, cannot be read as philosophical tracts, to regard him as a philosopher in the same class as Plato or Ficino is absurd. On the other hand, consistent ideas can underlie even a heterogeneous collection of poems, united only in their common authorship. And certain assumptions, certain trends of thought, are distinct in Wyatt's lyrics. What, then, is this distinctive 'philosophy'? The answer, already implied in the foregoing discussion, is, surely—the philosophy of courtly love in its medieval English form.

Even where Wyatt appears, superficially, to adopt untypical attitudes, the typical are evident. Thus it is unusual for him to acknowledge that he has no grounds for his grievances:

> I haue no wrong when I can clayme no right;
> Nowght tane me fro wher I nothing haue had.   (no. 90)

The belief in rights and claims is the thread connecting this with the grievance poems. Love is a bargain, a bond conferring rights and demanding obligations.

Wyatt's complaints are all based on the fact that he keeps his side of the bargain, while the mistress neglects hers. If there is one single love theme peculiarly his, it is betrayal:

> Ffortune and you did me avaunce;
> Me thought I swam and could not drowne; . . .
>
> Where are your plaisaunt wordes, alas?
> Where your faith, your stedfastnes?   (no. 53)

His sense of betrayal, at its height in respect of the traditional villains, Fortune and women, is extended to people in general. 'They fle from me' includes 'they' as well as 'she', while the line 'For none is wourse then is a frendly ffoo' occurs in a short comment on the stabber-in-the-back, who may be man or woman (no. 49). Let down, insecure, at the mercy of fair-weather friends or a mistress who blows hot and cold—this is a familiar Wyatt. He is the man who has travelled forth without his cloak, or the one who is kept dangling on a string. Hence his destiny is 'Continuelly inward to fret' (no. 58). As lover he lacks the Stoic patience which would enable him to control his reaction to change and of which he writes so convincingly in his non-amatory poems. He is frustrated, and in consequence his love turns into hatred.

> The hart and servys to yow profferd
> With ryght good wyll full honestly,
> Refuse yt not, syns yt ys offerd,
> But take yt to you gentylly. (no. 109)

Wyatt's ideal is a reciprocal and permanent love, in which gentle lady and servant are united, in which good will and honesty are mutual. Given the liberal reward of her gentleness, he is well prepared to observe his part in the pact:

> Byd ye me go and strayte I glyde
> At your commawndement humbly. (no. 109)

There is a rough honesty in Wyatt himself, and he certainly detests hypocrisy where he meets it, that is, always in others. Still his idea of 'gentleness' is limited by his rather legalistic thinking about human love—its due, just rights, rewards, and claims, &c. It is, in fact, like that of the English lyrists before him—in the last resort, somewhat barbarous. It is by no means on the Italianate-Chaucerian level.

Furthermore, for all his genuine love of truth, it is too much to regard the amorous and demanding Wyatt as joined in the quest, with St Paul and Plato, of 'Beauty through the light of truth'.[1] In his 'English' love poems he is, with the English poets, bent on satisfying his 'love as to a creature'. He has not Palamon's 'affeccioun of hoolynesse'. He is not searching for a transcendental reality or a spiritual satisfaction. It would, however, be unfair to the author of the view quoted above to leave the matter there. For Miss Foxwell, Wyatt is not only 'a student of Plato',[2] but of the platonism of Castiglione and the *École Lyonnaise*:

Castiglione's ideals corresponded with Wiat's own view of life, and the platonism which is expressed later in the poem 'Lo what it is to love' was quickened by his knowledge of the *Courtier*, and developed as he came into contact with the eager spirits of the literary circle at Lyons in later years.[3]

It may be noticed, in passing, that for all his visits to foreign courts and journeys through Lyons, Wyatt's life does not necessarily fit the

[1] Foxwell, ii, Introd., p. xii. [2] *Ibid.*, ii. 127. [3] *Ibid.*, ii, Introd., p. viii.

pattern Miss Foxwell has in mind. He is not really comparable with, say, the lyonnais author of *La Parfaicte Amye* (1542), Antoine Héroët, the hellenist and pensioner of Marguerite de Navarre, sharing her devotion to the study of Plato. Wyatt, as I have remarked elsewhere, probably did not know Greek. As far as we know he did not belong to a platonic circle, nor had he a Marguerite de Navarre among his patronesses.

Wyatt's supposedly platonic poem 'Lo, what it is to love!' (no. 87) is worth consideration. It is a debate on the nature of love of the kind favoured both by the Bembo–Castiglione circle in Italy, and Louise Labé's in France. Though debates are prominent in medieval love literature, the more modern influence of these neoplatonic debaters is possible. Wyatt's first speaker slanders love, calling it a 'snare', a thing unlasting, chancy, and incompatible with wisdom. It is a 'fervent fire, / Kendeld by hote desire'. This is the love which the Duke of Suffolk, making a routine distinction, dismissed as 'dotage'. Wyatt elsewhere calls it 'fancy' or 'fantasy', associating it with lack of reason and strength of mind:

> Of loue there ys a kynd
> > Whyche kyndlythe by abuse,
> As in a feble mynd,
> > Whome fansy may enduce ... (no. 124)

'Fantasy' directs a man's choice, and therefore 'Ffurst vnto love dyd me induse' (no. 121). But love must thereafter knit the 'faster knott', for fantasy itself 'lastyth nott'. There can be little doubt, therefore, that ideally Wyatt prefers the view of the second speaker in 'Lo, what it is to love!' He declares, in answer to the first, that the snare of love is not to be fled, for love guided by wisdom will last, while

> Love is a plaisaunt fire
> Kyndeled by true desire.

The third and last section of the poem is rather obscure, but it certainly does not seem to settle the debate once and for all in favour of the second speaker:

> Ye graunt it is a snare
> And would vs not beware. ....
>
> To love and to be wise,
> It were a straunge devise.

Moreover, even were the poem weighted more strongly than it is on its idealistic side, it would still not be platonic. The second speaker delights in the 'plaisaunt daies' and 'honest wayes' of love—things that Wyatt was often hankering after. His is a respectable ideal. But does he, with Castiglione's 'Peter Bembo',[1] 'take this love for a stayre (as it were) to climbe up to another farre higher than it'? There is, in fact, no mention of the platonic ladder or eventual contemplation of 'universall beautie'. 'Bembo' works up to a paean of praise of 'the most *holy* fire of true heavenly love', whereas Wyatt leaves love as, at its very best, a '*plaisaunt* fire'.

This, furthermore, is the best Wyatt ever says or implies of love. He never mounts the platonic ladder. He will either kick it away in disgust, to choose liberty, as in 'Ffarewell Love and all thy lawes for ever' (no. 13); or, as in the second section of 'Lo, what it is to love!', he will rest contentedly on a low rung. Placed here, he is far from rejecting sexual love outright or interesting himself in a state of mind beyond it. Indeed, he vindicates it as a desirable end, good in itself. He would agree not with Castiglione's neo-platonic 'Bembo', but with his 'Lord Julian', the exponent of fulfilled, reciprocal, human passion, 'that both the one and the other may have full and wholy his perfection'.[2]

Wyatt, therefore, is a thoroughly English courtly lover. Perhaps it is not so strange to find the quality of his 'subduedly sensual' feeling well summed up by a Victorian clergyman:

> The love of Wyatt is neither, on the one hand, the merely animal feeling to be found in Dryden, . . . nor is it, on the other hand, the fine etherealised rapture of a Crashaw or a Shelley.[3]

[1] See his speech in Castiglione's *The Courtier, ed. cit.*, pp. 317, 319.
[2] *Ibid.*, p. 241.
[3] Wyatt, *The Poetical Works*, ed. Rev. George Gilfillan (Edinburgh, 1858), Introd., p. xv.

CHAPTER VI

The First English Petrarchans

(i) Petrarch

LIKE his younger contemporary Chaucer, Petrarch (1304–74) was saturated in Latin literature, and especially in the poetry of 'Venus clerk, Ovide'. Following the Ovidian model *Amores* (I. ii), his *Trionfo d'Amore* describes a vision of the victorious god of love, riding in triumph on his fiery chariot and attended by a throng of captive lovers. Among them are love poets who, collectively, define Petrarch's whole literary heritage. For, having given priority to the classical poets, he comes on to his Italian predecessors of the thirteenth and early fourteenth centuries. There are the 'Siciliani', inventors of the sonnet; Guittone d'Arezzo, the first important Tuscan poet and the one noted, above all, for his extravagant exaggeration of the courtly commonplaces; Guido Guinizelli, Dante's 'padre mio', the poet *par excellence* of the gentle heart and divinized mistress; Dante himself, with his friends, Guido Cavalcanti and Cino da Pistoia, the three chief representatives of the *dolce stil nuovo*. From the Italians Petrarch makes but a short step back to their acknowledged masters, the Provençal Troubadours, headed by Arnaut Daniel, 'Gran maestro d'amor' (iv. 41).

'Petrarch was the final blossom and perfection of the Troubadours.'[1] Ten years of his life he spent in Provence, where, in 1327, he first set eyes on Laura. In describing his love for her, he follows an established tradition. Yet, with him, tradition means not only what is taken over from the past, but what is handed on to the future. The *Trionfi*, with all their baroque allegorizing, remain decidedly medieval, and it is significant that, as they succeeded in popularity to Petrarch's Latin

[1] S. T. Coleridge, a marginal note: see *Essays and Lectures on Shakespeare and Some Other Old Poets and Dramatists*, Everyman edition, p. 226.

149

works, so, in turn, they were succeeded by the *Rime*. The *Rime* comprise his sequence of 366 poems, mainly sonnets and mainly about his love for Laura. And this is the main channel through which the courtly love lyric, in its modern Petrarchan form, flows forward from the Middle Ages into the Renaissance.

Like Dante's, Petrarch's love for his mistress continues after her death. But there are differences. The Petrarch of the early 'In Vita' poems blesses the time and place at which his soul was first lifted up to Laura:

> Da lei ti ven l'amoroso pensero
> Che, mentre 'l segui, al sommo ben t' invia.   (*Rime*, no. xiii)

Does not Laura therefore become, like Beatrice, the lover's route to the *summum bonum*? She does so, but in a negative sense. Laura simply says 'no' to the dangerous mixture of flesh and spirit contained in Petrarch's 'amoroso pensero'. 'Cerchiamo 'l ciel': in one of the 'In Morte' sonnets, Petrarch again communes with his soul, and now, sadder and wiser, he asks it to forget Laura and turn to God (no. cclxxiii). This non-Dantesque rejection shows that his splendid love has been, in a last resort, earthly, human, and therefore sinful.

That is not, however, a classification of which Petrarch can always be sure. On the one hand his love has ennobled him, on the other endangered his soul. The issue, inconclusively argued between St Augustine and Petrarch in his dialogue, *The Secretum*, is the focus of psychological and religious interest in the *Rime*. Courtly love, it has often been remarked, rests on an equivocal basis, masking considerable evil under evident good. Petrarch, more conscious of the resultant dilemma than any predecessor, is not content with a purely formal recantation, the stock Provençal palinode. He constantly brings the possibility of equivocation into view. His problem is not so simple as that of the man who would 'be pardoned and retain the offence', because it is only slowly that he comes to know that his love is an offence. Self-blame and self-justification alternate. Petrarch, immobilized by their combined pressures, paints a self-portrait of a weak person, a 'whining dotard', as Byron dubbed him.[1] He can only regard himself as he is now and work for illumination. His lack of moral categorizing and unwillingness to generalize from anything but immediate experience is taken, by J. H. Whitfield, as a means of distinguishing a Renaissance Petrarch from a medieval Dante.[2] He is a self-conscious man, one

---

[1] *Letters and Journals*, ed. R. G. Prothero (London, 1898), ii. 379.
[2] *Petrarch and the Renascence* (Oxford, 1943), p. 79.

who strives to bring his conceptions into line with his perceptions. 'We had the experience but missed the meaning': not even to try for 'meaning' would have been anathema to Petrarch.

Petrarch's struggle to understand himself contains profoundly real and human interest. If he reveals little of Laura's inner self, he tells us all about his own. It is strange that this most personal of poets should ever have been taken for the mere theorist of love, the man of abstractions. The Petrarchan self-examination is, indeed, of major importance in the reminting of courtly love. Even had the *Vita Nuova* not remained unprinted till 1576, the *Rime* would probably have outrivalled it as the lover's text book of the Renaissance. For Petrarch's love is more ordinary, human, and accessible than Dante's, and less drastic and revolutionary in its relation to the main courtly tradition. There are but few examples, such as Lorenzo de' Medici, of love poets who wholeheartedly followed Dante. Petrarch's followers, on the other hand, are legion.

The range and style of Petrarch's sequence also account for its unique status as a literary model. Sweeping over the twenty-one years between his *innamoramento* and Laura's death, then, more swiftly, over the *post mortem* years, the *Rime* cover nearly every vicissitude of love. The attention of his followers was soon riveted not only by his psychology, but by his unprecedented technical skill in lyric structures, and, above all, by his brilliant rhetoric. These components of Petrarch's art have, in accounts of his influence and for convenience, often been separated. Nowadays it is perhaps more important, critically, to reunite them in that seamless union which characterizes the work of genius, and which distinguishes it from derivative and mechanical craftsmanship. Certainly Petrarch deserves to be distinguished from the Petrarchans in this respect. Undeniably many Petrarchans simply picked out from the *Rime* the plums of conventional rhetoric, leaving the psychological yeast to take care of itself. Hence, most unfairly, Petrarch himself has acquired the reputation for frigid and exaggerated conventionality, as though he were another Guittone. But if some few of his poems feed the Guittonian taste, that taste in Petrarch himself is by no means central.

All Europe was more or less preoccupied with Petrarch from somewhat before his death in 1374 till the decline of his reputation in the eighteenth century. His friend Boccaccio was an early, Milton a late, admirer. In between, the major Petrarchan schools rose and declined in Italy, France, Spain, and England. Chaucer, Wyatt, and Surrey, the subjects of this chapter, are simply the first pupils in the English school.

In the approach to them an effort of the historical imagination is naturally called for. It is perhaps as necessary with Petrarch as with Milton to separate the poet from the poet's influence. A good poet is not necessarily a good influence, and the Petrarchan imitation of the Renaissance has been criticized even more tartly than the Miltonic imitation of more recent times. Yet to precipitate an adverse criticism of early Petrarchan writing is to miss an opportunity to appreciate the enthusiastic pioneering of the age to which it belonged. It is to use too much hindsight, and to risk the injustice to which all prejudged cases are liable. To appreciate what Chaucer, Wyatt, and Surrey did with Petrarch, the inaner Petrarchan sequences of the 1590s—Barnes's, Tofte's, Lodge's, with their continental counterparts—must all be forgotten. History points to the initial freshness of what we now feel to be stale. In the early Renaissance the sonnet was an exciting new form, while courtly love was not as yet a dead letter. Petrarch provided both. And no doubt it was precisely this mixture of familiar and unfamiliar that constituted, then, a part of his charm. It was a time when England knew no Petrarchan sequences of her own, and, though she had produced courtly love lyrics, none was of such art as Petrarch's.

English Petrarchanism dawns with Wyatt, while Chaucer merely sings a dawn chorus. Yet his one version of a Petrarch sonnet is so arresting an event in literary history, that I shall accord it what might appear a disproportionately generous share of attention.

(ii) The Canticus Troili

Chaucer's use of one of Petrarch's sonnets for the 'Canticus Troili' in *Troilus and Criseyde* prompts numerous unanswerable questions on points of fact. Did Chaucer encounter all the sonnets, or only no. cxxxii, circulating independently? That is, did he deliberately choose it from the *Rime*, or did it simply cross his path by chance? Did he think Boccaccio the author, not only of *Il Filostrato*, the main narrative source for *Troilus and Criseyde*, but also of the sonnet? Or, on the other hand, did he suppose Petrarch to have written both? Is either of these contemporary Italian poets the unidentified 'Lollius' whom Chaucer actually cites as his source? The lack of certain answers to these factual questions makes it difficult even to speculate about Chaucer's response to Petrarch's sonnets. It is impossible to tell whether, with little first hand knowledge of them, he simply lacked opportunity to do more than he did in transplating them; or whether, knowing much, he nevertheless resisted these models as uncongenial to his own more cheerful and essentially narrative genius. Again, it is impossible to tell whether Chaucer sensed Petrarch's significance for European poetry, his 'modern' adaptation of the Troubadour conventions. And, finally, the answer to the question why Chaucer, never slow to experiment with foreign metrical forms, yet failed to attempt a quatorzain must remain lapped in mystery. All this depends on how far he was acquainted with Petrarch as vernacular poet as distinct from Petrarch as renowned Latinist.

> Fraunceys Petrak, the lauriat poete,
> . . . . whos rethorike sweete
> Enlumyned al Ytaille of poetrie.
>
> *(Clerk's Prologue*, lines 31–3)

Chaucer's anticipation of the sixteenth century's rapt admiration for Petrarch's sweet rhetoric does not, unfortunately, prove that he necessarily had much first-hand knowledge of it. He was aware, as no traveller and man of letters could fail to be, that Petrarch, having acquired widespread poetic fame in the Italy of his day, was honoured with the laurel crown. Chaucer was in Italy in 1372 and 1373, not long before Petrarch's death in 1374.

The Clerk's Tale, the only other Chaucerian text dependent on Petrarch, throws no light on the 'Canticus Troili'. *De Obedientia ac Fide Uxoria Mythologia*, Petrarch's Latin prose version of Boccaccio's story of the Patient Griselda, is stylistically very different from the vernacular love sonnet. There is also a radical difference in treatment, in attitude, and in the aspect of truth chosen for imitation. The Griselda story is uncourtly. Instead of a mistress imposing her will on a lover, there is a husband imposing his will—and most ungently— on a wife. Illustrating wifely obedience, the story proceeds from the abstract to the concrete. Founded on moral truth, it yields an ideal scheme for life, not a picture of actual life. Chaucer, reading the story as it was intended, that is, as 'mythologia', quickly perceives that it is not applicable to ordinary human psychology:

> No wedded man so hardy be t'assaille
> His wyves pacience in trust to fynde
> Grisildis, for in certein he shal faille.
>
> *(Clerk's Tale*, lines 1180-2)

Petrarch's sonnet no. cxxxii, an account of the feelings which probably, though not certainly, mean that he is in love, is no 'mythologia'.
It is based on human psychology, its method is empirical, and its
concern is not with how things should be, but how they are in one
particular case. It promotes no rule, moral, or ideal such as could be
applied to men in general. To abstract a general idea from this sonnet
would be to achieve only such a drastic simplification as 'love is an
indefinable sentiment'. Even so, this is not stated, only obliquely in-
ferred. The foreground is entirely occupied with Petrarch's thoughts
and feelings. These are obvious reasons why the sonnet is perfectly
suited to *Troilus and Criseyde*, a story itself diametrically opposed to
The Clerk's Tale, and one which owes its modern popularity largely
to the fact that it abandons the mode of medieval allegory for that of
the 'psychological novel' or 'drama of real life'. Whether by design or
accident Chaucer hit on a sonnet singularly appropriate to his purpose.
Neither the wittier of the 'In Vita' sonnets, nor the more philosophical
of the 'In Morte' ones would have fitted Troilus's helpless succumbing
to love.

> *S'amor non è*, che dunque è quel ch'io sento?
>> Ma, *s'egli è Amor*, per Dio *che cosa e quale?*
>> Se *bona*, ond' è l' effetto aspro mortale?
>> Se *ria*, ond' è sí dolce ogni tormento?
> S'a mia voglia ardo, ond' è 'l pianto e lamento?
>> *S'a mal mio grado*, il lamentar che vale?
>> O viva morte, o dilettoso male,
>> *Come puoi tanto in me*, s' io no 'l consento?
> E s' io 'l consento, a gran torto mi doglio.
>> Fra sí contrari venti in frale barca
>> Mi trovo in alto mar, senza governo,
> Sí lieve di saver, d' error sí carca,
>> Ch' i' medesmo non so quel ch' io mi voglio;
>> E tremo a mezza state, ardendo il verno.
>>>>> (Petrarch, *Rime*, no. cxxxii)

> *If no love is*, O God, what fele I so?
> And *if love is, what thing and which is he?*
> If *love be good*, from whennes cometh my woo?
> If *it be wikke*, a wonder thynketh me,
> When every torment and adversite
> That cometh of hym, may to me savory thinke,
> For ay thurst I, the more that ich it drynke.

And if that at myn owen lust I brenne,
From whennes cometh my waillynge and my pleynte?
If harm agree me, wherto pleyne I thenne?
I noot, ne whi unwery that I feynte.
O quike deth, O swete harm so queynte,
How may of the in me swich quantite,
But if that I consente that it be?

And if that I consente, I wrongfully
Compleyne, iwis. Thus possed to and fro,
Al sterelees withinne a boot am I
Amydde the see, bitwixen wyndes two,
That in contrarie stonden evere mo.
Allas! what is this wondre maladie?
For hete of cold, for cold of hete, I dye.

(Chaucer, 'Canticus Troili', *Troilus and Criseyde*, i. 400–20)

The italicized phrases indicate Chaucer's 'misunderstandings' of the Italian text as noted by Professor Ernest Hatch Wilkins.[1] His careful explanations form the basis for the following comments on Chaucer's deviation from Petrarch in the first stanza of the 'Canticus Troili':

(1) '*S'amor non è*' and '*s'egli è amor*' mean respectively 'if this be not love' and 'if it be love', not '*if no love is*' and '*if love is*'. (Petrarch is asking whether this incomprehensible feeling of his is love or not. Chaucer has put into the back of Troilus's mind a more basic and general question, the answer to which Petrarch takes for granted: 'does love exist or not?' This change could perhaps be argued as consistent with Chaucer's narrative and its hero: Laura's lover, a devotee of Love, can assume its reality, whereas Troilus, an all too recent scoffer, has first to readjust his ideas.)

(2) '*Che cosa e quale*', which is merely a variant for 'che . . . è quel ch'io sento', means 'what is this experience of mine', not '*what thing and which is he*'. (While Petrarch is still concentrating on himself, Troilus's first question has been superseded by another, equally general, one: 'what, then, is love?')

(3) Similarly '*bona*' and '*ria*' refer to the particular experience of Petrarch, and not, as in the 'Canticus Troili', to the general nature of love.

---

[1] *The Making of the 'Canzoniere' and other Petrarchan Studies* (Rome, 1951), p. 307.

Evidently, then, the first stanza of the 'Canticus Troili' is more theoretical and remote from the intensities of uniquely individual experience than its original. The difference is a 'Petrarchan' danger signal indicating the direction in which his imitators tended to deviate from Petrarch. It also contains a warning against a common misunderstanding among critics. For much argument against Petrarch's value as an 'influence' turns on objections natural in themselves but totally unconnected with sonnets like the one used by Chaucer: objections to Petrarch's supposedly abstract and impersonal style. Italian theorizing is felt to be uncongenial to the more down-to-earth English genius. Yet in the very first encounter of an English poet with Petrarch, it is the former who is likely to raise the stock objections. The truth of the matter is that the English poets had everything to learn from Petrarch in the expression of subjective experience and the analysis of complex states of mind. Did Chaucer, the 'misunderstandings' of the first stanza apart, learn anything?

After the first stanza, though two more mistakes in translation occur, Chaucer does closely follow Petrarch in dwelling on the experience of one lover to the exclusion of general ideas about Love. And even earlier, in fact in the very first line, Troilus's 'O God, what fele I so?' is a *cri de cœur* consistent with the Petrarchan presentation of a man immersed in his own feelings. This is more reassuring, both for the future of subjective poetry as a whole and for Chaucer's portrayal of Troilus in particular. Furthermore, the translation involves not only such violent expressions of strong feeling but also analysis, reflection upon feeling. Chaucer follows out Petrarch's form of logic, a 'scholastic' one that carefully balances two opposed points of view: 'if this is/ is not love', 'if this is good/bad'. The result is again reassuring for the future of introspective and metaphysical love poetry, as well as for the portrayal of Troilus.

While following, in this way, the main outline of Petrarch's thought, Chaucer makes a few additions and omissions. Most are unimportant, not affecting the Petrarchan content of the 'Canticus Troili', but the third stanza suffers a loss of concentration and richness which, again, points forward to future 'Petrarchan' insipidities. Here Chaucer embarks upon the metaphor of a sea voyage, which occupies most of Petrarch's sestet. But he omits the twelfth line of the sonnet in which the lover, a storm-tossed boat, is described as 'having no ballast of wisdom, loaded with error':'Sí lieve di saver, d'error sí carca'. The implied moral judgement is perhaps too solemn for Chaucer's love story, but unfortunately its omission makes the seafaring metaphor light in weight. One of Chaucer's own metaphorical variants—'Allas! what is this wondre maladie?'—fills the gap, leaving the seafaring image to contain only the vague feeling of helplessness. Petrarch, no less than Troilus, is 'possed to and fro' by the conflicting winds of feeling; but he also gives reasons for such emotional floundering: lack of reason ('governo'), wisdom ('saver'), and a propensity to 'error'. The Petrarchan image is a means of analyzing why, as well as describing what, the lover suffers. The Chaucerian image is merely descriptive and suggestive. Petrarch's parallel between self and boat is complete, logical, and yet unforced, for it does not deteriorate into witty ingenuity. Obviously the task of transplanting his highly metaphorical poetry is fraught with difficulties too great for all but Petrarch's equals. Stock criticisms of Petrarchan imagery are, on the one hand, that it is inane, purely decorative, or merely emotional, and, on the other hand, that it is over-ingenious in its clever pursuit of analogies between image and idea. It is towards the former that Chaucer, in rehandling Petrarch's seafaring image, tends.

Chaucer's expansion of fourteen lines to twenty-one obviously involves a further loss of concentration. His metaphorical variants, including the one already mentioned, serve primarily to increase the proportions of the poem. Nevertheless they are consistent and thoughtful. The feverish malady introduced into the penultimate line is not only generally suited to the picture of the love-sick Troilus tossing on his bed, but particularly connected with two earlier additions: in the first stanza, 'For ay thurst I, the more that ich it drynke', and, in the second, 'I noot, ne whi unwery that I feynte'.

Otherwise the result of the expansion is often puffy. For instance, in the first stanza, the first three lines correspond to those of the original, but it takes lines four to seven to cover Petrarch's fourth: 'Se ria, ond'è sí dolce ogni tormento?' Chaucer's 'a wonder thynketh me' is a blatant gap-filler, while 'torment and adversite' is a somewhat redundant phrase. The whole passage is clumsy and long-winded in contrast to Petrarch's compact phrasing of the question 'why so sweet each torment?'

Chaucer remedies this as he goes on. In the second stanza, he avoids using up his material too quickly and spreads its weight more evenly. Thus, lines one and two cover the first line of Petrarch's second quatrain; line three covers the second; line four is a metaphorical variant introduced by Chaucer; line five covers Petrarch's third; and lines six and seven cover his fourth. In the third stanza such problems hardly arise, since a sestet can be expanded to seven lines without much danger of puffiness. Notwithstanding, the 'Canticus Troili', taken as a whole, leaves the problem of concentration as a legacy to Chaucer's Petrarchan successors.

The structure of sonnet cxxxii presents a further array of the problems which not only beset Chaucer, but which also typify those of future English sonneteers. It is, of course, a regular Italian sonnet, the octave comprising two enclosed quatrains each linked by rhyme, the sestet two flowing tercets, also linked by rhyme: abba, abba, cde, dce. But this sonnet also has individual features. The ninth line—'E s'io'l consento, a gran torto mi doglio'—though linked by rhyme to the sestet, is linked by sense to the octave. It continues the initial series of agonized conditional arguments: 'if that I consente, I wrongfully / Compleyne'. At the same time it silences the earlier questions, by making, for the first time in this sonnet, a statement. So Petrarch slides into the completer statement of his case embodied in the extended seafaring image of the sestet. The ninth line hovers between the two parts of the sonnet after the manner of the 'crucial fifth line' of the Spenserian stanza 'which must give a soft bump to the dying fall of the first quatrain, keep it in the air, and prevent it from falling apart from the rest of the stanza'.[1] Consequently the sestet's introduction of the frail bark tossed on the sea is not so abrupt as it might have been; and the machine of the sonnet structure, with its octave-sestet division, does not creak at this point as in a poor Petrarchan imitation. This feature would, again, be difficult to imitate. Nevertheless it acts as a warning because it shows that to follow out or adapt Italian rhyme schemes, to comprehend the rough distinction between octave and sestet, do not of themselves produce the structural equivalents of Petrarch's sonnets. Many English sonnets have a comparatively disconnected and rigid structure.

Chaucer's reconstruction of sonnet cxxxii as three stanzas of the rhyme royal used throughout *Troilus and Criseyde* might suggest a total failure to understand even the bare rudiments of its structure. However, his distribution of its contents shows that the opposite is true. He devotes a stanza apiece to the two quatrains and a third to the sestet, including the 'crucial' ninth line in its metrically appropriate position in his sestet stanza. Clearly, then, he was thinking in terms of

[1] William Empson, *Seven Types of Ambiguity* (London, 2nd edition 1947), p. 33.

the metrical and formal scheme of the regular sonnet before him. In other words, Chaucer really can have the credit, before the Tudor poets, for 'discovering' the sonnet, for recognizing it as a special form with its own features. He was probably also aware of the sonnet's rhythmical continuity, and that his own stanzaic form was breaking it. For he made a noteworthy attempt to provide a syntactical substitute by the use of the connective phrase 'and if that' to introduce both the second and third stanzas.

But, in spite of his evident understanding of the sonnet's structure, Chaucer obviously did not intend to copy it closely. His division of the 'Canticus Troili' into three parts of equal weight is an arrangement identical neither with the two-part Italian nor four-part English sonnet. Yet it comes closer to the latter. The strict symmetry imposed by the stanzaic form foreshadows that of the three even, separable, and metrically self-contained quatrains of the English sonnet. Both contrast with the asymmetrical balance characteristic of Petrarch.

As for the rhyme royal stanza itself, it has in common with the English sonnet two main features: the interwoven 'abab' scheme of the quatrain, and the final couplet. (Petrarch and the Italians, while using these occasionally, give preference to the enclosed quatrain and tercet ending.) George Saintsbury even suggested that the discovery of the English sonnet form might have been the accidental result of the juxtaposition of a couple of rhyme royal stanzas.[1] Walter Bullock, emphasizing the many Italian variants of the sonnet, challenged this view, and asserted that only the final couplet of the rhyme royal stanza could have influenced Wyatt.[2] This scepticism, at any rate, leaves the couplets of Chaucer's stanzas open to conjecture as possible patterns for future English sonnets. It is at once apparent that in the first two Chaucer plans to avoid cutting the final couplet adrift from the rest of the stanza. It is continuous with the preceding line or lines:

> O quike deth, O swete harm so queynte,
> How may of the in me swich quantite,
> But if that I consente that it be?

On the other hand, the final couplet of the last stanza—the end of the whole 'Canticus'—is indeed detached, self-contained, after the manner of the English sonnet:

> Allas! what is this wondre maladie?
> For hete of cold, for cold of hete, I dye.

---

[1] *A History of English Prosody* (London, 2nd edition, 1923), i. 307–8.
[2] 'The Genesis of the English Sonnet Form', *P.M.L.A.*, xxxviii (1923), 737.

As though to enhance this effect, Chaucer, at this point in his translation, adjusts the metaphors. The 'malady', which is his own contribution, anticipates the 'heat' and 'cold' of the following line, in which Chaucer omits Petrarch's reference to the summer and winter seasons. Hence the emphasis falls exclusively on Troilus's description of love as a bodily fever; the terms bind the two lines more closely together, and dissociate them from the immediately preceding lines. To isolate the final couplet by metaphor, as well as by rhyme, was to be a Shakespearian procedure. For example, 'Farewell! thou art too dear for my possessing' sustains an intricate legal metaphor until the couplet breaks apart with

> Thus have I had thee, as a dream doth flatter,
> In sleep a king, but, waking, no such matter.   (Sonnet 87)

If, then, the rhyme royal stanza, as handled by Chaucer, was by no means the exclusive model for the English sonnet, the two forms certainly bear some affinity.

Chaucer's achievement in this pioneer effort compares very favourably with the next English translation of sonnet cxxxii, Passion V of Thomas Watson's *Passionate Centurie of Loue* (1582).[1] Watson, who corrects Chaucer's first mistranslation, is an accurate translator. But there are typical limits to his accuracy. His habitual interest in the 'familier trueths' of the laws of love led him to seek and find them everywhere in the *Rime*, and this produces further that un-Petrarchan tendency towards the abstract and general already incipient in the 'Canticus Troili'. His note on sonnet cxxxii draws attention to its application to the representative lover: it expresses 'certaine contrarieties, whiche are incident to him that loueth extreemelye'. The passion itself soon deserts the subject of the poet-lover's own 'hurtes' to dwell, unlike the original, on those of 'many men'. Later, probably in order to stretch the sonnet to his own eighteen-line unit, Watson adds two lines. And these embody a piece of proverbial triteness quite out of tune with Petrarch's subjectivity, and even with Troilus's:

> And touching him, whome will hath made a slaue,
> The Prouerbe saith of olde, *Selfe doe, selfe haue.*

One is almost persuaded that Watson's greater contemporary, Sir Philip Sidney, must have had all this in mind when he remarked that

Chaucer, vndoubtedly, did excellently in hys *Troylus* and *Cresseid*; of whom, truly, I know not whether to meruaile more, either that he in

---

[1] See Watson, *Poems*, ed. Edward Arber (London, 1870), p. 41.

that mistie time could see so clearely, or that wee in this cleare age walke so stumblingly after him.[1]

The compatibility of Petrach's sonnet cxxxii and *Troilis and Criseyde* extends much further than a mere reference to its local context— Troilus's love-sickness in Book I—implies. The sonnet's special value for Chaucer is enhanced by the fact that Chaucer and Petrarch were already united in their relation to the common tradition: that of courtly love poetry. Three aspects of this tradition are specially relevant to the present case: the psychology of falling in love, the character of the hero, and certain of the images and devices of 'rethorike sweete' used to express them.

To fall in love is to experience conflicting feelings, 'certaine contarieties', as Watson would have it: so the 'psychology' of sonnet cxxxii can be baldly summed up. Petrarch derived the definition of love as 'dulce malum' or 'doussa dolors' from Ovid and the Ovidian Troubadours, together with the rhetorical device, oxymoron, by which it is expressed. The definition and device became commonplaces of the courtly love poetry of the Middle Ages and Renaissance. Petrarch's own 'dilettoso male' and 'viva morte' are reproduced in Chaucer's translation as 'swete harm' and 'quike deth'. Close to this device and expressive of the same state of conflict is the antithesis, an example of which is found in the last line of sonnet cxxxii: 'E tremo a mezza state, ardendo il verno.' In what way, then, did Petrarch's individual genius act upon the tradition? Simply, he united this stock concept of love with personal experience, and argued about it. The octave of sonnet cxxxii describes a whole tissue of contradictions as felt and understood by the one lover. Definition of Love becomes description of a lover's feelings.

Petrarch's hero—himself—owes less to Ovid than to his Provençal and Italian predecessors. In the power of the god of love and the service of an adored lady, the courtly lover's situation makes him humble and helpless. Often in tears, always burning, sighing, groaning, and lamenting, he can but utter the stock 'complaint'. Sonnet cxxxii expresses the usual helplessness, the 'pianto e lamento'; but now the helplessness is as much an aspect of the lover's character as of his situation. And this hero therefore becomes less the vague 'I' of the medieval love lyric than a 'modern' melancholic personality: 'non so quel ch'io mi voglio'—he knows not what he wants or needs. All this emerges more fully

[1] *An Apologie for Poetrie* (written *c.* 1583), in *Elizabethan Critical Essays*, ed. G. G. Smith (London, 1904), i. 196.

as the arguments which occupy the octave are suspended; and it achieves its final expression through the sustained seafaring metaphor.

The seafaring image of sonnet cxxxii is Petrarch's main 'device' for projecting his hero: his character, feelings, thoughts, and personal experience. The image itself can again be traced to the common tradition, though, in this case, later love poets owe virtually everything to Petrarch and but little to Ovid and the medieval courtly poets. A stock ancient figure, renewed in the Middle Ages, is the comparison of the composition of a work to a sea voyage: Ovid, Petrarch, Boccaccio, and Chaucer are among the many poets to 'sail' through their stories.[1] But, obviously, the classical legacy here is rather to long narrative poems than to short love lyrics like sonnet cxxxii. The one is concerned with an outer circumstance, the progress of the poem, the other with an inner psychological state, the subject matter of the poem. The seafaring image as an expression of the lover's dilemma and state of mind is only occasionally found in Ovid, source of so many figures of courtly love poetry. However, a striking use of it opens *Amores*, II. iv. Ovid, hating his sins but lacking the strength to rule himself, is like a ship swept along and tossed about by raging water:

> Nam desunt vires ad me mihi iusque regendum;
> auferor ut rapida concita puppis aqua.   (lines 7–8)

Alfred Jeanroy, who thinks it by no means certain that the Provençal poets derived this image from Ovid, cites instances from Ventadour, Borneil, and Arnaut d'Aganges, all of whom compare the lover 'possed to and fro' between hope and despair to a boat on a stormy sea.[2] The seafaring image, which he used more frequently and developed much further than his predecessors, Petrarch transmitted to the European Renaissance. And the channels through which, in its Petrarchan form, it entered English love poetry were, first, Chaucer's translation of sonnet cxxxii, and, second, Wyatt's translation of sonnet clxxxix. The image, in fact, was to become one of the most firmly entrenched of Elizabethan Petrarchanisms. But this later phase is not to the present purpose; and it is sufficient to notice the key position of Petrarch in the history of the seafaring image.

Chaucer stands in the same relation as Petrarch to all these tradi-

[1] See E. R. Curtius, *European Literature and the Latin Middle Ages* (1948), trans. W. R. Trask. Bollingen Series no. 36 (New York, 1953), pp. 128–30.
[2] *La Poésie Lyrique des Troubadours* (Toulouse and Paris, 1934), pp. 125 and 126 n.

tional doctrines and rhetorical conventions. The extent of his acquaintance with them is revealed in the poems already discussed in Chapter V, and with these *The Romaunt of the Rose* may be included, if with some reserve. (The attribution to Chaucer has been questioned, but certainly, if it was not his, he was well acquainted with the work in its French original.) The 'I' of the poem is, of course, the obedient servant of the god of love and adorer of the Rose. The pleasure–pain sensation of loving is expounded at great length, through allegory and rhetoric, by precept, and, very occasionally, by direct description of the lover's feelings. For example, after the hero has been struck by an arrow, the god of love gives him an ointment, and, as the wound heals, he feels 'Bothe gret anoy and eke swetnesse', 'joie meynt with bittirnesse', 'harm and good', 'ese and anger' (lines 1919–26). Soon after, the god of love gives various charges and precepts to the lover, predicting that, while he loves, he shall

> no whyle be in o stat,
> But whylom cold and whilom hat.   (lines 2397–8)

And, accordingly, having kissed the rose, the lover does experience all these 'mixed' emotions and contrary states:

> I myght not be so angwisshous
> That I [ne] mote glad and joly be,
> Whanne that I remembre me.
> Yit ever among, sothly to seyne,
> I suffre noy and moche peyne.   (lines 3768–72)

Then directly following—the actual juxtaposition strongly suggesting sonnet cxxxii and the 'Canticus Troili'—is a long description of the sea of Love, sometimes calm, sometimes rough:

> The see may never be so stille
> That with a litel wynde it nille
> Overwhelme and turne also,
> As it were wood, in wawis goo.
> Aftir the calm the trouble sone
> Mot folowe and chaunge as the moone.
> Right so farith Love, that selde in oon
> Holdith his anker: for right anoon
> Whanne they in ese wene best to lyve,
> They ben with tempest all fordryve.   (lines 3773–82)

Right so fareth Love. This is doctrinaire, diffuse, and generalized compared with Petrarch's sonnet. But it provides a framework of familiar ideas and devices.

Le Roman de la Rose, then, prepares the ground for the 'Canticus Troili'. The contents of Petrarch's sonnet 'conformed too well to the rhetorical *exempla* of the poetics followed by Chaucer to escape his attention'.[1] That Troilus should address the god of love, that he should 'pleyne', that he should think love a 'swete harm' and feel it as a heat–cold sensation, that he should compare himself to a ship at sea: all these Petrarchan features conform to Chaucer's own knowledge of the code of love and to its 'poetics'.

The conclusion to be drawn is not necessarily that Petrarch's sonnet was, after all, of no special, only of general, value to Chaucer, providing items that he could have found elsewhere, or which were already before him in the text of his main source, Boccaccio's *Il Filostrato*. Take the 'Canticus Troili' again in its context. Troilus, like Boccaccio's Troilo, sees Criseyde in the temple, returns home to sit at the foot of his bed, and promptly makes up his mind 'Criseyde for to love, and nought repente' (i. 392). But Troilo's behaviour is much more precipitate than Troilus's, since he proceeds at once to address the god of love,

> con pietoso parlar:—Signor, omai
> L'anima è tua.   (Pt. I, stanza 38)[2]

Troilus sings his Petrarchan song before he utters the corresponding plea:

> And to the God of Love thus seyde he
> With pitous vois, 'O lord, now youres is
> My spirit . . .'   (i. 422–4)

So the 'Canticus Troili' makes a pause in which Troilus, baffled by the sudden onset of new and powerful feelings, attempts to sort them out and take stock of himself. More strikingly than anything in the early part of *Il Filostrato*, the 'Canticus Troili' also suggests future developments in the hero's personality. Sonnet cxxxii has been described as the expression of a weak spirit and wavering will, and as presenting a phenomenon, a certain state of mind, rather than a mere tissue of

[1] Mario Praz, *The Flaming Heart* (New York, 1958), p. 266.
[2] Giovanni Boccaccio, *Il Filostrato e il Ninfale Fiesolano*, ed. Vincenzo Pernicone. *Opere*, Vol. II (Bari, 1937).

thoughts.[1] Petrarch fails to find an issue in action or even to reach a decisive conclusion. In other words, his sonnet expresses a negative personality not unlike the future Troilus. If Troilus does become active, in accordance with the demands of the story, it is not before Pandarus has roused his 'mouse's heart'; and he is all too liable to lapse back into the mood foreshadowed in his 'song'.

Sonnet cxxxii does, then, make its own contribution to *Troilus and Criseyde*; but Chaucer's total debt to Petrarch remains quantitatively small. After the 'Canticus Troili' their paths do not cross again. Yet the study of their relationship would not be complete without a reference to a general similarity of achievement. Chaucer's independent advance in the art of characterization creates effects comparable with Petrarch's, particularly where the common conventions are handled. For instance, throughout *Troilus and Criseyde* Chaucer distinguishes conflict as inwardly felt from conflict as a conventional notion, outwardly adopted by the fashionable gallant. Nor does he overuse such traditional devices as the oxymoron. Pandarus's use of it savours strongly of conventionality, as when he mysteriously bears news to Criseyde: 'I have a joly wo, a lusty sorwe' (ii. 1099). Criseyde's rejoinder, for all its real alarm, also recognizes her uncle as the old hand at love's game, the man of 'olde ensaumples' in fact:

> Now, by youre fey, myn uncle . . .
> Tel us youre joly wo and youre penaunce.
> How ferforth be ye put in loves daunce? (ii. 1103, 1105–6)

Criseyde's own experience of contrariety, when told of Troilus's suit, had been quite another matter: 'What shal I doon?', 'Shal I nat love, in cas if that me leste?', 'Allas! how dorst I thenken that folie?', and so on, till

> . . . after that, hire thought gan for to clere,   /
> And seide, 'He which that nothing undertaketh,
> Nothyng n'acheveth, be hym looth or deere.'
> And with an other thought hire herte quaketh;
> Than slepeth hope, and after drede awaketh;
> Now hoot, now cold; but thus, bitwixen tweye,
> She rist hire up, and wente here for to pleye. (ii. 806–812)

It is not to be doubted that Criseyde, a universal favourite with readers, is a highly original Chaucerian character, owing little to Boccaccio

---

[1] See Francesco de Sanctis, *Saggio Critico sul Petrarca*. Scrittori d'Italia, no. 213 (Bari, 1869), pp. 116 and 68.

and nothing to Petrarch. Yet her wavering 'bitwixen' hope and dread, her feeling 'Now hoot, now cold' are, taken in isolation, conventional items: the very terms occur in *The Romaunt of the Rose*. Their assimilation into an original character study is simply the Chaucerian equivalent of the Petrarchan transformation of the Ovidian-Troubadour conventions: 'No poet, no artist of any art, has his complete meaning alone. His significance, his appreciation is the appreciation of his relation to the dead poets and artists.'[1]

(iii) Wyatt and Surrey

Well over a century passed before the experiment of transplanting Petrarch's poetry was repeated. Between Chaucer's death in 1400 and Wyatt's visit to Italy in 1527, Petrarch was not forgotten by Englishmen. His works, with Dante's and Boccaccio's, were among Humphrey Duke of Gloucester's bequests to Oxford. Lydgate, it will be recalled, cited the *De Remediis* in his *Fall of Princes*, while Skelton included the 'famous clerk' Petrarch in his long, boring roll calls in *Phyllyp Sparowe* and the *Garlande of Laurell*. These literary references are, typically, somewhat perfunctory. And such importance as this interim period has, in the story of English Petrarchan poetry, lies rather in its useful maintenance of the common currency of courtly love.

Very different was the situation in Italy. The imitation of Petrarch's *Rime* thrived uninterruptedly between early fifteenth-century examples like Giusto de' Conti's and early sixteenth-century ones like Bembo's. Under the literary dictatorship of Pietro Bembo, the Italy of 1527 was enthusiastically Petrarchan and was to continue so throughout the life-time of Wyatt and Surrey. Petrarch's vernacular poems, first printed in 1470, soon fell a prey to learned commentators, whose interpretations may well have influenced, as we shall see later, a studious reader like Wyatt. *The Divine Comedy* was printed in 1471, and it, too, received the scholarly treatment due to a classic. But, in the eyes of courtly imitators, Dante's religious epic, frequently vulgar in style, could never rival Petrarch's collection of elegant love poems. Giovanni della Casa (1503–56), Bembo's friend and Wyatt's exact contemporary, manifests the prevailing 'good taste' when he warns the would-be courtier against such words as 'epa', used in the *Comedy*: 'dirai piu tosto il Ventre (stomach) che l'Epa (belly)'. He continues with a con-

[1] T. S. Eliot, 'Tradition and the Individual Talent' (1919), in *Selected Essays*, 3rd edition (London, 1951), p. 15.

trasting illustration from Petrarch's 'Vergine bella' (no. ccclxvi), and with advice to follow this best of poets, who, in order to avoid reminding his audience of filth, seeks out an alternative to the offending 'epa': 'di niuna bruttura farai sovvenire all'uditore. Laqual cosa volendo l'ottimo Poeta nostro schifare, si come io credo, in questa parola stessa, procacciò di trouare altro vocabolo.'[1]

The Venice of Wyatt's day was the stronghold of both 'pure' Petrarchanism and Bembist imitation of it. From about 1500 Bembo was composing his own love sonnets, deliberately modelled on Petrarch's. In 1501 he prepared, from a manuscript in his possession, the beautiful and reliable Aldine edition of *Le Cose Volgari di Messer Francesco Petrarcha*. And, though this was followed, in 1502, by his edition of *The Divine Comedy*, Bembo continued to promote the study of Petrarch rather than Dante. His critical work, *Le Prose della Volgar Lingua* (1525), includes illustrations from earlier poets such as Dante, Cavalcanti, and Cino, but the mass is taken from Petrarch. An active promulgator of the neo-classical doctrine of Imitation, Bembo was also an upholder of the classic status of two modern models: Boccaccio's prose and Petrarch's poetry. Petrarch's poems, as models for diction, form, and metre, have all the virtues pleasing to modern, cultivated, courtly tastes: gravità, grandezza, leggerezza, vaghezza, piacevolezza, besides that quality most admired of all Renaissance critics, 'dolce varietà'. By contrast Dante, with Cavalcanti and Cino, is rather the great pioneer. The *Prose* gives emphasis to the fact that these poets are reputable forerunners, in vernacular poetry, of the unique and consummate artist, Petrarch: 'Seguì a costoro il Petrarca, nel quale uno tutte le grazie della volgar poesia raccolte si veggono.'[2]

Not that this adulation passed unchallenged. The anti-Petrarchans have a history nearly as long as the Petrarchans. Pietro Aretino, resident in Venice from 1527, and perhaps the most influential man of letters after Bembo, shared his admiration for Petrarch. Nevertheless this most virulent of satirists was, by 1537, protesting hotly against the 'sacking' of the *Rime*. He derides all forms of literary imitation. Instead of labouring uphill in 'l'orme del gran Petrarca', it is better to follow on the strength of one's own legs.[3] Meanwhile, the more cheerful Francesco Berni had produced his famous 'Sonetto alla sua Donna',

[1] From *Il Galateo*, the well-known book of manners: see Giovanni della Casa, *Rime, et Prose* (Venice, 1558), p. 136.
[2] Bembo, *Prose e Rime*, ed. Carlo Dionisotti (Turin, 1960), p. 130.
[3] Aretino, *Lettere*, ed. F. Nicolini (Bari, 1913, 1916), nos. 157 and 549.

a eulogy of a grey-haired hag, parodying the Petrarchan adulation of women:

> Chiome d'argento fino, irte e attorte
> Senz'arte intorno ad un bel viso d'oro. . . .
> Occhi di perle vaghi, luci torte
> Da ogni obietto diseguale a loro.[1]

Not long afterwards appeared the delightful dialogue, *Il Petrarchista* (Venice, 1539), by Niccolò Franco, who has new secrets from the shrine at Avignon to reveal to the worshippers of Petrarch and Laura. Nail scissors, a nightcap, a toothbrush, and fragments of a chamber pot can be seen among the relics of Saint Laura. The 'Petrarchist' has also reinvestigated the *Rime*. Did Petrarch fall in love amidst the vain pomps of the city? At a ball or a feast? On a balcony or in church? No, it was in the countryside, amidst flowers and grass, and he can 'prove' it from the text.[2] Thus, well before Shakespeare's fans gave occasion for it, the excesses of bardolatry were exposed to derision. And to the same effect—for the Petrarchans' ardour was no more easily snuffed out than the Shakespearians'. The year 1543 finds Benedetto Varchi, before the Florentine Academy, devoting a whole 'lezione' to the minute explication of a single 'bello, ed utilissimo Sonetto' by Petrarch.[3] It was but one of a series, and, though Varchi's lectures were mocked by such anti-Petrarchans as Alfonso de' Pazzi, there is no reason to think they were unsuccessful. He was still lecturing on Petrarch in 1565.

England was, of course, very much in the rear of all this. Yet, inevitably, English poets, like the French and Spanish, did eventually catch the Petrarchan infection. They then rapidly made up for lost time. An anonymous early Tudor poet describes Petrarch as 'hed and prince of poets all',[4] while Lord Morley thinks that 'neuer yet no poete nor gentleman could amend, nor make the lyke'.[5]

Wyatt and Surrey do not record their opinions of the *Rime*. But, what is more important, they honour it by translation and imitation. Of these two Petrarchans, Wyatt deserves the major emphasis. This is

---

[1] Berni, *Poesie e Prose*, ed. Ezio Chiòrboli (Geneva and Florence, 1934), *Rime*, no. xxiii.

[2] *Op. cit.*, ff. 18ᵛ and 14ʳ, in the edition published in Venice in 1541.

[3] See *Raccolta di Prose Fiorentine* (Florence, 1730), Pt. II. v. 46.

[4] Tottel, no. 218.

[5] *The Triumphes of Petrarch*, trans. Henry Parker, Lord Morley (1554), Roxburghe Club (London, 1887), p. 4.

not because he is judged *a priori* superior to Surrey. Wyatt was first in the field, Surrey being still a boy at the time of the 1527 embassy to Italy. Furthermore, in sheer bulk, Wyatt's Petrarchan poems outweigh Surrey's. Surrey translated three and imitated two of Petrarch's poems. But no less than twenty-five of Wyatt's poems—fifteen translations and ten imitations—depend on Petrarch. He, therefore, is the key figure in this pioneering phase of English Petrarchanism.

Pioneers can get overrated. Wyatt and Surrey—indeed all English lyrists before Sidney and Shakespeare—are amateurs compared with Petrarch. Not surprisingly, it is the Italian critics who underline this point. Emma Chini notes the English prejudice in favour of Wyatt and against Petrarch, who is mistakenly judged, outside Italy, to be 'sentimental and rhetorical'.[1] They also carry further E. K. Chambers's opinion that 'There is but little fundamental resemblance between Wyatt and Petrarch.'[2] Sergio Baldi speaks of an 'essential difference'. He finds that Wyatt's Petrarchanism is superficial and that Petrarch's most subtle images have few echoes in him.[3] As for Surrey's relationship to Petrarch, though Padelford finds Surrey, on at least one occasion, 'much the finer of the two',[4] it can hardly be seriously maintained that he is fundamentally akin to or greater than Petrarch.

Nevertheless I hope to show that some, at any rate, of Petrarch's meaning, quality, and style did enter English poetry through Wyatt, and rather less through Surrey. With the help of some valuable studies, among which those of J. M. Berdan, Hallett Smith, J. W. Lever, and Otto Hietsch stand out, it should be possible to understand their historical importance, intrinsic value, and comparative merits as Petrarchans. The chief touchstone for comparison is provided by Petrarch's sonnet cxl, the only one translated by both Wyatt and Surrey.

> Amor, che nel penser mio vive e regna
>   E'l suo seggio maggior nel mio cor tene,
>   Tal or armato ne la fronte vène,
>   Ivi si loca et ivi pon sua insegna.
> Quella ch'amare e sofferir ne 'nsegna,
>   E vòl che 'l gran desio, l'accesa spene,
>   Ragion, vergogna e reverenza affrene,
>   Di nostro ardir fra sé stessa si sdegna.

[1] 'Il Sorgere del Petrarchismo in Inghilterra e la Poesia di Sir Thomas Wyatt', *Civiltà Moderna*, vi (Jan.–Feb., 1934), 19.
[2] *Sir Thomas Wyatt and Some Collected Studies* (London, 1933), p. 129.
[3] *La Poesia di Sir Thomas Wyatt* (Florence, 1953), pp. 188, 182, 185.
[4] Padelford, p. 207.

Onde Amor paventoso fugge al core
   Lasciando ogni sua impresa, e piange e trema;
   Ivi s'asconde e non appar piú fòre.
Che poss'io far, temendo il mio signore,
   Se non star seco in fin a l'ora estrema?
   Ché bel fin fa chi ben amando more.   (Petrarch, no. cxl)

The longe love, that in my thought doeth harbar
   And in myn hert doeth kepe his residence,
   Into my face preseth with bolde pretence,
   And therin campeth, spreding his baner.
She that me lerneth to love and suffre,
   And willes that my trust and lustes negligence
   Be rayned by reason, shame and reverence,
   With his hardines taketh displeasur.
Wherewithall, vnto the hertes forrest he fleith,
   Leving his entreprise with payn and cry;
   And ther him hideth, and not appereth.
What may I do when my maister fereth
   But in the feld with him to lyve and dye?
   For goode is the liff, ending faithfully.   (Wyatt, no. 4)

Love that doth raine and liue within my thought,
And buylt his seat within my captyve brest,
Clad in the armes wherein with me he fowght,
Oft in my face he doth his banner rest.
But she that tawght me love and suffre paine,
My doubtful hope & eke my hote desire
With shamfast looke to shadoo and refrayne,
Her smyling grace convertyth streight to yre.
And cowarde Love, then, to the hart apace
Taketh his flight, where he doth lurke and playne
His purpose lost, and dare not shew his face.
For my lordes gilt thus fawtles byde I payine;
Yet from my lorde shall not my foote remove:
Sweet is the death that taketh end by love.   (Surrey, no. 4)

Wyatt and Surrey are on familiar courtly ground. Petrarch's sonnet is one of the many 'In Vita' ones in which he wages 'sweet warfare' with his mistress. He is a soldier of the god of love. His 'alto mio signore'—that stern, adult deity, distinct in personality from his colleague, the mischievous, chubby baby Cupid—is well known from the pages of Ovid, the *Romance of the Rose*, *Troilus and Criseyde* and *The Knight's Tale*:

> The god of love, a, *benedicite!*
> How myghty and how greet a lord is he!

Laura, however, with a characteristically chaste rebuff, is easily able to put him to flight. The god has been overbold, and, deserting the battle-field of Petrarch's face, takes frightened refuge in his heart. Petrarch remains, as orthodox lovers do, constant to love even in defeat, despair, and the hour of death. The warfare image figures forth the familiar tale of unsuccessful love in every detail.

Wyatt and Surrey have been blamed for their choice of this sonnet. J. M. Berdan expresses a strong distaste for it. 'This is a typical sonnet in Petrarch's conceited manner, a metaphor ridden to death for the purpose of closing with an epigram. . . . It is a purely intellectual concept worked out like a puzzle.'[1] A significant feature of this comment is its marked similarity to Dr Johnson's strictures on Cowley and Donne: 'they frequently threw away their wit upon false conceits. . . . The fault of Cowley, and perhaps of all the writers of the metaphysical race, is that of pursuing his thoughts to their last ramifications.'[2] However mistaken Johnson and Berdan may be in their final judgement of these poets, it is important to notice that Donne, commonly represented as the strongest opponent of Petrarchanism, actually has much in common with its founder—with Petrarch himself.

In sonnet cxl the military metaphor is sustained throughout and used as a means of expounding Petrarch's meaning and elucidating the lover's experience. Any image of Donne's—say, the moving sun of his 'Lecture upon the Shadow'—will illustrate the same 'conceited' usage. In neither Petrarch nor Donne is the image used in a merely associative, much less in a decorative, way. It is an essential part of the structure and meaning of the whole poem. The image, then, is, to use John Crowe Ransom's distinction, 'metaphysical' rather than 'romantic'.[3] That is, the poet's feelings and thoughts are expressed *through* his

[1] *Early Tudor Poetry* (New York, 1920), p. 520.
[2] The life of Cowley, in *Lives of the English Poets*, World's Classics edition, i. 16, 37.
[3] 'Shakespeare at Sonnets', in *The World's Body* (New York and London, 1938), pp. 270–303.

chosen image, and not simply associated *with* it in a vague, suggestive way. In the 'romantic style', Ransom indicates, is Shakespeare's

> Full many a glorious morning have I seen
> Flatter the mountain-tops with sovereign eye,
> Kissing with golden face the meadows green . . .
> Even so my sun one early morn did shine,
> With all-triumphant splendour on my brow . . . (Sonnet 33)

Triumph, glory, flattery, kissing—these obvious analogies probably do not exhaust the likenesses of weather and love in this case. Here the associations are rich indeed, as only Shakespeare can make them, but the relationship between image and idea is not fully, precisely, and coherently defined. Opinions will differ as to the relative value, poetically, of the metaphysical and romantic ways of handling imagery. The metaphysical conceit can be judged forced, unnatural, ingenious, and the product of mere cerebration. Nowadays, however, we are more likely than not to reverse the Johnsonian and Berdan's opinion. Since 1920, when Berdan wrote, metaphysical devices of style have ceased to need apology. They are recognized as having their own value. Packed with meaning, they prove marvellous instruments for handling intricate matters, clearly yet subtly. Petrarch is the original master in the metaphysical style, and Donne, not Shakespeare, his kindred spirit.

Wyatt is the pioneer through whom Petrarch's metaphysical manner enters English poetry. Chaucer, with his light-weight handling of Petrarch's sea-faring image, is here no rival. Nor is Surrey, who, as Hallett Smith points out,[1] takes the conceit in sonnet cxl much less seriously than Wyatt (of which more later). Furthermore, this metaphysical manner of handling imagery is a much more important part of the Petrarchan legacy than others familiarly associated with it, as, for example, the images themselves, or the idealization of the sonnet heroine. These the English poets could easily have derived from other sources, since they are ubiquitous in the courtly love poetry of medieval England and Europe. Petrarch, of course, helped to give them further currency, but he did not originate them. His style, on the other hand, is unique. His peculiar subtleties transform the usual medieval 'love longings', idealizations, and complaints into a new love poetry which was really worth the time and trouble bestowed on it by Wyatt. Quite simply, there is much more *in* the fourteen lines of 'The longe

---

[1] 'The Art of Sir Thomas Wyatt', *H.L.Q.*, ix (1946), 335.

love' than in any comparable English poem of the fourteenth or fift-
teenth centuries. This is perhaps the most important aspect of Wyatt's
historical importance as a Petrarchan sonneteer.

In various respects Wyatt serves Petrarch more faithfully than
Surrey. Both attempt metaphrase, and there are no deliberate inaccur-
acies. Yet it is difficult not to agree with Hallett Smith's thesis: that
while Surrey is 'smooth, suave, courtly',[1] Wyatt takes Petrarch altogether more seriously. There is little point in repeating the evidence
set out in Hallett Smith's well-known study, but an addition to it may
be welcome. It seems to me that Wyatt not only meets better than
Surrey the challenge of Petrarch's central conceit, but that he also—
and this really follows from the other—pays more heed to the framework of Petrarchan ideas. Laura, here, is not merely the cruel fair of
the courtly convention. She is also Petrarch's spiritual guide, closer to
Beatrice than to the heroine of an English sonnet sequence. That desire, therefore, should be restrained by the great moral imperatives,
'Ragion, vergogna e reverenza' is her doctrine, not her fad. Wyatt's
almost literal translation of the four lines that refer to the lover's
schooling does Petrarch's meaning justice:

> She that me lerneth to love and suffre,
> And willes that my trust and lustes negligence
> Be rayned by reason, shame and reverence,
> With his hardines taketh displeasur.

Surrey obliterates this serious moral content entirely:

> But she that tawght me love and suffre paine,
> My doubtful hope & eke my hote desire
> With shamfast looke to shadoo and refrayne,
> Her smyling grace convertyth streight to yre.

Reason, shame, and reverence are therefore lost except for what survives in Surrey's 'shamfast looke'. And this I think an unfortunate
touch in itself, since, together with his equally un-Petrarchan reference
to 'smyling grace', it suggests rather the simperings of lovers' faces
than the big moral issues on which Petrarch's love foundered. Surrey
also prefers a literal fact, a face blushing with shame, to the metaphor
of lust 'rayned' by shame used by Petrarch and Wyatt. This shows that
Surrey deserves all the credit he is usually given for the pictorial and
descriptive qualities of his poetry. He has visualized the 'face' of sonnet

---

[1] *Op. cit.*, p. 336.

cxl, giving it expression where neither Petrarch nor Wyatt do. But he sacrifices much, for his picture does not point to more than itself. It is a solid actuality, without the power that metaphor has to signify a reality other than itself.

Wyatt's sonnet is comparatively lacking in picturesqueness. Apart from a few details like the banner, its metaphors are grey, and its portentous abstract terms seem to gather like clouds. On the one occasion when Wyatt does venture to add a pictorial detail to his original, he goes, not with Surrey to the drawing-room, but with Petrarch to the wilds. In sonnet cxl, love flees to the 'heart', in Wyatt's version, to 'the hertes forrest'. Wyatt's image suits the rejected, lonely Petrarch who grieved so desperately as he paced the wooded valleys of Vaucluse. It also calls to mind the sombre forests of courtly romance, say, Malory's or Ariosto's, and, more particularly, the 'selva oscura' in which Dante's soul is lost in the mazes of error. Such connections a sixteenth-century reader would automatically make. Recalling Petrarch's account of how he has become 'un animal silvestro', John Harington remarks of Dante's 'selva oscura'—'This is that wandring wood of which the dolefull *Petrarke* complaines so often in those his sweet mourning sonets, in which he seemes to haue comprehended all the passions that all men of that humour haue felt.'[1] Wyatt's hart/heart is undisciplined and at bay. This is much what Petrarch has in mind in general, as well as in 'Amor, che' in particular. 'The hertes forrest' is a well-conceived and serious addition to the poem.

In handling Petrarch's rhyme scheme Wyatt is more obedient, less revolutionary, than Surrey:

abba,	abba,	cdc,	cdc (Petrarch)
abba,	abba,	cdc,	cdd (Wyatt)
abab,	cdcd,	efef,	gg (Surrey)

Their procedure is typical. And, since it would be tedious to go over the schemes of all my later examples, it is perhaps permissible here to interpolate a comment on the rhyming of all Wyatt's and Surrey's sonnets. Thus the twenty-eight sonnets among Wyatt's Egerton and Devonshire poems are all of the commonest Petrarchan type, but with the last two lines rhyming. The octaves invariably run abba, abba. Though the sestets admit of variety, it remains generally true that 'Wyatt regarded the sestet as a unit, tending rather to be divided into

---

[1] *Orlando Fvrioso in English Heroical Verse* (London, 1591), p. 30.

tercets than into a quatrain and couplet.'[1] On the other hand, with but one exception, Surrey's fourteen sonnets have interwoven rhymes, and, in all cases, his final couplet is detachable.

In 'The longe love', Wyatt's octave, with its two enclosed quatrains, bound together by rhyme but grammatically separate, is obviously Italianate (this being, in fact, the commonest structure with Petrarch). His sestet is also Italianate, if, at first sight, less obviously so. Wyatt's couplet ending, his only divergence from Petrarch, does not, after all, alter the original structure. His sense-divisions and rhythm follow Petrarch's closely in the sestet, so that it falls distinctly into two Italian tercets, and not into the English quatrain-and-couplet form. Furthermore, Wyatt's couplet is no more detachable by rhyme than it is by sense, for the 'd' rhyme has occurred as early as line ten, precisely as in Petrarch. Hence he has all the standard Italian features: the two major metrical parts (octave and sestet), subdivided into the two minor ones (two quatrains and two tercets).

Wyatt's slight alteration of the rhyme scheme, if structurally insignificant, is tantalizingly mysterious. If his final rhyming couplet did not derive from the English tradition, say, from rhyme royal, its probable source is in the general theory and practice of the sonnet in Italy. Italian Renaissance critics uniformly imply, and some state outright, that the sonnet is an essentially free, if difficult, form.[2] Their ideas spring from the practice of the *dolce stil nuovo*, and are usually so lavishly illustrated that their works resemble anthologies of poetry. The prosodists, Antonio da Tempo and Giangiorgio Trissino, set out a number of different rhyme schemes, the tercets being particularly varied, and admitting, in several cases, of a final rhyming couplet. The final couplet is used by Fazio degli Uberti and Cino da Pistoia, very occasionally by Dante and Petrarch, and, later, by Wyatt's contemporary, Benedetto Varchi. Hence, contrary to the popular opinion, there is no actual veto in Italy on the final rhyming couplet. Only, unlike the English, it must always remain linked by rhyme to the rest of the sestet. Hence Wyatt hardly appears even remotely un-Italianate.

Wyatt's is foreign territory for an English poet of the early sixteenth century, himself more likely to be expert in the interwoven quatrain and self-contained couplet, and in such combinations of the two as occur in the ever-popular rhyme royal. Surrey prudently

[1] H. B. Lathrop, 'The Sonnet Forms of Wyatt and Surrey', *M.P.*, ii (1905), 465.
[2] See Appendix H.

remains on home ground. In 'Love that doth raine', three interwoven quatrains, each with a fresh set of rhymes, succeed each other, and the whole is completed by a couplet, for which, again, a fresh rhyme is introduced. The sense-divisions correspond. Surrey's is, of course, the full-dress English or Shakespearian sonnet pattern. In general, if not invariably, this lends itself to non-Petrarchan effects. Most often, the Petrarchan sonnet is characterized by the asymmetrical balance of octave and sestet, the English by the symmetrical phases of its quatrains and the epigrammatic incisiveness of its couplet.

The Surrey–Shakespeare form 'is an English invention', but 'it was brought into existence on an Italian basis, by selection and adjustment'.[1] Surrey's feeding-in of fresh rhymes is wholly original and non-Italianate. His other novelties have precedents in Italy. Interwoven rhyming, like the final couplet, is admitted, in theory and practice, in the Italian sonnet. Both, moreover, form the stock in trade of the Italian epigram or strambotto. But Petrarch only occasionally writes sonnets in which the weight, as in an epigram, falls towards the end, or in which his conclusion is vested wholly in the last two lines. 'S'una fede amorosa' is an example to be discussed later, but its technique is not at all typical. The Italian precedent for the English form lies rather with Petrarch's fifteenth-century imitators, Serafino and the other Caritean Petrarchans, who constantly try to assimilate the style of the sonnet to that of the epigram.

In 'Love that doth raine', Surrey is not unmindful of the Petrarchan form. Like Wyatt he distributes Petrarch's matter in the structurally correct manner, balancing love's boldness (the octave) with love's discomfiture (the sestet). To support this structure Wyatt relies on grammar, rhyme, and rhythm. Surrey, instead, has recourse to the props of phrasing, which he makes as strong as possible. Much more emphatically than Wyatt, he enforces the contrast between 'Love that doth raine and liue' (the octave) and 'cowarde Love', a fugitive on the verge of death (the sestet). Wyatt, of course, gets the general sense of Petrarch here. But Surrey has studied and matched Petrarch's phrasing: 'Amor, che . . . vive e regna', 'Onde Amor paventoso'.

It is towards the end that Wyatt's conscientiousness reaps the reward of structural authenticity, while Surrey's independence militates against it. This judgement depends on one's reading of sonnet cxl. Berdan may be mistaken, for example, in imputing to Petrarch 'the purpose of closing with an epigram'. The final line, 'What a beautiful

[1] John S. Smart, *The Sonnets of Milton* (Glasgow, 1921), p. 20.

176

end he makes who dies loving well', is, indeed, a conclusive statement, though surely not the sum total of what Petrarch has to say. It is a logical consequence of what has passed: it is to be expected that Petrarch, when the lord of love is defeated, will choose to share his fate. But this final statement is preceded by a rhetorical question— 'What can I do but remain with my lord till the last hour?'—and has not the clipped incisiveness of an epigram. This is, rather, an effect of Surrey's English version, a direct consequence of his use of a detachable final couplet:

> Yet from my lorde shall not my foote remove:
> Sweet is the death that taketh end by love.

Contrast Wyatt's more faithful rendering of the end of the sonnet:

> What may I do when my maister fereth
>   But in the feld with him to lyve and dye?
>   For goode is the liff, ending faithfully.

Wyatt, while also using the couplet ending, retains the continuous flow of Petrarch's tercet and his rhetorical question. Both of these are destroyed, to be replaced by a couple of confident-sounding rhyming statements in Surrey's version. Petrarch and Wyatt, with their talk of the 'extreme hour', and of 'living and dying', set together with their emotionally wrought-up question, sound desperate. They are, indeed, the desperadoes and martyrs of love. Surrey sounds more like the brave and simple soldier, one who, it is perhaps not fanciful to suppose, would readily fall back upon a tidy epigram. Berdan seems to consider the comparison on this point in Surrey's favour: 'Wyatt's couplet is not complete in itself, whereas Surrey's may be detached as a quotation.'[1] This, in itself, is odd praise, only possible if some mysterious virtue is imputed to the detachable English couplet, and if it is forgotten that even Shakespeare uses it, too often, like the butt end of his rifle. At any rate, all this is profoundly unlike Petrarch, as well as unlike the Italianate Wyatt, who certainly imitates the original more closely, here, than Surrey. Petrarch is a poet who moves logically and often wittily towards his end, but not one who thinks in 'quotations' or snatches at epigrams and axioms.

   Their manipulation of individual lines provides yet another contrast between Wyatt and Surrey. Berdan concludes that Wyatt's close

[1] *Op. cit.*, p. 523.

adherence to the Italian rhyme scheme is a 'feat' that sacrifices 'whatever poetical value the original may have', while Surrey's sonnet 'shows the advance'.[1] Wyatt has to manage on four rhymes, and 'fleith' and 'appereth', for instance, make uncomfortable partners. English is not so rich in rhyming words as Italian, and Surrey's three extra rhymes must obviously help him.

> Amor, che nel penser mio vive e regna (Petrarch)
> The longe love, that in my thought doeth harbar (Wyatt)
> Love that doth raine and liue within my thought (Surrey)

Wyatt's first line, if the final e of 'longe' is sounded, runs smoothly. The sighing note, so typical of his own lyrical poetry, is, metrically, a result of the unstressed syllables at both the beginning and the end of his line. Surrey's first line is not only metrically perfect but sublimely true to Petrarch's emphasis. The initial Amor/Love is striking. Metrically, Surrey achieves this by using the initial trochee, the standard English device for varying the iambic pentameter line. His line also has a firmer tread than Wyatt's because he comes to rest on another strong stress. His line does not, like Wyatt's, tail off faintly and wearily. It is strongly trussed up. Surrey sounds unruffled, harmonious, Wyatt hesitant, and, if anything, melodic. Furthermore, whereas all Surrey's lines are regular, some of Wyatt's are clumsy. Unless Wyatt's secret be lost, 'She that me lerneth to love and suffre' is a line that must be gobbled. It is uncertain which of the first three syllables should receive a stress, or whether Wyatt was aiming at a four-stress or five-stress line. Clumsiness of rhythm is certainly un-Petrarchan. Professor Hietsch thinks the clumsiness that of a young and inexperienced Wyatt.[2]

The contrast, which holds good throughout, is not, however, quite uniformly in Surrey's favour. Italian is not a language of mono-syllables. Its numerous unstressed syllables create light rhythms. Petarch's lines have graceful feminine endings, 'estrema', 'signore', insegna', &c. These find an echo in Wyatt's rhythmically similar 'fleith', 'appereth', 'fereth', &c., rather than in Surrey's strong English beats 'thought', 'fowght', 'rest', 'brest', &c. By the time he reaches the last line, the reader will see the point of what Wyatt and Surrey, respectively, are doing:

[1] *Op. cit.*, pp. 521-2.
[2] *Die Petrarcaübersetzungen Sir Thomas Wyatts*. Wiener Beiträge zur Englischen Philologie, no. 67 (Vienna and Stuttgart, 1960), p. 79.

Chĕ bel fin fa chi ben amando morĕ   (Petrarch)
Fŏr goode is the liff, ending faithfullȳ   (Wyatt)
Swéet is the death that taketh end by lóve   (Surrey)

Wyatt, in the words of J. W. Lever, aims 'to capture the flowing rhythms of Petrarch'.[1] Surrey, on the other hand, aims at a wholly English rhythm.

Surrey gives English poetry a foretaste of the 'harmony of numbers' so highly rated in the eighteenth century. His syllabic regularity, though liable to monotony, is a valuable gift to his Elizabethan successors. This, with his rhyme scheme, constitutes Surrey's 'advance'. Further, he bequeaths to his successors pictorial solidity and an air of agreeable gallantry. Wyatt's metrical experiment is perhaps, comparatively speaking, a dead end. Yet, taken over all, his version of 'Amor, che' is much more authentic and interesting than Surrey's. Whatever he does elsewhere, in this instance Wyatt in all seriousness ushers much of Petrarch's meaning and quality into English. And this occurs through his attempt at exactness, and in spite of that 'essential difference' that, maybe, does exist, in general, between Wyatt and Petrarch.

(iv) Wyatt and Petrarch

Wyatt's other choices from the *Rime* resemble 'The longe love' in that they are consistent with the English poetic tradition and his own 'English' lyrics. Significantly, he chooses to translate only one poem and to imitate one other from Petrarch's 'In Morte' sequence. The first, 'Myne olde dere En'mye' (no. 8), is translated from the comparatively cheerful and impersonal canzone, 'Quell' antiquo mio dolce empio signore' (no. ccclx), a description of the trial of Love by Reason, set out as a legal debate. The second, 'The piller pearisht is' (no. 173), renders Petrarch's joint lament for Cardinal Colonna and Laura (no. cclxix) into an account of Wyatt's single loss, that of a patron, so that the result is not a love poem at all. Wyatt is therefore no more interested than his English predecessors in the love that survives the death of a beloved mistress, purifies the lover's soul through suffering and separation, and anticipates a reunion of souls in Heaven. If he learns to reject love, it is through chagrin, not repentance. The transcendental love and religious feeling of the 'In Morte' sequence do not appeal to the author of 'They fle from me'. The 'essential difference' between

---

[1] *The Elizabethan Love Sonnet* (London, 1956), p. 19.

Wyatt and Petrarch, together with his reputed rebelliousness and worldliness, follows logically from the rejection of Petrarch's transcendentalism. For if the lover's sufferings have no moral meaning and no eternal recompense, there is no reason why he should accept them as a willing penance on earth. Wyatt therefore prefers the poems from the 'In Vita' sequence that either describe, or can easily be converted into descriptions of, the lover's present and earthly pangs.

From the 'In Vita' sequence Wyatt continues to transplant common courtly *motifs*. His sheer faithfulness as a translator stands him in good stead. He takes to Petrarch's complaints as a duck to water, for they are like his own. The cruel Laura is an offender against the laws of love:

> Or vedi, Amor, che giovenetta donna
>   Tuo regno sprezza e del mio mal non cura.   (no. cxxi)

> Behold, love, thy power how she dispiseth!
> My great payne how litle she regardeth!   (no. 1)

The lover's sighs are of no effect:

> Ite, caldi sospiri, al freddo core;
>   Rompete il ghiaccio che pietà contende.   (no. cliii)

> Goo burnyng sighes vnto the frosen hert!
> Goo breke the Ise whiche pites paynfull dert
>   Myght never perse.   (no. 20)

Her enmity continues endlessly:

> Millefïate, o dolce mia guerrera,
>   Per aver co' begli occhi vostri pace,
>   V'aggio proferto il cor.   (no. xxi)

> How oft have I, my dere and cruell foo,
>   With those your Iyes for to get peace and truyse,
>   Profferd you myn hert.   (no. 32)

The tyranny of Laura's eyes is taken up repeatedly. The lover is brought to an extremity of frustration by gazing on them:

> Mirando 'l sol de' begli occhi sereno ...   (no. clxxiii)
> Auysing the bright bemes of these fayer Iyes ... (no. 29)

He is dazzled by them:

> Vive faville uscian de' duo bei lumi.   (no. cclviii)
> The lyvely sperkes that issue from those Iyes ... (no. 47)

And, unlike certain beasts, he cannot look upon such sunlight:

> Sono animali al mondo di sí altera
>> Vista che 'n contr' al sol pur si difende: ...
>> Lasso! ...
> Ch' i' non son forte ad aspettar la luce.   (no. xix)

> Som fowles there be that have so perfaict sight,
>> Agayn the Sonne their Iyes for to defend, ...
>> Alas, ...
> For to withstond her loke I ame not able.   (no. 24)

The novelty of Wyatt's Petrarchan enterprise continues to relate more to manner than to matter:

> Passa la nave mia colma d'oblio
>> Per aspro mare, a mezza notte, il verno
>> In fra Scilla e Cariddi; et al governo
>> Siede 'l signore, anzi 'l nimico mio.
> A ciascun remo un penser pronto e rio,
>> Che la tempesta e 'l fin par ch'abbi a scherno;
>> La vela rompe un vento, umido, eterno,
>> Di sospir, di speranze e di desio.
> Pioggia di lagrimar, nebbia di sdegni
>> Bagna e rallenta le già stanche sarte,
>> Che son d'error con ignoranzia attorto.
> Celansi i duo miei dolci usati segni;
>> Morta fra l'onde è la ragion e l'arte:
>> Tal ch'i' 'ncomincio a disperar del porto.   (no. clxxxix)

> My galy charged with forgetfulnes
>> Thorrough sharpe sees in wynter nyghtes doeth pas
>> Twene Rock and Rock; and eke myn ennemy, Alas,
>> That is my lorde, sterith with cruelnes;
> And every owre a thought in redines,
>> As tho that deth were light in suche a case.
>> An endles wynd doeth tere the sayll apase
>> Of forced sightes and trusty ferefulnes.
> A rayn of teris, a clowde of derk disdain,
>> Hath done the wered cordes great hinderaunce;
>> Wrethed with errour and eke with ignoraunce.
> The starres be hid that led me to this pain;
>> Drowned is reason that should me consort,
>> And I remain dispering of the port.   (no. 28)

Seafaring, no less than warfare, traditionally expresses the agonizing vicissitudes of love. This sonnet is structurally very similar to 'Amor, che'. The lord of love is at the helm. Every detail of the ship and its passage through the storm fits into a careful allegory of love, with rain as tears, cloud as disdain, guiding stars as Laura, &c. Wyatt, says Hietsch,[1] succeeds on the whole in bringing Petrarch's imagery into English, but the result is not uniform. He has so much material to concentrate within fourteen lines that it is not always possible to follow him without reference to Petrarch.

> A ciascun remo un penser pronto e rio,
>   Che la tempesta e 'l fin par ch'abbi a scherno.

> And every owre a thought in redines,
>   As tho that deth were light in suche a case.

This means that the oars, manned by the 'ready', cruel, thoughts of love, press on suicidally, as though scorning the tempest and death itself. Wyatt's lines do not immediately convey the idea of passion's self-destructiveness. His 'short manner', as in *Quyete of Mynde*, creates difficulties. By contrast, the succinct and beautiful line, 'The starres be hid that led me to this pain', deserves the constant praise it has had. I would draw attention, too, to the skill and sweep of Wyatt's opening:

> My galy charged with forgetfulnes
>   Thorrough sharpe sees in wynter nyghtes doeth pas
>   Twene Rock and Rock.

Like Petrarch's, his rhythm hurtles forward, over the line barriers. The second line succeeds with one of Shakespeare's favourite metrical rhythms: the spondaic 'sharpe sees' draws out the agony splendidly. In the third, 'between Scylla and Charybdis' is tellingly simplified to 'Twene Rock and Rock'. Thus 'My galy charged with forgetfulnes' illustrates a Wyatt struggling, by no means unsuccessfully, with the difficulty of anglicizing Petrarch's style.

In 'I fynde no peace', Wyatt's task ought to be easier, because the meaning of its original is simpler, the rhetoric more imitable, and the rhythmic units shorter. Warfare turns up again in the first line, to be quickly succeeded by other familiar courtly images, such as freezing fire and living death:

[1] *Op. cit.*, p. 105.

Pace non trovo e non ho da far guerra;
  E temo e spero, et ardo e sono un ghiaccio;
  E volo sopra 'l cielo, e giaccio in terra;
  E nulla stringo, e tutto 'l mondo abbraccio....
  E non m'ancide Amor e non mi sferra. (no. cxxxiv)

I fynde no peace and all my warr is done;
  I fere and hope, I burne and freise like yse;
  I fley above the wynde yet can I not arrise;
  And noght I have and all the worold I seson; (*i.e.* seize on) ...
  Nor letteth me lyve nor dye at my devise. (no. 26)

This time the one image is not pursued to its last ramifications, but many parallel images are fixed in a changeless pattern. Instead of a series of ideas unfolded through one image, there is a series of images riveting attention to one idea. Petrarch's rhetoric expresses the contrarieties of love. His antitheses, his half-line phrases, each deliberately repeating the same rhythm, express the sufferer's emotional deadlock. Evenly balanced contraries make any change impossible. Wyatt hammers away at the antitheses, but often misses the rhythmic evenness of his original. Its monotony he expresses in the first two lines, in which he uses a favourite monosyllabic thud of his. But he does not keep this up sufficiently long or with sufficient consistency. Perhaps, for once, Wyatt may justly be blamed for his choice of a sonnet more interesting for its rhetoric than for any psychological or other subtlety. At any rate, he appears, unusually, a prey to empty artifice. For success in this kind of writing, the polish must be perfect, as it is with Petrarch.

Structurally different, again, is the model provided by Petrarch's 'S'una fede amorosa'. Of all the sonnets chosen by Wyatt, this one most resembles the Caritean sonnet, with the weight falling towards the end. The late climax would have suited Surrey's English form. As it is, in Wyatt's version, the rhyming couplet has point:

S'una fede amorosa, un cor non finto,
  Un languir dolce, un desïar cortese;
  S'oneste voglie in gentil foco accese,
  Un lungo error in cieco laberinto;
Se ne la fronte ogni penser depinto,
  Od in voci interrotte a pena intese,
  Or da paura or da vergogna offese;
  S'un pallor di vïola e d'amor tinto;

S'aver altrui piú caro che sé stesso;
  Se sospirare e lagrimar mai sempre,
  Pascendosi di duol, d'ira e d'affanno;
S'arder da lunge et agghiacciar da presso
  Son le cagion ch'amando i'mi distempre;
  Vostro, donna, il peccato, e mio fia 'l danno. (no. ccxxiv)

Yf amours faith, an hert vnfayned,
  A swete languor, a great lovely desire,
  Yf honest will kyndelled in gentill fiere,
  Yf long error in a blynde maze chayned,
Yf in my visage eche thought depaynted
  Or els in my sperklyng voyse lower or higher
  Which nowe fere, nowe shame, wofully doth tyer,
  Yf a pale colour which love hath stayned,
Yf to have an othre then my self more dere,
  Yf wailing and sighting continuelly
  With sorrowfull anger feding bissely,
Yf burning a farr of and fresing nere
  Ar cause that by love my selff I destroye,
  Yours is the fault and myn the great annoye.   (no. 12)

Petrarch's main clause is delayed until the last two lines, lines one to twelve being occupied with conditional clauses, and no climax of any kind occurring at the end of the octave. There is suspense in anticipation of a statement. There is a strong forward motion, yet the steady repetition of 'se' (if) calls for patient listening. Petrarch is a logician, carefully amassing evidence, and, at last, suddenly clinching his case. If, he says, his wailing, sighing, burning, freezing, &c.—his hopeless loving, in fact—are causes of his self-destruction, then the fault lies with Laura, while the grief remains his. The unstated inference is that this is most unfair. Wyatt has certainly chosen a highly congenial sonnet. Blame is a subject that suits the nagging lover of his 'English' lyrics, always detailing his own woes and laying them at the door of an unjust mistress. He simply turns Petrarch word by word and line by line into English. All the main structural features are preserved. Wyatt's literalness, which at times appears dogged, recalls his *Quyete of Mynde*. But, as in *Quyete of Mynde*, his vocabulary has no awkward foreign flavour. Even 'depaynted', his rendering of 'depinto', has a perfectly good English precedent in *Sir Gawayne and the Grene Knight* (line 649).

But Wyatt's interest in Petrarch is not fully explained by his wish to transplant a difficult new form, and this some of his imitations, as distinct from his metaphrases, show. He is a born experimenter, and when he finds a sonnet he wishes to 'imitate' he does not invariably preserve its form. His stanzaic lyric 'O goodely hand' (no. 86) is taken from 'O bella man' (no. cxcix). 'Vinse Anibàl' (no. ciii) becomes the eight-line strambotto, 'Off Cartage he, that worthie warier' (no. 81). 'O cameretta' (no. ccxxxiv) is turned—and here there is a Chaucerian precedent—into three stanzas of rhyme royal (no. 115), a lengthening which involves Wyatt in much repetition. 'Ite, caldi sospiri' (no. cliii) is more successfully handled in two verses (the first of eight, the second of five lines), with the refrain 'Goo burning sighes!' (no. 20). It seems likely here, for instance, that Wyatt's experimental enthusiasm was aroused not so much by Petrarch's matter or form as by the beauty and emphasis of the initial phrase. 'Ite, caldi sospiri', which Petrarch later varies to 'Ite, dolci penser', is attractive because of its possible use as a lyrical refrain. Wyatt, himself so skilled in refrains, has a ready ear.

In handling the Petrarchan madrigal, Wyatt is so independent that its original character is virtually lost. He does not adhere closely either to its form or its matter. The madrigal is not, of course, rule-bound. Antonio Minturno, the sixteenth-century Italian critic, gives examples of from eight to eleven lines, with various rhyme schemes. But he insists, quite properly, that it is a diminutive form ('compositionetta'), dealing always with 'cose rustichette'.[1] Petrarch's 'Or vedi, Amor' (no. cxxi) is an example: a nine-line poem, describing Laura 'in mezzo i fiori e l'erba'. Wyatt's version, 'Behold, love' (no. 1), is a rondeau of fifteen lines, from which he has banished rusticity altogether.

Again, when handling Petrarch's canzoni, which he does on three occasions, Wyatt always alters the form. A 'canzone' is, of course, a 'big' song, just as 'sonetto' is a 'little' one. Minturno identifies the canzoni of Dante and Petrarch with Pindar's odes. Comparing them with the sonnets, he says they are similar in treatment and effect, but different in that they are 'divise in stanze' and in that, having no prescribed number of lines, stanzas or rhymes, they are freer.[2] The stanzas of the canzone vary then, both as to number and length. Each falls into two parts, 'fronte' and 'sirima', the first of which is always repeated, while the second may or may not be. The lines are of eleven and seven

---

[1] *L'Arte Poetica* (Venice, 1563), p. 261.
[2] *Ibid.*, pp. 240, 241.

syllables, variously distributed. The student of prosodic comments from Dante's *De Vulgari Eloquentia* to Minturno's *L'Arte Poetica* would understand the great complexity of the canzone's structure. The casual reader of the *Rime*, however, might take it as any kind of large-scale lyric. Wyatt may have rejected the original form as too difficult. On the other hand, he may simply not have recognized it as a distinct form. Certainly the canzoni he is known to have read present a varied picture, and their common structural elements are not immediately apparent. Furthermore, if Wyatt had any settled policy for dealing with the canzone, it escapes us. No general principle, no particular method, can be deduced from his three attempts. (1) Petrarch's 'Quell' antiquo mio dolce empio signore' (no. ccclx) comprises ten stanzas of fifteen lines apiece and a seven-line envoy. Wyatt's fairly accurate translation, 'Myne olde dere En'mye' (no. 8) is in twenty-one stanzas of rhyme royal. (2) 'Sí è debile il filo' (no. xxxvii) comprises seven sixteen-line stanzas and an eight-line envoy. Wyatt's 'So feble is the threde' (no. 96), again a fairly close version, is not even stanzaically divided but runs on to one hundred lines of poulter's measure. (3) 'S'i''l dissi mai' (no. ccvi) comprises six stanzas of nine lines apiece, and a five-line envoy. It is a technical achievement because Petrarch uses only three rhymes throughout, a feature which Wyatt does not attempt to imitate. Now translating rather more freely, he turns the original into the six light-weight eight-line stanzas of 'Perdye I saide yt not' (no. 134).

Thus in handling the canzone he approximately preserves its length, and, in two cases, its stanzaic structure. In one case, by the use of poulter's measure, with its alternate lines of twelve and fourteen syllables, he copies Petrarch's variation of line-length. He always ignores the envoy and always substitutes his own forms for Petrarch's. There is not enough evidence here, but what there is suggests that Wyatt has comparatively little importance as the purveyor of the Petrarchan canzone into English. Certainly he is the first to translate it, but Spenser should hold his place as the first to construct an English equivalent.

Wyatt's canzoni are not on this account necessarily bad reading. 'Myne olde dere En'mye', with its rhyme royal and court of love setting, reads like a dull medieval poem. Meanwhile the other two represent the best and the worst of Wyatt. 'So feble is the threde' may match Petrarch's canzone to the letter, but it is remote from its spirit. Contrast the delicate Italian endecasillabi and settenarii—

Il tempo passa, e l'ore son sí pronte
A fornire il viaggio,
Ch'assai spazio non aggio
Pur a pensar com'io corro a la morte.—

with Wyatt's lumbering poulter's measure

The tyme doth flete and I perceyve thowrs how thei bend
So fast that I have skant the space to marke my comyng end.

On the other hand, 'Perdye I saide yt not' is a brilliant rendering of
Petrarch in point of tone and style:

Perdye I saide yt not
Nor never thought to do,
As well as I ye wott
I have no powre thereto;
And if I ded, the lott
That first ded me enchaine
Do never slake the knott
But strayt it to my payne.

The whole of this torrential self-justification of the lover accused of
unfaithfulness is founded on the original. The persistent but varied
reiterations, 'S'i''l dissi mai', 'S'i''l dissi', 'Ma, s'io no'l dissi', &c., give
Wyatt his own series, 'And if I ded', 'Yf I saide so', 'And if I ded so
saye', 'Yf I be clere', &c. The whole effect is colloquial and vigorous,
a matter to which I shall have occasion to return in the next chapter.
Sufficient to remark now that Wyatt is here perfectly self-assured, even
building up the violence and bitterness implicit in his original. Thus
the line 'Per Rachel ho servito e non per Lia' gives him the cue for his
own pungent word-play;

Ye kno I never swervid,
Ye never fownd me *lyre*.
For Rachell have I seruid,
(For *Lya* carid I never)

This brings us to Wyatt's alterations, which are often violent and
bitter, of Petrarch's meanings. He is not always the faithful follower.
There is a clear distinction between his metaphrases on the one hand,
and, on the other, his paraphrases and imitations. For while the metaphrase, according to the Renaissance idea of 'Poetical Translation', is

bound to follow its original 'word by word, and line by line', the para-phrase is permitted 'latitude' and the imitation 'liberty'.[1]

Petrarch's 'Io non fu' d'amar' (no. lxxxii) describes how weary the lover is with long weeping for one who disdains him; and he protests that he would rather have an uninscribed tomb, 'un sepolcro bello e bianco', than one recording that he died for love of Laura. In 'Was I never yet of your love greved' (no. 9), Wyatt is far from repudiating the whole of Petrarch's central theme. But, availing himself of the para-phraser's latitude, he chooses to reject the tomb altogether, as a refuge for the disappointed lover: 'I will not yet in my grave be buried'. Petrarch concludes that he would be thankful to have no longer to love on in this hopeless way: 'Di che Amor e me stesso assai rin-grazio'. Wyatt concludes with something more like a threat to the lady, and a much severer note of blame: 'And ye yourself the cause therof hath bene'. Certainly the lover's behaviour, as rendered by Wyatt, is more rebellious, selfish, and human than the original warrants. It is 'courtly' after a different style. There is, very evidently, a difference between the amorous Tudor courtier and Dante's Italian successor.

Wyatt's conversion of Petrarch's lament for the deaths of his patron Colonna and mistress Laura into a lament for his own patron, Crom-well, involves considerable revision. The punning allusions of the first line could have no meaning for him: 'Rotta è l'alta colonna e'l verde lauro' (no. cclxix). He therefore at the outset departs from his model, giving also a more distinctly personal opening: 'The piller pearisht is whearto I lent' (no. 173). There follows in both sonnets an expression of personal grief, with Petrarch's 'sorrowful *soul*' (l'alma trista') becom-ing, characteristically, Wyatt's 'wofull *hart*'. But it is the conclusions that differ most markedly. Petrarch's reflects, in general terms, on how easy it is to lose in one morning what has taken many years to acquire. The tone is one of philosophical and elegiac melancholy:

> Oh nostra vita ch'è sí bella in vista,
> Com' perde agevolmente in un mattino
> Quel che 'n molti anni a gran pena s'acquista!

Wyatt's conclusion strikes a more intense note, that of personal mortification:

> My mynde in woe, my bodye full of smart,
> And I my self, my self always to hate,
> Till dreadfull death do ease my dolefull state?

[1] See John Dryden, *Essays*, ed. W. P. Ker (Oxford, 1900), i. 237.

Wyatt, who does not confine himself to Petrarch's love themes, achieves a rather similar effect in his imitation of 'Vinse Anibàl' (no. ciii). Petrarch's sonnet is an exhortation to his lord, Stefano Colonna, to pursue his victory over the Orsini, the general moral being the need to make effective use of advantages gained. Hannibal's failure in this respect contains a warning. In the strambotto, 'Off Cartage he' (no. 81), Wyatt applies all this very neatly, not to a patron but to himself. He is Hannibal. 'Restles ... in Spayne', when his personal fortunes hang in 'balaunce', he feels he has failed to exploit opportunities gained by 'long indeuer'. There is, again, a sense of personal frustration that is very far from Petrarch's considered advice.

In some of his imitations, Wyatt tends to simplify. He will elaborate upon only one of Petrarch's several themes or images. His content is consequently less rich, but he often intensifies a feeling, idea, or image to good purpose. If he ignored certain special features of the madrigal 'Or vedi, Amor' (no. cxxi), he found a congenial idea in it, for it invokes the vengeance of Love upon the disdainful Laura. 'Behold, love' dispenses with Petrarch's description of the careless young lady sitting barefoot among grass and flowers, in order to draw out more fully the lover's irritation:

> ... yet she bideth sure
> Right at her ease and litle she dredeth.   (no. 1)

Wyatt is no painter of nature or external beauty. It is characteristic of him to sacrifice the variety given by concrete visual detail to a monotonous emphasis on a dominant emotion.

He deals similarly with 'Vive faville' (no. cclviii), a sonnet on the bewildering effect of Laura's sudden favour, coming after so many rebuffs. Her eyes shine upon him, while wisdom and 'high eloquence' issue from her: a description that establishes her status as more that of the Dantesque instructress than of the wayward Tudor mistress, blowing hot and cold. But the lover's soul, schooled so long in sorrow, cannot readily adjust itself to this new treatment. He remains in a highly complex state of insecurity, the account of which at once sets Petrarch apart, for subtlety, from conventional dabblers in love's contrarieties. Wyatt's 'The lyvely sperkes' (no. 47) builds only on the initial image of the eyes. Excluding Laura's wisdom altogether, he describes at much greater length the dazzled state of the lover, which is only Petrarch's starting point. 'Dased ame I', 'Blynded with the stroke'— so Wyatt reiterates at points (lines 8 and 10) where Petrarch is reaching his analysis of the reactions of a soul nourished on sorrow: 'L'alma nudrita sempre in doglia e 'n pene' (line 9).

Wyatt's lyric 'O goodely hand' (no. 86) again simply takes an image, that of the hand, from Petrarch's sonnet 'O bella man' (no. cxcix); and, as both content and form are changed, he produces what is virtually a new poem. Petrarch reflects on the glove he has stolen and must return: 'O incostanzia de l'umane cose!' (O, inconstancy of human things!). But Wyatt, less concerned with general reflections, spends his energies on a characteristically urgent and personal plea: 'Consent at last'.

The Petrarchan poems, metaphrases apart, do therefore suggest an 'essential difference' between Wyatt and Petrarch. Indeed, scholars have usually found Wyatt's divergences from his sources more fascinating than his conformities with them. A. K. Foxwell long ago remarked on his habit of omitting Petrarch's descriptions of the beauty of nature or mistress to investigate more fully 'attitudes of mind'.[1] And since his own attitude of mind is his chief concern, he has frequently been found more egotistical than Petrarch. E. K. Chambers also noticed the absence of the 'circumambient penumbra of spirituality' in which Laura is veiled,[2] and J. W. Lever gives a striking instance of Wyatt's 'cynical and rebellious' handling of Petrarch.[3] The comparison of texts which I have made above does to a considerable extent bear all this out. So far so good. Yet a judgement of Wyatt as self-motivated rebel against Petrarch should not be precipitated. Some comparatively neglected precedents for what he does should first be taken into account: the precedents provided by the Petrarchan commentators.

(v) *Wyatt and the Petrarchan Commentators*

John Florio remarked, in 1598, that Petrarch might well disown his own commentators: 'A thousand strappadas coulde not compell him to confesse, what some interpreters will make him saie he ment.'[4] At about the same time, Henry Constable exploited their bewildering variety in a sonnet 'To his Mistrisse vpon occasion of a Petrarch he gaue her, shewing her the reason why the Italian Commenters dissent so much in the exposition thereof'.[5] Petrarch, he wittily contends, was

---

[1] Foxwell, ii. 48.

[2] *Sir Thomas Wyatt and Some Collected Studies* (London, 1933), p. 129.

[3] *Op. cit.*, p. 25.

[4] *A Worlde of Wordes* (London, 1598), sig. a 4ʳ.

[5] *The Poems of Henry Constable*, ed. Joan Grundy. English Texts and Studies (Liverpool, 1960).

foretelling in 'parables' the coming of Constable's mistress, and hence the Italians have all been baffled. Thus the Petrarchan glosses even provide a new conceit for Petrarchan love poetry. Every sixteenth-century student knew of their variety and disagreements.

Wyatt could hardly escape this common knowledge. His evident freedom in interpretation may therefore owe something to the editions and commentaries he consulted, while a general allowance should certainly be made for his awareness that the *Rime* could be approached and understood in more than one way. There is also a strong prior supposition that Wyatt did consult the Petrarchan commentaries. A large number of fifteenth- and sixteenth-century editions contain these alongside the text, so that the eye, even of a casual reader, cannot escape them. Consequently, editions and commentaries up to and including the years 1527–42 could have relevance to his interpretations.

Petrarch's vernacular poems were first printed in 1470, and in 1471 came the first of the annotated editions, Antonio da Tempo's. From then on there was a constant flow of new editions and commentaries, most of which were reprinted and added to again and again. Besides da Tempo, the chief of the early commentators were Francesco Filelfo and Girolamo Squarciafico. Filelfo's incomplete commentary was first published in 1476, and in successive editions (from about 1483) Squarciafico's additions were published with it. The notes of all three of these early interpreters of Petrarch are found together in *Li Sonetti Canzone Trivmphi del Petrarcha con li soi Commenti*, published by Bernardino Stagnino in Venice in 1519. (Stagnino carefully distinguishes his contributors, and so it will be convenient to quote their remarks below from this edition.) His volume illustrates some general features of the first phase in Petrarchan interpretation: for instance, it tends to perpetuate legends of Petrarch and Laura which have no foundation in fact or in the text, and also to abstract a philosophy or 'message' for all lovers even from Petrarch's most personal utterances.

A new phase was inaugurated in 1525 by Alessandro Vellutello, and, to a lesser extent, by Pietro Bembo. *Le Volgari Opere del Petrarcha con la Espositione di Alessandro Vellvtello da Lvcca*, published in Venice, incorporated the most thorough research to date into the lives of Petrarch and Laura, as well as the most scientific investigation of the text. Vellutello paid two visits to the scene of Petrarch's love for Laura, the district of Vaucluse in the Rhône valley, of which his edition includes a map. He satisfied himself that Laura was an unmarried woman, but was able, on historical grounds, to refute Antonio da Tempo's myth that the Pope had wished Petrarch to marry her. On such evidence as he could find Vellutello himself now reconstructed what has been called 'il vero romanzo di Messer Francesco e di Madonna Laura';[1] and, in handling the text, he tried to draw out the progressive story inherent in it and to give a sense of earthly happenings. He completely rearranged the order of the sonnets, remarking that while each exists for itself, yet some are obviously connected. Vellutello resembles certain interpreters of Shakespeare's sonnets in that he establishes his text as a highly personal document. His comments have no abstract tendencies but always refer particularly to the contents of the sonnet before him. For instance, to introduce 'Mie venture al venir son tarde e pigre' (no. lvii) he says simply that Petrarch is here lamenting his own unhappy fate: 'Duolsi il Poe. nel presente So. della sua trista sorte' (f. 65^r). Filelfo, by contrast, had emphasized its general purport as a demonstration of a quality common in all lovers, who always find themselves in unpleasant and 'contrary' situations: 'dimostra la qualita de gli innamorati: che sempre si trouano in possessione repugnante contrarie' (1519 edition ff. 49^v–50^r).

Concerned as he was with Petrarch's sentiments, Vellutello's references to style and technique are brief. His 'Proemio' does, however, draw attention to the fact that Pietro Bembo's study of 'l'arte, figure, et rettorici colori' had just been given to the press. The *Prose di M. Pietro Bembo nelle quali si ragiona della Volgar Lingua* was published in Venice in September 1525, only one month after Vellutello's edition. The two complement each other. The early piece of 'aesthetic' criticism—Bembo examines such matters as Petrarch's use of musical vowels and consonants—is also important in the history of Petrarchan interpretation. From this point on the sonnets to Laura could be read as a philosophical treatise or a biography, as a manual of love or of style.

Wyatt entered the arena at this particularly lively moment in the history of Petrarchan interpretation. When he visited Italy the 1519 edition (with the commentaries of da Tempo, Filelfo, and Squarciafico) was only eight years old and Vellutello's only two. In 1527 the tide was still turning. *Il Petrarcha colla Spositione di Misser Giovanni Andrea Gesualdo*, first published in 1533, continued Vellutello's work to a large extent; and Gesualdo himself is an interesting critic in that his fondness for refuting or confirming earlier interpretations keeps their

[1] L Baldacci, *Il Petrarchismo Italiano nel Cinquecento* (Milan and Naples, 1957), p. 52.

variety before the reader's eye. Meanwhile, Vellutello's commentary, of which there were twenty-seven editions between 1525 and 1584, established itself as the most popular of the sixteenth century. But it was not until 1558, after his death, that Bembo's comments were abstracted from the *Prose* and embodied in an edition of Petrarch's poems. The effect of all this on Wyatt's general attitude to Petrarch is open to surmise. He had probably heard of Bembo, one of whose canzoni he paraphrased,[1] but he need not have read the *Prose*. Of the editors, he had more in common with the modern Vellutello than with the old-fashioned Filelfo. For instance, his 'Ever myn happe is slack and slo in commyng' (no. 30) is a fairly accurate translation of the sonnet mentioned above, 'Mie venture'; and it is obvious that the strongly personal tone of this and other of Wyatt's renderings of Petrarch reflects more of Vellutello's subjective emphasis than of Filelfo's generalized one.

If nothing else, Wyatt simply gleaned information and cleared up obscurities by glancing at the commentaries alongside the text of Petrarch's poems. For instance, the reference to Scipio Africanus in stanza xiii of 'Myne olde dere En'mye' (no. 8) derives from a note on stanza vii of the original, Petrarch's canzone 'Quell'antiquo mio dolce empio signore' (no. ccclx). The text gives a list of great men who met disaster through the treachery of women, Agamemnon, Achilles, Hannibal, and 'another';

> E di tutti il piú chiaro
> Un altro e di vertute e di fortuna   (lines 93–4)

In the 1519 edition 'l'altro' is explained as probably Scipio but possibly Alexander the Great (f. 150ᵛ) while Vellutello, without any hesitation, states that he is 'lo primo Scipione Aphricano' (f. 160ᵛ). Hence Wyatt's 'the Affricane Scipion' (line 88).

A much greater difficulty is presented by the text of 'Perch'io t'abbia guardato di menzogna' (no. xlix), the original of 'Bicause I have the still kept fro lyes and blame' (no. 25). Petrarch's sonnet laments the fact that he can sigh and weep enough in solitude, but is tongue-tied and dry-eyed before Laura. The meaning is clear to Wyatt, except for one passage:

> Lagrime triste, e voi tutte le notti
> M'accompagnate, ov'io vorrei star solo,
> Poi fuggite di nanzi a la mia pace.

[1] See Rudolf Gottfried, 'Sir Thomas Wyatt and Pietro Bembo', *N.Q.*, cxcix (1954), 278–80.

And ye salt teres again my will eche nyght
That are with me when fayn I would be alone,
Then are ye gone when I should make my mone.

Petrarch's tears 'flee before his peace': 'Poi fuggite di nanzi a la mia pace'. Filelfo explains the inference of this somewhat obscure statement by indicating that Petrarch cannot utter the necessary sighs in the presence of one to whom he would like to reveal the griefs of his heart : 'non hauer potuto anche gittare sospiri grandi & focosi come sarebbero stati necessarii in presentia di lei a cui harebbe voluto in aguato aprire li soi cordiali affanni' (f. 43^r). Vellutello's simpler note states that Petrarch's tears disappear when he is in Laura's presence, that is, just at the very moment when they might effectively help to move her to compassion: 'quando egli è alla presentia di lei, & che per muouerla a compassione di lui vorrebbe lagrimare, non ne puo hauer una' (f. 66^r). Hence Wyatt's 'Then are ye gone when I should make my mone', a line owing more to the commentaries than to the text. On the face of it, to substitute 'when I should make my mone' for 'di nanzi a la mia pace' appears unduly 'free', and it certainly has the effect of emphasizing Wyatt's personal grievance. If, then, this is an instance of Wyatt's reputed rebelliousness and egotism, it is one which is sanctioned by the Petrarchan commentators. And what led him into it in this case was obviously simply the difficulty of understanding Petrarch.

The next example seems to illustrate Wyatt's habit of twisting Petrarch's meaning to suit his own more urgent and worldly interest in the business of wooing.

> Pien d'un vago penser, che mi desvia
>   Da tutti gli altri e fammi al mondo ir solo,
>   Ad or ad ora a me stesso m'involo,
>   Pur lei cercando che fuggir devria;
> E veggiola passar sí dolce e ria
>   Che l'alma trema per levarsi a volo,
>   Tal d'armati sospir conduce stuolo
>   Questa bella d'Amor nemica e mia.
> Ben, s'i' non erro, di pietate un raggio
>   Scorgo fra 'l nubiloso altero ciglio,
>   Che 'n parte rasserena il cor doglioso:
> Allor raccolgo l'alma, e, poi ch'i'aggio
>   Di scovrirle il mio mal preso consiglio,
>   Tanto gli ho a dir che 'ncominciar non oso.   (no. clxix)

Suche vayn thought as wonted to myslede me,
    In desert hope by well assured mone,
    Maketh me from compayne to live alone,
    In folowing her whome reason bid me fle.
She fleith as fast by gentill crueltie,
    And after her myn hert would fain be gone;
    But armed sighes my way do stoppe anone,
    Twixt hope and drede locking my libertie.
Yet, as I gesse, vnder disdaynfull browe
    One beame of pitie is in her clowdy loke,
    Whiche comforteth the mynde that erst for fere shoke;
And therwithall bolded I seke the way how
    To vtter the smert that I suffre within,
    But suche it is I not how to begyn.   (no. 56)

Petrarch's soul, overcome by the sweet agony of following the evasive Laura, trembles to be gone: 'l'alma trema per levarsi a volo' (line 6). But later, on discerning a ray of pity, he is cheered and recalls his soul: 'Allor raccolgo l'alma' (line 12). These are now generally taken to refer to Petrarch's wish for death (the flight of the soul from the body) and to a last minute revival of the wish to live. Wyatt, however, takes line six to imply a renewal of the chase of courtship, in which the heart, not the soul, is involved: 'And after her myn hert would fain be gone'. And likewise line twelve becomes a direct description of his state of feeling and progress in wooing: 'And therwithall bolded.' Yet Wyatt is not so unorthodox as he appears, for the early commentators do not mention the desire for death. Da Tempo and Squarciafico give very brief summaries of the whole sonnet, describing Petrarch's wish to declare his feelings to Laura and how eventually he sees pity in her eyes (f. 98v). Vellutello gives a much longer note with detailed paraphrases of the difficult lines (f. 91r). And this has a close bearing on Wyatt's rendering. Vellutello stresses throughout Petrarch's pursuit of Laura ('cercando pur M.L.') and the need for her to retreat ('dourebbe fuggire'). For him line six means that Petrarch's soul is trembling, because, seeing such sweetness in Laura, it dare no more: 'trema & non ardisce per la rigidita, dalla qual uede tal dolcezza in lei essere accompagnata'. And when Laura shows pity, Petrarch recalls his soul, that is, he regains his confidence: 'Allhor raccolgo l'alma, cio è allhor ripiglio l'ardire'. 'Ripiglio l'ardire' fully sanctions Wyatt's 'therwithall bolded', for 'ardire' means 'to dare' and 'ardimento' 'boldness'. 'And after her myn hert would fain be gone' remains somewhat free, nor has

Wyatt's omission of all Pertarch's references to the soul a source in Vellutello. Working upon Vellutello's hints, Wyatt makes this a sonnet solely about the adventures of the heart. He is an amorous poet who has no wish to carry his sorrows to the grave: the modern interpretation of Petrarch's sonnet would not have appealed to him. He may not have heard of other interpretations of it, though line six became a controversial matter. Gesualdo (1533) thought that Petrarch was alluding to the fact that in the act of sighing the soul breaks free of the body, in support of which he cited Diogenes.[1] The view that Laura's disdain caused Petrarch to desire death ('è cagione, ch'egli morir desidera') is found in Daniello's edition.[2] But these interpretations were not only uncongenial, they were probably also too late to cause any echoes in Wyatt's version. Vellutello's is the main influence here.

Even in one of his imitations—where, because he is working freely, it might be least expected—Wyatt takes hints from the commentators. 'Who so list to hount', interestingly enough, is not only among his most successful imitations, but also among his most un-Petrarchan, worldly, and egotistical. There is no intention to suggest, in what follows, that Wyatt minutely studied and sized up all the comments mentioned. Gesualdo's would, in any case, be too late if his poem is to be dated by affairs at the Tudor court, c. 1527. The inference merely is that the comments represent ideas in general circulation and that Wyatt read, or heard of, them or their like.

> Una candida cerva sopra l'erba
> Verde m'apparve, con duo corna d'oro,
> Fra due riviere, a l'ombra d'un alloro,
> Levando 'l sole, a la stagione acerba.
> Era sua vista sí dolce superba,
> Ch'i' lasciai per seguirla ogni lavoro;
> Come l'avaro che 'n cercar tesoro
> Con diletto l'affanno disacerba.
> 'Nessun mi tocchi.' al bel collo d'intorno
> Scritto avea di diamanti e di topazi;
> 'Libera farmi al mio Cesare parve.'
> Et era 'l sol già vòlto al mezzo giorno;
> Gli occhi miei stanchi di mirar, non sazi;
> Quand'io caddi ne l'acqua, et ella sparve.   (no. cxc)

[1] *Il Petrarcha* (Venice, 1541), f. 220ᵛ. (The first edition of 1533 has not been available.)

[2] *Sonetti, Canzoni, e Triomphi di Messer Francesco Petrarcha con la Spositione di Bernardino Daniello da Lvcca* (Venice, 1541), f. 113ʳ.

> Who so list to hount, I knowe where is an hynde,
>   But as for me, helas, I may no more:
>   The vayne travaill hath weried me so sore.
>   I ame of theim that farthest commeth behinde;
> Yet may I by no meanes my weried mynde
>   Drawe from the Diere: but as she fleeth afore,
>   Faynting I folowe. I leve of therefore,
>   Sins in a nett I seke to hold the wynde.
> Who list her hount, I put him owte of dowbte,
>   As well as I may spend his tyme in vain:
>   And, graven with Diamonds, in letters plain
> There is written her faier neck rounde abowte:
>   *Noli me tangere*, for Cesars I ame;
>   And wylde for to hold, though I seme tame.   (no. 7)

Petrarch's sonnet describes his symbolic vision of a white hind, which appeared before him one spring morning and which he gazed at avidly until it tragically disappeared from the beautiful landscape just before noon. The inscriptions on the hind's collar bear witness to its inaccessibility: 'Nessun me tocchi' and 'Libera farmi al mio Cesare parve' ('Touch me not' and 'It has pleased my lord to set me free'). The sonnet is open to a wide variety of interpretations, but all commentators naturally agree that, the white hind being Laura, it reflects a phase in Petrarch's protracted love for her. The atmosphere is dream-like, the imagery picturesque, and the sentiment pathetic.

Wyatt converts Petrarch's contemplation of the hind into a prolonged metaphor from hunting. Far from doting on his 'Diere' he has sickened of the 'vayne travaill'; and soon he advises others to abandon the pursuit of what is obviously a wayward court lady:

> Who list her hount, I put him owte of dowbte,
>   As well as I may spend his tyme in vain,

For the lady is already booked:

> *Noli me tangere*, for Cesars I ame;
> And wylde for to hold, though I seme tame.

The atmosphere is far from dream-like, the picturesque description of the countryside has gone, and the sentiment is arrogant and cynical. To describe the pursuit of an inaccessible lady as so much time spent 'in vain' is to aim a blow at the foundation of the sentiment of courtly love common to Petrarch and the Petrarchans. Wyatt takes only the idea for his hunting metaphor and a few details from Petrarch's text. But there are still the commentaries.

All the commentators give virtually the same note on the inscriptions on the hind's collar. 'Noli me tangere quia Caesaris sum', they say, was a well known Latin motto. It had been inscribed on the collars of Caesar's hinds, which were then set free but which no man ever presumed to touch or harm. Wyatt's *'Noli me tangere*, for Cesars I ame' is translated not from Petrarch's text but from the motto in the margin of one of the editions. There is consequently no need to refer Wyatt's phrasing to the influence of Romanello's 'Una cerva gentil', a sonnet itself based on Petrarch's:

> Tocar non lice la mia carne intera
> CAESARIS.   Enim sum . . .[1]

for both Wyatt and Romanello were drawing on the same source: the well-known story told by the commentators. This story could also have suggested to Wyatt the notion of 'Caesar's' exclusive ownership, which is by no means conveyed in Petrarch's 'it has pleased Caesar to *set me free*'.

Wyatt's hunting scene, with its lively impression of a crowd of eager rivals, is remote from the spirit of Petrarch. For, though Petrarch's whole story could be said to recount his pursuit of Laura, sonnet no. cxc has none of the heat of an active pursuit, and his contemplation of Laura also appears quite solitary. Squarciafico, however, hinted that others might be involved when he made the strange suggestion that the two rivers of the landscape represented the beauty of Laura which was desired by so many: 'la sua belleza che da molte era desiderata' (f. 103^r). Gesualdo, abandoning the contemplative element, described Petrarch's scene in terms very like Wyatt's. The poet, he says, is in pursuit of Laura and describes the 'amorous chase' by taking a metaphor from huntsmen: 'il Poeta descriue l'amorosa caccia prendendo la metaphora da cacciatori' (f. 236^{r-v}). Therefore, whether Wyatt had read Gesualdo's commentary or not, Petrarch's metaphor of the elusive hind impressed him in the same way.

Wyatt's portrait of the wild seeming-tame lady owes nothing to either Petrarch or the commentators. All the latter stress Laura's modesty: 'pudicitia' is Squarciafico's term (f. 103^r). Most comment on the moral force of the symbols: the whiteness of the hind indicates Laura's purity, the hind itself is sacred to the chaste Diana and so on. Wyatt retains only the symbol of the diamonds with which the hind's

---

[1] Giovanni Antonio Romanello, *Rhythmorvm Vvlgarivm* (Verona, n.d. ?1480), Sonnet no. iii. Cp. Foxwell, ii. 30.

collar is 'graven': and this suggests considerable irony, in view of its original force as a symbol of what Vellutello calls 'ferma costantia contra ogni ribolliment lasciuo' (f. 149^v).

Wyatt's lady, in a sense, 'disappears' just as Laura does: at least she is lost to him. But the implications of the disappearance and loss appear to differ widely in the two cases. The view that Petrarch's sonnet is a presage of Laura's death has proved acceptable, in spite of the fact that it occurs rather too early in the sequence. Among early interpreters, Vellutello says that Laura disappears in passing to the other life ('passando a l'altra uita sparue'); and that her death occurs just before noon because she was then, aged thirty-four, near to the middle of the life-span ('uicina al mezzo del suo corso uitale') (f. 150^r). That did not, however, settle the question, and a minor commentator, Silvano da Venafro, is content merely to say that Laura disappeared in the direction of her home: 'ella sparue andandosene nel suo albergo'.[1] At least, therefore, it was possible, in Wyatt's day, to interpret this episode more mundanely than Vellutello.

The loss of the lady is naturally closely connected with her relationship to Caesar, whatever it may be. 'Who so list to hount' may refer to Henry VIII's appropriation of Anne Boleyn. At any rate it describes the loss of a mistress to some lordly husband or master, and the consequent futility, even danger, of pursuing her further. This will again seem remote from Petrarch's sonnet if it is taken as a presage of Laura's death. For in this view, Laura has been set free from life by Caesar, and Caesar is inevitably God: 'M.L. fatta libera dal suo Cesare, inteso per lo suo & nostro sommo Iddio' is Vellutello's summing-up (f. 149^v). But, again, Wyatt could have chosen to interpret the sonnet on a more mundane level. Squarciafico cites Filelfo's opinion that Laura was married; and that 'Libera farmi al mio Cesare parve' is a reference to the imperial law that a married woman is subject to none but her husband: 'per legge imperiale nessuna donna maritata era subieta ad altro che al suo marito' (f. 103^v). This is certainly something more like the relationships that Wyatt has in mind; and Gesualdo's comments insist further on the legal danger of tampering with another man's property. Petrarch, he says, alludes to the marriage law decreed by Caesar and means that Laura must suffer no molestation: 'per Cesare intendono la maritale legge da Cesare ordinata, per laquale dee esser solo del suo marito e d'ogni altra persona libera si, che nessuno molesto esser le debba' (f. 237^r). Inclined to follow Vellutello in believing that

[1] *Il Petrarca col Commento di M. Sylvano da Venaphro* (Naples, 1533), f. 142^v.

Laura was unmarried, Gesualdo gives an alternative: in this case the reference is to the law *de Adulteris* of the dictator Julius Caesar: 'la Giulia legge de Adulteris ordinata da Cesare Giulio dittatore'. The explanation that follows becomes so confusing that Gesualdo breaks off with the excuse that it would take too long to expound it fully. It is obviously a fantastic notion. However, the present concern is not to establish the validity of any one interpretation of sonnet no. cxc, but to illustrate the variety of interpretations open to a sixteenth-century reader like Wyatt.

The inference is that it was not, as it were, obligatory for Wyatt to read 'Una candida cerva' as an unearthly vision of a sublime lady whose Lord and Master claimed her for Heaven. It is hardly necessary to add, on the other hand, that the commentaries do not yield the total meaning of 'Who so list to hount'. None equates the virtuous Laura with such a 'wild' court lady as Wyatt describes, or so much as hints that her admirers are wasting their time in loving her; and Filelfo, Vellutello, and Gesualdo would alike have been amazed at so cynical a 'version' of Petrarch's love story. Their freedom in interpretation becomes, perhaps, Wyatt's licence. And, as a born experimenter, as a habitual gleaner of foreign ideas, above all, as a genius, Wyatt would have little difficulty in combining academic notes with his own courtly experiences and transforming both into an original poem. Genius is not, I hope, too emotive a term here. 'Who so list to hount' is, at any rate, the product of a poet's mind, and 'The poet's mind is in fact a receptacle for seizing and storing up numberless feelings, phrases, images, which remain there until all the particles which can unite to form a new compound are present together.'[1]

Hence this attempt to explain Wyatt's rebelliousness partly in terms of the sixteenth-century climate of Petrarchan opinion is by no means aimed at undermining his reputation for originality. That originality will also appear in sharper relief by contrast with Surrey.

(vi) Surrey and Petrarch

Like Wyatt, Surrey chooses mainly from the 'In Vita' sequence. Only one of his five versions of Petrarch derives from the 'In Morte'. This one, 'The soote season' (no. 2), is an imitation of 'Zefiro torna' (no. cccx) and neglects entirely its love theme and its reference to Laura in Heaven. Surrey therefore appears no more interested than Wyatt in

---

[1] T. S. Eliot, *op. cit.*, p. 19.

Petrarch's transcendentalism. Indeed, he seems neither concerned, like Petrarch, with the value of love, not involved, like Wyatt, in the experience of loving. His original poems addressed to Geraldine bear this out. His feelings about his lady are neither so complex as Petrarch's nor so turbulent as Wyatt's.

> Bryght ys her hew, and Geraldine shee highte;
> Hampton me tawght to wishe her furst for myne;
> And Windesor, alas! doth chace me from her sight.
> Bewty of kind, her vertues from above,
> Happy ys he that may obtaine her love.   (no. 29)

Surrey's declaration that Geraldine's 'vertues' come 'from above' does not amount to more than a compliment. He is neither intellectually nor emotionally involved to the same degree as Petrarch and Wyatt. He is not interested in metaphysics. He is distinctly factual. The facts about Hampton Court and Windsor Castle are moving because they are simply stated, and this is where Surrey is strong. His manners, too, are good. His is a gallant love poetry, pointing forward to the gracious complimentary verse of Elizabeth's court. Petrarchanism is, with Surrey, made comparatively superficial, frothy, and gay.

Like 'Love that doth raine', the other two translations by Surrey have a confident regularity, and they are, if anything, rather more accurate.

> I neuer saw youe, madam, laye aparte
> Your cornet black, in colde nor yet in heate,   (no. 3)

follows Petrarch's fourteen-line ballata practically line by line:

> Lassare il velo o per sole o per ombra,
> Donna, non vi vid'io.   (no. xi)

All that Surrey has to do is to puff out the short lines to fit his own monosyllables. So, 'Sí mi governa il velo' becomes 'So doth this cornet governe me, *a lacke*!'

The puffiness is more marked in 'Set me wheras the sonne', and this translation also illustrates Surrey's tendency to replace Petrarch's metaphors by literal description.

> Pommi ove 'l sole occide i fiori e l'erba
> O dove vince lui il ghiaccio e la neve;
> Pommi ov' è 'l carro suo temprato e leve
> Et ov' è chi ce 'l rende o chi ce 'l serba:

Pommi in umil fortuna od in superba,
  Al dolce aere sereno al fosco e greve;
  Pommi a la notte, al dí lungo ed al breve,
  A la matura etate od a l'acerba:
Pommi in cielo od in terra od in abisso,
  In alto poggio in valle ima e palustre,
  Libero spirto od a' suoi membri affisso:
Pommi con fama oscura o con illustre:
  Sarò qual fui, vivrò com'io son visso,
  Continuando il mio sospir trilustre.   (no. cxlv)

Set me wheras the sonne dothe perche the grene,
Or whear his beames may not dissolue the ise,
In temprat heat, wheare he is felt and sene;
With prowde people, in presence sad and wyse;
Set me in base, or yet in highe degree;
In the long night, or in the shortyst day;
In clere weather, or whear mysts thickest be;
In lofte yowthe, or when my heares be grey;
Set me in earthe, in heauen, or yet in hell;
In hill, in dale, or in the fowming floode;
Thrawle, or at large, aliue whersoo I dwell;
Sike, or in healthe; in yll fame, or in good;
Yours will I be, and with that onely thought
Comfort my self when that my hape is nowght.   (no. 6)

Contrast their first lines:

Pommi ove 'l sole occide i fiori e l'erba
(Set me where the sun kills the flowers and the grass)
Set me wheras the sonne dothe perche the grene.

Petrarch's 'flowers and grass' become the 'green', while his metaphor 'kills' becomes the literal 'parch'. In the second line Surrey is again satisfied with 'ice' where Petrarch has 'ice and snow', and with the literal 'dissolve' in place of the metaphorical 'conquers':

O dove vince lui il ghiaccio e la neve
(Or where he conquers the ice and snow)
Or whear his beames may not dissolue the ise.

The omission of items like flowers and snow might not seem to matter much were it not that Surrey fills the gap with unimportant words such as 'doth', 'may', and 'not' (this last reversing Petrarch's sense). He seems slightly verbose. Fortunately, Petrarch's sonnet is one of his most leisurely in style and least concentrated in thought. The gist of it is simply 'set me here or there, high or low, &c., and I shall remain what I have been (*i.e.* constant to Laura)'. The simple listing, the catalogue of human states, together with a regular antithesis and much emphatic repetition of the 'Pommi' ('Set me') phrase, makes the sonnet adaptable to Surrey's particular gifts. The rhythmic balance of the antitheses is maintained far better than in Wyatt's 'I fynde no peace'. The key phrase 'Set me', introducing his three quatrains, gives solid support to Surrey's structure. He manifests, in fact, his usual firm control. He makes a sensible revision of the last line, which refers to Petrarch's fifteen-year-old sighs ('il mio sospir trilustre'). Otherwise the translation must have been plain sailing. Surrey's addition of 'With prowde people, in presence sad and wyse' to the list of human states is vivid, but the same cannot be said of his inane addition to line eleven, 'aliue whersoo I dwell'. Nevertheless, on the whole, this sonnet shows Surrey most at his ease with Petrarch, that is, with a Petrarch simpler, more relaxed, and less reflective than usual.

Surrey's two imitations manifest the expected 'liberty', but in rather different ways. 'The soote season' is a drastic simplification of 'Zefiro torna'. Surrey destroys the Petrarchan structure completely, and replaces it by a Caritean one. While its meaning resembles Petrarch's, its structure resembles, for example, that of 'Col tempo' by the Caritean poet Serafino. Here, for comparison, are the three sonnets:

Zefiro torna, e 'l bel tempo rimena,
　E i fiori e l'erbe, sua dolce famiglia,
　E garrir Progne e pianger Filomena,
　E primavera candida e vermiglia.
Ridono i prati e 'l ciel si rasserena;
　Giove s'allegra di mirar sua figlia;
　L'aria e l'acqua e la terra è d'amor piena;
　Ogni animal d'amar si riconsiglia.
Ma per me, lasso!, tornano i piú gravi
　Sospiri, che del cor profondo tragge
　Quella ch'al ciel se ne portò le chiavi;
E cantar augelletti e fiorir piagge
　E 'n belle donne oneste atti soavi
　Sono un deserto e fere aspre e selvagge.　(no. cccx)

The soote season, that bud and blome furth bringes,
With grene hath clad the hill and eke the vale;
The nightingale with fethers new she singes;
The turtle to her make hath tolde her tale.
Somer is come, for euery spray nowe springes;
The hart hath hong his olde hed on the pale;
The buck in brake his winter cote he flings;
The fishes flote with newe repaired scale;
The adder all her sloughe awaye she slinges;
The swift swallow pursueth the flyes smale;
The busy bee her honye now she minges.
Winter is worne, that was the flowers bale.
And thus I see among these pleasant thinges
Eche care decayes, and yet my sorow springes. (no. 2)

Col tempo passa glianni, i mesi, e lhore
  Col tempo le richezze, imperio, e regno
  Col tempo fama, honor, forteza, e ingegno
  Col tempo giouentú con beltá more
Col tempo manca ciascuna herba e fiore
  Col tempo ogni arbor torna un secco legno
  Col tempo passa guerra, ingiuria, a sdegno
  Col tempo fugge & parte ogni dolore
Col tempo el tempo chiar sinturba e imbruna
  Col tempo ogni piacer finisce e stanca
  Col tempo el mar tranquillo há gran fortuna
Col tempo in acqua uien la neue bianca
  Col tempo perde suo splendor la luna
  Ma in me giamai amor con tempo manca.
(sonnet no. cxxxii)[1]

Petrarch's octave describes the return of spring and universal love:
'L'aria e l'acqua e la terra è d'amor piena' (Air, water, and earth are
full of love). The sestet turns to his own woe: 'Ma per me, lasso!,
tornano i piú gravi / Sospiri' (But for me, alas, return the deepest
sighs). The contrast between statement and counter-statement is
strong. And it involves not only the contrast of joy with sorrow, but
also that of nature with self and that of loving fruitfulness with savage
barrenness. Surrey substitutes for Petrarch's octave a twelve-line list of
springtide joys. Only in the final couplet—indeed, in the last half-line
—does he remember the contents of the sestet:

[1] *Opere* (Florence, 1516), f. 33ᵛ.

And thus I see among these pleasant thinges
Eche care decayes, and yet my sorow springes.

This reads as an afterthought, not only because it literally comes too late, but also because it is tucked away in Surrey's final rhyming couplet. The conclusive air of this couplet, with the phrase 'And thus I see', gives the impression that Surrey has proceeded along a line of thought and achieved a valuable logical statement. But the thought process has been too simple to justify a display of logic. The whole effect, then, is un-Petrarchan. The couplet is too short to contain Petrarch's counter-statement. The balance of the sonnet is totally altered. In its new guise, it is much more like Serafino's. Serafino lists, line by line, all manner of things that change in the course of time. The reiterated 'Col tempo' is a simple device for suggesting universal, repetitive change. The list itself is static and arbitrary. It does not matter that riches are mentioned before youth, or the sea before the snow. If half the items were left out, the sense would remain the same. Similarly, Surrey's lines could be interchanged—say, the third with the twelfth—without any damage to the meaning or tone, which remains the same throughout. Serafino plods across the octave-sestet division, just as Surrey does, and, with his last line, suddenly twists round. 'Ma in me giamai amor con tempo manca.' Things are different with him, for the course of time leaves him as loveless as ever. So, in Caritean style, the weight falls to the end of the poem. It is not, as in 'Zefiro torna', distributed. The counter-statement is a quick, knock-out blow, negating all that has gone before. This simplest of structural formulas is used not only by Surrey, but by Shakespeare (as, for example, in Sonnet no. 66, 'Tir'd with all these').

Surrey's 'minute' observation of nature has been admired.[1] However, in at least one detail of 'The soote season', as well as in the style of the whole, he seems to be relying less on his own perceptions than on memories of Chaucer's *Parliament of Fowls*:

> The sparwe, Venus sone; the nyghtyngale,
> That clepeth forth the grene leves newe;
> The swalwe, mortherere of the foules smale
> That maken hony of floures freshe of hewe;
> The wedded turtil, with hire herte trewe;
> The pekok, with his aungels fetheres bryghte;
> The fesaunt, skornere of the cok by nyghte.   (lines 351–7)

[1] Edwin Casady, *Henry Howard, Earl of Surrey* (New York, 1938), p. 228.

Surrey's Chaucerian writing is pleasant. But surely most readers would willingly give up this harmonious listing for almost any one of Wyatt's 'clumsy' versions of Petrarch?

There remains Surrey's 'Alas! so all thinges', which is very much superior to 'The soote season':

> Or che 'l ciel e la terra e 'l vento tace
> > E le fere e gli augelli il sonno affrena,
> > Notte il carro stellato in giro mena
> > E nel suo letto il mar senz' onda giace;
> Vegghio, penso, ardo, piango; e chi mi sface
> > Sempre m'è inanzi per mia dolce pena:
> > Guerra è 'l mio stato, d' ira e di duol piena;
> > E sol di lei pensando ho qualche pace.
> Cosí sol d' una chiara fonte viva
> > Move 'l dolce e l' amaro ond' io mi pasco;
> > Una man sola mi risana e punge.
> E perché 'l mio martír non giunga a riva,
> > Mille volte il dí moro e mille nasco;
> > Tanto da la salute mia son lunge.   (no. clxiv)

> Alas! so all thinges nowe doe holde their peace:
> Heauen and earth disturbed in nothing;
> The beastes, the ayer, the birdes their song doe cease;
> The nightes chare the starres aboute dothe bring.
> Calme is the sea, the waues worke lesse and lesse;
> So am not I, whom loue, alas! doth wring,
> Bringing before my face the great encrease
> Of my desires, whereat I wepe and syng,
> In ioye and wo, as in a doubtful ease:
> For my swete thoughtes sometyme doe pleasure bring,
> But, by and by, the cause of my disease
> Geues me a pang that inwardly dothe sting,
> When that I thinke what griefe it is againe
> To liue and lacke the thing should ridde my paine.   (no. 1)

This is the occasion on which Padelford prefers the imitation to its original: 'Surrey's sonnet, with its abrupt opening, its more dramatic antithesis, and its superior interpretation of nature, is much the finer of the two. The opening verses, and especially the noble fifth verse, are prophetic of the Georgian poets.'[1] While he has identified the finest

[1] Padelford, p. 207.

qualities of Surrey's poetry, Padelford is less than just to Petrarch. In place of Petrarch's apparently rather tame opening, Surrey gives his 'abrupt' one:

> Or che 'l ciel e la terra e 'l vento tace
> (Now that the sky and earth and wind are silent)
> Alas! so all thinges nowe doe holde their peace.

Striking as the revised opening is in itself, its effect upon the whole sonnet is not altogether satisfactory. Why exclaim 'alas!' at that point? It has no bearing on what follows immediately. It anticipates too much of what Petrarch reveals only slowly, and the impact of the sixth line, repeating the 'alas', is consequently weakened. Petrarch's personal lament, on the other hand, does not begin to break upon the reader until his fifth line, that is, until after the quiet, gentle description of nature at rest has made its unabrupt impact. Otherwise, the Petrarchan contrast of resting nature and restless lover is kept fairly sharp in Surrey's version. Statement and counter-statement, this time, retain their Petrarchan proportions. Surrey's antitheses do not really appear 'more dramatic' than Petrarch's. But such phrases as 'I wepe and syng', 'In ioye and wo', and 'To liue and lacke' do genuinely convey the uncertain state of mind that Petrarch describes thus: 'Mille volte il dí moro e mille nasco' (A thousand times a day I die and a thousand am born), and 'Una man sola mi risana e punge' (One hand alone heals and hurts me). As for Surrey's 'superior interpretation of nature', his 'noble' line, 'Calme is the sea, the waues worke lesse and lesse' is, conceivably, an enhancement of Petrarch's 'E nel suo letto il mar senz' onda giace' (And in his bed the sea lies waveless). The difference here helps to characterize the two poets. Surrey certainly gives a more precise visual detail. But Petrarch's line is subtler. His image of the sea in bed is intimately connected with the meaning of the whole passage, for instance, with the birds and beasts falling asleep, in the second line. Surrey has made legitimate use of the imitator's liberty. His sonnet has qualities of its own. They are not the same as Petrarch's, and not, necessarily, to be preferred to his. But here, at his best, he is stately and impressive-sounding. As an imitator he is very different from Wyatt, but in his way also original. Had he composed more of the calibre of 'Alas! so all thinges' Surrey would certainly challenge Wyatt on Petrarchan ground.

As it is, Wyatt's translations and imitations of Petrarch deserve a higher place than Surrey's. Neither is profoundly Petrarchan in his attitude to love. But if their translations of 'Amor, che' are an indication, Wyatt understands Petrarch's attitude and meaning better than Surrey. Wyatt's divergences from Petrarch are either explicable in terms of current interpretations, or they represent a perfectly conscious and deliberate choice, an open act of repudiation in favour of opposite values. Surrey, none of whose changes of Petrarch's text can be referred to the commentators, is not aware of clashing values. He is not a rebel because, for him, there is nothing to rebel for or against. Surrey likes the descriptive rather than the metaphysical Petrarch, whereas, with Wyatt, the opposite is true.

CHAPTER VII
Wyatt and the School
of Serafino

T̤HE subject of this chapter is Wyatt's comparatively neglected connection with the Caritean Petrarchans: Benedetto Gareth or 'Il Cariteo' (c. 1450–1514), Antonio Tebaldi or 'Il Tebaldeo' (1463–1537), and Serafino de' Ciminelli or Serafino Aquilano (1466–1500). Serafino is the chief of this group. He is also Wyatt's biggest creditor after Petrarch, and provides, besides some general inspiration, the sources of five[1] of his translations and four of his imitations.

Between Petrarch's death in 1374 and Wyatt's visit to Italy in 1527 Petrarchan imitation in Italy had passed through three distinct phases: the derivative phase of the first half of the fifteenth century (Giusto de' Conti, Buonaccorso da Montemagno, Rosello Roselli); the 'conceited' or Caritean phase of the second half of the fifteenth century (Cariteo, Filosseno, Tebaldeo, Serafino); and the 'purist' or Bembist phase of the early sixteenth century (Bembo, Veronica Gambara, Vittoria Colonna). Mario Praz, discussing all three phases in relation to English poetry, points out that the Petrarchanism imported by Wyatt (and Surrey) was 'already tinged with Serafino's conceits'.[2] But Serafino's influence, though generally acknowledged, has been given little detailed attention by critics other than Praz and Sergio Baldi. It has also been

---

[1] A sixth translation, Blage no. xxix, identified by Annabel Endicott, may well be Wyatt's: see *A Critical Study of Metrical Effects in the Poetry of Sir Thomas Wyatt* (unpublished M.A. thesis, London, 1963), pp. 178–9.

[2] *The Flaming Heart* (New York, 1958), p. 6.

strongly deplored, and Hyder E. Rollins's opinion is a common one:

> Wyatt seldom failed to admire the worst features of his Italian masters, and by translating their stiff figures and images he set a bad example that helped to deform English poetry . . . It may be that he admired the conceited poems of Petrarch and Serafino because they could be easily translated.[1]

The Bembists of Wyatt's own day objected to Cariteanism for the same reasons, as well as some others. Pietro Bembo led the revolt not only against its deformed style, but against its eroticism and its cult of the strambotto. In all respects Cariteanism appeared a distortion of the original Petrarchan tradition, which Bembo laboured to restore. For Wyatt, however, this form of Petrarchanism had a positive value easily missed by the critics who concentrate on its deformities.

In the first place, Cariteanism probably represented a reaction against the derivative writing of Petrarch's immediate successors: Giusto de' Conti's poems on his Elizavetta, written in 1440, are largely a mosaic of phrases and ideas from Petrarch. The Cariteans' impulse to seek novelty of expression, and also to write of love-making as well as of love, if objectionable, is at least understandable. Cariteo's sequence *Endimion* (1506) is no servile copy of the sonnets to Laura. His strong predilection for the pagan love poets, Propertius, Tibullus, Catullus, Ovid, and Horace, modifies the attitude to the love theme derived from Petrarch. Petrarch's well-known sonnet 'Levommi il mio penser' describes a vision of Laura, who, taking her forlorn lover's hand, assures him that he will be with her, one day, in Heaven:

> Per man mi prese e disse—In questa spera
> Sarai ancor meco, se 'l desir non erra.   (no. cccii)

Cariteo's wish-fulfilment dream, on the other hand, is of the beloved's face and mouth, of their 'amorous sweetness', and of his victorious embrace:

> Quest' è pur quella fronte alta & gioconda
> Che turba & rasserena la mia mente;
> Quest' è la bocca, che soavemente
> D'amorosa dolcezza hor mi circonda . . .
> Hor ne le braccia io tengo il corpo adorno
> D'ogni valore, hor son con la mia dea,
> Hor mi concede Amor lieta vittoria.[2]

---

[1] *Tottel's Miscellany*, ed. cit., Introd., ii. 101.
[2] *Le Rime del Chariteo*, ed. E. Pèrcopo (Naples, 1892), sonnet no. xv.

Wyatt obviously has more in common, in general, with Cariteo than with Petrarch. And he ignores Bembist Petrarchanism. The sublime rhapsodizing and platonizing of, for example, 'O imagine mia celeste e pura'[1] finds no echo in Wyatt. He is more the poet of 'amorosa dolcezza', of 'tasted sweetness', of erotic fact and fantasy:

> but ons in speciall,
> In thyn arraye after a pleasaunt gyse,
>> When her lose gowne from her shoulders did fall,
>> And she me caught in her armes long and small;
> Therewithall swetely did me kysse,
> And softely saide, *dere hert, howe like you this?*

> It was no dreme: I lay brode waking . . . (no. 37)

Petrarch wrote no strambotti and Bembo accordingly despises them. The popularity of the strambotto as a literary medium dates from Cariteo's adoption of it in about 1480. The original Sicilian folk song had been formed of eight hendecasyllabic lines, their two rhymes alternating: ab, ab, ab, ab. The first five of Cariteo's strambotti follow the pattern of this *ottava siciliana*, while the remaining twenty-seven adopt the more modern one of the *ottava toscana*, distinguished by its final couplet: ab, ab, ab, cc. The predominant musical unit in both is the distich. There is also a pause at the end of the fourth line, to rest the singer's voice, and, often, to introduce fresh material. But the quatrain division remains subordinate to the distich. Consequently there can be little comparison between the eight lines of the strambotto and those of the commonest type of Italian sonnet-octave, with its two enclosed quatrains: abba, abba. And, perhaps more surprisingly, the strambotto is not related to the *ottava rima* stanza inherited by Ariosto from Boccaccio. Though metrically identical these are independent literary forms, the one essentially narrative, the other lyrical. In Cariteo's hands, then, the strambotto became a more sophisticated version of what had been a light love song, its style rather mannered, its matter by no means lofty. His strambotti are mainly a courtier's protests against the cruel lady who is driving him to death:

> Donna crudel, per culpa vostra & mia
> Si perderà quest' alma desperata. (no. xiii)

Such is the form inherited by Serafino, and, ultimately, by Wyatt and his French contemporaries. It is reckoned the most important lyric

---

[1] Bembo, *Prose e Rime*, ed. C. Dionisotti (Turin, 1960), sonnet no. xix.

development in the courtly poetry of the fifteenth century. And, as a light yet sophisticated form, filling a gap left by Petrarch's *Rime*, it must obviously have answered a need.

Wyatt wrote about thirty poems in this form, and they appear to derive from the strambotto, not from Ariosto's stanza.[1] It is even possible that he shared Marot's and Scève's belief that the strambotto, rather than the sonnet, was Italy's chief vehicle for love poetry. But, however that may be, the strambotto certainly provided Wyatt with the easier and more familiar pattern. The distich unit is congenial to him, the interwoven rhyming and couplet already familiar. Metrically rhyme royal (ababbcc) is not unlike the strambotto, and this was not only a dominant form in the English tradition, but one in which Wyatt was particularly expert.

An exaggeration of the rhetorical devices taken over from Petrarch is also incipient in Cariteo's poetry, but this notorious feature of fifteenth-century Petrarchanism is better illustrated from the excesses of Tebaldeo's sonnets, which were first published in 1499. When Petrarch writes, antithetically, of the fire of his passion and the flood of his grief, the metaphors, though wittily handled, have as their main object the illumination of his feelings and thoughts. For instance, in 'Quel foco ch' i' pensai che fosse spento' he examines himself in order to discover how far grief has killed his old passion, contrasting the two emotions strongly:

> Qual foco non avrian già spento e morto
> L'onde che gli occhi tristi versan sempre?   (no. lv)

Tebaldeo, on the other hand, treats the Petrarchan images and antitheses as literal realities, exaggerating them and relating them not to inner but to outer circumstances. 'Cinto da le montagne alte e superbe', an account of the lover's life in the wilds, describes a flame of passion and fountains of tears so great that they actually melt the snow around him:

> E si gran fiamma me arde dentro e di fora,
> E de gliocchi mi surgon dui tal fonti,
> Che non dura oue io sto la neue un hora.[2]

The contrast of heat and cold denotes, not an emotional conflict on Petrarch's lines, but an incredible freak of nature. The reader is impressed by ingenuity, not by insight. This 'conceited' or, as Praz calls

---

[1] See Appendix I.

[2] *Soneti & Capitoli di Misser Antonio Thebaldeo* (Modena, 1500), sig. b 8ᵛ.

it, 'flamboyant' style, modelled on Petrarch's rhetorical devices but excluding their sense and psychological value, has been subject to severe criticism. It is fantastic, absurd, artificial, hyperbolical, and, through repetition by Tebaldeo's successors, it also becomes trite. In spite of the Bembist attack, it has not lost all its appeal by 1527, nor is Wyatt likely to have been among its critics. On the contrary, his handling of Petrarch sometimes suggests a predilection for this manner. 'I fynde no peace and all my warr is done' (no. 26), from 'Pace non trovo e non ho da far guerra' (no. cxxxiv), is a series of the prolix antitheses so dear to the Cariteans.

Even before particular debts are examined, a general compatibility between Wyatt and the Cariteans is suggested by his occasional flirtation with flamboyant conceits, his frequent use of the strambotto, and the general tone of his poetry, which is that of the amorous courtier rather than the serious 'philosopher' of love. It is not surprising, therefore, that he found inspiration in Serafino, the chief of the Cariteans.

Serafino's supremacy needs to be understood in terms of contemporary tastes (Wyatt's included), not those of Bembist or modern criticism. At his death in 1500 the most popular poet of the day was mourned. He was the youngest of the major Cariteans, and also the first to die. His funeral in Rome was attended, according to his friend and biographer, Vincentio Calmeta, 'con grande honore, pompa e compagnia'.[1] He had been welcomed by such poets as Cariteo, Tebaldeo, Sannazaro and Pontano, and courted by such patrons as Ferdinand II of Naples, Cardinal Sforza, Isabella d'Este, the Duke of Mantua and the Duchess of Urbino. The first edition of his *Opere*, posthumously published in 1502, was followed, in 1504, by the joint publication of Calmeta's biography and a collection of elegies. Outside Italy his reputation was to become almost equally phenomenal, and Jean Lemaire de Belges, his first French follower, considered Serafino the equal of Dante and Petrarch.

It was generally recognized that Serafino outstripped his fellow Cariteans. Calmeta describes his emulation of Tebaldeo, whom he met, in about 1494, among the brilliant crowd at Isabella d'Este's court, and who was then at the height of his fame—'che 'l supremo culme tenneva'. To Cariteo's famous strambotti he was introduced by his friend, Andrea Coscia, who sang them to the lute. Serafino at once adopted the form, devoting himself to it with such enthusiasm that he soon

[1] *Vita Del Facondo Poeta Vulgare Seraphino Aquilano* (1504): see *Le Rime di Serafino*, ed. M. Menghini (Bologna, 1894), i. 1–15.

gained a reputation for the felicity of his style as a strambottist: 'in quello stile hebbe somma felicitade.' It remained his favourite medium. His strambotti number three hundred and fifty or more, his sonnets less than one hundred and fifty.

Serafino owed his success to his cultivation of popular taste: 'ad ogni cosa che potesse el vulgo tirare in ammiratione lo ingegno accomodava.' But he was first and foremost a musician, who, in his youth, had learned Petrarch's poems by heart and sung them with his lute. His own poems, which, in spite of his ambition, he did not even collect or publish, form no planned sequence of Petrarchan *canzoniere*. They are meant to serve occasions, to delight courts. Above all they are meant for performance, inseparable from their musical accompaniment. In their time they stirred the souls of all hearers, from the most learned to the most plebeian, because of Serafino's ardent delivery and the excellence of his judgement in fitting words to music: 'Nel recitare de' soi poemi era tanto ardente e con tanto giuditio le parole con la musica consertava che l'animo de li ascoltanti o dotti, o mediocri, o plebei, o donne equalmente commoveva.' He was, in fact, very much of his time and place. This was a period in which Italy produced little music and poetry of first-rate importance but much minor popular and courtly song for which the lute provided a favourite accompaniment.

The otherwise happy story of Serafino's success is marred only by his quarrels with Cardinal Sforza and intermittent periods of wandering through Italy without a patron's protection. Calmeta gives the impression that, socially, Serafino was a nonconformist, bitter at the indignity of having to sing for his supper, prone to satirize the vices of courts, loathing the Cardinal's zest for hunting, and merely veiling his dislike of the man. Hence the savage scepticism which appears so oddly in the work of a primarily suave and witty poet.

Though there is no strict parallel with Wyatt's life as courtier and diplomat, these two Petrarchans have much in common. From higher in the social scale, Wyatt, too, perceived the charms and evils of court life, the advantages and pitfalls of patronage. The poetry of both Serafino and Wyatt is courtly, light, occasional, suited to lute accompaniment, not planned to formulate a consistent narrative or exposition of love. Worldliness and disillusion are present in both. Serafino's poems are less formidable models than the sonnets to Laura, and, as Sergio Baldi points out, Wyatt has a greater temperamental affinity to Serafino than to Petrarch.[1]

[1] *La Poesia di Sir Thomas Wyatt* (Florence, 1953), p. 191.

Like Wyatt, only to much greater excess, Serafino delights in Caritean rhetoric. The exaggerated assertions of his sonnet cxxv equal any
of Tebaldeo's: if Love had lost his shafts, supply could be found in the
poet's heart, if the ocean bed were dried up he could fill it with his
tears, if Vulcan were short of flame or Aeolus of wind, his heart and
sighs could furnish them. Again like Wyatt, Serafino borrows whole
poems from Petrarch. Both, for instance, handle the allegorical intri-
cacies of the popular seafaring sonnet, 'Passa la nave mia'. Petrarch's
boat is 'colma d' oblio' ('charged with forgetfulnes'), Serafino's 'Carca
di fede' (loaded with faith), while the oars in each case represent
thoughts:

A ciascun remo un penser pronto e rio	(Petrarch: no. clxxxix)
And every owre a thought in redines	(Wyatt: no. 28)
Ciascun de remi è un pensier aspro & graue	(Serafino: f. 140^r)[1]

Yet Petrarch's influence is not invariably felt in terms of servile
imitation or frigid rhetoric, as the canzone 'S' i' 'l dissi mai' and its
derivatives in Serafino and Wyatt show. This model proves highly
adaptable to the expression of those gallantries in which Serafino,
Wyatt, and, presumably, their audiences delighted. It opens amidst a
violent outcry, the lover's defence of himself against some charge
which rumour has brought to Laura's ears: 'he did not say what he is
supposed to have said, but if he did, may he suffer for it':

> S' i' 'l dissi mai, ch' i' vegna in odio a quella
> Del cui amor vivo e senza 'l qual morrei:
> S' i' 'l dissi, ch' e' miei dí sian pochi e rei,
> E di vil signoria l'anima ancella:
> S' i' 'l dissi, contra me s'arme ogni stella.   (no. ccvi)

And so on throughout fifty-nine lines, constantly reiterating the initial
'if I said it' in a manner to suggest all the volubility of self-justification.
Petrarch's brilliant rhetorical repetition, an example of the naturalness
of much of his artifice, is turned to good purpose by Serafino and
Wyatt. Serafino, compressing the long tirade into the eight lines

---

[1] Quotations throughout this chapter will be taken from *Opere Dello Elegan-
tissimo Poeta Seraphino Aquilano* (Florence, 1516), the fullest of the early editions.
(No adequate modern one exists, Menghini's being incomplete.)

of a strambotto, achieves the more formal, lucid, and trenchant effect:

> Donna *se io dixi mai* contra tuo honore
> Te mostri à me crudel sempre e piú bella.
> *Se io el dixi* gran sospir me abrusci el core,
> E nasca ognhor di me peggior nouella.
> *Se io il dixi* uenga in ira al Dio de amore,
> E sii tu al mio uoler sempre ribella.   (f. 157^v)

Wyatt recaptures the original diffuseness, the volubility, and the opening *in medias res*. Without explaining exactly what the offending words have been, he launches directly into a flood of protests:

> Perdye *I saide yt* not
> Nor never thought to do,
> As well as I ye wott
> I have no powre thereto;
> And *if I ded*, the lott
> That first ded me enchaine
> Do never slake the knott
> But strayt it to my payne.
>
> And *if I ded*, eche thing
> That maye do harme or woo
> Contynuallye maye wring
> My herte whereso I goo; ...
>
> *Yf I saide so*, eche sterre ... &c.
>
> And *if I ded so saye*, ... &c.   (no. 134)

Hence the imitation of his rhetoric does not of necessity draw out the worst of Petrarch, deform the poetry modelled on his, or cramp the individual talent.

Serafino and Wyatt are indeed more akin to each other than either is to Petrarch, and Baldi suggests that the mark of Serafino's influence is found in precisely those aspects of Wyatt's art that are most remote from Petrarch—the sharp, the sardonic, and the downright satirical.[1] Compare Serafino's 'Contra Vna Vecchia', a derisive attack on the

---

[1] *Op cit.*, p. 191.

pretensions to beauty retained by the old, with Wyatt's abuse of an 'old mule':

> A Ha ha chi non ridesse
> Duna si difforme e uecchia,
> Che per bella ognhor si specchia
> Pur come altri li credesse.
> A ha ha chi non ridesse.   (f. 204ᵛ)

> Ye old mule, that thinck yourself so fayre,
> Leve of with craft your beautie to repaire,
> For it is time withoute any fable:
> No man setteth now by riding in your saddell;
> To muche travaill so do your train apaire,
> Ye old mule!   (no. 35)

Wyatt certainly read Serafino's poem, and, picking upon its jeering refrain, turns it to good effect in 'Tanglid I was yn loves snare':

> But ha, ha, ha, full well is me,
> For I am now at libretye.   (no. 154)

Again, he takes up the opening phrase of the 'Canzona de la Patientia':

> Patientia alla malora
> poi che vòl cosí fortuna.[1]

> Pacyence of all my smart,
> Ffor fortune ys tornyd awry.   (no. 118)

If Petrarch also cries out against fortune, it is not with the acrimony of his two followers. To Serafino the world is full of deception, scum only is valued nowadays:

> egli è pien tutto d'inganni;
> reputato è oggi i panni.

And to Wyatt,

> yt dothe well apere
> My frend ys tornyd my foo.

Indeed, both are poets rather of impatience than patience, overbearing opposition, consistently underrating, in a manner most unlike that of Petrarch's gentle, elegiac, reflective lamentations. Miss Foxwell may be right in stating that Wyatt's 'I abide and abide' is an adaptation of Serafino's 'Lasso, oimè'.[2] At any rate, both express the same irritation,

---

[1] Not in the 1516 edition. See Menghini, *ed. cit.*, pp. xxiv–v.
[2] *Ibid.*, pp. xxvi–vii. Cp. Foxwell, ii. 48.

that of being kept on a string by a lady (surely most unlike Laura) who raises but never satisfies hope and whose constant refrain is 'wait':

> ma s'io narro el mio dolore
> tu rispondi ch'i'ò bon tempo.

> And ever my ladye to me dothe say:
> 'Let me alone and I will prouyde.'   (no. 160)

The nagging monotony with which Serafino and Wyatt demand satisfaction is often directly dependent on the refrain, which both use with great skill. Serafino excells in the barzelletta, a form in which the opening phrase is repeated as a refrain, and this is also Wyatt's practice in 'Dysdaine me not'. Compare the following for both theme and lyrical effect:

> *Non mi negar signora*
> Di sporgermi la man
> Chio uó da te lontan.
> *Non mi negar signora*
> Vna pietosa uista
> Puó far chal duol resista
> Questalma afflicta e trista
> Che per te non mora.
> > *Non mi negar signora.*   (f. 208^v)

> *Refuse me not* without cause why
> Nor thynke me not to be vniust,
> Synce that by lot of fantasye
> The careful knot nedes knyt I must,
> > *Refuse me not.*   (no. 177)

Wyatt was not, as far as we know, a skilled musician like Serafino, and the England of his day had not a lute-song tradition like Italy's. Nevertheless he readily adopts the dramatic-lyrical pose of the lover as player and singer:

> My lute awake! perfourme the last
> Labor that thou and I shall wast,
> > And end that I have now begon;
> For when this song is sung and past,
> > My lute be still, for I have done.   (no. 66)

Wyatt's has been considered possibly the earliest English use of this lute *motif*.[1] He was undoubtedly inspired by the Italian precedent, and, probably, particularly by Serafino's.

[1] See John Hollander, *The Untuning of the Sky: Ideas of Music in English Poetry, 1500–1700* (Princeton, 1961), p. 128.

In the foregoing cases Wyatt was borrowing little, if anything, from particular poems by Serafino. While suggesting that he read him attentively, they illustrate chiefly the general affinity between the two poets. Wyatt's adaptations of poems by Serafino give further support to this idea, and also reveal him in his familiar guise as experimenter with foreign texts. For example, he bases a sonnet on two consecutive strambotti:

El cor ti diedi non che el tormentassi
  Ma che fosse da te ben conseruato,
Seruo ti fui non che me abandonassi
  Ma che fosse da te remeritato,
Contento fui che schiauo me acchatassi
  Ma non di tal moneta esser pagato,
Hor poi che regna in te poca pietade
  Non ti spiaccia sio torno in libertate.

La donna di natura mai si satia
  Di dar effecto à ogni suo desyderio,
E sempre ti stá sopra con audatia
  Del tuo martyr pigliando refrigerio,
Quanto piú humil li uai tanto piú stratia
  Perfin che thá sepulto in cymiterio,
Perche chi pone lo suo amor in femina
  Zappa nel acqua & nella harena semina.   (f. 151ʳ⁻ᵛ)

My hert I gave the, not to do it payn,
  But to preserue it was to the taken;
  I serued the not to be forsaken,
  But that I should be rewarded again.
I was content thy seruant to remayn,
  But not to be payed vnder this fasshion.
  Nowe syns in the is none othre reason
  Displease the not if that I do refrain.

Vnsaciat of my woo and thy desire,
  Assured be craft to excuse thy fault;
  But syns it please the to fain a default,
Farewell, I say, parting from the fyer:
  For he that beleveth bering in hand
  Plowithe in water and soweth in the sand.
                (no. 14, with octave and sestet separated)

In subject and tone these poems diverge from the sonnets to Laura. Both strambotti concern falling out of love, the first being a bitter explanation of the poet's decision to withdraw his affection, the second an attack on the sadism of women. Serafino does not fail to use the conventional terms of the Petrarchan complaint. He is—or has been—the 'slave' ('schiauo') of his lady, and his sufferings have been a long martyrdom. But his attitude is cynical and ill-tempered. Whereas Petrarch thinks of love's duties, Serafino thinks of its rights. After a generous investment of the heart, what dividend? Serafino uses an apt financial metaphor. He had not looked to be paid in the coin of pitilessness ('non di tal moneta esser pagato'). Yet since it is so—and his tone changes to an irony intended to hurt—let it not displease the lady if he returns to his old freedom: 'Non ti spiaccia sio torno in libertate'. All this is highly congenial to Wyatt, who also has an un-Petrarchan, bargaining attitude to the relationships he describes, and for whom falling out of love always proves a poetically richer subject than either falling in love, or, simply, being in love.

But however appropriate his choice of material, Wyatt's formal experiment is not altogether successful. The main problem was, of course, to avoid the impression that two poems were being clamped together to form a sonnet. 'El cor ti diedi' is literally translated, line by line, for the octave, and 'La donna di natura' more freely manipulated into the sestet. The structurally crucial point is the end of the one and the beginning of the next. Accordingly, all runs smoothly until Wyatt reaches the final couplet of the first strambotto. But at line seven he writes the feeblest line of the whole sonnet. 'Nowe syns in the is none othre reason' conveys no clear meaning, certainly not Serafino's 'since in thee is little pity'. Again, in line eight, 'refrain' is but a vague echo of 'torno in libertate'. Yet if Wyatt is intending to modify the drastic conclusiveness of Serafino's couplet, as unsuited to the middle of a sonnet, his decisive 'Nowe syns' undermines the purpose—it does in fact announce the logical end to his train of thought. The central hiatus is, if anything, deepened by the high pitched 'Vnsaciat of my woo' that introduces the sestet. By contrast the end of the sonnet, where Wyatt renders the second of Serafino's couplets, is well served by the original structure. This example is a useful pointer to the ways in which the strambotto may have influenced the structure of both the Caritean and the English sonnet. The Caritean strambotto pounces upon its couplet ending. The Caritean sonnet likewise gravitates towards its final statement, though without actually embodying it in a rhyming couplet. The English sonnet is akin to both, and Wyatt's 'My hert I gave the' at least approximates to the English form. Nevertheless, whatever lessons he learned from its composition, he did not return to the experiment of making two strambotti into a sonnet. And it was left to Surrey to develop a type of sonnet that has been called a 'fourteen-line strambotto.'[1]

Wyatt's other adaptations are much more successful, probably because they involve the comparatively easy task of expansion and because the originals are recast in familiar English forms. For if Wyatt as sonneteer was the pupil of Italy, he had nothing to learn in the structure of rhyme royal or quatrains. 'Resound my voyse, ye wodes that here me plain' takes its gist and scenic description from Serafino's strambotto:

> Laer che sente el mesto e gran clamore
> Diuulga in ogni parte la mia doglia
> Tal che per compassione del mio dolore
> Par che ne treme in arbore ogni foglia . . .   (f. 125^r)

The air, the leaves, the wild animals, each in their kind express compassion for the poet, echoing his grief. Wyatt merely adds rivers, hills, vales, and rain, as well as a stanza lamenting what Serafino leaves us to guess: that by contrast with nature his lady shows 'no pitie'. While the strambotto is neat and oblique, Wyatt's three stanzas of rhyme royal are explanatory, full, and grand:

> Oft ye Revers, to here my wofull sounde,
>   Have stopt your course and, plainly to expresse,
> Many a tere by moystor of the grounde
>   The erth hath wept to here my hevenes;
>   Which causeles to suffre without redresse
> The howgy okes have rored in the wynde:
> Eche thing me thought complayning in their kynde.   (no. 22)

'To seke eche where', a series of six-line stanzas, expands the theme common to two strambotti, in which Serafino offers his lady a treasure richer than adornments worked in gold and pearl—his heart:

> Donar non ti possio uago lauoro
>   Doro, di perle, ne ricchezza alcuna,
> Ma à me par doni assai riccho thesoro,
>   Chi lalma sua col cor franco ui dona.   (f. 119^r)

---

[1] H. B. Lathrop, 'The Sonnet Forms of Wyatt and Surrey', *M.P.*, ii (1905), 469.

I cannot gyve browches nor Ringes,
Thes goldsmythes work and goodly thinges,
   Piery nor perle oryente and clere;

   ... Frely, therefore, lo here
   Dare I well gyve, I say, my hert to yere. (no. 85)

Wyatt neglects the ensuing argument that all riches but true faith are
subject to the vicissitudes of fortune. So he avoids two problems set by
the strambotto, that of versifying argument and that of concentrating
it within eight lines. As before, he takes the leisurely 'English' course:

To seke eche where, where man doeth lyve,
The See, the land, the Rocke, the clyve,
   Ffraunce, Spayne and Ind and every where ...

Finally, 'Processe of tyme', a series of quatrains, takes its argument
and detail from a group of strambotti on the changes wrought by Time
in all things but the hard heart of a lady.

Processe of tyme worketh suche wounder,
   That water which is of kynd so soft
Doeth perse the marbell stone a sonder,
   By litle droppes faling from aloft.

And yet an hert that sems so tender
   Receveth no dropp of the stilling teres,
That alway still cause me to render
   The vain plaint that sowndes not in her eres.

   . . . .

Eche fiers thing lo! how thou doest exceede,
   And hides it vnder so humble a face;
And yet the humble to helpe at nede,
   Nought helpeth tyme, humblenes, nor place. (no. 82)

In one strambotto Serafino illustrates the idea from 'each beast' of the
woodland, which in time abates its ferocity, and then from water-drops
wearing down marble:

Con fede e con speranza io uiuo anchora
   Placar col ben seruir la tua dureza,
Ogni animal, che in boscho si dimora
   Col tempo abassa e tempra ogni fiereza,
Vedo una goccia dacqua adhora adhora
   Dar sopra el marmo tal che al fino lo speza,
Cosi spero il tuo cor si humilie e tempre,
   Pregando, amando, & lachrymando sempre. (f. 116ᵛ)

In the strambotto immediately following he actually starts, like Wyatt, with the water–marble illustration, and, in the next, uses it again, this time with a 'fier caual'. In yet another, again like Wyatt, he makes an immediate and specific connection between water-drops and the lover's tears:

> Suole una gotta dacqua à colpi lenti
> Cauare el marmo in longo tempo & hore
> E quel suo freddo cor turbato e obscuro
> Al mio gran lachrymar sempre è piú duro.   (f. 124^v)

This is obviously close to the first two stanzas of 'Processe of tyme', closer than anything in the sonnet 'Col tempo' (no. ciii), which has been cited as Wyatt's source.[1] But close as these analogies are, Wyatt may not have worked with Serafino's strambotti at his elbow. Quite probably, having once studied them, he drew from memory on their themes and images. (That the water–stone image established itself in his imagination is suggested by its recurrence in 'Passe forth, my wonted cryes' (no. 180), another Petrarchan complaint against his mistress's unnatural hardness.) As for the images of lion and tiger used in the fourth and fifth stanzas of 'Processe of tyme', they are so highly conventional that it is useless to try to trace them to particular sources. Wyatt took them either from such of Serafino's strambotti as 'Lasso debbio uoler' (f. 135^r) and 'Consuma el tempo' (f. 172^v), or (more likely) from the common Petrarchan stock. Wyatt's tearful sentiments and sense of ill usage are also very much part of the Petarchan tradition. In 'Processe of tyme' he brings out the sentiment; and in this he is closer both to Petrarch and to his own habitual vein than to the witty Serafino. Once again the effect is largely the result of his expansive stanzaic and thoroughly English form, which contrasts strongly with the compact strambotto-form. As each illustration comes up, Wyatt repeats his lamentations at length. The poem is consequently full, resonant, and emotional. It is successful in its way. But it is not unfair to add that this, for Wyatt, was easy writing.

The adaptations into English forms are by no means the work of a stumbling pupil. Nor have they historical importance, for Wyatt merely borrows ideas and images, without attempting to transplant unfamiliar forms or techniques. It is as a strambottist that Wyatt is the novice from the school of Serafino. And here too is found the most important part of Serafino's legacy to English poetry. Hence, however

[1] *E.g.*, following Koeppel, by Baldi (*op. cit.*, pp. 195 and 228), and myself (*C.L.*, xiii (1961), 302).

uncongenial, Serafino's strambotti must be fairly understood, assessed for what they are, not for what we should like them to be.

Serafino's strambotti range from the serious to the frivolous. There are groups on death, night, sleep, fortune, time's ravages—subjects on which his music confers sweetness and gravity:

> Placido somno, che dal ciel descendi
>> À tranquillar degli huomini ogni cura . . .   (f. 132ᵛ)

At the other extreme are such whims as the description of how so many of Love's arrows have found their mark that the poet's heart has become a target:

> Tirate mhai tante saette amore
>> Che del mio core hormai bersaglio hai facto.   (f. 140ʳ)

It is these light, fantastic strambotti that are most often associated with Serafino's name.

The strambotto has in fact earned a reputation not as the expression of profound passion but as a caprice. A group is devoted entirely to the mistress's mirror, and in one Serafino expressed his wonder that the frail glass does not break in reflecting her beauty:

> Marauigliome assai specchio, che hai intorno
> Madonna ognhor quando in beltá piú uale,
> Che non ti frangi al suo bel uiso adorno
> Essendo un uetro pur caduco & frale.

Why so? For the reason that when the poet first saw her his heart was shivered into fragments by an arrow. Could it be Love that struck?

> Che quando la uidi io quel primo giorno
>> Subito me sentí nel pecto un strale
> Non só sel colpo lo facesse amore,
>> Che mi fé drento in mille parte il core.   (f. 133ᵛ)

This is no more than froth, but its inventiveness, wit, and gallantry delight. Serafino and his reader do not really expect mirrors to break in this way. No more does anyone take seriously the notion that trees will 'crowd into a shade' where a lady sits, though pleasure is given by the poet's pretence that this is so. Serafino has simply sought out what the sixteenth-century critic calls an 'invention', in this case one that George Gascoigne would term a 'supernaturall cause wherby [his] penne might walke in the superlatiue degree'.[1] And Serafino's wit belongs not only to the original invention but to his whole structure: to the drawing of the parallel between mirror and heart, to the pursuit of reasons for their getting broken, and to the revelation of the point of it all, his love, at the very end—'Non só sel colpo lo facesse *amore*'.

The 'imagery' characteristic of the strambotto is neither suggestive nor symbolic. Usually a literal term of comparison is employed in the interests of the poet's intention to establish a predetermined truth. There are no excursions into the unknown. A high degree of consciousness and deliberation reigns over the use of metaphor and simile, and the latter predominates. The strambotto is not highly metaphorical, for the obvious reason that its comparisons are best made explicitly and 'wittily'. Coleridgians may detect the operation of the Fancy in the art of Serafino. But, considering the intention of the strambotto, this is no ground for criticism. For the intention was clearly to work out such similitudes as that of mirror and heart, and to impose an iron coherence upon materials formerly unrelated.

The strambotto is a form in which logic prevails. It frequently sets about an argument and strives towards a conclusion. Serafino's handling of the traditional *carpe diem* theme, with its stock imagery of roses, thorns, &c., illustrates his rigid control:

> Risguarda donna come el tempo uola,
> Et ogni cosa corre alla sua fine,
> In breue si fá oscura ogni uiola,
> Cascan le rose, & restan poi le spine,
> Cosi la tua beltá, che al mondo è sola
> Non creder come oro al foco affine,
> Dunque conosci el tuo tempo felice
> Ne sperar renouar, come phenice.   (f. 114ᵛ)

The logical transitions are heavily underlined as Serafino passes from concrete illustration (the fading flowers, &c., of lines 1–4) to the truth illustrated ('*Cosi* la tua beltá'—thus your beauty), and thence to the conclusion ('*Dunque* conosci'—therefore recognize). Though the scheme appears simple, its three phases—example, application, deduction—demand considerable discipline and concentration.

A simpler logic and structure involve the amassing of several

---

[1] *Certayne Notes of Instruction* (1575), in *Eliʒabethan Critical Essays*, ed. G. G. Smith (Oxford, 1904), i. 48.

equivalent illustrations of a general point, which, again, is stated at the end:

> Spesso nel mezo dun bel fabricare
> Manca lharena, ouer la calce bianca,
> Spesso per longo, & forte caualcare
> In mezo el corso el fier caual si stanca,
> Spesso al bon nauigante in mezo al mare
> Prima che giunga in porto el uento manca,
> Cosi questa fortuna è si fallace
> Che tal crede uolar, che in terra giace. (ff. 119ᵛ-120ʳ)

Often a building stops midway for lack of materials, a ride because the horse tires, and a sea voyage because the wind fails. Thus fortune is deceptive, and who thinks to fly is earthbound. Here, not only logic and structure, but grammar is as simple as possible. The short statements fall neatly into the familiar distich units of the strambotto. Such grammatical simplicity is common with Serafino, though not the invariable rule. 'Marauigliome assai specchio' (quoted above) is introduced by a fine, claused sentence which makes of lines 1–4 a sweeping musical cadence. 'Spesso nel mezo', by contrast, depends for its music on the metronomic use of the initial phrase, which recurs at lines three and five (compare the identical pattern in Serafino's 'Donna se io dixi mai'). The common feature of all the strambotti is, however, their combination of sense and music, and Calmeta was surely not wrong in praising Serafino's skill in this.

Its brevity, logicality, and termination in some witty statement make the strambotto a form of epigram. As such, it must have what Lorenzo de' Medici calls 'acume' and 'destrezza',[1] and Antonio Minturno 'agutezza di motteggio, ó di sentenza'.[2] As such, too, much of its effect will depend on the final couplet, which is given added point, musically, because it is detached by rhyme from the rest of the stanza (ababababcc). There are exceptions to the general rule that the couplet is treated as a self-contained, detached unit. In 'Son in mare di dolor smarrita naue', the seafaring allegory is maintained to the last and the couplet is logically and grammatically continuous with the preceding lines:

> Speme è il timon, le uel son uoglie praue
> Ciascuna ingorda, & di sospir gonfiata,
> Bussolo è il cor, tú tramontana e scorta
> Et persa te la mia speranza è morta.   (lines 5–8, f. 140ʳ)

[1] Commento . . . sopra Alcvni de' svoi Sonetti (c. 1490), in Poesie Volgari (Venice, 1554), f. 120ᵛ.

[2] L'Arte Poetica (Venice, 1563), p. 240.

But even here the end brings the novelty of an explicit, personal state-ment: 'if I lose you, my hope is dead.' More typically there is a distinct break and transition of thought at the final couplet, which, as in the Shakespearian sonnet, has an epigrammatic resonance. In the 'mirror' strambotto, a new and witty explanation strikes with slight surprise:

> Non só sel colpo lo facesse amore,
> Che mi fé drento in mille parte il core.

In 'Risguarda donna' a logical climax sounds triumphantly:

> Dunque conosci el tuo tempo felice
> Ne sperar renouar, come phenice.

And in 'Spesso nel mezo' a familiar truth rings out like a proverb:

> Cosi questa fortuna è si fallace
> Che tal crede uolar, che in terra giace.

These are some of the patterns provided by Serafino. By virtue of its comparatively simple structure, rhyme scheme, and grammar, the strambotto is possibly a more manageable model than the Italian son-net. On the other hand, difficulties meet the imitator because of the need to concentrate expression, to manipulate imagery, to combine argument with lyrical smoothness, to achieve an epigrammatic wit, and to maintain a general air of elegance, poise, and dexterity.

The task of transplanting the strambotto to England first fell to Wyatt. His strambotti are usually grouped with his 'epigrams', and, though not so designated in the Egerton MS or by their first editor Tottel, they do, in the opinion of Warton, Nott, and Whipple, legiti-mately belong to this kind.[1]

In two cases Wyatt chooses from the simplest of Serafino's stram-botti, and, with the care of a literal translator, proceeds to render the originals practically line by line:

> Sio son caduto interra inon son morto
>> Ritorna el Sol benche talhor si cele,
> Spero mi dará el ciel qualche conforto,
>> Poi che fortuna hará sfocato el fele
> Chi hó uisto naue ritornarsi in porto,
>> Dapoi che rotte há in mar tutte soe uele
> El salce anchora el uento abasso & piega
>> Poi si ridriza, & glialtri legni lega.   (f. 120ʳ)

---

[1] See T. K. Whipple, 'Martial and the English Epigram from Sir Thomas Wyatt to Ben Jonson', *University of California Studies in Modern Philology*, x (1925), 312 n.

He is not ded that somtyme hath a fall;
 The sonne retorneth that was vnder the clowd;
And when fortune hath spitt oute all her gall,
 I trust good luck to me shalbe allowd.
For I have sene a shippe into haven fall
 After the storme hath broke boeth mast and shrowd;
And eke the willowe that stowpeth with the wynde
Doeth ryse again, and greater wode doeth bynd.   (no. 60)

Ogni pungente & uenenosa spina
 Se uede à qualche tempo esser fiorita,
Crudel ueneno posto in medicina,
 Piú uolte torna lhom da morte uita,
El foco che ogni cosa arde & ruina,
 Spesso risana una mortal ferita,
Cosi spero el mio mal me fia salute,
 Chogni cosa che noce há pur uirtute.   (f. 117^r)

Venemus thornes that ar so sharp and kene
 Sometyme ber flowers fayre and freshe of hue;
Poyson offtyme is put in medecene
 And cawsith helth in man for to renue;
Ffyre that purgith allthing that is vnclene
 May hele, and hurt: and if thes bene true,
I trust somtyme my harme may be my helth,
Syns evry wo is joynid with some welth.   (no. 76)

Wyatt's alterations are of minimal importance. In 'He is not ded', the first line is made impersonal, 'uele' (sails) becomes 'mast and shrowd', and Serafino's third and fourth lines are inverted. As Wyatt soon reverts to the first person, even the first of these makes little difference to the original sense and tone. There can scarcely be a more literal translation than 'spitte oute … gall' for 'sfocare fièle'. In Wyatt's version of 'Ogni pungente', a few adjectives are transposed or omitted, and the fire 'che arde & ruina' (that burns and destroys) becomes the fire 'that purgith'. But again the sense is virtually unchanged. The originals also fall easily into the one or two line units which Wyatt can reproduce with ease. Both strambotti comprise merely a series of illustrations, uncomplicated statements of fact, all bearing out a single philosophical point. The technique would be already familiar to Wyatt. Exactly of a piece with it is Chaucer's proof that joy follows sorrow— the very theme of 'Ogni pungente':

> For thilke grownd that bereth the wedes wikke
> Bereth ek thise holsom herbes, as ful ofte
> Next the foule netle, rough and thikke,
> The rose waxeth swoote and smothe and softe;
> And next the valeye is the hill o-lofte;
> And next the derke nyght the glade morwe;
> And also joie is next the fyn of sorwe.
>
> (*Troilus and Criseyde*, i. 946–52)

'Sio son caduto' proclaims its point as much in the first line as the last. There is no climax, for the weight is spread evenly, and the argument is reiterative. Unity is given by the underlying idea and by the ruling image of weather (clouds hide the sun, storms toss the ship, wind bends the willow). Both are easily rendered into English. 'Ogni pungente', governed by the idea that 'every thorn has a rose', is only slightly more complicated. Following a pattern familiar with Serafino, it starts with an even series of illustrations to draw its conclusion in the couplet: 'Cosi spero' (thus I hope). This climax is further marked by a transition from the impersonal statement of reasons for optimism to the personal expression of confidence in the future. The emphasis of Wyatt's couplet is weakened by the introductory phrase cutting across the line-division: 'and if thes bene true, / I trust'. But for the rest he follows out the original structure conscientiously. It is unlikely that he found his task, in these two cases, particularly difficult or unfamiliar. The results, however, are stiff, and, if not exactly tending to deform English poetry, do little to refute Rollins's adverse opinion of Wyatt's translations from Serafino.

Elsewhere Wyatt's problems as a translator prove more difficult:

> Se una bombarda è dal gran foco mossa
> Spirando, ció che troua aterra presto.
> Ma segli aduien chella spirar non possa
> Se stessa rompe & poco offende el resto.
> Cosi io dentro ardo, el foco è giunto à lossa
> Sel taccio imor, sel dico altrui molesto.
> Sospeso uiuo, amor mi dá tal sorte,
> Che altro non è che una confusa morte.   (f. 145^v)

> The furyous gonne in his rajing yre,
> When that the bowle is rammed in to sore
> And that the flame cannot part from the fire,
> Cracketh in sonder, and in the ayer doeth rore

The shevered peces; right so doeth my desire,
  Whose flame encreseth from more to more,
Wych to lett owt I dare not loke nor speke:
So now hard force my hert doeth all to breke.   (no. 61)

The greater freedom of the translation has been necessitated by the
more complicated structure of the original. Unlike those discussed
above, it can hardly have been chosen because it was 'easy to translate'.
This time a single illustration is brought to bear on the several aspects
of a situation. The truth to be illustrated, and so the illustration itself,
are more detailed. The essence of such conceited writing is that the
comparison must be as complete as possible. The several phases in the
firing of a gun (lines 1–4) must be repeated exactly in the phases
through which the lover passes (lines 5–8). If fire reaches the gun-
powder in line one, in line five desire penetrates to the lover's bones.
The stanza falls into equally balanced halves, and within each section
a developing situation must be followed.

So concentrated, intricate, and rigid is the strambotto that Wyatt
proceeds at once to simplify and soften it. Serafino points out that the
gun if firing properly will throw down all before it (lines 1–2); if not,
it will destroy itself (lines 3–4). Likewise, if the lover speaks out, he
will harm another, and, if not, himself alone (lines 5–6). Wyatt rests
content with only one aspect of Serafino's situation—that a misfiring
gun will destroy itself, and so will he, through his inability to speak
or look his love. He says nothing of harming others by a successful
explosion of gunfire or passion, omissions which are consistent but
which leave unexplained the lover's inhibition. A further result is that
the first part of Wyatt's poem becomes a mass of technical details. The
description of the breaking gun is vivid, but too long in comparison
with the parallel description of the breaking heart. Wyatt's 'right so
doeth my desire' lags a half-line behind Serafino. The consequence is a
slight disproportion, as well as a loss of concentration; but it is of interest that Wyatt avoids some of the stiffness that might have resulted
from too close an adherence to Serafino.

In this case, too, Wyatt adopts a more complicated syntax. Upper-
most, therefore, is what was always a main problem with him—the
adjustment of a periodic sentence to the music of his stanzas. The first
main clause, initiated in line one and not completed till line four,
presses forward with magnificent urgency, to land with fierce emphasis on its verb: 'The furyous gonne . . . Cracketh'. These four
lines are widely different in effect from their Italian equivalents. They

are less sweet and harmonious, but more oratorical. Serafino, with habitual poise, balances two strictly symmetrical conditional sentences: 'Se . . . Ma se . . .' Wyatt's wild eloquence is, in its way, the bolder, more original effect. Unfortunately, his subordinate clauses are not handled with the 'Miltonic' skill of the main one. However the third line is uttered, the metre brings stress where it is not logically apt. 'And that' sets syntax and music at odds. Again, Wyatt's second sentence is marred by clumsy subordinate clauses. This time there is little compensating eloquence, though he does achieve the equivalent in sound of his subject's violence and disorder. He destroys not only the balance of section against section and line against line, but even the internal balance of single lines. Contrast the dainty swing of 'Sel taccio imor, sel dico altrui molesto' with the pounding irregularity of 'Whose flame encreseth from more to more'. And, finally, he cuts through the originally self-contained final couplet. The extent of his success must remain a matter of opinion; what was once dubbed 'clumsiness' in Wyatt does not nowadays lack champions. At any rate his intention in 'The furyous gonne' is clear. He strives towards a greater fullness and violence than Serafino's strambotto contains. His response to the subject of breaking guns and hearts has been more serious than Serafino's. Though this is one of the 'conceited' strambotti, generally deplored, to suggest that so promising a poem deforms English poetry or sets a bad example would surely be an exaggeration.

The preceding examples have comprised strambotti serious in the original, and, if anything, made more serious by Wyatt. Two more illustrate his attempt at this form in its better known guise, as a light piece of gallantry:

> À che minacci, à che tanta ira e orgoglio,
>   Per questo non farai chel furto renda.
> Non senza causa la tua man dispoglio
>   Rapir quel daltri non fú mai mia menda.
> Famme citar dauanti amor chio uoglio,
>   Che la ragion de luno & laltro intenda.
> Lei il cor mi tolse, & io gli hó tolto un guanto
>   Vorró saper da te se u cor ual tanto.   (f. 170^{r-v})

> What nedeth these thretning wordes and wasted wynde?
>   All this cannot make me restore my pray.
> To robbe your good, I wis, is not my mynde,
>   Nor causeles your fair hand did I display.

Let love be judge, or els whome next we meit,
   That may boeth here what you and I can say.
She toke from me an hert and I a glove from her:
Let vs se nowe, if th'one be wourth th'othre.   (no. 48)

Incolpa donna amor se troppo io uolsi
   Aggiungendo alla tua la bocca mia.
Se pur punir mi uoi di quel chio tolsi
   Fá che concesso replica mi sia.
Che tal dolceza in quelli labri accolsi,
   Chel spirto mio fú per fugirsi uia.
Só che al secondo tocco uscirá fora
   Bastar ti dé, che per tal fallo io mora.   (f. 179^v)

Alas! madame, for stelyng of a kysse,
   Have I so much your mynd then offended?
Have I then done so greuously amysse,
   That by no meanes it may be amended?
Then revenge you, and the next way is this:
   An othr kysse shall have my lyffe endid.
For to my mowth the first my hert did suck,
The next shall clene oute of my brest it pluck.   (no. 44)

These strambotti breathe the air of the court, its sophisticated amours
and frivolous gallantries. They are naughty but not vicious, flirtatious
but not passionate, overbearing but not brutal. They describe storms
in tea cups, blowing up in the first because the poet has stolen a glove,
and in the second a kiss. Unimportant feminine tantrums are seen from
the view-point of the worldly male. There is much of the scepticism
common to Serafino and Wyatt.

'À che minacci', literally translated by Wyatt, opens in apparent
seriousness with talk of 'minacci' (threats) and 'furto' (prey). The
triviality of their connection with 'tua man' (your hand) is not revealed
until line three in Serafino's strambotto, and line four in Wyatt's. The
second phase opens, at line five, with protests of the bombastic male
kind: 'Let love be judge'. 'Or els whome next we meit'—Wyatt, in
adding this, gets the appropriate spirit, almost the social environment,
perfectly. The rhythm is light, there are no attempts at eloquent
periods, and Wyatt cultivates the neatness and liveliness of Serafino's
short sentences, with their variety of questions and imperatives. The
reason for all this fuss has, however, been only partially revealed as to
do with a lady's hand. It remains for the final couplet to bring forward
the lover's theft of her glove, and, with the same air of discovery, her

theft of his heart. Is a heart worth a glove? The concluding witticism turns the tables on the temperamental lady of the opening threats. The translation has all the liveliest qualities of the original and of the kind of strambotto it typifies.

Wyatt translates 'Incolpa donna' more freely, not, this time, because he is unable to incorporate all the original detail, but because, in full possession of it, he works for enhancement. The recasting of the two opening sentences as questions at once reveals his confidence, as does the courtly, mock-serious phrasing of his opening 'Alas! madame'. He works well within the easy distich units of the strambotto. The opening talk of the grievous wrong of stealing a kiss gives way, with an even more suspicious submissiveness, to the lover's suggestion that he should be punished. Serafino begins to adumbrate this notion at line three, but Wyatt delays it until lines four and five. There are other signs that he is shifting the weight towards the end. Serafino suggests a return kiss ('replica') at line four, while Wyatt waits till line five. Serafino's assertion that the first kiss brought him to the verge of death occurs at line six. Wyatt shifts it to the final couplet, where, when it comes, it is both more surprising and more concentrated. Serafino's couplet pushes home the idea that the second kiss would successfully kill him. But Wyatt's gives the whole history of these deadly kisses in two witty lines, to which zest is added by the emphatic rhyming of 'suck' and 'pluck'. Yet his alterations are entirely in harmony with the spirit of the original. For frivolity and wit, they actually improve upon it. There can be no doubt that Wyatt, as translator, is most successful with light strambotti of this kind. And what of the 'stiff figures and images' supposedly the product of Wyatt's admiration for Serafino? In neither this nor the preceding example is there anything but ease and fluency.

If all five translations are taken together, it becomes clear that the case against their having either intrinsic or historical value, though not without some foundation, has been much exaggerated. Serafino was not a great poet, but it does not follow that he provided a useless model. True, Minturno dubbed him 'ingegnoso, ma indegno d'imitatione',[1] but that was a warning to Italian poets of 1563, not to English ones of c.1527. His concentration, his control of imagery and structure, were not unworthy objects of study for early Tudor poets. The unfortunate aspect of his influence, flamboyance and rhetorical stiffness, is reflected in Wyatt, but not nearly to the extent that Rollins would claim.

[1] *Op. cit.*, the prefatory table.

As far as Wyatt's debt to Serafino is concerned, the positive gain out weighs the negative. For his two most successful translations of Serafino's strambotti have historical value as the first good examples of the English epigram. And they also have literary value, unless this be solemnly denied to all light, social verse which is designedly limited in scope, and, in its origin and appeal, more fanciful than imaginative. This is a minor historical event and a minor poetic achievement which Wyatt's critics have not sufficiently valued.

The strambotto's general value—or lack of it—can also be observed in Wyatt's independent attempts at this form. The translations, whose themes range from the philosophical to the amorous, taught him something of Serafino's range. His own strambotti are equally varied. On the one hand are clever fancies like 'Off purpos Love chase first for to be blynd' (no. 98), a comparison of the blind Cupid with the seeing lover. On the other are macabre anecdotes, as, of a miser's gruesome end (no. 191) and of a mother who eat her own child (no. 80). Many, like 'In court to serue decked with freshe aray' (no. 193), are satirical. Some of the most interesting are personal: 'Syghes are my foode' (no. 168) is addressed to Sir Francis Brian from prison, while 'Tagus, fare well' (no. 97) commemorates Wyatt's departure from Spain in 1539. Here he finds the strambotto a useful vehicle for occasional utterances.

Wyatt's strambotti collectively imply that the medium was not uncongenial to him. He applied himself seriously to the literary problems presented by this medium, and two of the main ones concerned the use of the Italianate conventions and the adjustment of syntax to metrical music.

Certainly the independent strambotti yield instances of the stiff conventionality and rhetorical frigidity so often condemned:

> The fructe of all the seruise that I serue
>   Dispaire doth repe, such haples hap have I;
> But tho he have no powre to make me swarve,
>   Yet bye the fire for colde I fele I dye.
> In paradis for hunger still I sterve,
>   And in the flowde for thurste to deth I drye;
> So Tantalus ame I and yn worse payne,
>   Amyds my helpe and helples doth remayne.   (no. 135)

The torment endured in the unending service of love is a trite Petrarchan subject, made more trite, here, by the handling. The mass of oxymora and antitheses, favourite Caritean devices, acts exactly as in 'I fynde no peace' (no. 26), Wyatt's translation of Petrarch. It holds the argument to a single point. And though this was its original intention, the result will appear static to readers not attuned to Cariteanism (or to Euphuism, which, in prose, achieves the same effect by the same means). The image of the man who shivers by the fire, though un-original, serves to reveal the lover's despair. But when it is followed by hunger in paradise, thirst in the flood, and, at last, by Tantalus, attention strays from the matter to the manner. The devices take on a life independent of their meaning, which remains, as it were, spell-bound. There is so much repetition that when the summing up of the couplet comes it merely sounds obvious.

Where conventional devices of style are concerned, it is commonly asked—does the author make them his own? An answer is provided by a strambotto on a theme which can be called Wyatt's own, the de-sertion of friends who once took bread at his hands:

> Luckes, my faire falcon, and your fellowes all,
>   How well plesaunt yt were your libertie!
> Ye not forsake me that faire might ye befall.
>   But they that somtyme lykt my companye,
> Like lyse away from ded bodies thei crall:
>   Loe, what a profe in light adversytie!
> But ye, my birdes, I swear by all your belles,
>   Ye be my fryndes, and so be but few elles.   (no. 170)

The use of a central conceit is the most obvious convention here. Wyatt's falcons, like Serafino's mirror, establish a parallel and point a contrast. Mastery of the conventional technique is shown in Wyatt's skilful application of the image to two aspects of his own situation. The freedom of the falcons contrasts with his own lack of it, their loyalty with the disloyalty of his friends. His strambotto has the control, coherence and concentration proper to its kind. Much sheer intellectual effort has gone into it, but what raises it above the level of mere cleverness or ingenuity is the fine variation of tone that supports the contrasts worked out through the conceit. The free and friendly birds are offset against mean, earth-bound pests, and the exhilaration felt in 'Luckes, my faire falcon, and your fellowes all' gives way to a sneer at those who crawl 'Like lyse away from ded bodies'. The strambotto differs from 'The fructe of all the seruise', not because it has broken away from convention, but because it has broken away from mere derivativeness.

Some of Wyatt's most successful conventionalities exploit the skills learned in translating Serafino's strambotti on the revenge earned by stolen gloves or kisses. 'Who hath herd of suche crueltye before?' (no. 42) and 'She sat and sowde that hath done me the wrong' (no. 54) are two versions of the same lover's tale. They portray the kind of lady who goes on with her needlework while her lover utters his piteous 'plaint'. Indeed she pricks at her sampler in lieu of his heart. The wit of the revenge is trivial enough, but it comes with delightful surprise as the final couplet turns the tables:

> For as she thought this is his hert in dede,
> She pricked herd and made her self to blede.

As to the problem of syntax and music, Wyatt's difficulties lie between the rocks of stiffness and incoherence. Where he simplifies his grammar, allowing it to follow the distich unit and central pause of the Italian strambotto, he remains lucid, if, sometimes, rather mechanical:

> Desire, alas, my master and my foo,
> So sore alterd thi selff, how mayst thou se?
> Some tyme I sowght that dryvys me to and fro;
> Some tyme thow ledst that ledyth the and me. (no. 75)

Where he ambitiously overrides the conventional structure, the result is often garbled, unmusical, or, at best, of confused magnificence:

> With spurr and sayle for I go seke the Tems
> Gaynward the sonne that shewth her welthi pryd
> And to the town which Brutus sowght by drems
> Like bendyd mone doth lend her lusty syd. (no. 97)

On the whole, Wyatt's most promising solution is to retain a simple grammar while varying the pauses as much as possible. By so doing he achieves one of his finest results in a description of his undetermined future. Will he again put his head into the noose of love, and under what conditions?

> A face that shuld content me wonders well
> Shuld not be faire but louelie to behold,
> With gladsome cheare all grief for to expell;
> With sober lookes so wold I that it should
> Speake without wordes, such woordes as non can tell;
> The tresse also should be of crysped gold;
> With witt: and thus might chaunce I might be tyde,
> And knyt agayne the knott that should not slide. (no. 171)

He opens with a flowing distich to which the third line is loosely linked. Another follows, before, in line six, he utters an arresting one-line statement. A clipped addition—'with witt' —shortens the phrasing still further, before the couplet returns to something of the original fulness. The central pause is not observed, nor does Wyatt slavishly follow the distich-pattern. His variations realize in terms of rhythm the intriguing mixture of his open enthusiasm and narrow circumspection. Though still using the form taken over from Serafino, he is here at his furthest from stiff, derivative writing.

Wyatt found in Serafino what he did not find in Petrarch—a teacher whom he could surpass. Serafino, the most popular poet of his day, is now merely a text book name, and one, too, subject to contempt because his influence on his immediate successors far outstripped his intrinsic worth as a poet as judged by posterity. But it is often so. In their practical capacity as craftsmen, poets seek not so much great precedents as congenial and manageable modes of expression. It was easier for Restoration writers of comedy to extract a usable formula from Jonson than from Shakespeare. Serafino, in many ways his kindred spirit, provided Wyatt with an equally handy formula. What could he have extracted from *The Divine Comedy*? If he had had time, encouragement and inclination—all of which were lacking—to model himself on Dante, the result might well have stood in as absurd a relation to the sublime original as Haydon's large canvases do to Michelangelo's.

CHAPTER VIII
Neo-Classical Satire

Wyat appears a much more pleasing writer when he moralises on the felicities of retirement, and attacks the vanities and vices of a court with the honest indignation of an independent philosopher, and the freedom and pleasantry of Horace.[1]

I T was with a sigh of relief that Thomas Warton turned from Wyatt's 'overstrained' sonnets and epigrams to his three satires or verse letters; and these, since his day, have continued to enjoy a high reputation. They are the product of the last decade (1532–42) of his life, a time when Wyatt, while he was still ready for new ventures, may also be supposed to have assimilated much of his social and literary experience. More obviously than any other group of his poems the satires are *Erlebnisdichtung*, with Wyatt referring explicitly to his life at home and court, and to his friends Poynz and Brian. They also have literary sources which are indicated, in part, by Warton's reference to Horace. More fully, the satires may be defined as a synthesis of material from Wyatt's favourite sources—the literatures of England, Rome, and Italy. Common to all three is that most popular of moral and satiric themes, the complaint against the times, a complaint often accompanied by attacks on the 'vanities and vices of a court' and by nostalgia for the 'felicities of retirement'. Nor is the anti-court theme merely a literary matter. In an aristocratic or feudal society, whether in medieval England, Imperial Rome, or Renaissance Italy, the same abuses must

[1] Thomas Warton, *History of English Poetry* (1774–81), ed. W. C. Hazlitt (London, 1871), iv. 45.

obviously occur and be centred on the court. There are men like Ariosto and More who have really preferred retirement, that is, for whom the Sabine farm is not simply a literary fantasy.

Though satire was not a recognized literary kind in England before the 1590s, the satiric mode is prominent in the Middle Ages and early Renaissance. Through that period the anti-court theme runs an unbroken course. In medieval satire the attack is frequently generalized. The satirist is often self-characterized as a simple clown, who speaks less as an individual with a grievance than as the representative of an aggrieved, downtrodden people. He is democratic and progressive. Piers Plowman is introduced as a poorly clad rustic, alone on the Malvern hills and as far removed from civilization as may be. The court is but one of the abuses he attacks, and when he does so, it is as a complete outsider who neither has nor desires a footing there. Yet Langland's sketch of governing circles, early in his poem, contains much that the insiders would recognize. A rout of rats (lords) and small mice (commoners) is found at the mercy of the cat (king):

> For a cat of a courte · cam whan hym lyked,
> And ouerlepe hem lyghtlich · and laughte hem at his wille,
> And pleyde with hem perilouslych · and possed hem aboute.
> *(Piers the Plowman,* i. 149–51)[1]

The animal fable is a popular satiric vehicle of the Middle Ages, as is the elaborate allegory of which, in *Piers Plowman*, it forms a part. Both enable Langland to project his criticism of society in terms which are universally applicable. Through his main allegory he has much to say, in general terms, of vices which other satirists relate specifically to the court. In Passus II, for example, Mede (Reward and Bribe) marries Fals (Falsehood), while her father Favell (Flattery) 'thorw his faire speche' deceives the people into approbation of the event.

London Lickpenny,[2] the anonymous fifteenth-century satire, turns on the antithesis of town and country, stock emblems of wicked sophistication and innocent simplicity. The hero, another poor ploughman, goes up to London to obtain redress of a wrong, but, because he has no money, no one will take up his case. He cannot even get a ferry over the Thames, his cloak is stolen, and so he is glad to return to his Kentish plough. Though there are no bucolic musings, the inference

[1] *Op. cit.*, ed. W. W. Skeat (Oxford, 1886), i. 14.
[2] See *English Verse between Chaucer and Surrey*, ed. E. P. Hammond (Durham, N. Carolina and London, 1927), pp. 237–9.

distinctly emerges—that one is more worthily employed *chez soi*, in peace and quiet, than in the haunts of selfishness and greed.

Skelton represents the early sixteenth-century underdog:

> Thus I, Colyn Cloute,
> As I go aboute,
> And wandrynge as I walke,
> I here the people talke.
>
> *(Colyn Cloute*, 1519–20, lines 287–90)[1]

His rebukes are direct, unsubtle, vigorous. He is violently vituperative, and the Skeltonic verse which is 'helter-skelter John's' speciality reinforces the impression that his temper is quite out of control:

> Our shepe are shrewdly shorne,
> And trouthe is all to-torne;
> Wysdom is laught to skorne,
> Fauell is false forsworne,
> Iauell is nobly borne,
> Hauell and Haruy Hafter,
> Iack Trauell and Cole Crafter,
> We shall here more herafter;
> With pollynge and shauynge,
> With borowynge and crauynge,
> With reuynge and rauynge,
> With swerynge and starynge,
> There vayleth no resonynge,
> For wyll dothe rule all thinge,
> Wyll, wyll, wyll, wyll, wyll,
> He ruleth alway styll.
>
> *(Why come ye nat to Courte?* 1522–3,
> lines 89–104)

When, in the allegory *The Bowge of Courte* (1498), Skelton takes on the role of courtier it is in the guise of a completely helpless novice. The 'I' of the poem is Drede, who boards the ship of Fortune only to encounter Favell (Flattery), Suspect, Harvy Hafter (Swindler), Disdain, Riot, Dissimulation, Deceit—a crowd so terrible, a situation so frighteningly insecure, as to render wholly credible Drede's final attempt to leap overboard.

By contrast with these popular English satirists, the Scottish courtier-poet William Dunbar (*c.* 1460–?1522) writes more specifically,

---

[1] Quotations in this section are from *The Poetical Works of John Skelton*, ed. Alexander Dyce, rev. edition (Boston, 1856).

more as an insider, and more *in propria persona* of courtly abuses. His favourite medium is the *planctus*. In a complaint to James IV he declares that men of wit and wisdom, such as Dunbar himself, are not promoted, unlike the rogues whom he so vividly abuses:

> Stuffettis, strekouris, and stafische strummellis;
> Wyld haschbaldis, haggarbaldis, and hummellis;
> Druncartis, dysoris, dy[v]owris, drevellis,
> Misgydit memberis of the devellis.[1]

'Aganis the Solistaris in Court' contrasts the 'divers wyis and operatiounes', 'the besy labouris for premocione', of flatterers and deceivers with the 'sempillnes' of Dunbar himself.[2] With no pretensions to be a serious critic or moralist, he excels in these short self-righteous sallies, every bit as splenetic as Skelton's longer ones.

Alexander Barclay's neo-classical *Egloges* (*c.* 1515) make the first break with native forms, but remain in other respects wholly medieval. The first three derive their substance from Aeneas Silvius's *De Curialium Miseriis* (1444), a Latin prose account of the 'miseryes of Courtiers and Courtes of all princes in generall'. Barclay does not, however, borrow its epistolary form. Instead he models his poem on Mantuan's Latin eclogues, first published in 1498. Arcadian shepherds now take the place of the rustics of the native tradition, and the dialogues of Coridon and Cornix are a new thing in English literature. But, like Mantuan, Barclay is remote from the original classical masters. The Theocritan and Virgilian eclogue, while often including polemic and satire, served also to express the idyllic world of Arcadia. It was not meant to concentrate on 'miseryes'. Barclay, with his constant inveighing and complaining, is closer to Langland and Skelton; only he is much duller. He exposes vice in general (gluttony, lust, &c.), as well as the more specifically courtly abuses, like place-hunting. The picture is one of unrelieved gloom:

> The Court is in earth an ymage infernall,
> Without fayre paynted, within vggly and vile.
>
> . . . .
>
> This life is beastly and vtterly damnable.[3]

---

[1] *The Poems of William Dunbar*, ed. W. Mackay Mackenzie (London, 1932), no. 19.

[2] *Ibid.*, no. 29. Solistaris = suitors.

[3] *The Eclogues*, ed. Beatrice White, E.E.T.S., o.s. no. 175 (London, 1928), i. 1260–1 and ii. 571.

The Latin satirists Horace, Persius, and Juvenal were not forgotten in medieval England, but no attempt was made to imitate the classical form of satiric epistle or talk, and very little to catch its spirit. There was no immediate change after 1470, when printed editions of all three appeared. Skelton might quote Juvenal, but he did not think of working in a neo-classical framework, while Barclay ignored the proper classical vehicle for what he had to say. The Latin satirists shared in the general revival of learning. Nevertheless it was wisdom, not form and style, that the earliest Humanists were concerned to learn from the ancients. Lessons in abundance the earnest reader would find in Horace, Persius, and Juvenal. In fact a good deal of their wisdom is vested in attacks on courtly vices and in eulogies of retirement; and there was much here that would simply fill out, and at no point contradict, ideas already current in English thinking on these perennial topics.

Horace understands such things as the rat-race and boot-licker better than most men. His satires attack the race for wealth and position (I. i), or social and political ambition (I. vi). He tells a story of how a mere acquaintance joined him for a stroll in order to secure an introduction to Maecenas (I. ix), or describes a vulgar, ostentatious dinner at which Maecenas was guest of honour (II. viii). There is a witty account of his own conversation with Maecenas, which, while all envy Horace his supposed initiation into secrets of state, is actually about nothing but sport, the weather, or 'what's the time?' (II. vi). Rivalry for patronage, envy, flattery, deception, suspicion, ambition, &c.—Horace perceives the same courtly vices as Langland, Skelton, Dunbar, or Barclay. Yet to turn from their satire to his is to enter a different milieu. Horace is much more intimate and casual than the medieval English satirists. His personal background, Rome or the Sabine farm, is not readily forgotten. His satires are addresses to friends in the form of *epistolae* or *sermones*. He delights, he says, to do as Lucilius did, and to trust his secrets to his books, as if to faithful friends:

> ille velut fidis arcana sodalibus olim
> credebat libris.   (II. i. 30–1)

Compared, therefore, to such intricate constructions as *Piers Plowman* or *The Bowge of Courte*, Horace's satires seem informal. If he includes a fable or allegory it is within a conversation; these are not part of his structure. His sketches of contemporary life bear the appearance of being direct transcripts from his personal experience. *Piers* and the

Bowge contain life-like pictures—Langland's pardoner and Skelton's Harvy Hafter are as vivid as Horace's bore—but with Horace the individual character study stands in place of the typical or allegorical one. He is most unlike Barclay. His semi-dramatic dialogues contrast sharply with the stiff exchange of homilies between the shepherds in the *Egloges*. He is rather closer to Dunbar and Skelton. Horace often speaks in his own person or uses a mouthpiece, like the Apulian farmer, exponent of the quiet life (II. ii). But his monologues, for all their subjective and casual flavour, would not stand a close comparison with the personal effusions of Dunbar or the unbuttoned diatribes of Skelton. There is too big a difference of satiric tone and method. Horace is less direct, less uncontrolled, less abusive. True, he can be brutally insulting, as when attacking sensual indulgence (I. ii), but his more settled and mature manner is genial and detached. He is more the wit and ironist than any English satirist, except Chaucer, before the eighteenth century. Furthermore his detachment suggests a philosophical point of view. Horace does not aim at radical reform like Langland, nor inveigh like Skelton or Barclay. The ills he experiences in Rome merely make him long to return to the Sabine farm. He is less the moral or social reformer than the philosopher-critic, one who reflects on the contemporary scene, one who brings good sense rather than vehemence to his task. His philosophy is non-partisan, but partakes of the general individualism associated with the Stoics. He is not representative of 'every man' or even of a social group. He is merely himself, an independent thinker, discoursing to or with a small group of kindred spirits. Horace's is therefore more exclusive satire than the medieval English, more gentlemanly, civilized, and thoughtful. Several of his satires discuss the aims of this kind. He stipulates for an appropriate use of humour, for brevity, clarity, and smoothness, these last being characteristic of what was known, in poetry and oratory, as the plain style or *genus tenue* (I. x). Horace concludes that the satirist should aim at pleasing, not the multitude, but a small circle of good critics. (I. x. 72–91).

Horace's successor Persius lived to write only ten satires, and because of this, as well as a certain obscurity of style, he was less influential. His satires leave an impression similar to Horace's. The first, an attack on bad literature and taste in Rome, both taken as signs of a general corruption of manners, is in dialogue form. Are you afraid, Persius asks his friend, that people will rate Labeo (a poetaster) above me? Nonsense! Do not try to put the beef-witted Romans right about literature—or anything. 'Nec te quaesiveris extra' (I. 7): look to no one but yourself. Such philosophical detachment and self-sufficiency, such coolness and easy-goingness, is again remote from the English satirists.

Though Persius can also employ the direct rebuke, it is rather in Juvenal that this 'English' weapon finds its classical counterpart. Skelton claims to write *Why come ye nat to Courte?* 'at Juvenal's request', the corruption of Wolsey's England being so appalling to the good man, that 'Difficile est saturam non scribere'. This famous dictum from Juvenal's first satire (line 30) emerges from an enraged description of a Rome where eunuchs marry, barbers challenge the wealth of aristocrats, guttersnipes wear Tyrian purple, and retainers fawn on the man who has debauched his ward: 'Quid referam quanta siccum iecur ardeat ira?' (line 45). Juvenal's 'saeva indignatio', so often contrasted with Horace's urbanity, is certainly closer to the prevailing temper of Langland, Skelton, Dunbar, and Barclay. (The proper English contrast would be in Chaucer's obliqueness, geniality, and reserve.) Furthermore, Juvenal rarely describes or ridicules individual characters, making rather a total onslaught upon types and upon vice in general; and in this, too, he calls to mind the English invectives and allegories. Courtly abuses, such as the humiliation of suitors by patrons, are merely items in a universal social corruption, which is viewed with the utmost pessimism. Nevertheless Juvenal claimed Horace as his master. And if his mood is comparable with the English satirists', his form is still as far from theirs as is Horace's.

Like much else that was new to the Renaissance, the first modern vernacular imitations of classical epistolary satire appeared in Italy; and thence came Wyatt's immediate inspiration. But before his Italian background is considered, it will be useful to take stock of the English and classical.

The extent of Wyatt's reading in English literature is impossible to determine. Chaucer is the only English author he mentions: the unsatirical Chaucer of *The Knight's Tale*. He would, however, surely understand that the traditional anti-court theme had been and still was current in the national literature. That he knew the work of older contemporaries like Skelton—the laureate and a fellow-courtier—if not also Barclay is a natural assumption. Skelton died in 1529, and Barclay, though he survived till 1552, wrote nothing of importance after 1523. Wyatt succeeds to their matter, though not to their manner. Of his reading of classical literature there is more exact, if still limited, evidence. In 1527 he translated Plutarch's *Quyete of Mynde*, and, at a date unknown, a passage from Seneca's *Thyestes*. Neither is satirical, but both would serve to remind Wyatt of common classical satiric attitudes. There is Plutarch's condemnation of all worldly involvements, including the 'many cares and busynesses' of courts, those scenes of 'backbiting / of enuy / or nouhhty sclaundre' (sig. a 8ʳ⁻ᵛ). There is likewise Seneca's repudiation of the 'brackishe ioyes' of court in favour of the quiet life (no. 176). Seneca, with Epictetus, is also a moralist whom Wyatt recommended to his son. In addition it is likely that, as a university man, he read the Latin satirists; and Horace and Persius, at least, seem to have left traces in his own satires.

Apart from the general encouragement given by native and classical literature, there are reasons why Wyatt should turn to anti-court satire, reasons which lie outside literature. Of Wyatt's social and personal experience, the subject of an earlier chapter, only a brief reminder is necessary, sufficient to recall the fact that the European courts of his day were not beds of roses. Nor were they thought of as such. Criticism was in the air. Even Castiglione's *Courtier* (1528), entirely concerned to promote positive ideals, recognizes the seamy side of court life: 'sauciness', flattery, rivalry for 'favour and promotion', contentiousness, &c.: 'There is a storme in courtes that carrieth this condition with it.'[1] In 1539 appeared, from Spain, Antonio de Guevara's *A Dispraise of the Life of a Courtier*, to use the title of the English translation published in 1548. The translator was Wyatt's friend, Sir Francis Brian. 'Fauor and coueetuousnes guideth the Courtier', 'Courtiers . . . forgettyng themselfes, for the obteinyng of a litle fauour, do against nature, flatter, & begge', 'among courtiers is neither kept amitie nor faythfulnes: And howe muche the Court is full of trauail, of enuye & rancour'.[2] Though the comments of the noble Castiglione provoke no smile, there is irony in the fact that Brian, whose career is one long illustration of Favell, Riot, and Dissimulation, should condemn the passions he was unable to surmount.[3] The example nevertheless shows that anti-court sentiments were considered perfectly *en règle* —Brian dedicated his work to Catherine Parr's brother—and were, indeed, almost to be expected of sixteenth-century courtiers. The Guevara–Brian *Dispraise* is a mass of clichés. In Wyatt's case, unlike Brian's, the anti-court sentiments were touched off by personal

[1] *Op. cit.*, trans. Thomas Hoby. Everyman edition, p. 106.
[2] *Op. cit.*, trans. Brian, sigs. c 7ᵛ, d 1ʳ, k 7ᵛ.
[3] See Appendix C.

experience. He was not so uniformly successful as his friend. He knew the rancour of Suffolk, the envy of Bonner, the bitterness of imprisonment and banishment. His first satire refers to his retreat, probably in 1536, from Henry VIII's court to Allington Castle:

> homeward I me drawe,
> And fle the presse of courtes wher soo they goo,
> Rather then to lyve thrall, vnder the awe
> Of lordly lokes, . . .
> But here I ame in Kent and Christendome
> Emong the muses where I rede and ryme.
>
> (no. 196, lines 2–5, 100–1)

Wyatt is thinking the thoughts of his time. But it remains to explain his Italianate expression of them.

Given the impulse to express anti-court sentiments, there is every reason why Wyatt should seek a literary model in Italy. Italian poetic form always attracted him. The same interest that led him to Petrarch and the sonnet, to Serafino and the strambotto, now led him to the neoclassical satires in Italian terza rima published by Luigi Alamanni in 1532. Petrarch wrote three sonnets against the court of Rome and Serafino launched many sarcastic attacks on his courtier-patrons, but there was evidently something more suited to Wyatt's purposes in the more modern satire of Alamanni. As Wyatt's third Italian master, he deserves close attention.

Luigi Alamanni (1495–1556) was born in Florence, where, as a young man, he consorted with Machiavelli, Diacceto, Trissino, and the brothers Bernardo and Giovanni Rucellai—authors who used to read their poems and plays to each other, but who were also apt to talk of politics and the dangerous subject of Florentine liberty. Under the oppressive régime of Cardinal Giulio de' Medici, appointed by the Pope to govern Florence, they soon came to grief. The discovery of an anti-Medici plot in 1522 resulted in arrests and flights. Alamanni, pursued by the Cardinal's wrath, repaired to France, making Lyons his centre and the Provençal countryside his second home. He was well received by Francis I, who delighted in his Italian recitation and even employed him on diplomatic embassies. But the King was to prove a better patron to his poetry than to his cause. Alamanni's republican ardour did not flag. It was constantly applied to the thankless task of enlisting Europe's aid for the Florentine republic. Inevitably he suffered much disillusionment with the courts of princes, and often longed to retire from the fray. And, in moments of frustration, amid the sorrows of exile, these feelings found a ready outlet in verse. His satires belong to this first period of exile. In 1527, just after Wyatt's visit to Italy, Alamanni was able to return home, but it was to a Florence agitated by factions. The republican interlude was short-lived. On the return of the Medici in 1530, Alamanni took up the life of exile again. Proud and dauntless, he continued to win much respect from his sympathizers. Wyatt may even have been among them. They could have met in Lyons or at the French court, but there is no record of this. Both were poets, diplomats, courtiers, and travellers. Wyatt knew enough of Italian affairs—he had seen the beleaguered Florence and futile Medici Pope of 1527—to understand Alamanni's plight. Though he did not love liberty with Alamanni's high-minded republican zeal, Wyatt, too, became a patriotic hater of papal tyranny. Alamanni is bound, indeed, to appeal to men of Protestant sympathies.

The literary group to which Alamanni originally belonged was strongly neo-classical, cultivating Imitation of the Ancients with a thoroughness that leaves the England of Wyatt's day far behind. Indeed, its activities are not paralleled outside Italy before the generations of Du Bellay in France and of Sidney in England. Niccolò Machiavelli (1469–1527), if best remembered as political theorist, also has a reputation as an Italian Ben Jonson: his *Mandragola* is one of the liveliest modern classical comedies. But it was Giangiorgio Trissino (1478–1550) who gave the lead, devoting all his energies to the capture of the various classical kinds for Italy: Pindaric and Horatian odes, a tragedy *Sofonisba*, were followed, at last, by his life's work, the epic *L'Italia Liberata dai Goti* (1547). Under his influence Giovanni Rucellai (1475–1525) produced the tragedies of *Rosmunda* and *Oreste*, as well as *Le Api*, an imitation of Virgil's *Georgics*. At the group's meetings in the Oricellari Gardens in Florence *Sofonisba* and *Rosmunda* were read aloud. Alamanni, younger than the others, recited his sonnets and elegies. Soon he too was following in Trissino's footsteps, with Pindaric odes and the tragedy *Antigone*.

Opere Toscane (Lyons, 1532–3) is a two-volume collection of Alamanni's works in both Italian and classical forms. His preface justifies the inclusion of love poetry by reference to Tibullus and Propertius, 'i miei primi maestri', and the use of rhyme by reference to Tuscan and Provençal usage. There are sonnets of love and other personal matters like exile, his country, his friends; versions of the Penitential Psalms in terza rima; classical elegies and satires, also in terza rima; A *Favola di Narcisso* in ottava rima; a *Favola di Athlante, Diluvio Romano* and some eclogues in blank verse. The classical flavour is unmistakable, as, for example, in the *Lycidas*-like eclogue lamenting the death of Cosimo Rucellai: 'Lasciate, o ninfe, i freschi erbosi fondi'. To Wyatt, when he read it, the whole volume would seem profoundly unEnglish. Up to this point he had himself produced no neo-classical poetry. In Alamanni's satires he found his first neo-classical model.

Alamanni's thirteen Provençal satires, twelve of which are published in the first volume of the *Opere Toscane*,[1] form an important contribution to what was, even in 1532, a fairly new Italian neo-classical kind. The first Italian poems with the name of satires and in the classical form are those of Antonio Vinciguerra (fl. 1480),which were printed in 1495 and again in 1527. Their style being rough and uncultivated, his successors, Ariosto and Alamanni, still had pioneer work to do. Their satires are contemporaneous and complementary. Ariosto's, posthumously published in 1534, are imitations of Horace. They are unbitter, moderate, and peaceful in tone. Ariosto talks easily of himself, and of life in his beloved retreat from the court and the world at Ferrara. Alamanni's satires are, by contrast, primarily Juvenalian, though not without Horatian interludes. They are, for the most part, addresses to friends and sympathizers—his wife, Florentine expatriates like Tommaso Sertini and his brother the Bishop of Santes, or Giuliano Buonaccorsi, the Treasurer in Provence of the Florentine merchants. The first declares the reason prompting Alamanni to write satire: the ancient peace and virtue are dead, 'Tra che stolti pensier, tra quanti 'nganni'. Again, in the third, he announces that the greed, lust and ignorance of his time have put a whip in his hand. He is 'loaded' with scorn: 'Carco forse talhor di sdegnio'. He must expose a universal vice and folly:

> Mostrando al mondo quanto basse & uile
> È 'l suo 'imperfetto oprar.

He can no longer remain silent:

> Non posso piu tacer, chi tanto, o quanto
> Tacer porria?

'Difficile est saturam non scribere' is therefore as much Alamanni's motto as Juvenal's; and perhaps his reference to Ariosto as 'Il Fer-

---

[1] The numbering of the satires and the text is taken, throughout this section, from the first edition of *Opere Toscane*, I, 357–418.

rarese mio chiaro & gentile', which comes towards the end of the third satire, denotes his own recognition of the difference between them. Except that they are spiced with patriotic hopes, Alamanni's satires are as pessimistic as Juvenal's. His weapons are invective and sarcasm. He uses, too, a grim irony, as when exhorting the nations in turn to enjoy their favourite vices. Let France, for example, rejoice in wine and women:

> Godi pur Francia, & poi che sol ti piace
> Segui Vener, le piume, & l'ocio, e'l uino,
> Virtù fuggendo.   (no. xii)

Alamanni's style is grave and lofty, straining at times after its 'sublime' effects and generally lacking in wit and delicacy. There are times, however, when, in answer to the demands of his subject, he drops into the gentler Horatian manner. He does not lack the intimate touch when addressing friends, or when he describes, in truly classical spirit, the charms of country life. There are the flocks, the fruits, the fireside, the life of the family, the table spread with simple foodstuffs by a loving wife—what a contrast to 'le soglie regal' and the big city:

> Beato quel che 'n solitarie riue
> Lunge dal rozzo uulgo, al nudo cielo
> Fuor dall' ampie città contento uiue.   (no. ix)

Alamanni's tenth satire, which is the one imitated by Wyatt, was, probably, inspired by Juvenal's third. Juvenal here commends his friend Umbricius, who is fleeing to the country from a corrupt Rome. And Umbricius explains that the honest man stands no chance in Rome, where merit is not rewarded. For himself, he cannot lie— 'mentire nescio'—cannot, in fact, fit in. The satire is mainly a description of Roman life, done in brilliant detail, even down to the pigeons, tiles, and wagons. Alamanni, on the other hand, is telling his friend Tommaso Sertini of his own reasons for preferring country to town. His satire is a boast, and to hear a satirist who praises his own superiority to the common herd is less pleasing than to hear one who praises his friend's. Furthermore, Alamanni's description of corruption is not accompanied by such life-like detail as Juvenal provides. It remains comparatively vague and general. Nevertheless, its passionate expression of Alamanni's disillusionment with contemporary courts is, in its way, impressive, and this would not be lost on Wyatt.

The whole substance of Wyatt's 'Myne owne John Poynz' (no.

196) derives from Alamanni's tenth satire. The poet explains to his friend the reasons for his withdrawal from court to country. It is not because he scorns the due rights of his rulers over him, or because he lacks desire for glory and honour. It is because he knows nothing of the arts by which men rise at court. This is the main body of the argument in both satires which are almost entirely given over to an amplification and illustration of the courtly 'arts' rejected by the poet. He cannot honour lecherers and drunkards or lick the boots of unworthy patrons. He cannot keep silent about wrongs or otherwise conceal what he really thinks. He is no flatterer, double-dealer, or turncoat. He cannot use wiles or sanction injustices; and of these he gives a series of examples from history, including literary history. And so on, with a good deal of repetition. The poet concludes that he is freer at home, where no one interferes with him and he can cultivate the muses. And he is glad of his home—in Provence or Kent—for it contrasts with epicurean France, wily Spain, drunken Germany (or Flanders), and, above all, with Rome, in which Christ is betrayed.

The satire takes the form of an address or letter to a friend—Tommaso Sertini or John Poynz—in whom the poet can confide his inmost thoughts:

> Io ui dirò poi che d' udir ui cale,
> > Thommaso mio gentil, perch' amo, & colo
> > Piu di tutti altri il lito Prouenzale.
> Et perche qui cosi pouero & solo,
> > Piu tosto che 'l seguir Signiori & Regi
> > Viuo temprando 'l mio infinito duolo.   (x. 1–6)

> Myne owne John Poynz, sins ye delight to know
> > The cause why that homeward I me drawe,
> > And fle the presse of courtes wher soo they goo,
> Rather then to lyve thrall, vnder the awe
> > Of lordly lokes, wrappid within my cloke,
> > To will and lust lerning to set a lawe;
> It is not . . . &c.   (no. 196. 1–7)

Alamanni has conferred on Wyatt this classical epistolary form, and with it a man-to-man intimacy that is not found in earlier English satire. Alamanni's introduction—he has yet to hurl his Juvenalian attack on courtly corruption—is Horatian in its moderation and reflectiveness. He considers whether any unjustifiable resentment could account for his rejection of court, deciding the point in his own favour:

Ne cio mi uien perch' io fra me dispregi
  Quei, ch' han dalla Fortuna in mano il freno
  Di noi, per sangue, & per ricchezze egregi.
Ma ben' è uer ch' assai gli estimo meno
  Che 'l uulgo, & quei ch' à cio ch' appar di fuore
  Guardan, senza ueder che chiugga il seno.   (lines 7–12)

It is not for becawse I skorne or moke
  The powar of them, to whome fortune hath lent
  Charge over vs, of Right, to strike the stroke:
But true it is that I have allwais ment
  Lesse to estime them then the common sort,
  Of owtward thinges that juge in their intent,
Withowt regarde what dothe inwarde resort.   (lines 7–13)

The poet weighs up himself and his situation. His tone is level and
suggests critical discernment. There is also much of the classical satirist's intellectual exclusiveness here. He speaks as a philosopher, and
like all classical satirists, from a generally Stoic point of view. Far from
identifying himself with 'the common sort', as Langland's Piers and
Skelton's Colin do, he is at pains to separate himself from them. For he
stands only for himself, the true individualist. All satirists, almost by
definition, must stand in isolation. They must be separate from what
they attack. By criticizing society, they become its outcasts. But Alamanni
and Wyatt emphasize this in the classical way. They have a fastidious,
intellectual, and self-conscious impulse to define the nature of their
own seclusion. They separate themselves not only from the common
people, but also from society's aristocrats, those whom Fortune, by
blood or wealth, allows to rule. They are themselves aristocrats, but
of a different—and, by implication, a superior—kind. Theirs is the
aristocracy of the mind. They judge not by 'outward' but by 'inward'
things. 'Fortune' is but casually referred to, for the good man is im-
pervious to its diverse chances and changes. This philosophy is itself
not unfamiliar to the English literature of Wyatt's day, but his assimilation of it into a satirical *persona* is new. As the classical *vir bonus* he
can command a social authority lacking in the outsider Langland and a
moral authority lacking in the irresponsible Skelton. Yet in this role,
Wyatt, owing to the skill with which he transposes it into a personal
key, appears sublimely English. The English, indeed, take well to the
idea of the honest, blunt man, incapable of flattery. Thomas Wyatt of
Allington Castle is like Shakespeare's Kent and like the 'honest' man
his Iago pretends to be. The effect is to inspire confidence. These men

can say what they like. There is a firm core of indifference in them, the kind of indifference to one's own prospects that the mud-slinging Dunbar lacks. They have too much proper pride to air their own grievances and call for justice as Dunbar does. They prefer to retire, in dignified order, from the fray they despise. They are more informed than Skelton's Drede. They are not novices at court but mature men who have seen through it. They are not frightened into jumping overboard, but sail away freely to their own private havens, with a glance of contemptuous pity at those who remain behind.

All this receives strong reinforcement at the end of Alamanni's and Wyatt's satires in the account of the poet's turning to his private resources:

> Questo fa che 'l mio regnio, e 'l mio thesoro
> — Son gli 'nchiostri & le carte, & piu ch' altroue
> Hoggi in Prouenza uolentier dimoro.
> Qui non ho alcun, che mi domandi doue
> Mi stia, ne uada, & non mi sforza alcuno
> À gir pe'l mondo quando agghiaccia & pioue . . .
> Sono in Prouenza . . .
> Con le mie Muse in solitario loco.   (lines 76–81, 97, 108)

> This maketh me at home to hounte and to hawke
> And in fowle weder at my booke to sitt.
> In frost and snowe then with my bow to stawke,
> No man doeth marke where so I ride or goo;
> In lusty lees at libertie I walke, . . .
> But here I ame in Kent and Christendome
> Emong the muses where I rede and ryme.
>
> (lines 80–4, 100–1)

Alamanni and Wyatt both like the freedom to read and write. It matters little that, in frosty weather, Alamanni is glad not to be forced out of doors, while Wyatt seizes the chance to go forth with his bow. Alamanni would have approved the change. The gist of all these personal passages is that the poet's occupation is a free choice, a reflection of his independence and integrity, of his refusal to go the world's way.

But this is not proclaimed to the world at large. What would be the use? 'They' would not understand. It is told to a friend, one who 'delights to know'. Wyatt's framework—that of a personal letter to a friend—is essentially Alamanni's. He even gives it a better finish. Alamanni seems to forget 'Thommaso mio gentil' towards the end, where he reverts again to the attack on the vices of the age. Wyatt

omits this rather tame retrogression, which would spoil the climax of
'here I ame in Kent and Christendome'; and substitutes an invitation
to 'my Poynz' to visit him: 'Thou shalt be judge how I do spend my
tyme.'

But Alamanni's personality also expresses itself in a specifically
Juvenalian way; and here, too, Wyatt follows him. Following the
ruminative introduction, which I have called generally 'classical' or
'Horatian' in tone, Alamanni launches into a ferocious Juvenalian
attack upon the vices he opposes. This occupies the centre of the poem
so as almost to crowd out the more reflective passages. Alamanni remains strongly personal and individualistic, but now he is so after a
different manner. His aristocratic exclusiveness increases, to become a
lofty, angry pride.

> *Io non saprei* Sertin porre in disparte
>   La uerità, colui lodando ogni hora
>   Che con piu danno altrui dal ben si parte.
> *Non saprei* reuerir che soli adora
>   Venere & Bacco, ne tacer saprei
>   Di quei che 'l uulgo falsamente honora.
> *Non saprei* piu ch' à gli immortali Dei
>   Render honor con le ginocchia inchine
>   À piu ingiusti che sian, fallaci, & rei.
> *Non saprei* nel parlar courir le spine
>   Con simulati fior, nell' opre hauendo
>   Mele al principio, & tristo assentio al fine.
> *Non saprei no,* . . .   (lines 19–31)

> My Poynz, *I cannot* frame me tune to fayne,
>   To cloke the trothe for praisse withowt desart,
>   Of them that lyst all vice for to retayne.
> *I cannot* honour them that settes their part
>   With Venus and Baccus all theire lyf long;
>   Nor holld my pece of them allthoo I smart.
> *I cannot* crowche nor knelle to do so grete a wrong,
>   To worship them, lyke gode on erthe alone,
>   That ar as wollffes thes sely lambes among.
> *I cannot* with my wordes complayne and mone,
>   And suffer nought; nor smart wythout complaynt,
>   Nor torne the worde that from my mouthe is gone. . . .
> *I cannot, I. No, no,* it will not be.   (lines 19–30, 76)

Wyatt is not only translating as closely as possible here but copying the
rhetorical effect of Alamanni's enumeration, tercet by tercet, of vices

he knows not of. For effect the tirade depends, of course, largely on the repetition of 'Non saprei' / 'I cannot', and the climax reached in 'Non saprei, no' / 'I cannot, I. No, no.' Alamanni repeats the key phrase sixteen times, Wyatt only eight; either because it proves too difficult or because he finds the formality frigid and boring. Little of the general impression is lost, however, and the prominence given to 'I' brings forward the idea of the satirist's now boastful assertiveness. He is self-appointed the scourge of society. A further series follows:

> *Non sono* in Francia à sentir beffe & danno
> > S' io non conosco i uin, s' io non so bene
> > Qual uiuanda è miglior di tutto l'anno.
> *Non* nella Hispagnia oue studiar conuiene
> > Piu che nell' esser poi nel ben parere,
> > Oue frode, & menzognia il seggio tiene,
> *Non* in Germania oue 'l mangiar e 'l bere
> > M' habbia à tor l'intelletto, & darlo in preda
> > Al senso, in guisa di seluagge fere.
> *Non sono* in Roma, oue chi 'n Christo creda,
> > Et non sappia falsar, ne far ueneni
> > Conuien ch' a casa sospirando rieda.
> *Sono* in Prouenza.... (lines 85–97)

> *I ame not* now in Ffraunce to judge the wyne,
> > With saffry sauce the delicates to fele;
> *Nor* yet in Spaigne where oon must him inclyne
> > Rather then to be, owtewerdly to seme.
> > I meddill not with wittes that be so fyne,
> *Nor* Fflaunders chiere letteth not my sight to deme
> > Of black and white, nor taketh my wit awaye
> > With bestlynes, they beeste do so esteme;
> *Nor I ame not* where Christe is geven in pray
> > For mony, poison and traison at Rome,
> > A commune practise vsed nyght and daie:
> But here *I ame* in Kent and Christendome. (lines 89–100)

Following Alamanni to the letter, Wyatt repeats the negative phrase four times, to sweep round finally to the splendid antithetical affirmative: 'But here I ame in Kent.' The whole tirade is, in fact, based on antitheses—between 'I' and 'they', the poet and the vulgar, the poet and the courtier, what people seem and what they are, what the poet is and what he is not, &c. In the detail of single lines Wyatt does not or cannot always follow out Alamanni's antitheses with their matching rhythmic balance. The clumsy 'Nor torne the worde that from my mouthe is gone' (line 30), if like in sense, is remote in effect from 'Mele al principio, & tristo assentio al fine' (line 30). This is an obstacle that Wyatt constantly met in translating Italian poems, for it is a feature of Petrarch's and Serafino's as well as of Alamanni's. However, in the present case, it is clear that, while he handles the music of individual lines and tercets freely, Wyatt is definitely imitating Alamanni's rhetorical repetition and antithesis. The whole sweep of his tirade is modelled on the original, and the original aggressiveness is also retained. This is an important aspect of Wyatt's new English satire. Anger is always difficult to handle artistically, and when it is the anger of a Stoic, who should above all exemplify self-control, the problem becomes acute. What confidence can we have in a satirist who, while attacking uncontrolled vice, himself loses his temper? The undisciplined manner of the Skeltonics is a case in point. It is terrifying, but does not command authority. It would not have done for Wyatt. By contrast, Alamanni's rhetoric supplies him with a model suggestive of an anger, which is real indeed, but still held within the bounds of decorum.

In achieving the sweeping effect of the tirade, Wyatt uses some rhythmic methods of his own. He is not so much bent on altering Alamanni's rhythm for the sake of alteration as on finding an English equivalent for his personal, angry speech. His handling of line 30 is probably, indeed, an instance of sheer ineptitude. But elsewhere his rhythms are often arresting, where Alamanni's are merely smooth. Contrast 'Non saprei no, doue 'l contrario intendo' (line 31) with the more sharply broken 'I cannot, I. No, no, it will not be' (line 76). There is only one marked medial line break (line 17) in Alamanni's satire, whereas Wyatt has several effective ones; for example, 'My wit is nought—I cannot lerne the waye' (line 57). Furthermore, such rhythmically self-contained and abrupt lines contrast with Alamanni's consistent three-line units. True, there is only a slight break between Alamanni's first tercet and his second, and he allows his last tercet to run on into the final line. Otherwise, following a common Italian practice, he does not permit enjambement between the tercets. They are self-contained units, comparable with the enclosed heroic couplet in eighteenth-century English poetry. Now Wyatt is using the Italian terza rima. In fact he is the first English poet to do so (with the very doubtful exception of Chaucer). And Alamanni is his instructor. The passage of close translation quoted above (lines 19–30) shows that he can make a sustained attempt to preserve the Italian character of the tercets. On the other hand, the more informal introductory passage (lines 1–7, also quoted above) is very differently constructed. Alamanni makes two distinct grammatical statements in his first two tercets. Wyatt does not complete his first grammatical statement until the beginning of his third tercet, with 'It is not . . .' (line 7). Thus by delaying the main clause he urges the voice to sustain the forward movement. And, having completed this first statement, he launches upon another of considerable length:

> But true it is that I have allwais ment
>> Lesse to estime them then the common sort,
>> Of owtward thinges that juge in their intent,
> Withowt regarde what dothe inwarde resort.   (lines 10–13)

Here again Wyatt has ridden over the barrier between the tercets. In all, he does this in ten out of the total of thirty-four. The verse, therefore, is looser than Alamanni's. Sometimes it flows forward more urgently than his, sometimes it is more abrupt. In both respects it achieves a more natural, speech-like result. 'Myne owne John Poynz' is therefore a mixture of formal Italianate and informal English rhetoric. Metrically and rhythmically it is experimental, though this does not mean that it is not also successful.

Wyatt tones down some of Alamanni's lofty rhetorical expressions, though again not consistently.

> I cannot honour them that settes their part
>> With Venus and Baccus all theire lyf long;   (lines 22–3)

is as high flown as

> Non saprei reuerir chi soli adora
>> Venere & Bacco.   (lines 22–3)

But, immediately after, Alamanni's extravagant reference to 'immortal gods' and his crowd of vague general terms ('cruel', 'deceptive', 'unjust') are remodelled into a concrete, fable-like description:

> Non saprei piu ch' à gli immortale Dei
>> Rendere honor con le ginocchia inchine
> À piu inguisti che sian, fallaci, & rei.   (lines 25–7)

> I cannot crowche nor knelle to do so grete a wrong,
>> To worship them, lyke gode on erthe alone,
>> That ar as wollffes thes sely lambes among.
>>>> (lines 25–7)

Wyatt's lines are more homely, and more consonant with the English satiric tradition. Then the vague generalities of

> Non trouare ad ogni hor false cagioni
> Per abbassare i giusti, alzando i praui,
> D' auaritia, & di 'nuidia hauendo sproni,   (lines 34–6)

become a precise, personal, metaphorical statement:

> I cannot wrest the law to fill the coffer
> With innocent blode to fede my sellff fat,
> And doo most hurt where most hellp I offer.
> (lines 34–6)

Following this, Wyatt omits two tercets in which Alamanni, having dealt with avarice and envy, proceeds to inveigh against ambition and pitilessness, and in the same hollow-sounding general terms. There is more ordinariness in Wyatt's idiom in general. He does not aim at sublimity through 'walking on tiptoe' to the same extent as Alamanni.

The nature of Wyatt's imitation is evident. While he retains Alamanni's argument, form, approach, and much of his rhetoric, he is transposing the tenth satire into an English and personal key. Provence becomes Kent, Alamanni's amusements Wyatt's. Unlike Alamanni, Wyatt, as he leaps hedge and dike, has a 'clogg' upon his heel (line 86); and this, as has already been noted, probably refers to the limitations set on his freedom in 1536, when he was banished from court to Allington. In retirement, Alamanni, 'pouero & solo', is learning to temper his 'infinito duolo' (lines 4 and 6). Wyatt is 'To will and lust lerning to set a lawe' (line 6). Besides a difference of circumstance, a difference of poetic personality is reflected here. 'Infinito duolo' expresses Alamanni's romantic Italian disposition. It is like a poor echo of Petrarch's, as he wandered, solitary, sorrowing, yet half-enjoying his sorrow, in the Vaucluse. The literary judgement implies no moral judgement on Alamanni. His sufferings were real, largely altruistic, and borne with dignity. But this does not emerge fully through the dim allusion to 'infinito duolo'. Wyatt, who also ignored some of Petrarch's melancholy musings, is tougher and more precise.

Wyatt's anglicizing is especially noticeable in the long section in which historical examples illustrate dishonourable conduct. Alamanni cannot laud Sulla and Caesar, and condemn Brutus:

> Non di loda honorar chiara immortale
> Cesare & Sylla, condannando à torto
> Bruto, & la schiera che piu d' altra uale.   (lines 43–5)

It was well and good for the republican Florentine to condemn Sulla, the dictatorial, aristocratic oppressor of the Roman *populares*, and to admire Brutus's party, which, by the murder of Caesar, struck a blow for political liberty. Not so for the Tudor monarchist. Brutus and Cassius were, in any case, dubious moral *exempla*. If Plutarch understood their motives, Dante saw them, simply, damned among the treacherous. Wyatt accordingly substitutes Livy's story of Brutus's uncle, Cato of Utica, who also fought for freedom against Caesar, and, having lost, committed suicide:

> I am not he that can alow the state
>> Off highe Cesar and dam Cato to dye,
>> That with his dethe dyd skape owt off the gate
> From Cesares handes (if Lyve do not lye)
>> And wolld not lyve whar lyberty was lost:
>> So did his hert the commonn wele aplye.   (lines 37–42)

Not, of course, that the new story avoids condemning absolute rulership. But with Cato, Wyatt has come on to safe, orthodox, moral ground. Cato represented the medieval idea of pagan virtue—Dante has him guard the entrance to Purgatory—and his death was regarded, traditionally, as the martyrdom of liberty. In excising Sulla, Brutus, and Caesar's murder, Wyatt has avoided controversial subjects, unsuited for discussion in the England of Henry VIII. It is to be noticed, too, that he adds an explanation, merely implied by Alamanni, of his hero's love of liberty and the common weal. This addition must be one of the reasons for his reduction of the total number of historical illustrations in this passage. Others are, perhaps, their redundancy, their formality, and the fact that Wyatt, unlike his Italian masters, has, in general, no taste for classical allusions. He prefers allusions applicable and meaningful to Englishmen. Though a reference to Alexander is retained, those to Thersites and Aeneas are rejected. Alamanni cannot swear that, for beauty of style, the palm is taken by Maevius (the poetaster of Virgil's third eclogue and Horace's tenth epode):

> Dir non saprei Poeta alto, & gentile
>> Meuio, giurando poi che tal non uide
>> Smirna, Manto, & Fiorenza ornato stile.   (lines 55–7)

Wyatt, preferring *The Canterbury Tales*, swears that he cannot

> Praysse Syr Thopas for a nobyll talle,
> And skorne the story that the knyght tolld.   (lines 50–1)

Later comes another sign of Wyatt's readiness to think in terms of English literature. Alamanni cannot admire 'L' amico lusinghier', the flattering friend (line 64), while Wyatt cannot 'say that Favell hath a goodly grace' (line 67). That is, he adopts an English allegorical term, Favell being familiar to him from some such source as *Piers Plowman* or *The Bowge of Courte*.

Though its theme is traditional and its idiom English, 'Myne owne John Poynz' resembles no earlier native satire in its form, metre, and satiric *persona*. It is a profoundly original neo-classical imitation, paralleled, in its time, only by the other two satires by Wyatt. These again join classical form to Italian metre and English idiom. But they are not quite the mixture as before. They differ, in the first place, in being free imitations, not based on particular texts of Alamanni's or any other master's, but taking hints from various quarters.

> My mothers maydes when they did sowe and spynne,
>   They sang sometyme a song of the feld mowse,
>   That forbicause her lyvelood was but thynne,
> Would nedes goo seke her townysshe systers howse.
>   (no. 197, lines 1–4)

Aesop's fable of the town and country mice occupies the first sixty-nine lines of 'My mothers maydes', while the remaining forty-three form a long tail-piece in which Wyatt moralizes on the fable and applies it to the human lot:

> Alas, my Poynz, how men do seke the best,
>   And fynde the wourst by error as they stray! ...
>   O wretched myndes, there is no gold that may
> Graunt that ye seke! ...   (lines 70–1, 75–6)

Immediately evident is Wyatt's departure, in verse and narrative, from Alamanni. His influence survives in the use of terza rima, but this is now almost totally emancipated from the original Italian model. The first nineteen lines, for example, reveal no attempt to work in tercet units, falling into successive groups of 4, 4, 5, 2, 2, 2, lines. Here Wyatt is aiming at narrative fluidity. He is telling a homely tale, and this is an activity which Alamanni is too selfconsciously sublime ever to indulge in. Wyatt quite unselfconsciously drops into the medieval English Aesopian manner. Chaucer's Cock and Fox fable, humorously told, is followed by a solemn *moralitas*:

Lo, swich it is for to be recchelees
And necligent, and truste on flaterye.
But ye that holden this tale a folye,
As of a fox, or of a cok and hen,
Taketh the moralite, goode men.
                    (*The Nun's Priest's Tale*, lines 3436–40)

Wyatt's fable of the mice fits into the same pattern, and there is an equally sharp difference of tone between the lively narrative and the sombre moral sections.

Nevertheless 'My mothers maydes' is recognizably a classical satire. It is a companion piece to 'Myne owne John Poynz'. It is another informal address to Wyatt's friend, intimate enough to start with a childhood reminiscence of the maids at Allington and to interject an affectionate 'My Poynz' at intervals. The *moralitas* is confided to this one good friend, not declared, as with Chaucer, to the crowd of 'goode men'. The theme, too, remains that of 'Myne owne John Poynz'. Wyatt now attacks not courtly vice in particular, but that general townish vice to which courtiers are among the most prone. And he now approaches his moral statement not through subjective experience but through a well-known fable. It is as though he has broadened out a discussion that began with 'Myne owne John Poynz'.

Wyatt combines the classical and English modes in such just proportion that one is not predisposed in favour of either a classical or an English source for the fable of the two mice. Aesop's fable was retold by poets as far apart as Horace and Robert Henryson, Wyatt's immediate predecessor who died some time before 1508. Rollins, following Nott and Foxwell, calls 'My mothers maydes' an 'imitation' of Horace's satire II. vi, but suggests that Wyatt 'possibly' also knew Henryson's 'Taill of the Uponlandis Mous, and the Burges Mous'.[1] Baldi, on the other hand, thinks Horace's satire a precedent rather than a source, and states that Wyatt 'certainly' knew Henryson's analogous fable.[2] I think that Wyatt probably knew several versions of what was, after all, a well-known fable; that the resemblance between his satire and Horace's is merely generic; that he is closer to Henryson but still not using the 'Taill' as a major source; that there is no reason to ignore his own statement to the effect that his immediate inspiration was a sewing-women's song: and that he reworks the story and moral-

---

[1] *Tottel's Miscellany, ed. cit.*, ii. 213–4.
[2] *La Poesia di Sir Thomas Wyatt* (Florence, 1953), p. 237.

izes it in accordance with his own conceptions. The evidence is as follows.

Here, first, are the details of Wyatt's version of fable and moralization. The country mouse 'would nedes' seek out her sister in town because her 'lyvelood was but thynne'. She acts of her own volition, without persuasion. She is sorry for herself, and dislikes the hard work of gleaning. 'She thought her self endured to much pain' (line 5). Wyatt further emphasizes the country mouse's unprompted sinfulness in her envious, greedy soliloquy on the comforts her sister enjoys. 'She fedeth on boyled, bacon meat, and roost' (line 27). 'The dyrt doeth not defile / Her tender fote' (lines 21–2). There is more than one hint of feminine folly, of giddy aspirations to gentility. The mouse sets off with the intent 'To lyve a Lady while her liff doeth last' (line 35). On scraping at her sister's door, she meets a scared response, 'Of every noyse so was the wretche agast' (line 39). Anyone but a fool would take this for warning, and Wyatt is again stressing the mouse's free will, her responsibility for what happens. Nothing daunted, she calls out 'Pepe . . . I ame here', and is then welcomed by her sister:

> She fested her, that joy it was to tell
> The faere they had: they drancke the wyne so clere.
>
> (lines 46–7)

In the midst of a cheerful bumper, the country mouse spies two glaring eyes, a round head and sharp ears beneath a stool, and though she has never seen a cat before, she instinctively recognizes her foe. Her sister knows where to hide. She herself skips to the door, her foot trips,

> And ere she myght recover it again
> The traytor Catt had caught her by the hippe
> And made her there against her will remain.   (lines 65–7)

The punishment fits the crime, but whether the mouse is killed or let off with a bad fright remains untold. This is the starting point for some very serious reflections on sin and folly, and on sin *as* folly. Men want much and find little. Even with head 'howpt with gold' you cannot avoid trouble, for 'Eche kynd of lyff hath with hym his disease' (line 80). Lust, once satisfied, becomes itself irksome. A man is not so stupid as to seek grapes on brambles, yet he will seek his happiness in the wrong places. He should be satisfied with what he has, and seek happiness where alone it is to be found—within. At this point, Wyatt, approaching his favourite classical theme of 'quiet of mind', appears to draw on Persius's expression of it. 'Nec te quaesiveris extra' develops into

> Then seke no more owte of thy self to fynde
> The thing that thou haist sought so long before,
> For thou shalt fele it sitting in thy mynde.   (lines 97–9)

And as for adherents to worldly pleasures, may God punish them only in the one way—by letting them look on virtue and long for what they have lost:

> Magne pater divum, saevos punire tyrannos
> haut alia ratione velis, cum dira libido
> moverit ingenium ferventi tincta veneno:
> virtutem videant intabescantque relicta.   (III. 35–8)

> These wretched fooles shall have nought els of me
> But to the great god and to his high dome
> None othre pain pray I for theim to be
> But when the rage doeth led them from the right
> That lowking backwards vertue they may se
> Evyn as she is so goodly fayre and bright;
> And whilst they claspe their lustes in armes a crosse,
> Graunte theim, goode lorde, as thou maist of thy myght,
> To frete inwards for losing suche a losse.   (lines 104-12)

In this splendid conclusion, Wyatt has moved a long way, yet by perfectly logical and natural steps, from the mouse caught by the hip and held 'against her will'. The punishment again fits the crime and the final image is of the self-deluded sinner, grievously tantalized. No other known version of the fable is exactly like Wyatt's, and no moralization so serious as his.

In the original fable, Aesop's forty-first, a country mouse, quite innocently, invites a friend from town to dine. When the town mouse finds that country fare consists only of corn, he is none too polite, exclaims against living like an ant, and invites his friend to town for a decent meal. This proves a revelation to the country mouse, who congratulates the other and curses his own lot. The door opens and the mice scuttle away, but are soon able to return. They are about to tackle some dried figs when someone again enters the room and once more they take cover. Whereupon the country mouse decides that hunger is preferable and bids his friend goodbye. The moral is then stated in a single sentence: a simple life with peace is better than a luxurious one with fear. Like all Aesop's fables, this is short and the

moralization is one slice of pithy wisdom. Fable and moral were amplified and modified in detail, but not altered in essentials, in the two
thousand years before Wyatt rewrote them.

Horace's version serves as conclusion to one of his most autobiographical satires (II. vi). He first contrasts his life in Rome, fretted with
business and trifles, with his carefree life on the Sabine farm, with his
books and friends. Turning to the conversation of country-dwellers,
he emphasizes its concern with fundamentals, as, whether wealth or
virtue makes man happy, whether self-interest or uprightness produces friendship, what is the nature of goodness and its highest form.
It is at this point, and as part of the conversation proper to country
life, that the fable of the mice is introduced. It occupies the thirty-eight
lines from line 79 to the end of the satire. Horace's neighbour Cervius
often recounts timely 'fabellae', the present being his answer to un-
thinking admiration for the wealthy. The fable follows Aesop's or an
intermediate version very like Aesop's. The country mouse's hospitality is more fully described than in Aesop. He grudges nothing in
the attempt to overcome the town mouse's squeamishness—including
bacon scraps (a luxury envied by Wyatt's country mouse). The town
mouse is more philosophical than Aesop's, persuading his friend that
since all must die, it is well to live one's brief span happily. The misleading of the ignorant by the sophisticated remains a dominant *motif*.
The mice make for town, take up residence in a palace, and start on the
remains of last night's banquet. But, in the midst, there is a terrific
banging of doors. They rush off in a panic which increases when the
barking of Molossian hounds is heard. So the country mouse declares
that he has no use for this life and will return to the secure frugality of
his home:

> tum rusticus, 'haud mihi vita
> est opus hac,' ait 'et valeas: me silva cavusque
> tutus ab insidiis tenui solabitur ervo.'   (II. vi. 115–7)

This summary should make it clear that the resemblances between
Wyatt and Horace (even those bacon scraps) are more likely than not
to be accidental, and to derive either from the classical form or from
the ideas implicit in Aesop's fable. Certainly Wyatt resembles Horace
in that he philosophizes freely, talks as one intelligent gentleman to
another, and is aware that the fable is unsophisticated fare—an old
wives' tale or sewing women's song. But these things he would derive,
not from this particular satire, but from classical satire in general. (The

order of the satires' composition is unknown, but he may be building on his own precedent, 'Myne owne John Poynz', as well as on his general reading.) Wyatt gives no autobiographical sketch of his life in town or country. In particular he paints no idyllic portrait of country life. For him it is grim, hard, gleaning, and not relieved by books or friendship. The only joy he recognizes belongs to all manners of living, and consists in accepting one's lot. It is not exclusive to the country dweller. It is entirely an inward joy. Though Horace talks of the highest good, he is, in practice, less radical than Wyatt. He does not practise complete non-attachment to material well-being, but a modified form of it, which consists in cultivating the civilized, healthy pleasures of country life. As for the fable, Wyatt does not seem to be following Horace. The role of the town mouse is totally altered. Wyatt's is already scared stiff when she comes upon the scene. She does not visit the country mouse, philosophize, or in any positive way egg her on to her folly. She simply fits in with her sister's plan. Wyatt has a different slant on the story. His country mouse, who needs no persuasion, is also guilty of many more faults than simply wanting a good meal. Banging doors and barking dogs are enough to bring Horace's mouse to his senses, while Wyatt's incurs the severer punishment which is proportionate to her severer sin. It therefore seems unlikely that Wyatt was imitating Horace's satire.

Similar differences exist between Wyatt's fable and the English prose versions in print in his time. There are but a couple of details that he might have gathered from this quarter. In 1484 William Caxton published his translation from the French of the *Fables of Esope*, Book I, no xii comprising the fable 'of the two rattis'; and of this Richard Pynson published an almost identical version in about 1500.[1] As in the original fable and Horace's version, the fat town rat is responsible for luring his lean country friend to town, where he lives in a rich man's cellar. 'Be mery & make gode chere & ete & drinke Joyously' exclaims the town rat, in terms which might have suggested Wyatt's

> they drancke the wyne so clere. . . .
> She chered her with 'How, syster, what chiere?' (lines 47, 49)

A butler, this time, interrupts the feast. The town rat flees to his hole, but the country one, like Wyatt's, 'wyst neuer whether he shulde goo ne fle'. He hides behind the door, is not seen, and escapes back to the fields, having told his friend that 'it is better to lyue porely & suerly

---

[1] The following quotations are from Pynson's edition, sig. e 2^{r-v}.

than to lyue rychely & withoute suraunce'. The story remains one of mere ignorance and folly, adequately punished with a bad fright.

The earliest extant edition of Henryson's *Morall Fabillis of Esope*[1] is dated 1570, so that if 'The Taill of the Uponlandis Mous, and the Burges Mous' be taken as a source of Wyatt's, he must be assumed to have read a manuscript or a lost printed text. Certainly in various features, not found in Aesop or Horace, Henryson anticipates Wyatt. The mice are now 'Sisteris dere' (line 163) and, in behaviour, recognizably feminine. The 'grit distress' of country life is mentioned at the outset (line 170). One mouse squeaks 'peip' to greet the other (lines 187 and 308). The country mouse does not know a hiding place (line 298). 'Gib hunter, our Jolie Cat' now appears as the villain of the piece (line 326). He catches the country mouse, and before her escape, 'Fra fute to fute he kest hir to and ffra' (line 330), so that the climax is very like Wyatt's. Then, Henryson's *moralitas*, in four stanzas, is more fully developed and more ruminative than Aesop's. Like Wyatt, he observes that no earthly state is 'Without trubill and sum vexatioun', and that those who climb high are specially apt to find this so (lines 370–3). He too expostulates sternly with mankind:

> O wanton man! that usis for to feid
> Thy wambe, and makis it a God to be,
> Lieke to thy self; I warne the weill but dreid,
> The Cat cummis, and to the Mous hes Ee.   (lines 381–4)

On the other hand, Henryson's fable is far from identical with Wyatt's, preserving far more of the original Aesopian material. He treats in full the preliminary episode in which the country mouse entertains the town mouse, exploits the tension between them, and reveals two characters almost the opposite of Wyatt's. Henryson's town mouse 'fredome had to ga quhair ever echo list' (line 174). She is full of bravado, and actually boasts that 'Off Cat, nor fall trap, I have na dreid' (line 251). She is the elder sister, which helps to explain, though not to excuse, her extreme rudeness about the frugal country fare. There is a lively row in which the country mouse, far from complaining at her own lot in life, protests against snobbery and greed. It is much against her better judgement that she consents at last to go to town. The feast there follows the usual lines, except that, unlike Wyatt's, Henryson's

---

[1] See *The Poems and Fables of Robert Henryson*, ed. H. Harvey Wood, rev. edition (Edinburgh and London, 1958).

mice drink 'watter cleir / In steid off wyne' (lines 272–3). Two inter-
ruptions occur, the first by the 'spenser', after which the country
mouse swoons, the second by the cat, after which her reaction is 'I told
you so'. Confirmed in her original opinion, she launches a parting
shot: 'Fairweill, sister, thy feist heir I defy!' (line 343). Furthermore,
for all the solemn admonitions, Henryson's *moralitas* ends with a cosy
Scottish–Horatian picture, most unlike Wyatt's chilly vision of virtue
lost:

> Thy awin fyre, my freind, sa it be bot ane gleid,
> It warmis weill, and is worth Gold to the.   (lines 389–90)

Arguably, too, the resemblance between their moralizings is chiefly
generic, deriving from the medieval Aesopian manner as used by
Chaucer, a favourite with both. Henryson therefore accounts, not so
much for the moral and psychological essence of Wyatt's satire, as for
some of its lively touches.

The rest must be guesswork. The idea of a lost source, often enough
a convenient refuge for lost academics, is given a real foundation, in
this case, by Wyatt's opening statement that his story is one sung by
his mother's maids at their sewing and spinning. If this is not a fiction,
made to give a homespun verisimilitude to the poem, it is a reference to
a contemporary *chanson de toile*. Something like the following, known
as early as the reign of Edward I and found in a fifteenth-century manuscript, is to be imagined:

> The fals fox camme unto owre croft,
> And so oure gese ful fast he sought;
> With how, fox, how, with hey, fox, hey.
> Comme no more unto oure howse to bere oure gese aweye.
>
> The fals fox camme unto oure stye,
> And toke oure gese there by and bye;
> With how, fox, how, with hey, fox, hey, &c.[1]

The song would be easily memorable, because simple and repetitious;
and, needless to say, it would have no moral or philosophical tail-piece
of any length or complexity. At most, therefore, it supplied Wyatt's
fable with its popular air and its narrative details. If it was also known
to Henryson, then it might well account for items, like the 'traytor
Catt' and 'Sisteris dere', that he and Wyatt have in common. Just possibly, it could explain Wyatt's omission of the preliminary episode of

---

[1] See *Reliquiae Antiquae*, ed. T. Wright and J. O. Halliwell (London, 1841), i. 4.

the country meal, though this I am inclined to relate rather to his own conception of the story as one of self-delusion. The hypothetical song could not possibly account for the form and structure of 'My mothers maydes', which is an unsonglike narrative and moral satire. Above all, it leaves still unexplained Wyatt's reconstruction of Aesop's story as one of sin and freewill, and the philosophical gravity with which he moralizes its theme.

These things appear unique to Wyatt. No known source explains them. And I am the more willing to believe them his own in that they bear the stamp of his individual genius, in its most sombre aspect. The tone is not unlike that of the two letters to his son, written in 1537. Even in 1527 his courtly life had produced *Quyete of Mynde* as well as light love poetry, and there is every reason to think that the next ten years brought an increase of seriousness. 'My mothers maydes' therefore has claims to be as serious and as original a poem as 'Myne owne John Poynz'.

'A spending hand' (no. 198), in fluid terza rima and dialogue form, is equally remote from Alamanni, and also, in its own way, equally original. There were already signs in 'Myne owne John Poynz' that Wyatt was willing to desert the Juvenalian for the Horatian manner. He now drops entirely the direct rebuke and savage, pessimistic onslaught on mankind's vices. He commands the new and perhaps more trenchant weapon of irony. Tottel aptly entitled the satire 'How to vse the court'. It attacks courtly vices by ironically commending them. At the beginning Wyatt commends a quiet home life, and Sir Francis Brian a life of service to 'my prynce, my lord and thyn'. Brian only wants to know how to rake in as much money as he spends in the course of this hectic activity, and Wyatt undertakes to advise him:

> Ffle therefore trueth: it is boeth welth and ese.   (line 34)

> Vse vertu as it goeth now a dayes:
> In word alone to make thy langage swete,
> And of the dede yet do not as thou sayse.   (lines 37–9)

> Lend in no wise, for fere that thou do want.   (line 43)

And so on. Possibly Alamanni's grim irony—say, that of the twelfth Provençal satire, in which he advises the nations to indulge their vices—could have suggested this technique to Wyatt. But the combination of dialogue form and ironic advice, the special emphasis on money-making and the insinuating, friendly manner, point rather to the influence of Horace's satire on legacy-hunting (II. v). As before, where Foxwell finds a model, Baldi finds only a generic resemblance.[1] But, this time, I prefer a compromise. Wyatt is obviously not imitating Horace's satire closely, as he did Alamanni's, yet he might well be taking his cue from its matter and manner. Horace's Tiresias instructs Ulysses in such arts as flattery, and advises him to cultivate some wealthy man with a sickly son. Likewise Wyatt instructs Brian to 'pourchase frendes where trowght shall but offend' (line 33); and, reminding him that eventually 'riche age begynneth to dote', continues

> Se thou when there thy gain may be the more.
> Stay him by the arme, where so he walke or goo;
> Be nere alway: and if he koggh to sore,
> When he hath spit tred owte and please him so. (lines 52–5)

The Horatian influence does not extend further. Wyatt does not adopt Horace's mock-heroic manner or his witty subtlety. If he burlesques any literary mannerism, it is his own and Brian's proverbial style. At first his friend is represented as a rolling stone that gathers no moss, at last as one whose purse is a sieve: 'these proverbes yet do last' (line 4). Just possibly, Wyatt, whose satiric *persona* is now that of a selfish, cunning boor, mocks such tedious homely wisdom. What cannot be mistaken, at any rate, is the deliberate coarseness of the talk in this satire. Horace, with sophisticated subtlety, suggests, for example, that to woo a childless man would look too crude—hence the sickly son. Wyatt advises pretty blatant, though ingenious, behaviour. And he uses terms which do not amuse like Horace's, but revolt, like Swift's:

> For swyne so groyns
> In stye and chaw the tordes molded on the grownd,
> And dryvell on perilles, the hed still in the maunger,
> Then of the harp the Asse to here the sownd.
> So sackes of durt be filled vp in the cloyster
> That servis for lesse then do thes fatted swyne. (lines 18–23)

Thus Brian describes the unbusy life, while Wyatt, on the other hand, peoples the busy life with a rich old dotard who spits on the ground and his 'old mule' of a widow with 'ryveld skyn', 'stynking breth', and 'tothles mowth'. The satire is effective because, as with Swift's *Modest Proposal*, the reader's gorge is bound to rise at the thought of the life he is supposed to be willing to lead.

---

[1] Foxwell, ii. 108; Baldi, *op. cit.*, p. 237.

The actual terms of Wyatt's advice do not, of course, demand a search for literary sources. He is thinking of Brian's and his own courtly experience, of the alternatives of the ambassadorial life and life at Allington:

> I thowght forthwith to write,
> Brian, to the, who knowes how great a grace
> In writing is to cownsell man the right.
> To the, therefore, that trottes still vp and downe,
> And never restes, but runnyng day and nyght
> Ffrom Reaulme to Reaulme, from cite, strete and towne.
> Why doest thou were thy body to the bones,
> And myghtst at home slepe in thy bed of downe
> And drynck goode ale so noppy for the noyns,
> Fede thy self fat and hepe vp pownd by pownd? (lines 8–17)

Possibly the fact that Brian had already married his first wealthy widow is relevant to Wyatt's afterthought on the cultivation of rich dotards:

> But if so chaunce you get nought of the man,
> The wedow may for all thy charge deburse.   (lines 59–60)

But the whole satire cannot safely be regarded as a rebuke to Brian until evidence is forthcoming that Wyatt shared the Roman Catholic opinion of him as 'vicarius inferni'.[1] The opening compliment to this literary friend as one 'who knowes how great a grace / In writing is to cownsell man the right' can be taken at its face value. And even at the end, when Brian is made to state his preference for an 'honest name', Wyatt is probably not delivering his final stroke of irony. As for money, Wyatt did once lend Brian £200, but Cromwell arranged repayment. And, in the satire, doubtless the régime rather than a culpable individual is in his mind, for every Tudor ambassador knew the difficulty of milking the exchequer. His own ambassadorial letters are full of worry about his 'diets', while 'Lend in no wise, for fere that thou do want' is well nigh the same advice as Cromwell gave the 'gentle', over-generous Wyatt. My point is not, however, to argue for this or that experience as his inspiration. It is simply to suggest that he knows what he is talking about, and to add that no better source than such knowledge exists.

The final emphasis ought not to be on Wyatt's sources but on his

---

[1] Nicholas Sander *De Origine ac Progressu Schismatis Anglicani* (Cologne, 1585) f 16r.

art. He achieves the naturalization of classical satire. Certainly he wishes to create the illusion that he is transcribing experience. That is proper to his classical form. It is what Horace did. Wyatt's presentation has got to be realistic. That being so, there is for him no better procedure than to use his own experience as a primary source. But to conclude that the satires therefore contain the whole reality of his life would be absurd. That, if its ups and downs, its sheer muddle, be recalled, would suggest a chaotic diary rather than a work of art. Wyatt, in fact, does what every artist does. He makes a selection. He chooses a 'rivelled skin', where, for a love poem, he would have chosen a 'look all soul'. He ignores the beautiful for the ugly, or the ugly for the beautiful, in order to express, not his whole experience, but his love or his hate.

Nevertheless the satires may well be judged as Warton judged them, as Wyatt's most 'pleasing' poems. There is no reason why both his amorous and his satirical poetry should not be enjoyed. But if I were called, as in an examination, to admire one at the expense of the other, I should look askance at the love poetry, as Yeats did at his 'Stolen Child': 'that is not the poetry of insight and knowledge but the poetry of longing and complaint'.[1] And certainly the satires are Wyatt's greatest achievement in the poetry of insight and knowledge. In the long run courtly wisdom was a richer source of inspiration than courtly love.

[1] Letter to Katharine Tynan, quoted in her *The Middle Years* (London, 1916), p. 39.

Appendices A–I

A. The Wyatt MSS

'The Wyatt MSS' is a bound volume, with this title, forming part of the collection of Wyatt family books and papers deposited in the British Museum Manuscripts Department (loan no. 15). The contributors to it include Wyatt's grandson, George, and two great-grandsons, Sir Roger Twysden and Thomas Scott. The papers were put together by another descendant, Richard Wyatt, in 1727.

George Wyatt (1554–1624), the most versatile contributor to the manuscripts, is the descendant most like Sir Thomas the elder, for he appears here as poet, adviser to his son, and student of war and history. There is much to suggest that he gathered materials for, and began to prepare, a much more ambitious work than the 'Life of Anne Boleyn' (Wyatt MSS no. 7) which was eventually published in 1817. 'This Princely lady was elect of God' he claimed for her in a general 'Vindication of the Reformation' (no. 18, f. 2^r), and he also penned a defence of Henry VIII's divorce (no. 21). The defence of his grandfather was merely part of a larger design, though probably the part which most stimulated George Wyatt. As the son of a rebel executed for treason, though himself restored to his hereditary rights, he had personal motives. To re-establish the tradition of family loyalty was an act both pious and prudent. 'Wyatt's Rebellion', had it succeeded, would have made Elizabeth Queen in 1554, yet it was still one of those civil commotions that she dreaded. The vindications of Sir Thomas Wyatt the elder and his son (nos. 10 and 24), though not by George Wyatt, were probably collected by him, as was the account of Henry's reign (no. 19), while Thomas Scott's family anecdotes (no. 29) were perhaps recorded for him. Scott's record, which includes the anecdotes of Sir Henry and Sir Thomas Wyatt used early in Chapter I, was made about 1612. It was used by John Bruce in his 'Unpublished Anecdotes of Sir Thomas Wyatt the Poet, and of other members of that Family' (*Gentleman's Magazine*, xxxiv (1850), ii. 235–41). See also Agnes Conway's 'The Wyatt MSS in the Possession of the Earl of Romney', *Bull. Inst. Hist. Res.* i (1925) 73–6, and R. Flower's 'The Wyatts of Allington Castle', *B.M.Q.* ix (1934–5) 117–9.

B. Wyatt's 'Daughter Besse'

That Wyatt had a daughter, named Bess, was first suggested by Albert McHarg Hayes in 'Wyatt's Letters to his Son' (*M.L.N.*, xlix (1934), 446–9). It has been accepted by most later authorities: for example by Muir (p. ix) and Baldi (*La Poesia di Sir Thomas Wyatt*, Florence, 1953, p. 3 and note). Hayes identified Bess, conjecturally, with 'Eliz. Wyott', a nun, who was at Barking when its abbey was dissolved in 1539.

There is no older tradition or family record to support this. The only evidence is found in Wyatt's second letter of advice to his son, written, probably, in 1537, and the product of the anxiety he felt, while absent in Spain, as to his son's moral welfare. The letter concludes: 'I remitt you wholie to youre father-in-lawe. Recomend me to my daughter Jane and my daughter Besse' (Letter no. 2). Thomas Wyatt the younger was, in 1537, aged about sixteen and newly married to Jane, the daughter of Sir William Hawte, in whose charge he had evidently been left. 'My daughter Jane' is, therefore, Wyatt's daughter-in-law. And 'my daughter Besse' is, I would suggest, her sister Elizabeth Hawte, and no child of Wyatt's own. That Jane and Elizabeth were Hawte's only children is shown by a record concerning the division of his property after his death in 1539 (LP, xiv (i), 867, cap. 28). For Wyatt to bracket these two 'daughters' together, in an affectionate farewell, would seem quite natural.

C. Sir Francis Brian

Sir Francis Brian (d. 1550) is remembered by the label which Henry VIII and Cromwell fixed on him, but which only opponents of the Reformation took seriously: 'vicar of hell'. The date of his birth is unknown, but he was at court by 1513, and in 1517 married Philippa, the wealthy widow of Sir John Fortescue. He acquired an unrivalled reputation for dissoluteness, was a boon-companion of Henry VIII's, and retained his favour by disloyalty and sycophancy. In 1548 he published a translation of Antonio de Guevara's *A Dispraise of the Life of a Courtier, and a Commendacion of the Life of the Labouryng Man*. But it is unlikely that this signifies a change of heart. In the very same year, Brian obliged the government by preventing a marriage alliance between the two chief Irish houses: he himself snapped up the wealthy Countess of Ormonde, who was being wooed by the Earl of Desmond.

Wyatt's friendship with this man had troubled his admirers. But Brian, a poet, translator, diplomat, and, obviously, a highly intelligent person might well have attracted the young Wyatt, who was about ten years his junior. It is difficult to discover his later feelings. Brian is not among the great friends mentioned in Leland's elegies. On the other hand, 'Syghes ar my foode' (no. 168), addressed to Brian from prison, probably in 1541, suggests trust. The third satire, also addressed to him, is ambiguous. It could infer either that Brian was himself under attack or that Wyatt regarded him as a partner in noble-minded criticism of courtly ways. In Chapter VIII, I incline to the latter interpretation, while acknowledging the force of Wyatt's irony in handling such matters as the futile diplomatic life, which he as well as Brian led. There is mockery, too, of the habit of marrying wealthy widows. But though Wyatt may have had in mind Brian's marriage to Philippa Fortescue, we do not know that she resembled the 'old mule' derided in the satire. Wyatt also seems to poke fun at the contemporary liking for proverbs. And here it is of interest that Brian, like Wyatt himself, indulged it. One hundred and eighty-four lines of proverbial sayings by Brian are extant in a Huntington Library MS. (Their identification by Elsa Chapin is reported by H. E. Rollins in his edition of *Tottel's Miscellany*, ii. 82–83 n.)

Foxwell (ii. 109) suggests that Brian may have undertaken the *Dispraise* in acknowledgement of Wyatt's satire. If so, it is unlikely that Wyatt ever saw the acknowledgement. Brian's translation was done from the French version, by Antoine Allègre, of Guevara's work, and this was not in print until 1542.

D. Wyatt's May Day Sonnet

In his May Day sonnet (no. 92) Wyatt writes retrospectively of some or all of the following occurrences: his return to England in May 1527, to find Catherine of Aragon's divorce under way and Anne Boleyn earmarked as her successor; his imprisonment in May 1534, and again at the fall of Anne's 'lovers' in May 1536; and, finally, his return from Flanders in May 1540, when he found his master Cromwell's fall imminent. 'Sephame' is the pseudonym of an astrologer (Cp. 'Sepharial', the modern astrologer, these names being taken, probably, from the cabbalistic term 'sephiroth'). An Edward Sephame has been put forward as Wyatt's man. His 'natiuitie' is his birth horoscope, in which, apparently, Venus (the astrological 'ruler' of Taurus, and hence of May) was afflicted. Afflictions to Venus are said to affect chiefly, but not exclusively, success in love:

> In May my welth and eke my liff, I say,
> Have stonde so oft in such perplexitie.

'Welth' is a word Wyatt frequently uses to mean the happiness of love. Compare the usage in the sonnet describing his refraining from the love of Anne Boleyn/Brunet, 'that set my welth in such a rore' (no. 95). As for the danger to his 'liff', this was most apparent in 1536 and 1540.

E. Opinions on Wyatt's Affair with Anne Boleyn

After George Wyatt's death, the story of Wyatt's affair with Anne Boleyn became a matter of hearsay. Thomas Fuller (1662) and David Lloyd (1665) rely solely on popular tradition. Wyatt, says Fuller, 'was Servant to King Henry the Eighth, and fell (as I have heard) into his disfavour, about the business of Queen Anna Bollen, till, by his *innocence, industry,* and *discretion,* he extricated himself' (*The History of the Worthies of England,* ed. John Nichols, London, 1811, i. 506). Lloyd follows Fuller almost verbatim (*State-Worthies, or, the States-Men and Favourites of England since the Reformation,* 2nd edition, London, 1670, p. 76).

Modern interpreters differ widely. G. F. Nott attacked with scholarly weapons, the only important document not available to him being the Spanish *Chronicle,* rediscovered in 1873. He was sceptical as to scandal, but took a romantic view of Wyatt's and Anne's love (see *The Works of Henry Howard Earl of Surrey, and of Sir Thomas Wyatt,* vol. II (London, 1816)). W. E. Simonds took a moderate view (see *Sir Thomas Wyatt and his Poems,* Boston, 1889). A. K. Foxwell, in her *Study of Sir Thomas Wyatt's Poems* (London, 1911), showed confidence only in the idea of a short, sweet intimacy. J. M. Berdan, in *Early Tudor Poetry* (New York, 1920), was extremely sceptical, rejecting the evidence of poems based on Petrarch and taking Wyatt's imprisonment at the time of Anne's fall as mere coincidence. Recent opinion, as represented in E. K. Chambers's *Sir Thomas Wyatt and Some Collected Studies* (London, 1933), and Kenneth Muir's edition (1949), reacts in the other direction, though without going to romantic extremes. There is no sign of the controversy's settling. Thus, quite recently, R. C. Harrier has attacked R. O. Evans for not taking the highly-coloured Spanish accounts of Anne's love-life with a sufficiently large pinch of salt, and for building too much biography into Wyatt's poems (see R. O. Evans, 'Some Autobiographical Aspects of Wyatt's Verse', *N.Q.,* cciii (1958), 48–52, and R. C. Harrier, 'A New Biographical Criticism of Wyatt', *ibid.,* cciv (1959), 189).

F. Boethius, Chaucer, and Wyatt

Wyatt's 'If thou wilt mighty be' (no. 195) is an adaptation of metres 5, 6 and 3 of Boethius's *De Consolatione Philosophiae*, Book, III, it being generally believed that he used Chaucer's translation (see Baldi, *op cit.*, p. 236, and the less categorical statement by Muir, p. 181 n). Boethius's work was not only very popular with readers, but fairly popular with translators between Alfred and Elizabeth. John Walton, in the 'Prefacio Translatoris' to his version of 1525, mentions 'diuerse' predecessors, a phrase which suggests a larger number than we know of (see *De Consolatione Philosophiae*, trans. Walton, ed. Mark Science, E.E.T.S. o.s. no. 170, London, 1927). Hence the possibility that Wyatt used a lost source exists. But, until another is found, he must be regarded as an independent translator, who gave few or no glances at Chaucer's *Boece*.

Wyatt and his contemporary Walton, both as translators of Boethius and as Chaucerians, present a marked contrast. Walton aimed to 'keep the sentence in hys trewe entent', consulting the Latin conscientiously, as is revealed in his numerous Latinisms. At the same time he helped himself out by opening *Boece*. 'Chaucer that is floure of rhethoryk' is Walton's acknowledged master, whose phrasing he often plagiarizes, and some of whose glosses he incorporates into his own version. Wyatt is faithful to Boethius's 'sentence' in a more general way. While the gist is retained, ideas are omitted and transposed freely. Hints for the rehandling, furthermore, are not derived from Chaucer's translation or glosses.

In their versions of metres 5 and 6 the resemblances between Wyatt and Chaucer are more apparent than real. 'Mighty' is an obvious translation of 'potens', as is 'cruel' of 'ferox' and 'beginning' of 'primordia'. The common statement 'he gave the moon her horns' is striking until we ask how else the simple 'dedit . . . cornua lunae' could be translated. By contrast with Wyatt, Walton takes over whole phrases, such as 'it is no power that thou hast', from Chaucer.

In their versions of metre 3, the resemblances between Chaucer and Wyatt are rather more impressive. 'All were it so' is a phrase in common, derived from Boethius's 'Quamuis'. 'Cura mordax' yields Chaucer's 'bytynge bysynesse' and Wyatt's 'busye bytyng', while 'oneretque bacis colla' yields Chaucer's 'nekke charged' and Wyatt's 'ycharged . . . backe'. Even so, it is noticeable that neither Chaucer nor Wyatt gets beyond the dictionary definitions of the Latin words. At this point Wyatt possibly remembered the Chaucerian terms, which, since he was a reader of Chaucer, is not remarkable. To say that he used *Boece* is a very different matter. There is nothing, in fact, common to Chaucer and Wyatt, which is not also in Boethius. Furthermore, Wyatt's main omission (the omission of Boethius's and Chaucer's reference to 'the soules that comen from his heye sete', discussed in Chapter IV) would argue that he was working, not from Chaucer's text, but from a Latin one incorporating the glosses attributed, at the time, to Aquinas. I argue the matter further in 'Wyatt's Boethian Ballade,' R.E.S. XV (1964).

G. Clichés in the Medieval Lyric

Here are a few lyrical parallels to the conventional love-statements found in *The Knight's Tale*.

The god of love

Lines 1785–6 from *The Knight's Tale* was used verbatim to introduce the apocryphal 'Of the Cuckowe and the Nyghtingale' in Thynne's edition of Chaucer's *Workes* (1532), f. 378ʳ. Complaints, if not, as most commonly, made to the mistress or to Fortune, are addressed to the superior powers of the religion of love, *e.g.*

> O Lord of loue, here my complaynt, . . .
> Syth thou haste set me on the fyere.   (SL, no. 128)

May

This *motif* is so common that a bare reminder of the spring morning openings of many *chansons d'aventure* is sufficient.

'Wommanly pitee'

Robert Henryson's 'Garmont of Gud Ladeis' includes a 'hals ribbane of rewth' (*Poems and Fables*, ed. H. Harvey Wood, rev. edition (Edinburgh, 1958)). 'Nor out of gentill harte is fundin petie': the Italianate-Chaucerian doctrine is actually made part of William Dunbar's amusingly exaggerated complaint, 'Quhone he list to feyne' (*Poems*, ed. W. Mackay Mackenzie, London, 1932, no. 50).

Wounds, death, mercy, grace, love and service

The terms used of Palamon's and Arcite's experience occur *en masse* in SL, no. 140. 'With dedely wounde thus am I slayne,' cries this lover, who also pleads for 'grace' and 'mercy' and resolves that he will 'trewely serue and wilfully obeye' his mistress.

Death-dealing eyes

> 'your lokyng wold me peressh to the hert' (SL, no. 205)

Absence

The numerous 'farewell' songs are obviously nearly related to those on the general theme of absence summed up in the cliché, 'Alas, departyng ys ground of woo!' (SL, no. 156).

Sighs and tears

Absence causes a lyrist to 'sygh and playne' and his 'yen oft for to rayne' (SL, no. 168).

Suicide

Few lyrists mention self-slaughter, but many threaten to die, even going so far as to plan, self-indulgently, a 'last wyll' and 'tombe' (SL, no. 206).

Sleeplessness

'ane hour I may nocht sleip' (SL, no. 133)

Solitude

'alone, I lyue alone' (SL, no. 163)

Captivity

Chaucer's words (line 1552) are found in the lamentations of more than one 'cative bound & thrall' (e.g., SL, no. 196).

H. Italian Sonnet Theory

Antonio Minturno, summing up the character of the sonnet, with that of the canzone and other lyric forms, emphasizes its freedom: 'la Poesia sempre si riseruô, e si riseruerà questa libertâ nel comporre' (L'Arte Poetica, Venice, 1563, p. 267). However, it was not on this account regarded as an easy form. Lorenzo de' Medici, the most modern-sounding of Italian Renaissance critics, argues the sonnet's difficulty from its brevity, and from the consequent need to achieve concentration without obscurity: 'La breuità del sonetto non comporta, che una sola parola sia uana, & il uero subietto & materia del sonetto debbe essere qualche acuta, & gentile sentenza, narrata attamente, & in pochi uersi ristretta, et fuggendo la oscurità & durezza' (Commento . . . sopra Alcvni de' svoi Sonetti, written c. 1490, published in Poesie Volgari, Venice, 1554, f. 120ᵛ).

The prosodists are not unduly dogmatic about structure, except as regards the main two-part, and minor four-part, division of the sonnet. The sestet, particularly, admits of considerable freedom in rhyming, and the final rhyming couplet characteristic of the English form is certainly not ruled out by Italian theory. Antonio da Tempo sets out five varieties of sestet, including one composed of rhyming couplets (ccddee) (*De Ritimis Vulgaribus*, written 1332, published in Venice, 1509, ff. 6ʳ–7ᵛ). Giangiorgio Trissino gives six types, including two in which the last two lines rhyme together (abb, abb; abb, baa), and for which Cino da Pistoia serves as illustration (*La Poetica*, Vicenza, 1529, ff. 38ᵛ–39ᵛ). Varieties of octave are also quoted by the prosodists. The abba, abba form is the commonest, with abab, abab as runner-up. Other variants (like Petrarch's abab, baba and abab, baab) are noted, sometimes with the remark that they are 'rare'. What never occurs, in Italian theory or practice, is the introduction of new rhymes as early as the second quatrain: for that the sestet is the proper place. The Italian octave always sticks to its two rhymes throughout. The practice of introducing new rhymes with the second quatrain is specifically English.

I. Wyatt and Ariosto

The external facts would favour the idea that Wyatt read Ariosto's poetry. In 1527 he visited Ferrara, where Ariosto, a protégé of the powerful d'Este family, was in permanent residence. Two versions of *Orlando Furioso* had already been published, in 1516 and 1521, and the third and last was to follow in 1532. These events, occurring in the midst of Wyatt's active career, are likely to have drawn his attention.

The internal facts do not, however, support the idea that Wyatt, having read *Orlando Furioso* and perhaps other works like the *Capitoli Amorosi* (*c.* 1537), went on to glean from Ariosto. The case rests on two strambotti, and is, in my view, weaker than has been supposed.

The wandering gadlyng (no. 46)

Recent scholars, such as H. E. Rollins and Sergio Baldi, have dismissed *Orlando Furioso*, I, ii. 5–8 as a source for this poem. Wyatt describes a man who bursts in on him when he is with the lady whom both admire, and immediately starts back like a 'wandering gadlyng' 'That fyndes the Adder with his recheles fote'. Ariosto describes Angelica, fleeing alone through a wood, her sudden meeting with a knight, and how she starts back as timid shepherdess from 'serpo crudo'. The common image is, however, a classical one. Alexander starts back at the sight of Menelaus, like a man at the sight of a snake (*Iliad*, III, 33–6). Androgeus, on discovering that the men he has greeted in friendly fashion are Trojans, starts back like a man who treads on an adder (*Aeneid*, II, 378–81).

From thes hye hilles (no. 94)

Ariosto is still universally accepted as the inspiration of this strambotto, though the matter has not been discussed in detail. Foxwell (ii. 71 and 218) simply states that *Orlando Furioso* (xxxvii. 110) is Wyatt's source. Rollins (*Tottel's Miscellany*, ed. cit., ii. 175) and Baldi (*op. cit.*, p. 230) cite this and another possible source in *Capitoli Amorosi* (Cap., v. 1–18), while Muir (p. xxx) gives 'Ariosto' as the source.

Wyatt describes a mountain stream which gradually gathers force, till 'at the fote it ragith ouer all'; then, neatly draws the parallel: 'So faryth love.' The same image and structure are found both in *Orlando Furioso* and 'Capitolo V'. In the first, Wyatt's image is found in reverse, and the context is not love but war. A proud torrent, swollen with rains and snow, can lose force on its way down the mountain, enabling a child, at last, to cross it at any point. 'Cosí già fu che Marganorre. . . .' In the next stanza, Ariosto goes on to explain how this tyrant's powers also failed, enabling Ruggiero's party to overcome him easily. The resemblance is not close, but, it may be argued, Wyatt and Ariosto also have in common their metre (ottava rima), their clear cut parallelism of image and idea, and their strongly marked correlative phrasing. These similarities are, I think, accidental. They are features typical of the strambotto, which Wyatt picked up from Serafino and not from Ariosto. In the case of the capitolo, which, like all its kind, is in terza rima, a metrical debt is obviously ruled out. And though this 'source' again employs the correlative structure I do not think the fact particularly significant. Its interest lies in the fact that the river image is here both present in a love context, and, in itself, very much more like Wyatt's. Ariosto knows that it would be best to hide his joy because it provokes envy, but to hide it is impossible. Joy is like a river gathering force and overflowing. It bursts its banks. There is the same suggestion as in Wyatt's poem of an emotion beyond control. The case for a debt therefore gains some substance, or would do if the possibility of a common source, used by Ariosto and Wyatt, did not also exist.

Petrarch's 'Rapido fiume' (no. ccviii)

In this sonnet the parallel between Petrarch and the Rhône is carefully worked out. Both tend towards Laura's home, the one led by Love, the other by Nature (line 4). Petrarch bids the river press forward, as he would do, its course, this time unlike his own, unchecked by weariness (lines 5–6, 14). Passing Laura's home, the river is to become the bearer of messages, and, more than that, the actual representative of the absent lover (lines 9–14). The fact that Wyatt was a student of Petrarch would be a strong reason for preferring the sonnet to Ariosto's poems as a source for 'From thes hye hilles'. 'Off Cartage he' (no. 81), would provide a precedent for the change of form. On the other hand, the case is not clinched because there is insufficient similarity of detail between the two poems. Petrarch has in mind only a possible variation, not a real change, in the river's force. His comparison, though essential to his meaning, has not the explicitness of Wyatt's, being, rather, a matter of sympathetic identification of lover and river. He is more personal, the river is his mirror image, where Wyatt is defining love's growth in its general and invariable features.

Serafino's strambotto (1516 edition, f. 145ʳ)

> Vdito hó giá che una acqua se è ueduta
>   Cader duno alto monte in basso loco
> Et per la uiolente alta caduta
>   Talhor nel fondo generar gran foco,
> Tal cosa è pur in me non cognosciuta,
>   Che ogni gran cosa apresso amore è poco
> Lachrymo sempre, el pianto há tal furore,
>   Che percotendo el pecto marde el core.

The source-hunter is bound to favour this poem, at the outset, for two reasons. First, as sources for Wyatt's Italianate poems, Serafino's strambotti are second only, in importance, to Petrarch's sonnets. Second, 'Vdito hó giá' is the only one of the possible sources under discussion to employ the same form as 'From thes hye hilles'. Of course, *Orlando Furioso* is composed of ottava rima stanzas. But, in the passage cited above, Ariosto does not complete his comparison of image and idea within a single stanza. The stanza describing the river is part of a narrative sequence, and is not a statement completely meaningful in itself. On the other hand, the strambotto stanza, which by a historical accident has the same rhyme scheme as Ariosto's octaves, is a self-contained unit.

Serafino's image bears a marked resemblance to Wyatt's. And, though the love situation it illustrates is quite different, it is applied in the same explicit, strambotto-like way. Serafino has heard of a strange phenomenon. Water has been seen falling from a high mountain, gathering on its way such violent force that, on reaching the ground, it actually generates fire. Likewise the lover's tears fall so fast and furious that they shatter his breast and his heart catches fire. Such ingenious working out of analogies (often absurd analogies) is typical of the witty strambotto, as practised by Serafino and imitated by Wyatt. An example, discussed in Chapter VII, is 'The furyous gonne' (no. 61), Wyatt's version of 'Se una bombarda' (incidentally, the strambotto immediately following 'Vdito hó giá' in the 1516 edition). The gun explodes: 'right so doeth my desire'. Likewise, in 'From thes hye hilles', the river rages: 'So faryth love.' In both cases, Wyatt, unlike Serafino, allows his image-description to extend beyond the fourth line. And so, in both cases, while exceeding Serafino in the tumultuous, imaginative force of his images, he falls short of him in wit, in the ingenious application of image to idea. As an example of 'Serafino rendered by Wyatt', 'The furyous gonne' provides a formula. And 'From thes hye hilles' fits that formula.

With the literature of an age of common conventions, certainty about sources is notoriously difficult. In the present case Serafino's strambotto has been put forward as the likeliest candidate. The most satisfactory alternative view is to suppose that the combination of Wyatt's knowledge of Petrarch's imagery and his practice in writing strambotti accounts for 'From thes hye hilles.' Ariosto's claims would stand a poor third.

Index

Aesop, 41; fable of the two mice, 259, 260, 262–3, 265; and Wyatt, 259, 260, 262–5, 267; Caxton's translation of, 264–5
Aganges, Arnaut d', 162
Aigues Mortes, meeting of Charles V and Francis I at, 54, 64
Alamanni, Luigi, 43, 54, 58, 68, 246–7; *Opere Toscane*, 68, 247–8; satires in, 247, 248 ff.; and Wyatt, 43, 58, 68, 246 ff., 259, 267, 268
Alfred, King, 277
Allègre, Antoine, 275
Amyot, Jacques; translation of Plutarch's *Lives*, 101–2
Anaxagoras, 85, 101
Anne Boleyn, Queen, 21, 23, 25, 27, 275; in the Tower, 33 ff.; and Henry VIII, 15, 17, 21, 23, 25 ff., 33 ff., 273; and Wyatt, 17, 18 ff., 33 ff., 59, 60, 276; 'Life' by George Wyatt, 27–8, 273
Anne of Cleves, Queen, 52, 68, 70, 73
Aquinas: *see* Thomas
Aretino, Pietro, 167
Ariosto, Lodovico, 58, 239; *Orlando Furioso*, 58, 174, 280–3; ottava rima stanza, 211, 212, 281, 282; satires, 248–9; *Capitoli Amorosi*, 280, 281; Ariosto and Wyatt, 58, 280–3
Aristotle, 12, 86
Arnold, Matthew, ix
Ascham, Roger, 11–12, 51, 94–5, 99, 106
Audeley, Lord, 87
Augustine, Saint, 150

Ausonius; Wyatt's version of, 95
Austen, Jane, 132

Bacon, Sir Francis, 102
Bacon, Roger, 79
Baldacci, L., 192
Baldi, Sergio, ix, 169, 209, 214, 223, 260, 274, 277, 280
Barclay, Alexander, 241–4
Barnes, Barnaby, 152
Baskervill, C. R., xiii, 59, 101
Baynton, Sir Edward, 31
Beatrice: *see* Dante
Beaufort: *see* Margaret
Becon, Thomas; on Wyatt, 73–4
Bedingfeld, Thomas, 50
Bembo, Cardinal Pietro, 57, 67, 147, 166, 167, 191–3, 209, 211; and Wyatt, 57, 193, 211; 'Peter Bembo' in Castiglione's *Courtier*, 148
Berdan, J. M., 169, 171–2, 176–8, 276
Berners: *see* Bourchier
Berni, Francesco, 56, 57, 167–8; and Wyatt, 56
Blage MS, Wyatt's poems in, xiii, 42, 67
Blage, George; and Wyatt, 7, 66–7, 72, 109
Blundeville, Thomas; translation of Plutarch's moral essays, 86, 105; of Plutarch's *De Tranquillitate*, 86, 102 ff.; compared with Wyatt's, 102 ff.
Boccaccio, Giovanni, 151, 162, 166, 167, 211; *Il Filostrato*, 152, 164, 165; 'Patient Griselda' (in *Decameron*), 153; *Teseide*, 113

285

Boethian commentators, 79; *and see* Thomas

Boethius, xiv, 92, 95; *De Consolatione*, 91–3, 277; Chaucer's translation of (*Boece*), 92, 93, 277–8; Walton's translation of, 93, 277; Wyatt's version of, 79–80, 91 ff., 95, 277–8

Boleyn family, 5, 21, 35, 39; and Wyatt, 8

Boleyn group, 33, 39; and Wyatt, 39 ff.

Boleyn, Anne: *see* Anne

Boleyn, George, Viscount Rochford, 31, 32, 33, 35, 36, 39, 41–2; and Wyatt, 32, 39–42, 43, 91

Boleyn, Mary, 17, 18

Boleyn, Thomas, Viscount Rochford and Earl of Wiltshire, 6, 18, 21, 25, 26

Bonner, Edmund, Bishop of London; and Wyatt, 10, 20, 43, 63–5, 67–9, 71–2, 75, 109–10, 246; on Wyatt, 10, 20, 43, 64–5, 67, 75

Bonvisi, Antonio, 26

Borneil, 162

Boscán, Juan; and Wyatt, 67

Bosworth, Battle of, 4, 5, 53

Bourbon, Constable, 55, 58

Bourchier, John, Lord Berners, 30, 98; and Wyatt, 30

Boxley, Abbot of, 5

Brancetour, Robert; and Wyatt, 69, 74, 109

Brandon, Charles, Duke of Suffolk, 16, 20, 28–9, 37, 71; and Wyatt, 20, 26–9, 37–8, 43, 44, 71, 72, 73, 246

Brereton, William, 33, 35, 36, 41; and Wyatt, 41–2

Brews, Margery, 12–13

Brian, Sir Francis, 20, 28, 32, 33, 36, 64, 65, 245; proverbs by, 268, 275; Wyatt's poem addressed to, 71, 72, 234, 275; Wyatt's satire addressed to: *see* Wyatt, third satire; Brian and Wyatt, 20, 28, 32,

Brian, Sir Francis, *continued—* 44, 63, 64, 71, 72, 238, 245–6, 267–9, 274–5; Foxwell on Brian, 275

Brian, Lady Philippa, 269, 274, 275

Brodeau, Victor, 55

Brooke family, 5

Brooke, Elizabeth: *see* Wyatt

Brooke, George, Lord Cobham the elder, 8

Brooke, George, Lord Cobham the younger; and Wyatt, 19, 20, 43

Bruce, John, 64, 273

Buckingham, Henry Stafford, Duke of, 4

Budé, Guillaume, 81, 83, 100; and Wyatt, 54; translation of Plutarch's *De Tranquillitate*, 54, 79, 82, 95, 102 ff.; compared with Wyatt's, 102 ff.

Bullock, Walter, 159

Buonaccorsi, Giuliano, 248

Buonaccorso da Montemagno, 209

Burckhardt, Jacob, 57

Byron, Lord, 150

Calmeta, Vincentio, 213–14, 226

Cambrai, Peace of, 60

Cambridge, University of, 48; Wyatt at, 7–8

Camden, William, 4

Canterbury, John Whitgift, Archbishop of, 27

Cardinal's College, Oxford, 48

Cariteo, Il (Benedetto Gareth), 67, 209–13

Carlisle, Bishop of, 39

Casa, Giovanni della, 166–7

Casady, Edwin, 205

Casale, Giovanni; and Wyatt, 57, 58

Casale, Sir Gregory, 58; and Wyatt, 56

Castiglione, Baldassare, 147; and Wyatt, 57; *Courtier*, 50, 51, 57, 146, 148, 245; 'Peter Bembo' in, 148

Catherine of Aragon, Queen, 19, 20, 21, 25, 27, 29, 39, 46–7, 50, 59, 60,

Catherine of Aragon, Queen, *continued*—
61, 275; and Wyatt, 20, 46, 52, 59–60, 80, 82, 88, 91, 108

Catherine Howard, Queen, 17, 19, 29, 70; and Wyatt, 71–2

Catherine Parr, Queen, 245

Catullus, 210

Cavalcanti, Guido, 149, 167

Caxton, William, 7, 86; translation of Aesop, 264–5

Cellini, Benvenuto, 54, 59

Challoner, Sir Thomas; elegy on Wyatt, 74–5

Chambers, E. K., 19, 169, 190, 276

Chapin, Elsa, 275

Chapuys, Eustace (Spanish ambassador), 25, 27, 34, 35, 36, 37, 39

Charles V, Emperor, 48, 50, 53, 54, 55, 57, 58, 60–6, 69, 70; and Wyatt, x, 46, 62–6, 69

Chaucer, Geoffrey, ix, 95, 149, 151–2, 162, 166, 185, 243, 244, 255; *Anelida and Arcite*, 142; 'Balade de Bon Conseyl', 94; *Boece* (translation of Boethius), 92, 93, 277–8; *Canterbury Tales*, 101, 114; *Clerk's Prologue* and *Tale*, 153–4; courtly love lyrics, 111 ff.; compared with Wyatt's 'English' lyrics, 135–6, 142–3; *House of Fame*, 112; *Knight's Tale*, 113–15, 121, 126–9, 142, 171, 244, 278–9; Duke Theseus in, 113–14, 121; Palamon in, 146; *Legend of Good Women*, 116; *Monk's Tale* stanza, 116, 130; *Nun's Priest's Tale*, 259–60; *Parliament of Fowls*, 205–6; *Romaunt of the Rose* (translation), 112, 163–4, 166; *Squire's Tale*, 114; *Troilus and Criseyde*, 114, 118, 121, 127, 130, 152 ff., 171, 228–9; 'Canticus Troili' in (translation of Petrarch), 116, 152 ff., 172, 185; Pynson's edition of Chaucer, 94, 101, 113; Thynne's, 9, 94, 113, 278; Chaucer's influence on his successors,

Chaucer, Geoffrey, *continued*—
112–13; on Wyatt's translation of Boethius, 93–4, 277–8; on Wyatt's 'English' lyrics, 115, 126 ff.; on Wyatt's satire, 266; Wyatt on Chaucer, 9, 113, 126, 128, 244, 258

Cheney family, 5

Cheney, Sir John, 53

Cheney, Sir Thomas; and Wyatt, 53–4

Chini, Emma, 169

Chorónica del Rey Enrico Otavo (*Chronicle of King Henry VIII*), 25; *and see* Spanish Chronicle

Chronicle of Calais, 42

Cino da Pistoia, 149, 167, 175, 280

Clapham, John; translation of Plutarch, 86

Claude, Queen (wife of Francis I), 64

Claudio: *see* Shakespeare

Clement VII, Pope, 16, 53, 55–60; and Wyatt, 56, 59, 247

Clippesby, John, 11

Cobham: *see* Brooke

Cognac, League of, 53–4, 55

Coleridge, S. T., 149; Coleridgians, 225

Colonna, Cardinal Giovanni (Petrarch's patron), 70, 179, 188

Colonna, Cardinal Pompeo, 55

Colonna, Stefano (Petrarch's patron), 189

Colonna, Vittoria, 209

Constable of France, 109

Constable, Henry, 190–1

Conti, Giusto de', 166, 209, 210

Conway, Agnes, 273

Cornwallis, William, 102

Corrierez, Montmorency de, 74

Coscia, Andrea, 213

Coverdale, Miles, 11–12

Cowley, Abraham, 171

Coxe, Leonard, 98–100, 110

Crashaw, Richard, 148

Cromwell, Sir Thomas, Earl of Essex, 4, 26, 33–4, 38, 43, 46, 49–53, 60, 64, 68, 70, 73, 274;

Cromwell, Sir Thomas, Earl of Essex, *continued*—
and Wyatt, x, 9, 19, 25, 30, 33, 37–8, 43, 46, 49, 50, 52, 53, 62–6, 68, 70, 71, 72, 75, 76, 179, 188, 269; on Wyatt, 68, 76
Culpeper, Thomas, 17
Curtius, E. R., 162

Daniel, Arnaut, 149
Daniello, Bernardino, 196
Dante Alighieri, 54, 122, 149, 150, 166, 167, 175, 185, 188, 213, 258; *De Vulgari Eloquentia*, 186; *Divine Comedy*, 166, 174, 237; *Vita Nuova*, 114, 142, 151; Beatrice in, 173; Dantesque, 189
Darrell, Elizabeth; and Wyatt, 19, 20, 64, 65, 67, 70, 71
Dauphin of France, 16, 54
Dereham, Francis, 17, 29
Desmond, Earl of, 274
Devonshire MS, xi, 14, 21, 24, 39; Wyatt's poems in, xi, 14, 21–2, 24–5, 115, 174
Diacceto, Jacopo del, 246
Digby, Sir Kenelm, 29
Digby, Lady Venetia (*née* Stanley), 29
Diogenes, 104–5, 107, 196
Dolce stil nuovo, poets of, 112, 149, 175; *and see* Cavalcanti, Cino, Dante
Donne, John, 97, 122, 171–2; poems by, 123, 143–4, 171; compared with Wyatt, 115, 143–5
Drayton, Michael, 32
Drede: *see* Skelton
Dryden, John, 148, 187–8
Du Bellay, Cardinal, 247
Dudley, Edmund, 5, 6
Dudley, Sir John; and Wyatt, 62
Dunbar, William, 112, 240–1, 242, 243, 244, 252; poems by, 117, 118, 241, 278

École Lyonnaise; and Wyatt, 68, 146–7; *and see* Héroët, Labé, Scève
Edward I, King, 266
Edward IV, King, 13
Edward, Prince, 62
Egerton MS; Wyatt's poems in, xi, 22, 115, 133, 174
Eliot, T. S., 166, 200
Elizabeth, Queen, 26, 27, 30, 273, 277
Elyot, Sir Thomas, 12, 47; translation of Plutarch, 86–7
Empson, Richard, 5, 6
Empson, William, 158
Endicott, Annabel, 209
Epictetus; Wyatt on, 7, 88, 245
Erasmus, Desiderius, 8, 12, 41, 47, 79, 81, 82, 83, 84–6, 90, 100; *Adagia*, 40, 80; *Apophthegmata*, 80; Erasmian Humanism and Humanists, 79 ff.
Este family, 280
Este, Alfonso d', Duke of Ferrara, 55, 57; and Wyatt, 57–8
Este, Isabella d', 213
Evans, R. O., 276
Exeter, Henry Courtenay, Marquis of, 65

Ferdinand II, King of Naples, 213
Ferrara: *see* Este
Ficino, Marsilio, 145
Filelfo, Francesco, 191–4, 199–200
Filosseno, Marcello, 209
Fisher, Cardinal John, 8, 47, 49, 50, 61
Flodden, Battle of, 6, 32
Florio, John, 41, 190
Flower, R., 273
Fortescue, Sir John, 274
Foxwell, Agnes K.; on Wyatt, 20, 57, 75, 276; on his poems, xi, xiii, 146–7, 190, 217, 260, 281; on Brian, 275
Francis I, King of France, 48, 53–4, 55, 60–1, 63, 64, 65, 68, 69, 70, 246; and Wyatt, 54, 63, 65, 69

Franco, Niccolò, 168
Froissart, Jean, 98
Fuller, Thomas, 53; on Wyatt, 276

Gainsford, Anne, 27
Gambara, Veronica, 209
Gascoigne, George, 32, 224–5
Gawayne and the Grene Knight, Sir, 184
Geraldini, Alessandro and Antonio, 47
Gesualdo, Andrea, 192–3, 196, 198, 199–200
Giberti, Matteo; and Wyatt, 56
Gilfillan, Rev. George, 148
Giulio de' Medici, Cardinal, 246
Gloucester, Humphrey, Duke of, 166
Gottfried, Rudolf, 193
Gower, John, 112, 117, 120
Grainfield, Sir Richard; and Wyatt, 33
Grandvela, Cardinal Antoine Perrenot, sieur de; and Wyatt, 62, 65
Grant, Edward; translation of Plutarch, 86
Gray, Thomas, xi
Grimald, Nicholas, 95
Guevara, Antonio de, 245, 274, 275
Guinizelli, Guido, 149
Guittone d'Arezzo, 149, 151

Hales, John; translation of Plutarch, 86–7
Halle, Edward, 17, 31, 50; Chronicle cited, 16, 17–18, 20, 31, 50
Hamlet: see Shakespeare
Harington, Sir John, 174
Harpsfield, Nicholas, 25–6, 27, 29
Harrier, R. C., 22, 276
Hatton, Lady Alice, 15
Hatton, Sir Christopher (husband of Lady Alice, cousin of the Chancellor), 15
Hatton, Sir Christopher (the Chancellor), 50
Haute, Anne, 13
Hawes, Stephen, 112

Hawte, Elizabeth; and Wyatt, 274
Hawte, Jane: see Wyatt
Hawte, Sir William; and Wyatt, 19, 43, 89, 274; Wyatt on, 89
Haydon, B. R., 237
Hayes, Albert McHarg, 274
Henry VI, King, 13, 120
Henry VII, King, 3, 4, 5, 6, 52, 76
Henry VIII, King, 3, 6, 7, 9, 14, 16, 17, 20, 33, 46–8, 49, 51, 52, 53–4, 55, 59, 60–6, 68, 70, 79, 258, 273, 274; Letters and Papers, xiii; songs by, 17, 32, 38–9; and Anne Boleyn, 15, 17, 21, 23, 25 ff., 33 ff., 273; and Wyatt, 9, 20, 21, 24, 25–9, 32, 33, 37, 43, 44, 46, 53–4, 59, 61–6, 68–9, 71, 72, 73, 76, 108–9, 246, 258; on Wyatt, 7, 26, 69
Henryson, Robert, 112, 131, 143, 278; 'Taill of the Uponlandis Mous, and the Burges Mous', 260, 265; and Wyatt, 260, 265–6
Herbert, George, 8
Héroët, Antoine, 68, 147
Heynes, Simon; and Wyatt, 63–4, 72, 109–10
Heywood, John, 40
Hietsch, Otto, 169, 178, 182
Hoccleve, Thomas, 112
Holbein, Hans; portrait of Wyatt, 75
Holland, Elizabeth, 17
Holland, Philemon; translation of Plutarch compared with Wyatt's, 105–7
Hollander, John, 218
Homer, 280
Horace, xiv, 90, 210, 238, 258; satires, 242–3, 244; fable of the two mice, 260, 263–4, 265; and Wyatt, 238, 245, 260, 263–4, 267–8, 270
Howard family, 16; and Wyatt, 72, 73
Howard group, 33
Howard, Agnes, Dowager Duchess of Norfolk, (wife of 2nd Duke), 17
Howard, Catherine: see Catherine

Howard, Elizabeth, Duchess of Norfolk, (wife of 3rd Duke), 17
Howard, Frances (*née* Vere), Countess of Surrey, 16
Howard, Henry, Earl of Surrey, 4, 14–15, 16, 32, 95, 151–2, 166, 201; versions of Petrarch's *Rime*, 168 ff., 200 ff., 209; compared with Wyatt's, 169 ff., 200–1, 203, 206–8; sonnet form, 174 ff., 205, 221; relationship with and elegies on Wyatt, 73, 74–5
Howard, John, 1st Duke of Norfolk (1430–85), 4
Howard, Mary, daughter of 3rd Duke of Norfolk: *see* Richmond
Howard, Thomas, 2nd Duke of Norfolk (1443–1524), 4, 6; and Wyatt, 8
Howard, Thomas, 3rd Duke of Norfolk (1473–1554), 9, 16, 17, 18, 36, 52, 70; and Wyatt, 70, 73
Howard, Lord Thomas, (younger brother of 3rd Duke of Norfolk, husband of Margaret Douglas), 14, 16
Huizinga, J. H., 18
Husee, John, 36, 38

Iago: *see* Shakespeare
Idley, Peter, 87–9
Infant of Portugal, 61, 62
Isabella of Castile, Queen, 47
Italian diplomats in Spain; and Wyatt, 67
Italy, attitudes to, 51–2; and Wyatt's, 55–6, 59

James I, King of Scotland, 112
James IV, King of Scotland, 241
Jane Seymour, Queen, 36, 62
Jeanroy, Alfred, 162
Johnson, Samuel, 171–2
Jonson, Ben, 237, 247
Juvenal, xiv, 242, 244, 248, 249; and Wyatt, 253

Kendal, Sir John, 11
Kent: *see* Shakespeare
Kingston, Lady, 38
Kingston, Sir William, 33–5, 38
Knox, John, 12
Koeppel, Emil, 223
Kyd, Thomas, 115

Labé, Louise, 68, 147
Langland, William, 239, 241–4, 251, 259
Lannoy, General, 57
Lathrop, H. B., 86, 174–5, 221
Le Fèvre, Jean, 39
Lear: *see* Shakespeare
Lee, Sir Antony, 14
Lee, Lady Margaret (*née* Wyatt), 5, 43
Leland, John, 31, 32, 47; and Wyatt, 7, 74; elegies on Wyatt, 7, 67, 74, 275
Lemaire de Belges, Jean, 213
Lever, J. W., 169, 179, 190
Lewis, C. S., 12, 31–2
Linacre, Thomas, 47
Livy, 258
Lloyd, David, 48–9; on Wyatt, 75–6, 109, 276
Lockwood, Henry; and Wyatt, 30
Lodge, Thomas, 152
London Lickpenny, 239
Lorenzo de' Medici, 151, 226, 279
Louis XII, King, 16
Lucian, 82, 86
Lucilius, 242
Lucilius, the younger, 102
Lupset, Thomas, 49
Lycidas: see Milton
Lydgate, John, 14, 112, 113, 115, 120, 129, 130; ballade by, 116, 118–19; *Fall of Princes*, 82, 85, 166; Lydgatian style, 122

Machiavelli, Niccolò, 50–1, 52, 55, 58, 246, 247; and Wyatt, 58; Machiavellian ideas, 50, 52, 66
Madrid, Treaty of, 53

Malfi, Duchess of (in Webster's *Duchess of Malfi*), 11
Malory, Sir Thomas, 174
Manox, Henry, 17
Mantua, Duke of, 213
Mantuan (Baptista Mantuanus), 241
Margaret Beaufort, Lady, 8, 48
Margaret Douglas, Lady (Henry VIII's niece), 14, 16
Marguerite d'Anjou, Queen consort of Henry VI, 120
Marguerite de Navarre, Queen, 54, 147
Marillac, Charles de, 71
Marlowe, Christopher, 119
Marot, Clément, 212; and Wyatt, 54; Wyatt's debt to, x
Mary Tudor, Princess, daughter of Henry VII, 16, 18, 27
Mary Tudor, Princess, daughter of Henry VIII, 7, 16, 25, 47, 61, 62
Mason, H. A., ix, x, xi; on Wyatt's lyrics, xi, 111 ff.
Mason, John, 48–9; and Wyatt, 7, 48, 62, 63, 65, 66, 71, 72, 75, 109
Medici; 58, 247; and *see* Giulio *and* Lorenzo
Menghini, M., 213, 217
Merbury, Charles, 41
Merriman, R. B., xiii
Metcalfe, Nicholas, 8
Michelangelo Buonarroti, 237
Milan, Christina, Duchess of, 62–3
Milton, John, 74, 151, 152; *Lycidas*, 248; Miltonic style, 231
Minturno, Antonio, 185–6, 226, 233, 279
Mont, Christopher, 49–50, 52
Montague, Henry, Baron, 65
Montaigne, Michel de, 102
More, Sir Thomas, 3, 9, 12, 47, 48, 49, 50, 61, 75, 106, 239; *Dialogue concernynge Heresyes*, 99–100; *Dyalogue of Comforte*, 85–6; *Utopia*, 47, 83
Morison, Richard, 49, 50, 52

Morley, Henry Parker, Lord, 47, 51, 60; translation of Petrarch's *Trionfi*, 168; translations of Plutarch's *Lives*, 82
Mortimer, Lady, 16
Muir, Kenneth, xi, xiii, 23, 42, 90, 274, 276, 277, 281
Mundt: *see* Mont

Navagero, Andrea, 67; and Wyatt, 57
Nice, meeting of Catholic powers at, and truce between Charles V and Francis I, 54, 63–4
Norris, Henry, 20, 33, 34, 35, 36, 41–2; and Wyatt, 20, 41–2
Norfolk: *see* Howard
North, Sir Thomas; translation of Plutarch's *Lives*, 86, 87
Nott, Rev. George Frederick, xi, 227, 260, 276

Orleans, Charles d', 111, 115, 119–20, 130, 140
Ormonde, Countess of, 274
Orsini family, 189
Ovid, 112, 149, 161, 162, 171, 210; Ovidian conventions, 166
Oxford, University of, 48, 166

Padelford, Frederick Morgan, xiii, 169, 206–7
Palamon: *see* Chaucer, *Knight's Tale*
Palgrave, F. T., 143
Pampyng (servant of the Pastons), 11
Paris, meeting of Charles V and Francis I at, 54, 69
Parr, William, Marquis of Northampton (Queen Catherine Parr's brother), 245
Paston family, 13
Paston Letters, 10, 11, 13–15
Paston, Anne, 11
Paston, Constance, 11
Paston, Edmund, 10
Paston, Sir John, 13
Paston, Margaret, 11
Paston, William, 10

Paul III, Pope, 50, 60–1, 63
Paul, Saint, 12, 146
Pavia, Battle of, 53
Pazzi, Alfonso de', 168
Percy, Lord Henry, 19
Persius, xiv, 90, 242, 243–4; and Wyatt, 245, 262
Petrarch (Francesco Petrarca), xiii, 54, 70, 79, 81, 82, 85, 89, 96, 97, 213, 214, 257, 280; *De Obedientia*, 153–4; *De Remediis*, 59, 81–3, 85, 95–6, 166; Wyatt on, 80–1; Wyatt's translation of, 59, 79, 80–2, 85, 95–6, 100, 137; Twyne's translation of, 81; *Rime*, xiii, 24, 96, 150 ff., 210, 212–13, 215; sonnet from, translated by Chaucer, 116, 152 ff., 172, 185; sonnet from, translated by Watson, 160–1; Petrarch's poetry in, and Wyatt, 67, 80, 131, 144–5, 151–2, 167, 168 ff., 209, 210, 214, 216, 219–20, 223, 246, 255, 257, 281–2, 283; Wyatt's autobiographical adaptations of, x, 24, 41, 67, 70; Wyatt's versions of, x, 23–4, 95–6, 179 ff., 208, 213, 215–16, 234–5, 276; Wyatt's sonnets translated from, 162, 169 ff., 193 ff., 208; compared with Surrey's, 169 ff., 200–1, 203, 206–8; Wyatt's version of madrigal from, 185, 189; Wyatt's versions of canzoni from, 185–7; Wyatt's paraphrases and imitations of, 23–4, 67, 70, 185, 187 ff., 196–200; Surrey's versions of, 168 ff., 200 ff., 209; commentators on, 166, 190 ff., 208 (*and see* Daniello, Filelfo, Gesualdo, Squarciafico, Stagnino, Tempo, Vellutello, Venafro); *Secretum*, 150; *Trionfi*, 50, 149; translated by Morley, 168; *Trionfo d'Amore*, 149
Pilgrimage of Grace, 43
Pindar, 185
Plato, 51, 85, 95, 103, 104, 105, 145, 146, 147

Plattard, Jean, 100
Plutarch, 82, 85, 86, 87, 89, 92, 96, 102, 258; *De Tranquillitate*, 54, 83–6; Budé's translation of, 54, 79, 82, 95, 102 ff.; Blundeville's translation of, 86, 102 ff.; Holland's translation of, 105–7; Wyatt's translation of (*Quyete of Mynde*), ix, x, xiii, 40, 46, 54, 59 ff., 79–80, 82 ff., 86–8, 90–1, 95, 98 ff., 108, 137, 182, 184, 245, 267; 'Of Education'; Elyot's translation of, 86–7; 'Of Health'; Hale's translation of, 86–7; other moral essays translated by Blundeville, Clapham, Elyot, Grant, 86; *Lives*; Amyot's translation of, 101–2; Morley's translation of, 82; North's translation of, 86, 87
Pole, Cardinal Reginald, 49, 51, 61, 69, 74; and Wyatt, 63, 66, 72, 75; on Wyatt, 66
Pole, William de la, Duke of Suffolk (d. 1450), 87, 116, 120, 121, 126, 147
Polonius: *see* Shakespeare
Pontano, Giovanni, 213
Poynings family, 5
Poynings, Sir Edward, 7
Poynings, Lady (wife of Sir Thomas); and Wyatt, 7, 71
Poynings, Sir Thomas; and Wyatt, 7
Poynz, John; and Wyatt, 20, 43–4, 238, 250, 253, 260; Wyatt's satires addressed to: *see* Wyatt, first and second satires
Praz, Mario, 164, 209, 212–13
Propertius, 210, 247
Provençal poetry: *see* Troubadour and Provençal poetry
Proverbs, 40–1, 144; Wyatt's liking for, 40, 88, 89, 144, 268, 275; Idley's, 88; Brian's, 268, 275
Puttenham, George, 80
Pynson, Richard, 59, 264; edition of Chaucer, 94, 101, 113

Raleigh, Sir Walter, 30
Ransom, John Crowe, 171–2
Relation of England, 10, 46–7
Reliquiae Antique, 266
Richard III, King, 3, 4, 6, 53
Richmond, Henry Fitzroy, Duke of, 14, 15, 17
Richmond, Mary (*née* Howard), Duchess of, 14, 17
Ringley, Sir Edward, 30
Rochford: *see* Boleyn
Robbins, R. H., xiii
Rollins, H. E., xiii, 210, 229, 233, 260, 275, 280, 281
Romance of the Rose (*Le Roman de la Rose*), 18, 112, 163–4, 165, 171; and see Chaucer, *Romaunt of the Rose*
Romanello, Giovanni Antonio, 198
Rome, Sack of, 58
Roper, William, 9
Rosalind: *see* Shakespeare
Roselli, Rosello, 209
Royal MS; Wyatt's connection with, 39–41
Rucellai, Bernardo, 246
Rucellai, Cosimo (son of Bernardo), 248
Rucellai, Giovanni, 246–7
Russell, Sir John; embassy to Italy, 55 ff.; and Wyatt, 19, 21, 55 ff., 59, 60, 89

Saint John's College, Cambridge, 7–8, 48
St Leger, Sir Anthony, 49, 52; elegy on Wyatt, 74
Saint-Gelais, Mellin de; and Wyatt, 54–5; Wyatt's debt to, x
Saintsbury, George, 159
Salel, Hugues; and Wyatt, 55
Sanctis, Francesco de, 164–5
Sander, Nicholas, 25, 26, 27, 29, 30, 34, 269
Sannazaro, Jacopo, 213
Santayana, George, 118
Santes, Bishop of, 248
Scarisbrick, J. J., 69

Scève, Maurice, 67, 68, 212
Scott, Thomas, 273
Secular Lyrics of the XIVth and XVth Centuries, xiii, 116 ff., 278–9
Seneca, xiv, 82, 88, 90, 92, 102; moral epistles and dialogues, 90; *Hippolytus*, 91; *Thyestes*, 90–1, 245; Wyatt's versions of, 79–80, 90–1, 245; Wyatt on Seneca, 7, 88, 90, 245
Sephame (astrologer), 21, 275
Serafino Aquilano (Serafino de' Ciminelli), 54, 176, 203–5, 209 ff.; reputation, 213–14, 237; poems by, 215 ff.; style of his strambotti, 224 ff.; compared with Wyatt, 214 ff., 235, 237; echoed by Wyatt, 217; Wyatt and his poetry, 95, 130, 209 ff., 236, 237, 246, 255, 281, 282–3; Wyatt's versions of his poems, 209, 217, 219 ff., 236; in sonnet form, 219–21; in English forms, 221–3; in strambotto form, 223, 227–34, 282–3
Sertini, Tommaso, 248, 249, 250, 252
Sforza, Cardinal (Serafino's patron), 213, 214
Sforza, Massimiliano, Duke of Milan, 55
Shakespeare, William, 11, 168, 169, 182, 237; *Antony and Cleopatra*, 29; Rosalind in *As You Like It*, 23; *Hamlet*, 115; Hamlet in *Hamlet*, 76; Polonius in *Hamlet*, 88, 89; Lear in *Lear*, 138; Kent in *Lear*, 251; Claudio in *Much Ado*, 10, 11; Iago in *Othello*, 251; *Sonnets*, 117, 160, 172, 176, 192, 205, 227
Shelley, P. B., 148
Sherry, Richard, 99
Sicilian poets of thirteenth century, 149
Sidney, Sir Philip, 160–1, 169, 247
Silvano da Venafro, 199
Silvius, Aeneas, 241
Simnel, Lambert, 6
Simonds, W. E., x, 276

Skelton, John, 32, 47, 130, 241–4, 251; *Bowge of Courte*, 240, 242–3, 259; Drede in, 252; *Colyn Cloute*, 240, 251; *Garlande of Laurell*, 112, 118, 166; *Phyllyp Sparowe*, 112–13, 166; *Why come ye nat to Courte?*, 240, 244; Skeltonics, 255; Skelton and Wyatt, 32, 130, 244

Skinner, Anne: *see* Wyatt

Skinner, John, 5

Smart, J. S., 176

Smeaton, Mark, 33, 34, 35, 36, 41; and Wyatt, 40–2

Smith, Hallett, 169, 172–3

Smith, Lacey Baldwin, 17

Smith, Richard, 32

Sonnet form; English, 159–60, 176, 220–1, 280; Caritean, 183, 203–5, 220; Italian, 159, 175–6, 211, 227, 279–80; Surrey's, 174 ff., 205, 221; Wyatt's, 159, 174 ff., 183–4, 220–1

Spanish Chronicle and Spanish chronicler, 25, 26, 29, 30, 34, 35, 37, 41, 276; on Wyatt, 25, 29, 37, 41, 43

Spenser, Edmund, 30, 122, 186; Spenserian stanza, 158

Spurs, Battle of the, 6

Squarciafico, Girolamo, 191–2, 195, 198–9

Stagnino, Bernardino, 191; edition of Petrarch (1519) cited, 191–200

Stanley: *see* Digby

Starkey, Thomas, 49

Stevens, John, xi, 31–2; on Wyatt's lyrics, xi, 111 ff.

Stoke on Trent, Battle of, 6

Strype, John, 34, 38

Suckling, Sir John, 122

Suffolk, Dukes of: *see* Brandon *and* Pole

Surrey: *see* Henry Howard

Swift, Jonathan, 268

Tebaldeo, Il (Antonio Tebaldi), 209, 212–13, 215

Tempo, Antonio da, 175, 191–2, 195, 280

Theocritus; the Theocritan eclogue, 241

Theseus: *see* Chaucer, *Knight's Tale*

Thomas Aquinas, Saint, 93, 278

Thompson, John, ix

Thynne, William; edition of Chaucer, 9, 94, 113, 278

Tibullus, 210

Tilley, M. P., 109

Tofte, Robert, 152

Toledo, Treaty of, 66

Tottel, Richard and Tottel's 'Miscellany', xi, xiii, 22, 32, 86, 95, 142, 143, 267; anonymous poet in the 'Miscellany', 168

Tournon, Cardinal de, 68

Trissino, Giangiorgio, 175, 246, 247, 280

Trivulzi family, 68

Troubadour and Provençal poetry, 112, 116, 149, 150, 153, 161, 162, 166, 247

Tuke, Sir Brian; introduction to Thynne's 'Chaucer', 9, 113; and Wyatt, 9, 113, 128

Twyne, Thomas; translation of Petrarch's *De Remediis*, 81

Twysden, Sir Roger, 273

Tynan, Katharine, 270

Tyndale, William, 75, 99–100

Uberti, Fazio degli, 175

Udall, Nicholas, 31

Urbino, Duchess of, 213

Urbino, Francesco Maria della Rovere, Duke of, 55

Varchi, Benedetto, 168, 175

Vaudemont, Count de, 56

Vega, Garcilaso de la, 67

Vellutello, Alessandro, 191–6, 199–200

Venice, Signory of, 55, 57

Ventadour, 162

Vere, Frances: *see* Howard

Vinciguerra, Antonio, 248

Virgil, 247, 258, 280; the Virgilian eclogue, 241
Vives, Juan Luis, 47

Wallop, Sir John, 69, 71; and Wyatt, 30, 71, 72, 73
Walpole, Horace, xi
Walton, John; translation of Boethius, 93, 277
Warton, Thomas, 227, 238, 270
Watson, Thomas; translation of sonnet from Petrarch's *Rime*, 160-1
West Malling, Abbess of, 32
Weston, Francis, 33, 34-5, 36, 41-2; and Wyatt, 41-2
Whipple, T. K., 227
Whitehead, A. N., 124-5
Whitfield, J. H., 150
Whythorne, Thomas, 14, 25
Wiatt, William H., 33
Wilkins, Ernest Hatch, 155
Wilson, Thomas, 99
Wireker, Nigel, 41
Wolsey, Cardinal Thomas, 4, 6, 17, 21, 48, 49, 52, 53, 58, 59
Wood, Anthony à, 8
Wriothesley, Thomas, 52; and Wyatt, 62, 68
Wyatt MSS, xiv, 27, 273; *and see* George Wyatt
Wyatt, Lady Anne (*née* Skinner), 5
Wyatt, Lady Elizabeth (*née* Brooke); and Wyatt, 8, 19, 23, 43
Wyatt, Elizabeth, 274
Wyatt, George, 27, 29-30, 75, 273, 276; 'Life' of Anne Boleyn, 27-8, 273; other contributions to Wyatt MSS, 273; on Wyatt, 27-9, 72, 273
Wyatt, Sir Henry, 4-9, 18, 38, 43, 273; and Wyatt, 3-4, 7-9, 30, 37-8, 43, 52-3, 60, 67, 72, 74; on Wyatt, 37-8; Wyatt on, 3, 9, 88-9
Wyatt, Jane (*née* Hawte); and Wyatt, 43, 71, 274
Wyatt, Margaret: *see* Lee
Wyatt, Richard, 273

Wyatt, Sir Thomas, **Biography**: birth, 5-6; early life, 7 ff.; at Cambridge, 7-8; marriage, 8; separation, 19, 43; finances, 9, 30, 68, 269; grants to, 32-3, 70, 73; Clerk of the King's Jewels (1524), 5, 8; Esquire of the Body (1525), 8; as a young courtier, 18; Christmas at court (1524-5), 20; as court poet, 31-2, 38-9, 43, 111; poems in the Devonshire MS, xi, 14, 21-2, 24-5, 115, 174; poems in the Egerton MS, xi, 22, 115, 133, 174; poems in the Blage MS, xiii, 42, 67; affair with Anne Boleyn and its aftermath, 17, 18 ff., 30-1, 33 ff., 59, 60, 196, 199, 276; poems about Anne, x, 22-4, 27, 59, 196-200, 276; autobiographical adaptations of Petrarch, x, 23-4, 41, 67, 70, 276; on Cheney's embassy in France (1526), 24, 53 ff.; on Russell's embassy in Italy (1527), 21, 24, 55 ff., 80, 166, 169, 192, 209, 247, 280; return from, 21, 59, 275; May Day sonnet, 21, 126-7, 275; translation of Petrarch's *De Remediis* (1527), 59-60 (*and see below, under* LATIN, TRANSLATIONS FROM); translation of Plutarch's *Quyete of Mynde* (1527), ix, x, xiii, 40, 46, 54, 59-60 (*and see below, under* LATIN, TRANSLATIONS FROM); Marshal of Calais (1528-30), x, 24, 25, 30, 60; in 1532, 30; at Anne Boleyn's coronation, 30-1; in the Fleet prison, 32, 37, 275; knighthood, 33; in the Tower (1536), 33, 37 ff., 89, 275; release and exile from court (1536), 43-4; poems on events of May 1536, 42, 91; adaptation of Alamanni, 43, 246-7 (*and see below, under* SATIRES); the first satire and the exile from court (1536), x, 43-4, 113, 238, 246, 257, 260 (*and see*

Wyatt, Sir Thomas, *continued—*
below, under SATIRES); the third
satire and Wyatt's courtly experience, 44, 238, 267–9 (*and see
below, under* SATIRES); connection with Royal MS, 39–41;
military service (1536), 43; sheriff
of Kent (1536), 43; 1536–7 as a
turning point, 42, 43, 45; Letters
to his son (1537), 3, 10, 11–12, 45,
87–90, 92, 267, 274; ambassador
to the Imperial court in Spain
(1537–9), 45, 46, 61 ff., 89; visit to
England (1538), 64; poems written
in Spain (1537–9), x, 61, 66, 67, 189,
234; recall from Spain (1539), 66;
ambassador in France and Flanders (1539–40), 68 ff.; at Cromwell's execution (1540), 70; sonnet on Cromwell's fall, x, 70, 179,
188; translation of Psalms, ix, 70;
in the Tower (1541), 71 ff.; poem
to Brian from prison, 71, 72, 234,
275; 'Declaration' (1541), x, 71;
'Defence' (1541), x, 37, 40, 67,
71–2, 108–10; M.P. (1542), 73;
captain in fleet (1542), 73; death
(1542), 74; epitaphs and elegies on
Wyatt, 74–5. CHARACTER:
discussed 74–6; extravagance, 8–9,
68, 75, 269; Holbein's portrait, 75;
idea of service, 3, 9, 72; liking for
proverbs and maxims, 40, 88, 89,
144, 268, 275; patriotism, 72, 74;
Protestantism and enmity towards Inquisition, 62, 66, 67, 68,
69, 75, 247; seriousness, 45, 59–60,
89, 267. *For opinions of Wyatt, see*
Becon, Bonner, Challoner, Cromwell, Foxwell, Fuller, Henry
VIII, Leland, Lloyd, Pole,
Spanish chronicler, Surrey,
George Wyatt, Sir Henry Wyatt.
OPINIONS: on Bonner, 72, 75,
109; on Charles V's marriage
projects, 63, 75; on Chaucer, 9,
113, 126, 128, 244, 258; on the
court, 42–4, 91, 94, 245–6, 249 ff.;

Wyatt, Sir Thomas, *continued—*
on the English language, 81, 108–
9; on Epictetus, 7, 88, 245; on
Hawte, 89; on Henry VIII, 71–2,
108; on Heynes, 72, 109; on his
imprisonment, 43, 65, 89; on
Italy, 55–6, 59; on Latin, 81; on
love and marriage, 10, 11–12, 19–
20, 22–4, 96–8, 145 ff.; on
Petrarch, 80–1; on Russell, 59,
89; on Seneca, 7, 88, 90, 245; on
Sir Henry Wyatt, 3, 9, 88–9.
RELATIONSHIPS: Alamanni,
58, 247; Anne Boleyn, 17, 18 ff.,
33 ff., 59, 60, 276; Ariosto, 58,
280; Bembo, 57, 147–8; Berners,
30; Berni, 56; Blage, 7, 66–7, 72,
109; Boleyn family, 8; Boleyn
group, 39 ff.; George Boleyn, 32,
39–42, 43, 91; Bonner, 10, 20, 43,
63–5, 67–9, 71–2, 75, 109–10, 246;
Boscán, 67; Brancetour, 69, 74,
109; Brereton, 41–2; Brian, 20,
28, 32, 44, 63, 64, 71, 72, 238,
245–6, 267–9, 274–5; Brodeau, 55;
Budé, 54; Giovanni Casale, 57,
58; Gregory Casale, 56; Castiglione, 57; Catherine of Aragon,
20, 46, 52, 59–60, 80, 82, 88, 91,
108; Catherine Howard, 71–2;
Charles V, x, 46, 62–6, 69; Thos.
Cheney, 53–4; Clement VII, 56,
59, 247; George Cobham (brother-
in-law), 19, 20, 43; Cromwell, x,
9, 19, 25, 30, 33, 37–8, 43, 46, 49,
50, 52, 53, 62–6, 68, 70, 71, 72,
75, 76, 179, 188, 269; Elizabeth
Darrell, 19, 20, 64, 65, 67, 70, 71;
John Dudley, 62; *École Lyonnaise*, 68, 146–7; Alfonso d'Este,
57–8; Francis I, 54, 63, 65, 69;
Giberti, 56; Grainfield, 33; Grandvela, 62, 65; Elizabeth Hawte,
274; Sir William Hawte, 19, 43,
89, 274; Henry VIII, 9, 20, 21,
24, 25–9, 32, 33, 37, 43, 44, 46,
53–4, 59, 61–6, 68–9, 71, 72, 73,
76, 108–9, 246, 258; Heynes,

Wyatt, Sir Thomas, *continued*—
63–4, 72, 109–10; Howard family, 72, 73 (*and see* Catherine Howard, Norfolk, Surrey); Italian diplomats in Spain, 67; Leland, 7, 74; Lockwood, 30; Machiavelli, 58; Marot, 54; Mason, 7, 48, 62, 63, 65, 66, 71, 72, 75, 109; Navagero, 57; 2nd Duke of Norfolk, 8; 3rd Duke of Norfolk, 70, 73; Norris, 20, 41–2; Reginald Pole, 63, 66, 72, 75; Lady Poynings, 7, 71; Thos. Poynings, 7; Poynz, 20, 43–4, 238, 250, 253, 260; St Leger, 74; Russell, 19, 21, 55 ff., 59, 60, 89; Saint-Gelais, 54–5; Salel, 55; Skelton, 32, 130, 244; Smeaton, 40–2; Suffolk, 20, 26–9, 37–8, 43, 44, 71, 72, 73, 246; Surrey, 73, 74–5; Tuke, 9, 113, 128; Wallop, 30, 71, 72, 73; Weston, 41–2; Wriothesley, 62, 68; Lady Elizabeth Wyatt (wife), 8, 19, 23, 43; Elizabeth Wyatt, 274; Sir Henry Wyatt (father), 3–4, 7–9, 30, 37–8, 43, 52–3, 60, 67, 72, 74, 88–9; Jane Wyatt (daughter-in-law), 43, 71, 274; Thomas Wyatt (son), 7, 9, 10, 11, 20, 43, 45, 59, 74, 87–90, 92, 245, 267, 274. **Works:** ARIOSTO'S POETRY, WYATT AND: 280–3. 'DECLARATION': x, xi, 71. 'DEFENCE': x, xi, 10, 40, 67, 71–2, 108–10. BEMBO'S POETRY, WYATT AND: 193, 211. 'ENGLISH' LYRICS: 111, 115–16, 121, 125, 126 ff., 179–80, 184; Mason and Stevens on, xi, 111 ff.; their medieval and Chaucerian background, 111 ff.; Chaucer's influence on, 115, 126 ff.; compared with Chaucer's, 135–6, 142–3; plain style of, 130 ff.; metrical forms, 130–1, 185; conventionality of, 111, 133 ff.; compared with Donne's, 115, 143–5; 'philosophy' in, 145 ff. FRENCH POETRY, DEBT TO:

Wyatt, Sir Thomas, *continued*—
Marot and Saint-Gelais, x. LATIN, TRANSLATIONS FROM: 79 ff.; translation of Plutarch's *Quyete of Mynde*, ix, x, xiii, 40, 46, 54, 59 ff., 79–80, 82 ff., 86–8, 90–1, 95, 98, 100–1, 108, 137, 245, 267; its prose style, 98 ff., 182, 184; compared with Budé's, Blundeville's, Holland's, 102 ff.; translation of Petrarch's *De Remediis*, 59, 79, 80–2, 85, 95–6, 100, 137; versions of Seneca, 79–80, 90–1, 245; version of Boethius, 79–80, 91 ff., 95, 277–8; influence of Chaucer on, 93–4, 277–8; version of Ausonius, 95. LETTERS: ambassadorial, xi, xiii; style of, 109; to his son, 3, 10, 11–12, 45, 87–90, 92, 267, 274. PETRARCH'S POETRY, WYATT AND: 67, 80, 131, 144–5, 151–2, 167, 168 ff., 209, 210, 214, 216, 219–20, 223, 246, 255, 257, 281–2, 283 (*and see immediately below*); Petrarch's *Rime*, versions of, x, 23–4, 95–6, 179 ff., 208, 213, 215–16, 234–5, 276; sonnets translated from, 162, 169 ff., 193 ff., 208; compared with Surrey's, 169 ff., 200–1, 203, 206–8; sonnet form, 159, 174 ff., 183–4, 220–1; version of madrigal from, 185, 189; versions of canzoni from, 185–7; paraphrases and imitations of, 23–4, 67, 70, 185, 187 ff., 196–200; autobiographical adaptations of, x, 24, 41, 67, 70; versions influenced by Petrarchan commentators, 166, 190 ff. (*and see* Daniello, Filelfo, Gesualdo, Squarciafico, Stagnino, Tempo, Vellutello, Venafro). PSALMS, TRANSLATIONS OF: ix, 70. SATIRES: 94, 238 ff.; their English background, 238 ff., 244, 259; their classical background, 238–9, 242 ff.; their Italian neoclassical

Wyatt, Sir Thomas, *continued*—
background, 238–9, 244, 246; and
Alamanni, 43, 58, 68, 246 ff., 259,
267–8; and Horace, 238, 245, 260,
263–4, 267–8, 270; and Persius,
245, 262; and Juvenal; 253, and
Aesop, 259, 260, 262–5, 267; and
Henryson, 260, 265–6; and
Chaucer, 266; the first satire
('Myne owne John Poynz'), x,
20, 43–4, 113, 238, 246, 249 ff.,
257, 260, 264; the second satire
('My mothers maydes'), 7, 259 ff.;
the third satire ('A spending
hand'), 20, 44, 63, 94, 238, 267–9,
275. SERAFINO'S POETRY, WYATT
AND: 95, 130, 209 ff., 236, 237,
246, 255, 281, 282–3 (*and see
immediately below*); the Caritean
background, 183–4, 209 ff.; Wyatt

Wyatt, Sir Thomas, *continued*—
compared with Serafino, 214 ff.,
235, 237; his echoes of Serafino,
217; his versions of Serafino's
poems, 209, 217, 219 ff., 236; in
sonnet form, 219–21; in English
forms, 221–3; in strambotto form,
223, 227–34, 282–3; his independent strambotti, 234–7

Wyatt, Thomas, the younger, 8,
43, 273; and Wyatt, 7, 9, 10, 11,
20, 43, 45, 59, 74, 87–90, 92, 245,
267, 274; Wyatt's Rebellion, 27,
74, 273

Wyer, Robert, 86

Yeats, W. B., 97, 270

Yelverton, William, 11

Zeeveld, W. G., 49

LuLu

LuLu

LuLu Roman

Fleming H. Revell Company
Old Tappan, New Jersey

Unless otherwise identified, Scripture quotations are from the King James Version of the Bible.

Scripture quotations identified LB are from The Living Bible, Copyright © 1971 by Tyndale House Publishers, Wheaton, Illinois 60187. All rights reserved.

Library of Congress Cataloging in Publication Data

Roman, LuLu.
    LuLu.

       1. Roman, LuLu. 2. Christian biography—United States. 3. Entertainers—United States—Biography. I. Title.
BR1725.R65A34   248'.24 [B]   78-15510
ISBN 0-8007-0956-X

Copyright © 1978 by LuLu Roman
Published by Fleming H. Revell Company
All rights reserved
Printed in the United States of America

To Claudine Hable, my beloved grandmother—
who was always there for me, no matter how many times I let her down, no matter how far down I went. Through her faithful and undying love, she bore the shame, the hurt, and the humiliation with her head held high.

I could always run to her, and she never, never left me for any reason. To me, that is the highest example anyone on this earth could give—the example of never-ending patience, a steadfast hope, and an everlasting faith.

To me, she is the world's greatest grandma. She is "my Claudine," and I love her more than words can ever tell.

Contents

Our Friend LuLu   11

1   Everything Had Turned White   17

2   Whistles and Bells   22

3   Worst Days/Best Days   38

4   The Whistle Blew for Me   49

5   What I Thought I Didn't Have   56

6   Myclaudine   65

7   The Girls Called "Fast"   72

8   We're Free!   80

9   The Wrong Kind of People   96

10   They're Going to Call It "Hee Haw"   109

11   My Baby! He Must Be Dead!   116

12   God Will Take Care of It   130

13   You've Changed, Kiddo!   147

14   The Scars on My Heart Prove It   155

15   Struggle, a Necessary Part of Growth   162